Blender Cycles: Materials and Textures Cookbook

Third Edition

Over 40 practical recipes to create stunning materials and textures using the Cycles rendering engine with Blender

Enrico Valenza

[PACKT]
PUBLISHING

BIRMINGHAM - MUMBAI

Blender Cycles: Materials and Textures Cookbook
Third Edition

First published: January 2011

Second edition: June 2013

Third edition: February 2015

Production reference: 1200215

Published by Packt Publishing Ltd.
Livery Place
35 Livery Street
Birmingham B3 2PB, UK.

ISBN 978-1-78439-993-1

www.packtpub.com

Cover image by Enrico Valenza (envval@gmail.com)

Credits

Author
Enrico Valenza

Reviewers
Romain Caudron
John E. Herreño
Sanu Vamanchery Mana

Commissioning Editor
Ashwin Nair

Acquisition Editor
Sam Wood

Content Development Editor
Rahul Nair

Technical Editor
Madhunikita Sunil Chindarkar

Copy Editor
Vikrant Phadke

Project Coordinator
Aboli Ambardekar

Proofreaders
Simran Bhogal
Maria Gould
Paul Hindle
Bernadette Watkins

Indexer
Rekha Nair

Production Coordinator
Komal Ramchandani

Cover Work
Komal Ramchandani

About the Author

Enrico Valenza, also known as "EnV," on the Web is an Italian freelance illustrator who mainly collaborates with publishers such as Mondadori Ragazzi and Giunti as a cover artist for science fition and fantasy books.

He graduated from Liceo Artistico Statale in Verona, Italy, and was later a student of Giorgio Scarato, an illustrator and painter.

When he started to work, computers weren't very common. He spent the first 15 years of his career doing illustration with traditional media, usually on cardboard. At that time, he specialized in the use of the air-graph, a technique particularly esteemed for advertisements.

When the movie *Jurassic Park* was released, he decided to buy a computer and try out the computer graphics that everyone was talking about. Totally self-taught for what concerns the many aspects of CG, it was his encounter with the open source philosophy that actually opened up a brand new world of possibilities—Blender in particular.

In 2005, Enrico won the Suzanne Award for Best Animation, Original Idea, or Story, for the movie *New Penguoen 2.38*. In 2006, he joined the Orange team in Amsterdam for two weeks. He helped them in finalizing the shots of *Elephants Dream*, the first open source animated short movie produced by the Blender Foundation.

In 2007 and 2008, Enrico was the lead artist in the Peach Project team for the production of *Big Buck Bunny*, Blender Foundation's second open movie. In 2010 and 2011, he was the art director at CINECA in Bologna, Italy, for the *Museo della Città di Bologna* project. This was the production of a stereoscopic, computer-graphics-animated documentary made in Blender explaining the history of Bologna.

For Packt Publishing, Enrico is also writing *Blender 2.7 3D Modeling Cookbook*, which explains the complete workflow in Blender to build an animated fantasy monster. Being a Blender Certified Trainer, he often collaborates as a CG artist with production studios that decide to switch their pipeline to open source.

Enrico uses Blender almost on a daily basis for his illustration work, rarely to have the illustration rendered straight by the 3D package, more often as a starting point for painting with other open source applications. He has done several presentations and workshops about Blender and its use in productions.

Acknowledgments

I would like to say thanks to my family: my father, Giuseppe, and my mother, Licia, for giving me the possibility to follow what I always thought was my path in life, and my wonderful wife, Micaela, and my beautiful daughters, Sara and Elisa, for being there and encouraging me in the making of this book.

Then, I would like to thank (obviously) Ton Roosendaal for Blender and Brecht Van Lommel for Cycles. Also, I would like to thank all the "Blender-heads" at the Blender Artist and Kino3d forums for all the testing, experiments, explanations, and examples about feature and material creation in Cycles that were (and still are) often posted almost at the same time as they were implemented in the software.

About the Reviewers

Romain Caudron is a French 3D modeler and game designer passionate about Blender and ZBrush. He has worked on jewellery design, short film animation, and independent video games. He has mostly self-learned for his career, but he studied 3D animation with CGITrainer. Romain received a master's degree in cinema and game design from Paul Valéry University, Montpellier III, France. You can check out his most recent work at www.romain-caudron.net.

John E. Herreño is 31 years old. At the early age of 13, he developed a curiosity for the "magical" things that modern digital computers can do. He graduated as an electronics engineer from the National University of Colombia. This helped him understand how computers are built, and he studied some principles of software development himself to understand how to get the most out of them. John became interested in Blender 3D after finding version 1.72 in a CD inside a magazine he bought for a different reason, and he has been learning it since then from the awesome community of users on Internet forums and tutorials. Today, he's highly convinced of the power of open source software and the business models around it to improve the general quality of life in developing countries.

Above all, he's just a human being who wants to know and serve Jesus Christ.

John authored *Blender 2.5 Hotshot*, *Packt Publishing*, which was published in 2011. Currently, he spends entire days on web development with Drupal.

Sanu Vamanchery Mana is a 3D artist from India with over 16 years of experience in the fields of animation, gaming, and special effects. He is a lecturer on interactive media design and animation at Dhofar University, Salalah, Oman. In this role, he has run many workshops, training sessions, and presentations in many countries in Europe, Asia, and Latin America. He was the reviewer of two books on Blender by Packt Publishing.

Sanu has worked on gaming projects such as *GoldenEye 007* (*Electronic Arts*), *Neopets* (*Sony Entertainment*), and *World Series of Poker* (*Sony Entertainment*). He has also worked on the short movie *JackFrost*, which was nominated for a BAFTA award.

www.PacktPub.com

Support files, eBooks, discount offers, and more

For support files and downloads related to your book, please visit www.PacktPub.com.

Did you know that Packt offers eBook versions of every book published, with PDF and ePub files available? You can upgrade to the eBook version at www.PacktPub.com and as a print book customer, you are entitled to a discount on the eBook copy. Get in touch with us at service@packtpub.com for more details.

At www.PacktPub.com, you can also read a collection of free technical articles, sign up for a range of free newsletters and receive exclusive discounts and offers on Packt books and eBooks.

https://www2.packtpub.com/books/subscription/packtlib

Do you need instant solutions to your IT questions? PacktLib is Packt's online digital book library. Here, you can search, access, and read Packt's entire library of books.

Why subscribe?

- Fully searchable across every book published by Packt
- Copy and paste, print, and bookmark content
- On demand and accessible via a web browser

Free access for Packt account holders

If you have an account with Packt at www.PacktPub.com, you can use this to access PacktLib today and view 9 entirely free books. Simply use your login credentials for immediate access.

Table of Contents

Preface

Since the Blender interface and code were rewritten from scratch, starting with the 2.5 series and throughout the production of the open movie Sintel, a lot of good things have happened to the famous open source 3D modeling and animation suite.

One of them has been the announcement (in April 2011) of Cycles, a new rendering engine developed by Brecht Van Lommel with the goal of modernizing Blender's shading and rendering systems. It could be used as alternative to the Blender Internal rendering engine.

Cycles has finally been integrated with Blender with the 2.61 release, as an add-on that is a Python script, enabled in the Preferences panel by default. It suffices to set this as the active render engine in the User Interface main header.

While Blender Internal is a scan-line rendering engine, Cycles is a physically based path tracer. This approach allows simplification of material creation, support for Global Illumination, and much more realism in the results.

But the best feature of Cycles is probably the rendering you get in the 3D viewport. When you set the Draw mode of any 3D viewport to Rendered, an interactive rendering starts in the viewport. From then onwards, the pre-visualization rendering of the scene is continuously updated almost in real time (depending on the power of your graphics card) as a material, a light, or object. Even the entire scene can be modified.

Using Cycles, a lot of astonishing images and a few animations have been produced, both for testing and for real productions. You can find most of them at the Blender Artists forum (`http://blenderartists.org/forum/`), but it's enough to mention *Tears of Steel*, the fifth open movie produced by the Blender Foundation with the codename *Mango*—a short science-fiction movie entirely rendered in Cycles to accomplish the visual effects; well, not entirely, but actually 95 percent. The team used Blender Internal for the then unsupported features. In fact, being included in the same software also provided an integrated compositor. Both the Blender Internal and the Cycles render engines can actually be paired to make full use of all the needed features.

If you are not a beginner in Blerder, you are probably already using your customized version of the User Interface, with your personal preferences as add-ons, modified screens, and all that is already set in the User Preferences panel.

In this book, we'll start our workflow with the Factory Settings, which is the basic interface and preferences situation we have the very first time we start Blender, just after downloading the ZIP file and uncompressing it into some location on our hard drive.

Instructions about any required add-on to be enabled or particular settings are provided in the *Getting ready* section of the recipes.

In the making of this Cookbook, I've used versions of Blender from 2.71 to 2.73. Therefore, you could sometimes find a screenshot showing buttons or features not appearing in other pictures; for example, there are differences in the Node Editor toolbar between versions 2.71 and 2.72, as shown in the following screenshot (actually, this is only relevant to Cycles):

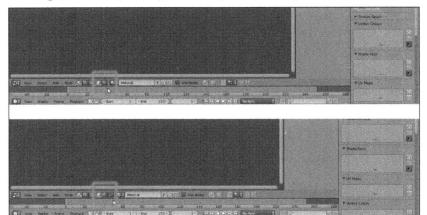

Things like this shouldn't be an issue, however, because there are no big differences in these three versions; only improvements. Moreover, the files provided have been tested under the three versions. Obviously, new features introduced in version 2.73 are not available in the previous versions, so always use the last official Blender release.

You can see a list of the new features available in version 2.73, at `http://wiki.blender.org/index.php/Dev:Ref/Release_Notes/2.73`.

What this book covers

Chapter 1, *Overview of Materials in Cycles*, explains how Cycles materials work and their main characteristics. You will learn how to build a basic Cycles material, add textures, use lamps or light-emitting objects, use volume materials, set displacement, and set the World.

Chapter 2, *Managing Cycles Materials*, shows you how to manage and organize the Cycles textures and materials, create node groups, and build libraries to link or append the materials from.

Chapter 3, *Creating Natural Materials in Cycles*, covers the process of creating several types of basic natural materials using mainly procedurals but also some image textures.

Chapter 4, *Creating Man-made Materials in Cycles*, explains the creation process of several types of man-made materials using procedurals and textures.

Chapter 5, *Creating Complex Natural Materials in Cycles*, teaches you the creation of more complex natural materials using mainly procedurals.

Chapter 6, *Creating More Complex Man-made Materials*, covers the creation of some more elaborate man-made materials using procedurals and textures.

Chapter 7, *Subsurface Scattering in Cycles*, explains the use of the Subsurface Scattering node, some ways to simulate the Subsurface Scattering effect in Cycles, and how to build a fake Subsurface Scattering node group.

Chapter 8, *Creating Organic Materials*, demonstrates the creation of several types of organic shaders that try to use only procedural textures where possible. You will learn how to create hair, fur, and a layered human skin shader in Cycles.

Chapter 9, *Special Materials*, explains the use of volume materials. You will then be able to create clouds, smoke, fire, and many other special effects.

What you need for this book

The only piece of software necessary for the recipes of this book is the last official 2.73 Blender release (version 2.73a, with several bug fixes, is already out). You need to download it from www.blender.org/download/get-blender. Any particular texture needed for the exercises in the book is provided as a free download on the Packt Publishing website itself.

An image editor is not essential, but it can be handy if you want to adapt your own textures to replace the provided textures. I advise you to try the GIMP, an open source image editor that you can download from www.gimp.org. Any other editor that you prefer is also fine.

Who this book is for

This book is mainly for the intermediate Blender user, who already knows Blender but still hasn't dealt with the new Cycles rendering engine. It's assumed that you already know how to navigate through the Blender interface, and that you have at least basic knowledge of the standard Blender material creation interface. However, this knowledge is not strictly necessary.

Sections

In this book, you will find several headings that appear frequently (Getting ready, How to do it, How it works, There's more, and See also).
To give clear instructions on how to complete a recipe, we use these sections as follows:

Getting ready

This section tells you what to expect in the recipe, and describes how to set up any software or any preliminary settings required for the recipe.

How to do it...

This section contains the steps required to follow the recipe.

How it works...

This section usually consists of a detailed explanation of what happened in the previous section.

There's more...

This section consists of additional information about the recipe in order to make the reader more knowledgeable about the recipe.

See also

This section provides helpful links to other useful information for the recipe.

Conventions

In this book, you will find a number of styles of text that distinguish between different kinds of information. Here are some examples of these styles, and explanations of their meanings.

Sequences of operations, for example, adding nodes to the Node Editor or objects to the 3D view, are written as follows:

Open the **Blender User Preferences** panel (*Ctrl + Alt + U*) and go to the **System** tab, which is the last tab to the right of the panel.

This means that you need to press the keys at the same time, then place the mouse arrow on the Texture item in a pop-up menu, and click on the item.

New terms and **important words** are shown in bold. Words that you see on the screen, in menus or dialog boxes for example, appear in the text like this: "clicking on the **Next** button takes you to the next screen."

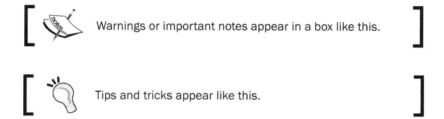

Warnings or important notes appear in a box like this.

Tips and tricks appear like this.

Reader feedback

Feedback from our readers is always welcome. Let us know what you think about this book—what you liked or may have disliked. Reader feedback is important for us to develop titles that you really get the most out of.

To send us general feedback, simply send an e-mail to feedback@packtpub.com, and mention the book title via the subject of your message.

If there is a topic that you have expertise in and you are interested in either writing or contributing to a book, see our author guide on www.packtpub.com/authors.

Customer support

Now that you are the proud owner of a Packt book, we have a number of things to help you to get the most from your purchase.

Downloading the example code

You can download the example code files from your account at http://www.packtpub.com for all the Packt Publishing books you have purchased. If you purchased this book elsewhere, you can visit http://www.packtpub.com/support and register to have the files e-mailed directly to you.

Downloading the color images of this book

We also provide you with a PDF file that has color images of the screenshots/diagrams used in this book. The color images will help you better understand the changes in the output. You can download this file from `http://www.packtpub.com/sites/default/files/downloads/9931OS_ColorImages.pdf`.

Errata

Although we have taken every care to ensure the accuracy of our content, mistakes do happen. If you find a mistake in one of our books—maybe a mistake in the text or the code—we would be grateful if you could report this to us. By doing so, you can save other readers from frustration and help us improve subsequent versions of this book. If you find any errata, please report them by visiting `http://www.packtpub.com/submit-errata`, selecting your book, clicking on the **Errata Submission Form** link, and entering the details of your errata. Once your errata are verified, your submission will be accepted and the errata will be uploaded to our website or added to any list of existing errata under the Errata section of that title.

To view the previously submitted errata, go to `https://www.packtpub.com/books/content/support` and enter the name of the book in the search field. The required information will appear under the **Errata** section.

Piracy

Piracy of copyrighted material cn the Internet is an ongoing problem across all media. At Packt, we take the protection of our copyright and licenses very seriously. If you come across any illegal copies of our works in any form on the Internet, please provide us with the location address or website name immediately so that we can pursue a remedy.

Please contact us at `copyright@packtpub.com` with a link to the suspected pirated material.

We appreciate your help in protecting our authors and our ability to bring you valuable content.

Questions

You can contact us at `questions@packtpub.com` if you are having a problem with any aspect of the book, and we will do our best to address it.

1
Overview of Materials in Cycles

In this chapter, we will cover the following recipes:

- An overview of material nodes in Cycles
- An overview of procedural textures in Cycles
- How to set the World material
- Creating a mesh-light material
- Using volume materials
- Using displacement

Introduction

Cycles' materials work in a totally different way than in Blender Internal.

In Blender Internal, you can build a material by choosing a diffuse and a specular shader from the **Material** window, by setting several surface options, and then by assigning textures (both procedurals and image maps as well) in the provided slots. All of these steps make one complete material. After this, it's possible to combine two or more of these materials by a network of nodes, thereby obtaining a lot more flexibility in a shader's creation. However, the single materials themselves are the same as those set through the **Material** window—shaders made for a scan-line-rendering engine—and their result is just an approximation of the simulated absorption-reflection behavior of light on a surface.

In Cycles, the approach is quite different. All the names of the closures describing surface properties have a **Bidirectional Scattering Distribution Function** (**BSDF**), which is a general mathematical function that describes the way in which light is scattered by a surface in the real world. It's also the formula that path tracers such as Cycles use to calculate the rendering of an object in a virtual environment. Basically, light rays are shot from the camera. They bounce on the objects in the scene and keep on bouncing until they reach a light source or an empty background (which, in Cycles, can emit light as well). For this reason, a pure path tracer such as Cycles can render in reasonable times an object set in an open environment. The rendering times increase a lot for closed spaces, for example, furniture set inside a room, because light rays can bounce on the floor, the ceiling, and the walls many times before reaching one or more light sources.

In short, the main difference between the two rendering engines is due to the fact that, while in Blender Internal, the materials use all the traditional shader tricks of a scan-line rendering engine such as the simulated specular component, the Cycles rendering engine is a path tracer that tries to mimic the real behavior of a surface as closely as possible as if the surface were real. This is the reason we don't have an arbitrary Specular factor simulating the reflection point of light on the surface in Cycles, but instead have a glossy shader that actually mirrors the light source and the surroundings to be mixed with other components in different ratios. Thus the glossy shader behaves in a more realistic way.

Just for explanatory purposes, in this book, I will refer to the more or less blurred point of light created by the reflection of the light source on a mirroring glossy surface as *specularity*.

Be aware that the rendering speed in Cycles depends on the device you use to render your scenes—CPU or GPU. This means that basically, you can decide to use the power of the CPU (default option) or the power of the graphic card processor, the GPU.

To set the GPU for the rendering, perform the following steps:

1. Call the **Blender User Preferences** panel (*Ctrl + Alt + U*) and go to the **System** tab, the last tab to the right of the panel.

2. Under the **Compute Device** tab to the bottom-left corner of the panel, select the option to be used for computation. To make this permanent, click on the **Save User Settings** button or press *Ctrl + U*. Now close the **Blender User Preferences** panel.

3. In the **Properties** panel to the right of the screen, go to the **Render** window and, under the **Render** tab, it's now possible to configure the GPU of the graphics card instead of the default CPU (this is possible only if your graphic card supports CUDA, that is, for NVIDIA graphic cards. OpenCL, which is intended to support rendering on AMD/ATI graphics cards, is still in a very incomplete and experimental stage, and therefore, not very usable yet).

A GPU-based rendering has the advantage of literally increasing the Cycles' rendering speed several times, albeit with the disadvantage of a small memory limit, so it's not always possible to render big complex scenes made up of a lot of geometry. In such cases, it's better to use the CPU instead.

There are other ways to reduce the rendering times and also to reduce or avoid the noise and the fireflies (white dots) produced in several cases by the glossy, transparent, and light-emitting materials. All of this doesn't strictly belong to shaders or materials. By the way, you can find more information related to these topics at the following addresses:

Information on *Cycles Render Engine* can be found at `http://wiki.blender.org/index.php/Doc:2.6/Manual/Render/Cycles`.

More information on *Reducing Noise* is available on the Cycles wiki page, at `http://wiki.blender.org/index.php/Doc:2.6/Manual/Render/Cycles/Reducing_Noise`.

A list of supported graphic cards for Cycles can be found at `https://developer.nvidia.com/cuda-gpus`.

Material nodes in Cycles

A Cycles material is basically made up of distinct components named **shaders**. They can be combined to build even more complex surface or volume shaders.

In this recipe, we'll have a look at the basic, necessary steps required to build a basic surface Cycles material, to activate the rendered preview in the 3D window, and to finally render a simple scene.

Getting ready

In the description of the following steps, I'll assume that you are using Blender with the default factory settings. If you aren't, start Blender and just click on the **File** menu item in the top main header bar to select **Load Factory Settings** from the pop-up menu, as shown in the following screenshot:

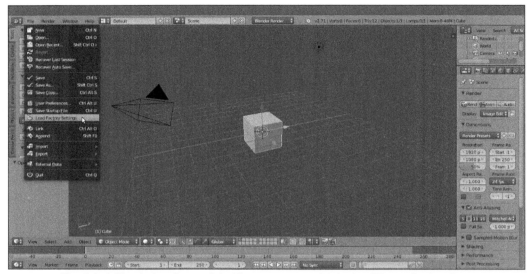

The default Blender interface and the File pop-up menu with the Load Factory Settings item

Now perform the following steps:

1. In the upper menu bar, switch from **Blender Render** to **Cycles Render** (hovering with the mouse on this button shows the engine to use to render a label).

2. Now split the 3D view into two horizontal rows, and change the upper row to the **Node Editor** window by selecting the menu item from the **Editor Type** button in the left corner of the bottom bar of the window. The **Node Editor** window is, in fact, the window we will use to build our shaders by mixing the nodes (actually, this is not the only way, but we'll see this later).

3. Put the mouse cursor in the 3D view and add a Plane under the Cube (press *Shift + A* and navigate to **Mesh | Plane**). Enter **Edit Mode** (press *Tab*), scale it 3.5 times bigger (press *S*, enter *3.5*, and then press *Enter*) and go out of **Edit Mode** (press *Tab* again). Now move the Plane one Blender unit down (press *G*, then *Z*, then enter *-1*, and finally, press *Enter*).

4. Go to the little icon (**Viewport Shading**) showing a sphere in the bottom bar of the 3D view and click on it. A menu showing different options appears (**Bounding Box**, **Wireframe**, **Solid**, **Texture**, **Material** and **Rendered**). Select **Rendered** from the top of the list (or press the *Shift + Z* shortcut) and watch your Cube being rendered in real time in the 3D viewport.

5. Now you can rotate and translate the view or the Cube itself, and the view gets updated in real time (the speed of the update is restricted only by the complexity of the scene and the computing power of your CPU or graphics card).

Let's learn more by performing the following steps:

1. Select the **Lamp** item in the **Outliner** window (by default, it's a Point lamp).
2. Go to the **Object data** window under the **Properties** panel on the right-hand side of the screen.
3. Under the **Nodes** tab, click on **Use Nodes** to activate a node system for the selected light in the scene. This node system is made by an **Emission** shader connected to a **Lamp Output** node.
4. Go to the **Strength** item, which is set to 100.000 by default, and start increasing the value. As the intensity of the Lamp increases, you will see the Cube and the Plane rendered in the viewport getting brighter, as shown in the following screenshot:

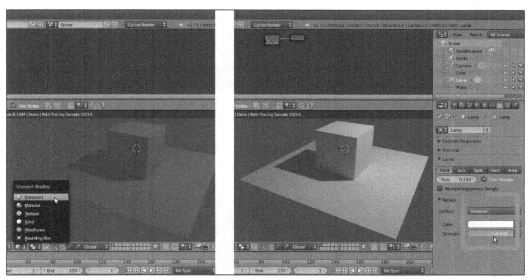

The Viewport Shading menu with the Rendered item and the Lamp Object data window with the Strength slider

How to do it...

We just prepared the scene and took the first look at one of the more appreciated features of Cycles since its first inclusion in Blender—the real-time-rendered preview (which, by the way, is now also available in Blender Internal but seems to work faster in Cycles).

Now let's start with the object's materials:

1. Select the Cube to assign the shader to by clicking on the item in the **Outliner** window or right-clicking directly on the object in the **Rendered** viewport (but be aware that in the **Rendered** mode, the object selection outline usually around the mesh is not visible because it's obviously not renderable).

2. Go to the **Material** window under the **Properties** panel. The Cube already has a default material assigned (as you can precisely see under the **Surface** subpanel within the **Material** window). By the way, you need to click on the **Use Nodes** button under the **Surface** subpanel to activate the node system for the material. Instead of this, you can also check the **Use Nodes** box in the toolbar of the **Node Editor** window.

3. As you check the **Use Nodes** box, the content of the **Surface** tab changes, showing that a **Diffuse BSDF** shader has been assigned to the Cube and that, accordingly, two linked nodes have appeared inside the **Node Editor** window. The **Diffuse BSDF** shader is already connected to the **Surface** input socket of a **Material Output** node.

4. Put the mouse cursor in the **Node Editor** window, and by scrolling the mouse wheel, zoom in to the **Diffuse BSDF** node. Click on the **Color** rectangle. A color wheel appears, where you can select a new color to change the shader color by clicking on the wheel itself or by inserting the **RGB** values (note that there is also a color sampler and the alpha channel value, although the latter, in this case, doesn't have any visible effect on the object material's color).

The color wheel of a Diffuse shader node in the Node Editor window and the Rendered 3D viewport preview

5. The Cube rendered in the 3D preview changes its material's color in real time. You can even move the cursor in the color wheel and watch the rendered object switching the colors accordingly. Set the object's color to a greenish color by changing its **RGB** values to 0.430, 0.800, and 0.499, respectively.

6. Go to the **Material** window, and under the **Surface** tab, click on the **Surface** button, which is showing the **Diffuse BSDF** item at the moment. From the pop-up menu that appears, select the **Glossy BSDF** shader item. Now the node changes in the **Node Editor** window, and so does the Cube's material in the **Rendered** preview, as shown in the following screenshot:

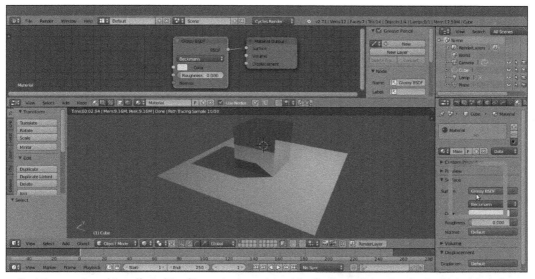

Real-time preview of the effect of the Glossy shader node and the Surface subpanel under the Material window

Note that although we just switched a shader node with a different node, the color we set in the former has been kept in the new one. Actually, this happens for all the values that can be kept from a node to a different one.

Now, because a material having a 100 percent matte or reflective surface could hardly exist in the real world, a more accurate basic Cycles material should be made by mixing the **Diffuse BSDF** and the **Glossy BSDF** shaders, blended together by a **Mix Shader** node, which in turn is connected to the **Material Output** node:

1. In the **Material** window, under the **Surface** tab, click again on the **Surface** button, which is now showing the **Glossy BSDF** item, and replace it with a **Diffuse BSDF** shader.

2. Put the mouse pointer on the **Node Editor** window, and by pressing *Shift + A*, make a pop-up menu appear with several items. Move the mouse pointer on the **Shader** item. It shows one more pop-up, where all the shader items are collected. Alternatively, press the *T* key to call the **Node Editor** tool shelf, where you can find the same shader items under the different tabs.

3. Select one of these items (in our case, the **Glossy BSDF** shader node again). The **Shader** node, which is already selected, is now added to the **Node Editor** window, although it is not connected to anything yet (in fact, it's not visible in the **Material** window but only in the **Node Editor** window).

4. Again press *Shift + A* in the **Node Editor** window, and this time, add a **Mix Shader** node.

5. Press *G* to move the node to the link connecting the **Diffuse BSDF** node to the **Surface** input socket of the **Material Output** node (you'll probably need to first adjust the position of the two nodes to make room between them). The **Mix Shader** node gets automatically pasted in between, and the **Diffuse** node output gets connected to the first **Shader** input socket, as shown in the following screenshot:

Mix Shader node pasted between a preexisting nodes connection inside the Node Editor window

6. Click on the green dot output of the **Glossy BSDF** shader node, and grab the link to the second input socket of the **Mix Shader** node. Release the mouse button now and see the nodes being connected.

7. Because the blending **Fac** (factor) value of the **Mix Shader** node is set by default to 0.500, the two shader components, **Diffuse** and **Glossy**, are now showing on the Cube's surface in equal parts, that is, each component at 50 percent. Click on the **Fac** slider with the mouse and slide it to 0.000. The Cube's surface now shows only the **Diffuse** component because the **Diffuse BSDF** shader is connected to the first **Shader** input socket, which is corresponding to a value of 0.

8. Slide the **Fac** slider value to 1.000 and the surface now shows only the **Glossy BSDF** shader component, which is, in fact, connected to the second **Shader** input socket corresponding to a value of 1.

9. Set the **Fac** value to `0.800` (keep *Ctrl* pressed while you are sliding the **Fac** value to constrain it to `0.100` intervals). The Cube is now reflecting the white Plane on its sides, even though it is blurred, because we have a material that is reflective at 80 percent and matte at 20 percent (the white noise you see in the rendered preview is due to the low sampling we are using at the moment. You will learn more about this later). This is shown in the following screenshot:

The Rendered preview of the effect of the mixed Diffuse and Glossy shader nodes

10. Lastly, select the Plane, go to the **Material** window, and click on the **New** button to assign a diffuse whitish material.

How it works...

In its minimal form, a Cycles material is made by any one of the node shaders connected to the **Surface** or the **Volume** input sockets of the **Material Output** node. For a new material, the node shader is **Diffuse BSDF** by default, with the **RGB** color set to `0.800` and connected to the **Surface** socket, and the result is a matte whitish material (with the **Roughness** value at `0.000`, actually corresponding to a **Lambert** shader).

Then the **Diffuse BSDF** node can be replaced by any other node of the available shader list, for example, by the **Glossy BSDF** shader as in the former Cube scene, which produced a totally mirrored surface material.

As we have seen, the **Node Editor** window is not the only way to build the materials. In the **Properties** panel on the right-hand side of the UI, we have access to the **Material** window, which is usually divided as follows:

- ▸ The material name, user, and the **datablock** subpanel.

- ▸ The **Preview** window.

- ▸ The **Surface** subpanel, including only the shader nodes added in a vertically ordered column in the **Node Editor** window, and already connected to each other.

- ▸ The **Volume** subpanel, with the similar feature as that of the **Surface** subpanel.

- ▸ The **Displacement** subpanel.

- ▸ The **Settings** subpanel, where we can set the object color, the alpha intensity, the specularity color, and the hardness as seen in the viewport in non-rendered mode (**Viewport Color, Alpha, Viewport Specular**, and **Hardness**). It also contains the **Pass Index** value of the material, a **Multiple Importance Sample** checkbox, the Volume sampling methods, the Interpolation, the Homogeneous item to be activated to accelerate the rendering of volumes, and an option to disable the rendering of the transparent shadows to accelerate the total rendering.

The **Material** window not only reflects what we do in the **Node Editor** window and changes accordingly (and vice versa), but can also be used to change the values to easily switch the shaders themselves, and to some extent, to connect them to the other nodes.

The **Material** and the **Node Editor** windows are so mutual that there is no prevalence in which window to use to build a material. Both can be used individually or combined, depending on preferences or practical utility. In some cases, it can be very handy to switch a shader from the **Surface** tab under **Material** on the right (or a texture from the **Texture** window as well, but we'll see textures later), leaving all the settings and the links in the node's network untouched.

There is no question, by the way, that the **Material** window can become pretty complex and confusing as a material network grows more and more in complexity, while the graphic appearance of the **Node Editor** window shows the same network in a clearer and much more readable way.

There's more...

Looking at the **Rendered** viewport, you'll notice that the image is now quite noisy and that there are white dots in certain areas of the image. These are the infamous fireflies, caused mainly by transparent, luminescent, or glossy surfaces. Actually, they have been introduced in the rendering of our Cube by the glossy component.

Here is one way to eliminate the fireflies:

1. Go to the **Render** window under the **Properties** panel.

2. Uncheck both the **Reflective** and **Refractive Caustics** items under the **Light Path** subpanel.

3. This will immediately eliminate the white noise, but alas! It also eliminates all the caustics (which we would like to keep in the rendering in most cases).

Therefore, a different approach is as follows:

1. Go to the **Render** window under the **Properties** panel. In the **Sampling** tab, set **Samples** to 100 for both **Preview** and **Render** (they are set to 10 by default).

2. Set the **Clamp Direct** and **Clamp Indirect** values to 1.00 (they are set to 0.00 by default).

3. Go to the **Light Paths** tab, re-enable the **Reflective** and **Refractive Caustics** items, and then set the **Filter Glossy** value to 1.00.

4. The resulting rendered image, as shown in the following screenshot, is now a lot smoother and noise-free, and also keeps the reflected caustics on the Plane:

Noise-free Rendered preview and settings under the Render window

5. Save the blend file in an appropriate location on your hard drive with a name such as start_01.blend.

6. The **Samples** set to 10 by default are obviously not enough to give a noiseless image, but are good for a fast preview. We could also let the **Preview** samples remain at the default value and increase only the **Render** value, to have longer rendering times but a clean image only for the final render (which can be started, as in Blender Internal, by pressing the *F12* key).

Using the **Clamp** value, we can reduce the energy of the light. Internally, Blender converts the image color space to linear, which is from 0 to 1, and then reconverts it to **RGB**, which is from 0 to 255, for the output. A value of 1.00 in linear space means that all the image values are now included inside a range starting from 0 and arriving to a maximum value of 1, and that values greater than 1 are not possible, thus avoiding the fireflies problem in most cases. Be aware that **Clamp** values higher than 1.00 might also lower the general lighting intensity of the scene.

The **Filter Glossy** value is exactly what the name says, a filter that blurs the glossy reflections on the surface to reduce noise.

Remember that even with the same samples, the **Rendered** preview does not always have a total correspondence to the final render with regards to both noise and the fireflies. This is mainly due to the fact that the preview-rendered 3D window and the final rendered image usually have very different sizes, and artifacts visible in the final rendered image may not show in a smaller preview-rendered window.

See also

As you have seen, the several nodes that can be used to build Cycles shaders have both input and output sockets to the left and to the right of the node interface, respectively, and the color of these sockets is actually indicative of their purpose; green sockets are for shaders, yellow sockets are for colors, gray sockets for values, and blue sockets for vectors.

Each color output socket of one node should be connected with the same color input socket of another node. By the way, connecting differently colored sockets also works quite often; for example, a yellow color output can be connected to a gray value input socket and to a blue vector input.

A general overview of all the Cycles nodes can be found at `http://wiki.blender.org/index.php/Doc:2.6/Manual/Render/Cycles/Nodes`.

Procedural textures in Cycles

In this recipe, we'll see several kinds of textures available in Cycles, and learn how to use them with the shaders.

Similar to Blender Internal, we can use both procedural textures and image textures in Cycles. However, the Cycles procedural textures are not exactly the same as in Blender Internal. Some textures are missing because they have been replaced by an improved version (for example, the **Clouds** procedural texture has been replaced by particular settings of the **Noise** procedural texture), and a few textures are new and exclusive to Cycles.

Getting ready

We have already seen a simple construction of a basic Cycles material by mixing the diffuse and the glossy (specular) components of a surface. Now let's take a look at the textures we can use in Cycles to further refine a material.

Because Cycles has a node-based system for materials, textures are not added in their slot under a tab as they are in Blender Internal. They get added in the **Node Editor** window, and are directly connected to the input socket of the shaders or other kinds of nodes. This gives a lot more flexibility to the material creation process because a texture can be used to drive several options inside the material network.

Let's see how they work:

1. Starting from the previously saved `start_01.blend` blend file, where we already set a simple scene with a Cube on a Plane and a basic material, select the Cube and go to the **Object modifiers** window inside the **Properties** panel to the right of the UI.

2. Assign to the Cube a **Subdivision Surface** modifier, set the **Subdivisions** level to 4 for both **View** and **Render**, and check the **Optimal Display** item.

3. Go to the **Tool** tab at the left of the 3D window, navigate to **Edit | Shading**, and set the subdivided Cube (let's call it Spheroid from now on) to **Smooth**.

4. Just to make things clearer, click on the color box of the **Glossy BSDF** shader to change it to a purple color (RGB set to `0.800`, `0.233`, and `0.388`, respectively). Note that only the glossy reflection part on the Spheroid is now purple, whereas the rest of the surface, which is the diffuse component, is still greenish.

5. Save the blend file and name it `start_02.blend`. The effect visible in the real-time **Rendered** preview is as follows:

The Rendered preview of the effect of two differently colored Diffuse and Glossy components on the Spheroid

How to do it...

Perform the following steps to add a procedural texture to the object:

1. Put the mouse pointer in the **Node Editor** window and press *Shift + A*.

2. In the contextual pop-up menu, go to the **Texture** item, just under **Shader**, and click on **Wave Texture** to add the texture node to the **Node Editor** window.

3. Grab and connect the yellow **Color** output socket of the texture to the yellow input socket of the **Diffuse** shader, the socket close to the **Color** rectangle that we formerly set as a greenish color, as shown in this screenshot:

The Rendered preview of the effect of a Wave texture assigned as color to the diffuse component of the material

4. In the **Wave Texture** node, change the **Scale** value to 8.500, **Distortion** to 12.000, **Detail** to a maximum value of 16.000, and the **Detail Scale** value to 6.000.

5. Now disconnect the texture color output from the **Diffuse** node and connect it to the color input socket of the **Glossy** shader, as shown in the following screenshot:

The effect of the Wave Texture assigned as color to the Glossy component of the material

6. Disconnect the texture color output from the **Glossy** shader. Grab and connect the texture node's **Fac** output to the **Roughness** input socket of the **Glossy BSDF** shader, as shown in this screenshot:

The effect of the Wave Texture assigned as Roughness factor to the Glossy component of the material

7. Disconnect the texture color output from the **Roughness** input socket of the **Glossy BSDF** shader. Move the **Wave Texture** node to the left and add a **Bump** node (*Shift + A* and navigate to **Vector | Bump**). Connect the **Fac** output of the **Wave Texture** node to the **Height** input node of the **Bump** node, and the **Normal** output of the **Bump** node to the **Normal** input socket of both the **Diffuse** and the **Glossy** nodes. Set the **Strength** to 0.300. Here is a screenshot showing the effect of the **Wave Texture** node as bump:

The effect of the Wave Texture Fac output as Bump for both the components of the material

8. Save the file.

9. Delete the **Wave Texture** node (*X* key), press *Shift + A* with the mouse pointer in the **Node Editor** window, and add a **Checker Texture** node.

10. Connect the **Fac** output of the **Checker Texture** node to the **Fac** input socket of the **Mix Shader** node and to the **Height** input socket of the **Bump** node, as shown in the following screenshot:

The effect of a Checker Texture used as bump and especially as blending factor to mix the two components of the material

11. Save the file as start_03.blend.

How it works...

From step 1 to 3, the changes are immediately visible in the **Rendered** viewport. At the moment, the **Wave Texture** node color output is connected to the color input of the **Diffuse BSDF** shader node, and the Spheroid looks as if it's painted in a series of black and white bands. Actually, the black and white bands of the texture node override the green color of the diffuse component of the shader, while keeping the material's pink glossy component unaltered.

In step 5, we did exactly the opposite. We disconnected the texture output from the **Diffuse** shader to connect it to the **Glossy** shader color input. Now we have the diffuse greenish color back and the pink has been overridden, while the reflection component is visible only inside the white bands of the wave texture.

In step 6, in addition to the color output, every texture node also has a **Fac** (factor) output socket, outputting gray-scale linear values. When connected to the **Roughness** input socket of the **Glossy** shader, the texture output works as a factor for its reflectivity. The Spheroid keeps its colors and gets the specular component only in the white areas on the surface (that is, white bands represent total reflection and black bands represent no reflection).

In step 10, the **Checker Texture** node's **Fac** output connected to the **Fac** input socket of the **Mix Shader** node works as a mask, or a stencil, based on the black and white values of the output. The numeric slider for the mixing factor on the **Mix Shader** node has disappeared because now we are using the black and white linear values of the **Checker Texture** output as a factor to mixing the **Diffuse** and **Glossy** components. Therefore, these components appear on the Spheroid surface according to the black and white quads of the checker.

Every texture node has several setting options. All of them have in common the **Scale** value to set the size of the procedural. The other settings change according to the type of texture.

The **Fac** output of the texture node can be used to feed the **Height** input socket of the **Bump** node (actually, the **Color** output also works quite well here). Hence, the **Normal** output of the **Bump** node can be connected to the **Normal** input sockets of each shader node, giving a per node bump effect. So, the bump can have an effect only on the diffuse component, or only on the glossy component, or on both, and so on.

Let's create an example of **Wave** and **Voronoi** textures:

1. Re-open the `start_02.blend` file.

2. Add a **Voronoi Texture** node (press *Shift + A* and navigate to **Texture | Voronoi Texture**) and a new **Bump** node (press *Shift + A* and navigate to **Vector | Bump**).

3. Connect the **Fac** output of the **Voronoi Texture** node to the **Height** socket of the new **Bump** node, and connect the latter to the **Normal** input socket of the **Glossy BSDF** shader node. Set its **Strength** value to `0.650` and the **Voronoi** scale to `6.000`.

4. Save the file as `start_02bis.blend`.

Two different procedural textures, a Wave and a Voronoi, used as bumps for the two components to have a per shader effect

In this case, we have two different bump types, affecting the diffuse and the glossy components independently, and building an effect of a layered bump.

There's more...

At this point, you could wonder: "Okay, we just mapped textures on the Spheroid, but what's the projection mode of these mappings?"

Good question! By default, if the projection mode is not specified and if the object doesn't have any UV coordinates, the mapping is **Generated**, which is the equivalent of the **Original Coordinates** mode (now renamed **Generated** as well) in Blender Internal.

But what if you want to specify a mapping method? Then follow these steps:

1. Press *Shift + A* with the mouse pointer in the **Node Editor** window again, go to the **Input** item, and select the **Texture Coordinate** item, which is a node with several mapping modes and their respective output sockets.

2. Try to connect the several outputs to the **Vector** input (the blue socket on the left-hand side of the node), which can be found from **Checker Texture**, to see the texture mapping on the Spheroid change in real time, as shown in the following screenshot:

The Object output of the Texture Coordinate node connected to the Vector input of the Texture node

By the way, I'd like to point your attention to the UV coordinates output. Connect the link to the texture's vector socket, and you will see the mapping on the Spheroid disappear. Why is this so? Because we haven't assigned any UV coordinates to our Spheroid yet.

Go to the **UV Maps** tab in the **Object data** window, under the **Properties** panel on the right, and click on the **+** sign. This just adds a one-to-one **Reset UV projection UV** layer to the object, which means that every face of the mesh is covering the whole area of the **UV/Image Editor** window. Remember that although the Cube looks like a Spheroid now, this is only due to the effect of the assigned **Subdivision Surface** modifier. The UV coordinates work at the lowest level of subdivision, which is still a six-faced Cube.

A second option is to place the proper seams on the Cube's edges and directly unwrap the object in the **UV/Image Editor** window, as demonstrated in the following steps:

1. Press *Tab* to go to **Edit Mode**, select the appropriate edges, press *Ctrl + E*, and in the **Edges** pop-up menu, select the **Mark Seam** item.

2. Now press *A* to select all the vertices (if deselected), press *U*, and choose an unwrapping method from the **UV Mapping** pop-up menu (**Smart UV Project** and **Cube Projection** don't even need the seams). Then go out of **Edit Mode** to update the **Rendered** preview.

The **Texture Coordinate** node is not mandatory to map an image texture on an unwrapped object; in such a case, Cycles will automatically use the (first) available UV coordinates to map the image map anyway.

Often, the only **Texture Coordinate** node is not enough. What we need now is a way to offset, rotate, and scale this texture on the surface:

1. First delete the **Bump** node, then select the **Texture Coordinate** node, and drag it to the left of the window as far as suffices to make room for a new node. In the **Add** menu, go to **Vector** and choose **Mapping**.

2. Grab the **Mapping** node in the middle of the link that connects the **Texture Coordinate** node to the **Checker Texture** node. It will be automatically pasted between them, as shown in the following screenshot:

The Mapping node pasted between Texture Coordinate and the Texture nodes

3. Now start playing with the values inside the **Mapping** node. For example, set the **Z Rotation** value to 45°, set the **X Scale** value to 2.000, and then slide the **X Location** value, while seeing, in the **Rendered** viewport, how the texture changes orientation and dimension and actually slide along the *x* axis.

4. Save the blend file as start_04.blend.

The **Min** and **Max** buttons on the bottom of the **Mapping** node are used to clip the extension of the texture mapping. Check both **Min** and **Max** to prevent the texture from being repeated *n* times on the surface, and it will be shown only once. A minimum value of 0.000 and a maximum value of 1.000 give a correspondence of one-to-one to the mapped image. You can tweak these values to limit or extend the clipping. This is useful to map decals, logos, or labels, for example, on an object and avoid repetition.

See also

In Cycles, it is possible to use normal maps by adding the **Normal Map** node (by navigating to **Add | Vector | Normal Map**) and connecting its output to the **Normal** input socket of the shader nodes.

To see an example of a **Normal Map** node used in a Cycles material, go to *Chapter 8, Creating Organic Materials*, of this cookbook and look at the `bark_seamless` material of the *Creating trees shaders – the bark* recipe.

Here is a link to the official documentation talking about the **Normal Map** node:

`http://wiki.blender.org/index.php/Doc:2.6/Manual/Render/Cycles/Nodes/More`

Setting the World material

In this recipe, we'll see the properties and the settings of the World in Cycles.

The main characteristic of the Cycles World is that it can emit light, so it practically behaves as a light source. Actually, its effect is the famous Global Illumination effect.

As in Blender Internal, the World is considered as a virtual dome at a large distance from the camera, never touching the scene's objects. Nothing in the 3D scene can affect the World. Actually, only the World can emit light on the scene and the objects.

Getting ready

1. Open the `start_04.blend` file and go to the **World** window under the **Properties** panel to the right of the screen. This is where we see the usual **Use Nodes** button under the **Surface** tab.

2. Although no node system for the **World** window is set by default, the **World** window already has a dark, medium gray color slightly lighting the scene. Delete the default Lamp or put it in a different and disabled layer to see that the Spheroid in the scene is dark but still visible in the rendered 3D viewport.

3. It's already possible to change this gray color to some other color by clicking on the **Color** button right under **Use Nodes** (the color at the horizon). This brings up the same color wheel that we saw for the shader colors. Set the color to R 0.179, G 0.152, and B 0.047, and save the file as `start_05.blend`.

Note that both the intensity and the general color graduation of the World are driven by this color. To have more light, just move the **Value** slider (the vertical slider) to a whiter hue. To give a general color mood to the scene, pick a color from inside the wheel. This will affect all of the scene's illumination but will show the effect mainly in the shadows, as shown in the following screenshot:

To the right is the color wheel to set the World's color, inside the World window, under the main Properties panel

How to do it...

However, to get access to all the options for the World, we have to initialize it as a node system, which is shown in the following steps:

1. Look at the bottom header of the **Node Editor** window. On the left-hand side of the material data block, there are two little icons: a little cube and a little world. The cube icon is used to create materials, while the world icon is for the World. At the moment, because we were working on the Spheroid material, the cube icon is the one selected.

2. Click on the little world icon. The material's node disappears, and the **Node Editor** window is empty now because we entered the World mode. Check the little **Use Nodes** box on the right of the data block to make a default world material appear. Alternatively, go to the **World** window under the **Properties** panel and click on the **Use Nodes** button under the **Surface** tab. This is shown in the following screenshot:

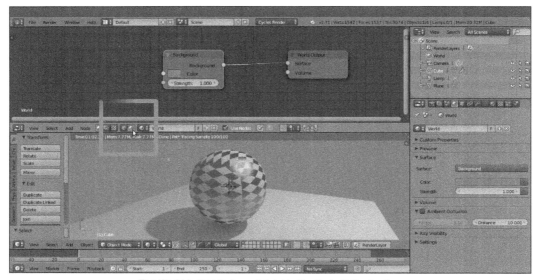

The World button to be switched in the Node Editor toolbar

Just like the materials, the default material for the World is simply made up of two nodes. A **Background** node is connected to a **World Output** node. In the **Background** node, there are two setting options: the **Color** box and the **Strength** slider. Both of them are quite self-explanatory. Now, perform the following steps:

1. Go to the **World** window under the **Properties** panel, and click on the little square with a dot to the right side of the **Color** slot.

2. From the resulting menu, select the **Sky Texture** node item. This replicates a physical sky model with two **Sky** types, an atmospheric **Turbidity** value slider, a **Ground Albedo** value slider, and a **Strength** slider, as shown in this screenshot:

The Sky Texture node with options connected as Color to the Background node

Note that you can also modify the incoming direction of the light, that is, the location of the sun, by rotating the sphere icon inside the node interface. This control isn't that much precise, by the way, and will hopefully improve in the future. The next steps are as follows:

1. Save the file as `start_06.blend`.

2. Click on the **Color** button, which is now labeled **Sky Texture**, under the **Surface** tab in the **Properties** panel, and select the **Environment Texture** node to replace it, as shown in the following screenshot:

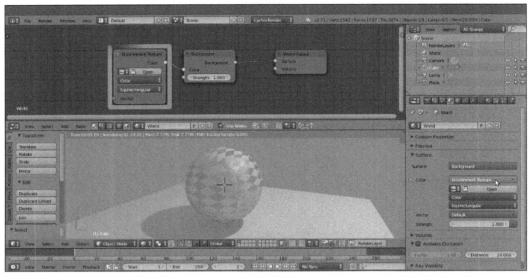

The pink warning effect of a missing texture in the Environment Texture node of the World setting

3. Look in the **Rendered** view. You'll see that the general lighting has changed to a pink color. This is to show that the World material is now using an image texture to light the scene, but that there is no texture yet.

4. Click on the **Open** button in the **World** window, either under the **Properties** panel or in the recently added node inside the **Node Editor** window. Browse to the textures folder and load the Barce_Rooftop_C_3k.hdr image (a free, **High-dynamic-range** (**HDR**) image licensed under the Creative Commons Attribution-NonCommercial-ShareAlike 3.0 License from the sIBL Archive, at http://www.hdrlabs.com/sibl/archive.html).

5. To appreciate the effect, click on the little eye icon on the side of the **Lamp** item in the **Outliner** to disable its lighting. The Spheroid is now exclusively lit by the HDR image assigned to the World material. Actually, you can see the image as a background in the **Rendered** preview. You can also rotate the viewport and watch the background texture, pinned to the World coordinates, rotate accordingly in real time.

6. As for the object's materials, the mapping of any texture you are going to use for the World can be driven by the usual **Mapping** and **Texture Coordinates** nodes we have already seen. Generally, for the World materials, only the **Generated** coordinates output should be used, and actually, the **Generated** coordinates output is used by default if no mapping method is specified. Add the **Mapping** and **Texture Coordinates** nodes and connect them to the **Vector** input socket of the **Environment Texture** node, as shown in the following screenshot:

The Rendered preview of an HDR image assigned as a background to the World through the Environment Texture node

7. Save the file as `start_07.blend`.

Now let's imagine a case in which we want to assign a texture to the World material and use it for the general lighting of the scene, but we don't want it to show in the background of the render. In other words, we are using the HDR image to light the Spheroid and the Plane, but we want the two objects rendered on a uniform blue background; so how do we do it? This is how:

1. One way is to go to the **Render** window and check the **Transparent** option under the **Film** tab. This will show our Spheroid and Plane rendered in both the 3D viewport and the effective final rendered image on a transparent background, with a premultiplied alpha channel, as shown in the following screenshot:

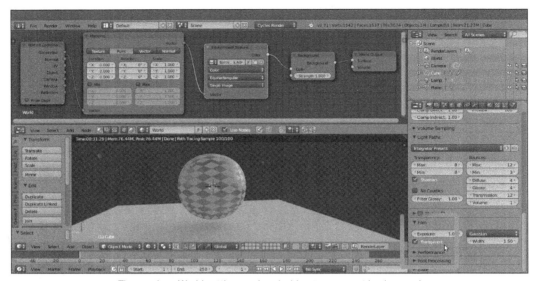

The previous World setting rendered with a transparent background

2. Now we can compose the rendered image with a blue background, both in external image editing software (such as GIMP, to stay inside FOSS) or directly in the Blender compositor.

A different way to render the two objects on a uniform blue background is to use a **Light Path** node:

1. If this is the case, deselect the **Transparent** item checkbox in the **Render** window to restore the sky background in the preview and in the rendering.

2. Click on the **World Output** node in the **Node Editor** window, press *G*, and move it to the right.

3. Add a **Mix Shader** node (press *Shift + A* and navigate to **Shader** | **Mix Shader**) and move it to the link connecting the **Background** node to the **World Output** node, to paste it automatically between the two nodes.

4. Select the **Background** node in the **Node Editor** window. Press *Shift + D* to duplicate it and move it down.

5. Connect its output to the second input socket of the **Mix Shader** node. Click on its **Color** box to change the color to R 0.023, G 0.083, and B 0.179.

6. Now, add a **Light Path** node (press *Shift + A* and navigate to **Input | Light Path**).

7. Connect the **Is Camera Ray** output of the **Light Path** node to the **Fac** input socket of the **Mix Shader** node, and voilà! The objects in the scene are lit by the HDR image connected to the first **Background** node, but they appear in a sky that is colored as set in the **Color** box of the second **Background** node. This is shown in the following screenshot:

The use of the Path Light node as a factor to have a different background than the HDR image still illuminating the scene

8. Save the file as start_08.blend.

How it works...

To explain this trick better, let's say we just created two different world materials: the first material with the texture and the second material with a plain blue color (this is not literally true; actually, the material is just one, containing the nodes of two ideally different worlds).

We mixed these two materials using the **Mix Shader** node. The upper green socket of the **Mix Shader** node is considered equal to a value of 0.000, while the bottom green socket is considered equal to a value of 1.000. As the name suggests, the **Light Path** node can set the path for the rays of light that are shot from the camera, if you remember. **Is Camera Ray** means that only the rays directly shot from the camera have a value of 1.000, that is, not the reflected ones, or the transmitted ones, or whatever, which have a value of 0.000.

Thus, because the textured world is connected to a socket equal to the value of 0.000, we don't see it directly as a background, but only see its effect on the objects lit from the reflected light or from the HDR image. The World of the blue sky, which is connected to the input socket of value 1.000 instead, is seen as a background because the light rays shot from the camera directly hit the sky.

There's more...

Just after the **Surface** subpanel, in the **World** window, there is the **Ambient Occlusion** subpanel. **Ambient occlusion** is a lighting method used to emphasize the shapes or the details of a surface, based on how much a point on that surface is occluded by the nearby surfaces. Ambient occlusion can replace the Global Illumination effect in some cases, though not the same. For example, to render interiors with fast and noise-free results, ambient occlusion is a cheap way to get an effect that looks a bit like indirect lighting.

There is a checkbox to enable **Ambient Occlusion**, along with the following sliders:

 ▸ **Factor**: This is used for the strength of the ambient occlusion. A value of 1.00 is equivalent to a white World.

 ▸ **Distance**: This is the distance from a shading point to the trace rays. A shorter distance emphasizes nearby features, while a longer distance takes into account objects that are further away.

The **Ambient Occlusion** feature is only applied to the **Diffuse BSDF** component of a material. The **Glossy** or **Transmission BSDF** components are not affected. Instead, the transparency of a surface is taken into account. For example, a half-transparent surface will only half-occlude other surfaces.

Creating a mesh-light material

In this recipe, we will see how to create a mesh-light material to be assigned to any mesh object and used as a source to light the scene.

Getting ready

Until now, we have used the default Lamp (a Point light) already present in the scene to light the scene. By enabling the node system for the Lamp, we have seen that it uses a material created by connecting an **Emission** node to the **Lamp Output** node.

The good news is that just because it's a material node, we can assign an **Emission** shader to a mesh, for example, to a Plane conveniently located, scaled, and rotated to point to the scene that is the center of interest. Such a light-emitting mesh is called a mesh-light. Being a mesh, the **Emission** shader node output must be connected to the **Surface** (or the **Volume**) input socket of a **Material Output** node instead of the **Lamp Output** node.

Light emission coming from a surface and not from a point is a lot more diffused and softer than the light from a Lamp. A mesh-light can be any mesh of any shape, so it can be used as an object taking part in the scene and be the real light source of the rendering at the same time, for example, a table lamp, or a neon sign, or a television screen. As a pure light-emitting Plane, it's usually used as a sort of photographic diffuser. Two or three strategically placed mesh-lights can realistically simulate a photo studio situation. To replace the Lamp with a mesh-light, Plane perform the following steps:

1. Call the **Blender User Preferences** panel (*Ctrl + Alt + U*), navigate to the **Addons** tab, and click on **3D View** under **Categories** on the left. Check the **Copy Attributes Menu** box to the right-hand side of the **3D View** option, and click on the **Save User Settings** button in the bottom-left corner of the panel. Then close the panel.

2. Starting from the `start_07.blend` file, click on the eye icon of **Lamp** in the **Outliner** to enable its visibility again.

3. Right-click on the **Lamp** in the 3D view and press *Shift + S* to bring up the **Snap** menu. Click on the **Cursor to Selected** item.

4. Press *Shift + A* with the mouse pointer in the 3D view and add a Plane to the scene at the 3D Cursor's location.

5. Press *Shift* and select the Lamp. Now you have both the recently added Plane and the Lamp selected, and the latter is the active object.

6. Press *Ctrl + C* to open the **Copy Attributes** menu and select the **Copy Rotation** item.

7. Rename this Plane as `Emitter`.

8. Right-click on the Lamp in the 3D view and press *X* to delete it.

9. Put the mouse pointer on the 3D view and press *0* from the numeric keypad to go to Camera view.

10. From the **Viewport Shading** menu in the window's header, select the **Rendered** mode (or put the mouse cursor on the **Camera** view and press *Shift + Z*):

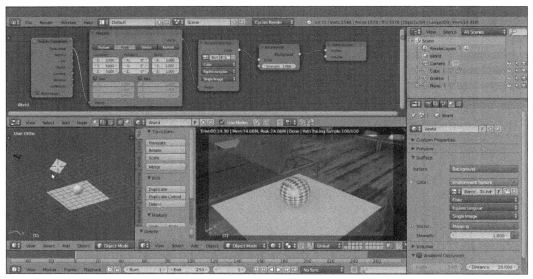

A Plane set as a mesh-light to replace the Lamp, and the previous HDR image as the background

11. Save the file as `start_09.blend`.

How to do it...

Now let's create the emission material and also take a look at the setup for the softness of the projected shadows:

1. Select the **Emitter** plane and click on the little cube icon on the header of the **Node Editor** window.

2. Click on the **New** button in the header and rename the material as `Emitter`.

3. In the **Properties** panel, go to the **Material** window, and under the **Surface** tab, click on the **Surface** button to switch the **Diffuse BSDF** shader with an **Emission** shader. Leave the default color unchanged (**RGB** `0.800`) and set the **Strength** slider to `25.000`.

4. Save the file.

   The situation so far is as follows:

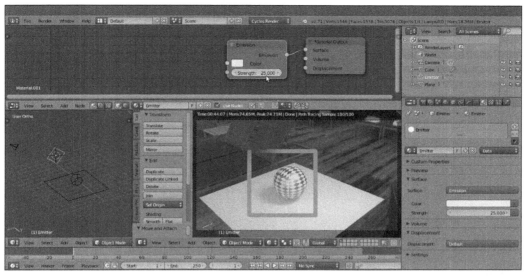

The mesh-light emission material with increased strength

5. In the 3D view, scale the **Emitter** plane five times bigger (press S, then enter 5, and press *Enter*), and then set the **Strength** slider to 2.500.

6. Save the file as start_10.blend. Now look at the softer shadow, as shown in the following screenshot:

Scaling the mesh-light bigger and decreasing the emission strength to have softer shadows

7. Now let's scale the **Emitter** plane a lot smaller (press S, then type *0.05*, and press *Enter*) and set the **Strength** slider to 450.000.

8. Save the file as `start_11.blend`. Look at the crisper shadow in the **Rendered** preview, as shown in this screenshot:

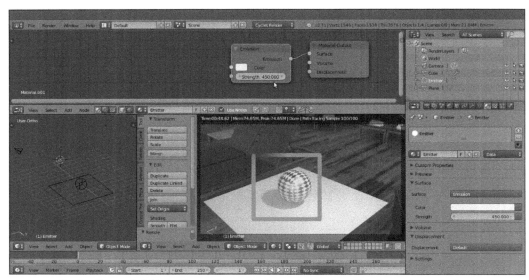

Scaling the mesh-light smaller and increasing the emission strength to have crisper shadows

How it works...

From steps 5 to 7, we saw how a mesh-light can be scaled bigger or smaller to obtain a softer (in the first case) or a sharper (in the second case) shadow, respectively. The **Strength** value must be adjusted for the light intensity to remain consistent, or the mesh-light must be moved closer or more distant from the scene.

Scaling the mesh-light is basically the same as setting the size value for a Lamp. For Lamps, the softness of shadows can be set by the **Size** value to the left of the **Cast Shadow** option in the **Lamp** window, under the **Properties** panel (by default, the **Size** value is set to `1.000`). At a value of `0.000`, the shadow is at its maximum crispness, or sharpness. If the **Size** value is increased, the softness of the shadow increases too.

Unlike the mesh-light, varying the **Size** value of a Lamp doesn't require us to adjust the **Strength** value to keep the same light intensity.

There's more...

In several cases, you might not want the emitters to appear in your rendering. There are node arrangements to accomplish this (such as using the **Light Path** node in a way quite similar to the *Setting the World material* recipe we have seen before), but the easiest way to do this is as follows:

1. Start with the last saved blend (`start_11.blend`) and put the mouse cursor on the orthogonal 3D view to the left of the screen. Press the *3* key to navigate to the **Side** view. Then press *Shift + Z* to go in the **Rendered** mode to also see the **Emitter** plane rendered (be warned that if your computer can't easily render two windows at the same time, you must temporarily turn off the rendering for the **Camera** view).

2. With the Emitter plane still selected, navigate to the **Object** window under the **Properties** panel.

3. Look at the **Ray Visibility** tab (usually at the bottom of the **Properties** panel), where there are five items: **Camera**, **Diffuse**, **Glossy**, **Transmission** and **Shadows**, with the corresponding checked boxes.

4. Uncheck the **Camera** item and watch the **Emitter** plane disappear in the rendered 3D window, but the scene still lit by it, as shown in the following screenshot:

Disabling the Camera item in the Ray Visibility subpanel to hide the mesh-light Plane from the rendering

When you disable any one of the items, the corresponding property won't take part in the rendering. In our case, when the **Camera** box is unchecked, the mesh-light won't be rendered but it will still emit light. Be careful that the **Emitter** plane is not renderable at this moment, but because all the other items in the tab are still checked, it can be reflected and could cast its own shadow on other objects.

5. Now reselect the Spheroid (remember that unless you have renamed it, its name in the **Outliner** remains as Cube). Next, from the **Ray Visibility** tab in the **Object** window under the **Properties** panel, uncheck the **Camera** item.

Now the Spheroid has disappeared, but it's still casting its shadow on the floor Plane, as shown in this screenshot:

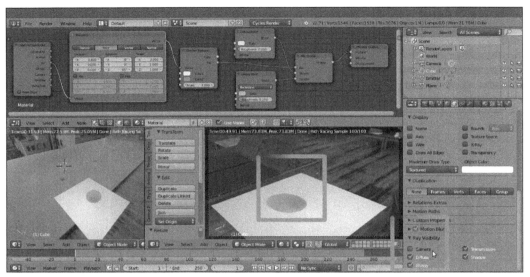

Disabling the Camera item to hide the Spheroid object from the rendering (but keeping the shadows on the floor)

6. Now check the **Camera** item again and uncheck the **Shadow** box. In this case, the Spheroid is visible again but doesn't cast a shadow, as shown in the following screenshot:

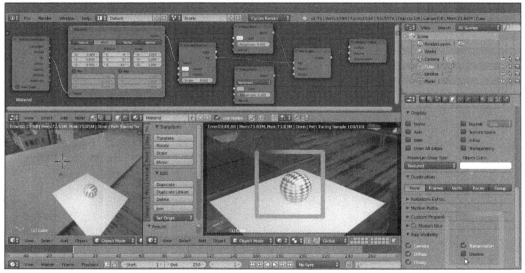

Disabling the Shadow item to have the Spheroid object rendered but without the shadows on the floor Plane

7. Save the file as `start_12.blend`. Let's try tweaking this a little.

8. Check the **Shadow** box for the Spheroid again, and select the floor Plane. Go to the **Material** window under the **Properties** panel, and click on the **New** button to assign a new material (**Material.001**).

9. Still in the **Material** window under the **Properties** panel, switch the **Diffuse BSDF** shader with a **Glossy BSDF** shader. The floor Plane is now acting as a perfect mirror, reflecting the Spheroid and the HDR image we formerly set in the World material.

10. Go back to the **Object** window and reselect the Spheroid. In the **Ray Visibility** tab, uncheck the **Glossy** item and watch the Spheroid, which is still rendered but not reflected by the mirror floor Plane, as shown in the following screenshot:

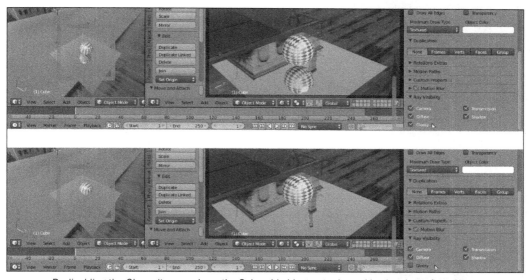

By disabling the Glossy item, we have the Spheroid object not mirrored by the glossy floor Plane

11. Save the file as `start_13.blend`.

Of course, the **Ray Visibility** trick we've just seen is not needed for Lamps because a Lamp cannot be rendered at all. At the moment, only **Point**, **Spot**, **Area**, and **Sun** lamps are supported inside Cycles. **Hemi** lamps are rendered as **Sun** lamps.

Both Lamps and mesh-lights can use textures too, for example, project colored lights on the scene, but only a mesh-light can be unwrapped and UV-mapped with an image map.

One advantage Lamps have over mesh-lights is that they can be made unidirectional easily, that is, apart from **Point** lamps, they cast light in only one direction. The following screenshot shows the casting of light with a Spot Lamp:

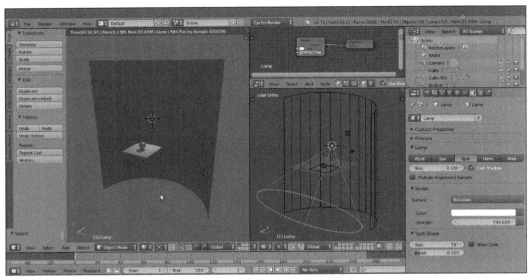

A Spot Lamp allows light to point in just one direction

In the preceding screenshot, you can see that only the Plane and the Spheroid in front of the Spot lamp receive light. With a mesh-light plane replacing the Spot lamp, objects in both the front and the back (the half-cylindrical **Wall** and the second Spheroid) receive light.

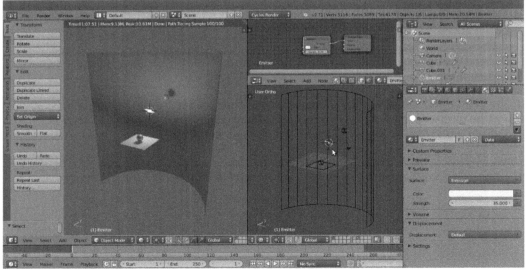

A mesh-light emitter illuminates the region backward and forward by default

What if we want to light the object in only one direction (Plane and Spheroid in front) with a mesh-light? Is there a way to make a light-emitting plane emit light only from one side and not the opposite side? Yes, there is; follow these steps:

1. Open the `01_meshlight.blend` file, which has prepared the scene used for the preceding screenshots, and be sure to enable only the first and the seventh layer.

2. Put the mouse cursor on the left vertical 3D view, and press *Shift + Z* to navigate in **Rendered** view mode.

3. Click on the **Emitter** item in the **Outliner** to select it (if not already selected), and put the mouse pointer in the **Node Editor** window. Add a **Mix Shader** node (press *Shift + A* and navigate to **Shader | Mix Shader**) and move it to the link connecting the **Emission** node to the **Material Output** node to paste it in between them.

4. Add a **Geometry** node (press *Shift + A* and navigate to **Input | Geometry**) and connect its **Backfacing** output to the **Fac** input socket of the **Mix Shader** node.

5. Switch the **Emission** node output from the first **Shader** input socket of the **Mix Shader** node to the second node, as shown in the following screenshot:

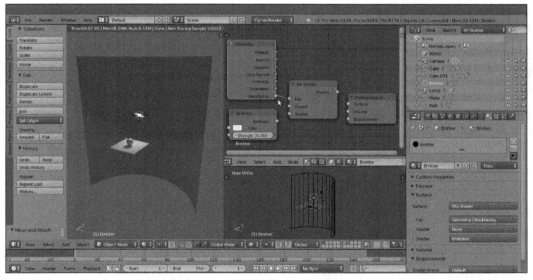

Thanks to the Backfacing output of a Geometry node as Factor, a mesh-light can illuminate in only one direction

6. Save the file as `01_meshlight_final.blend`.

We have already seen that in a **Mix Shader** node, the first (upper) green **Shader** input socket is considered equal to a 0 value, while the second socket is considered equal to a 1 value. So, the **Backfacing** output of the **Geometry** node is telling Cycles to make the mesh-light plane emit light only in the face-normal direction, and to keep the opposite back-facing side of the plane black and non-emitting (just like a blank shader).

By switching the **Emission** node connection to the first **Mix Shader** input socket, it's obviously possible to invert the direction of the light emission.

Using volume materials

Very briefly (because there are dedicated recipes in the last chapter of this Cookbook), let's take a look at how volumetric materials work in Cycles.

Volumetric materials are exactly what they sound like. Instead of the surface of an object, Cycles renders the inner volume of that object, and this gives space to a lot of interesting possibilities—not only can elusive materials such as smoke, fire, clouds, or light transmission effects through the medium be realized, but peculiar shapes can also be obtained from the volume itself by Boolean operations made through material nodes.

The drawback is that volume materials are slow—a lot slower compared to the surface materials, but hopefully, this is an issue that will be fixed in some way in the future (be aware that from Version 2.72, volume materials are available on GPUs too).

Getting ready

Let's start with our usual Spheroid blend file:

1. Open the `start_02.blend` file and delete the material assigned to the Spheroid.
2. Put the mouse cursor in the 3D view and press *Shift + Z* to navigate to the **Rendered** view.
3. Click on the **New** button to add a new material, and then switch the **Diffuse** node link from the **Surface** input socket to the **Volume** input socket of the **Material Output** node.

How to do it...

Now let's go to the volume section of the **Material** window with the following steps:

1. Go to the **Material** window under the **Properties** panel, and click on the **Diffuse BSDF** labeled button to the side of the **Volume** item. In the pop-up menu, select the **Volume Scatter** node as shown in this screenshot:

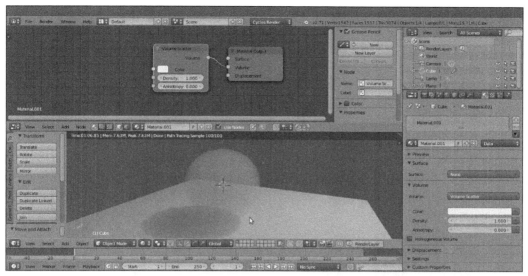

The Rendered preview of a Volume Scatter node assigned to the Spheroid

2. Change the **Density** value of the **Volume Scatter** node from 1.000 to 50.000. The Spheroid looks a lot more solid now, as shown in the following screenshot:

The effect of the Volume Scatter node with increased density

3. Add a **Voronoi Texture** node (Press *Shift + A* and navigate to **Texture | Voronoi Texture**). Connect the **Fac** output to the **Density** input socket of the **Volume Scatter** node. Set the **Voronoi** scale to 3.800.

4. Add a **Math** node (Press *Shift + A* and navigate to **Converter | Math**) and paste it in the link between the **Voronoi Texture** and the **Volume Scatter** nodes. Set **Operation** to **Less Than** and second **Value** to 0.100.

5. Add a second **Math** node and paste it right after the first node. Set the **Operation** to **Multiply** and second **Value** to 50.000. Here is a screenshot of the output of a **Voronoi Texture** node for your reference:

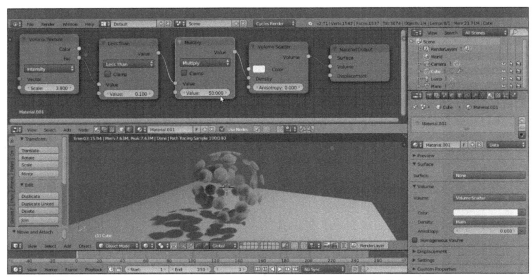

The output of a Voronoi Texture node used as Factor for the density of the Volume Scatter node

6. Click on the **Color** button of the **Volume Scatter** node. Set the **RGB** values to `0.800`, `0.214`, and `0.043`, respectively.

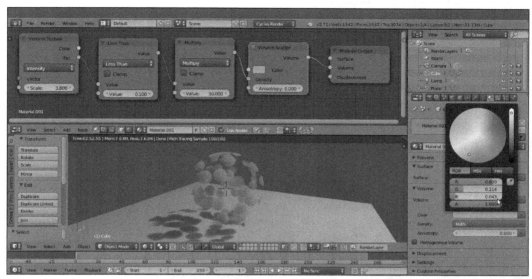

The scattered light is obviously of a hue complementary to the color assigned to the volume

7. Save the file as `01_volumetric.blend`.

How it works...

We have seen that when we increase the **Density** value of the **Volume Scatter** node, the Spheroid starts to look more and more solid. So, we used the output of a **Voronoi Texture** node and clamped it with a **Less Than** node to show only the values that are not beyond the `0.100` limit. Then we multiplied the value by `50.000`, thus increasing the density of the Voronoi spheres and making them appear as solid objects inside the Spheroid volume.

Remember that in this case, we rendered only the inside of the object and not the surface. Anyway, a combination of **Surface** and **Volume** is possible and can give interesting results, as shown in the following screenshot:

Combining a Glass shader for the surface with a Volume Scatter node for the inside of the mesh

There's more...

Volumes also work in the World. In fact, the **World Output** node now has a **Volume** input socket. By connecting a **Volume Scatter** or **Volume Absorption** node to the **World Output** node, it is possible to obtain several special effects, for example, fog, mist, atmospheric perspective, atmospheric scattering effects, and a body of water for an underwater scene. Clearly, it's also possible to fill this environment volume with textures.

In any case, you won't usually fill the entire World with a volumetric material because the World in Blender is considered as going to an infinite distance, and this would make the volume calculation too heavy. It's better to use a scaled Cube, properly placed and filled with the volume material.

To know more about volume materials, go to the last chapter of this Cookbook or to the documentation on the wiki at `http://wiki.blender.org/index.php/Doc:2.6/Manual/Render/Cycles/Materials/Volume`.

Using displacement

The last input socket of the **Material Output** node is **Displacement**. Sadly, it seems that at the moment, its use is limited.

Getting ready

By enabling **Experimental** in the **Feature Set** option under the **Render** tab in the **Render** window, it's possible to have access to an incomplete displacement feature:

1. Open the `start_03.blend` file, select the Spheroid, and delete its material.

2. Go to the **Render** window under the **Properties** panel. In the **Render** tab, click on the **Feature Set** button, labeled with **Supported** by default, and select **Experimental**.

3. Go to the **Object data** window to find a new tab named **Displacement**, where we can choose between three options: **Bump**, **True**, and **Both** (the **Use Subdivision** and **Dicing Rate** buttons don't seem to work yet).

> **Bump** will give us the average bump effect, which is the same as connecting the texture output in the **Displacement** input of the **Material Output** node (this is a different way to have an overall bump effect, and it works without the need to set the **Feature Set** option to **Experimental**).
>
> By setting the method to **True**, we can have a displacement effect that is not different from the **Displace Modifier** output, and the mesh must be subdivided.
>
> **Both** will use the texture gray-scale values' information for a displacement and the bump effect together.

4. Select **True**.

How to do it...

1. Go to the **Material** window under the **Properties** panel and click on the **New** button. In the **Displacement** tab, click on the **Default** button, and in the pop-up menu, select the **Image Texture** node.

2. Click on the **Open** button, browse to the `textures` folder, and load the `quads.png` image.

3. Split the bottom 3D window to open a **UV/Image Editor** window.

4. Press *Tab* to go to **Edit Mode**. Then press *U* with the mouse pointer in the 3D window. In the **UV Mapping** menu, select **Smart UV Project**, then load the `quads.png` image in the `UV/Image Editor`, and press *Tab* again to go out of **Edit Mode**. Note that this is the quicker way to unwrap the Spheroid, which is still a Cube at its lower level of subdivision. If you want, you can do a better unwrapping by placing seams to unfold it and by selecting a normal **Unwrap** option from the pop-up menu.

5. Go to the **Object modifiers** window and raise the **Subdivisions** levels for both **View** and **Render** to `6`.

6. Add a **Math** node (press *Shift + A* and navigate to **Converter | Math**) and paste it between the **Image Texture** node and the **Material Output**. Set **Operation** to **Multiply**, and the second option, **Value**, to 2.000 (if you don't see any modification in the rendered preview, it's an update issue, which can be solved by pressing *Tab* twice to go in and out of **Edit Mode**).

7. Add a **Glossy** node (press *Shift + A* and navigate to **Shader | Glossy BSDF**) and a **Mix Shader** node (press *Shift + A* and navigate to **Shader | Mix Shader**), and connect them to build the average basic material we already know.

8. Add two **MixRGB** nodes (press *Shift + A* and navigate to **Color | MixRGB**) and connect them to the color input sockets of the **Diffuse** and the **Glossy** nodes.

9. Finally, connect the color output of the **Image Texture** node to the **Color1** input sockets of the **MixRGB** nodes, and set colors for the **Color2** sockets. Here is a screenshot of a checker image texture used as displacement for your reference:

A checker image texture used as a color and output for the Rendered displacement of the Spheroid

Instead of the **Smart UV Project** option to unwrap the Spheroid, try the default 1:1 UV Mapping (the **Reset** item in the menu, which gives the whole image mapped on each face). The following screenshot shows the checker image texture used with the different unwrap:

The checker image texture used as a color and output for the rendered displacement of a Spheroid with a different unwrap

10. Save the file as 9931OS_01_displacement.blend.

In any case, this is just for a temporary demonstration; the feature is still incomplete. At the moment, it seems to work quite well only if the texture is mapped with UV coordinates. This is definitely going to change in the future.

How it works...

Simply put, the gray-scale values of the texture are multiplied by the value we put in the second slider of the **Math** node. For example, if we set a value of 0.500, the intensity of the effect will be the half of the default value (*1.000 x 0.500 = 0.500*). With a value of 3.000, the effect would be three times the default value, and so on. Similar to Blender Internal, the value can also be set as negative, thereby inverting the direction of the displacement.

2
Managing Cycles Materials

In this chapter, we will be covering the following recipes:

- ▶ Preparing an ideal Cycles interface for material creation
- ▶ Naming materials and textures
- ▶ Creating node groups
- ▶ Grouping nodes under frames for easier reading
- ▶ Linking materials and node groups

Introduction

As with Blender Internal materials, Cycles materials can (and should) be organized to optimize your workflow.

Material nodes in Cycles can easily grow quite complex, and it's sometimes a good idea to split and label the different parts of a shader's network, just to make the meaning of the different sections clearer (even to yourself because maybe at a certain point of your workflow, you will forget how exactly that 120-node material you made a couple of months ago works). Moreover, organized materials can be easily reused in other files and projects or as parts of bigger and different materials.

Organization of materials is basically done by grouping them or giving them proper names and defined locations so that they can be easily found in the hard disk.

Preparing an ideal Cycles interface for material creation

Before starting with the actual organization, it's a good idea to prepare a material creation screen to be saved in your Blender preferences.

It is possible, in fact, to prepare a basic scene setup that includes the elements and the settings we need to do the job best.

In any case, just take this recipe with a grain of salt, that is, take it as more of a suggestion or as a starting point that you can eventually modify to better suit your needs.

Getting ready

Start Blender and in the upper menu (the **Engine to use for rendering** button), switch to **Cycles Render**.

How to do it...

We are now going to customize the **Default** screen:

1. Split the 3D view into two horizontal rows. To do this, move the mouse cursor onto the lateral edge of the window. The cursor changes to a double arrow icon. Right-click on the edge, and from the little pop-up menu that appears, select **Split Area** (or click in the top-right corner of the window and move it).

2. Change the upper window to a **Node Editor** window by selecting the item from the **Editor Type** button in the left corner of the bottom bar (or by putting the mouse cursor in the window and pressing the *Shift + F3* keyboard shortcut).

3. Select the default Cube in the scene if it is not selected already, and go to the **Object modifier** window under the **Properties** panel to the right of the screen. Assign a **Subdivision Surface** modifier to the Cube, which is now a Spheroid, and set the **Subdivisions** levels for both **View** and **Render** to 4. Check the **Optimal Display** item.

4. Set the Spheroid shading mode to **Smooth** by clicking on the appropriate button under the **Shading** subpanel in the **Tools** tab on the left.

5. Move the Spheroid upward by 2 units on the *z* axis (press *G*, then press *Z*, enter digit *2*, and finally, press *Enter*).

6. Ensuring that the cursor is still at the center of the scene (if not, press *Shift + C* to center it), press *Shift + A* and navigate to **Mesh | Plane** to add a Plane.

7. Press *Tab* to go to **Edit Mode** and scale the Plane four times bigger (press *Tab*, then press *S*, enter digit *4*, and finally, press *Enter*). Exit **Edit Mode**.

8. Split the bottom row into two parts, put the mouse cursor in the 3D window on the right, and press *0* in the numeric keypad of the keyboard to go to the **Camera** view. Then press *T* to close the **Tool Shelf** panel with the tabs on the left. Scroll the mouse wheel to fit the **Camera** view field into the window (or for a finer control, press *Ctrl +* the middle button of the mouse and move the mouse).

This screenshot shows where we are now:

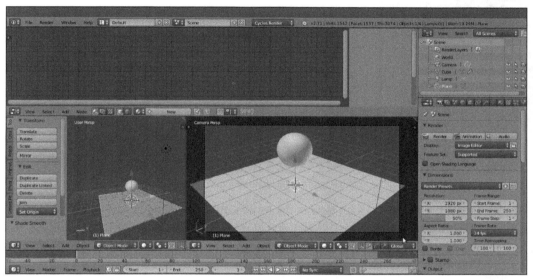

The first steps of the Default screen customization for Cycles material creation

9. In the **Editor Type** button in the left corner of the bottom bar of the left 3D window, select **UV/Image Editor**.

10. Select the Spheroid, go to **Edit Mode**, and scale it to twice the current size (press *Tab*, then press *S*, enter digit *2*, and finally, press *Enter*). Exit **Edit Mode**.

11. Move the mouse to the **Camera** view and press *Shift + F* to enter Walk Navigation mode (a viewfinder appears to show the center of the camera field). By moving the mouse to pan and by pressing the *W* or the *S* key to go forward or backward, respectively, adjust the **Camera** view to fit the Spheroid better. Then press *Enter* or click to confirm, as shown in the following screenshot:

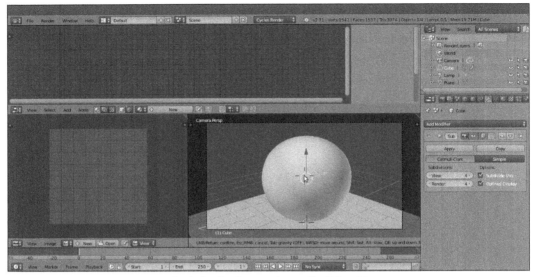

Centering the Camera view on the Spheroid

12. Select the Plane. Click on **New** in the **Node Editor** toolbar to assign a new material (**Material.001**). Rename it `Plane` and leave all the settings as they are.

13. Select the Spheroid and click on **Use Nodes** in the **Material** window under the **Properties** panel to the right of the screen or in the **Node Editor** toolbar.

14. Put the mouse in the **Node Editor** window and scroll the wheel to zoom to the nodes.

15. Under the **Surface** subpanel in the **Material** window, switch the **Diffuse BSDF** shader with a **Mix Shader** node. Then click on the first **Shader** slot to select a **Diffuse BSDF** shader and on the second slot for a **Glossy BSDF** shader (the two **Shader** slots I'm referring to are highlighted in the next screenshot).

16. In the **Node Editor** window, adjust the position of the nodes to make them more readable, as shown in this screenshot:

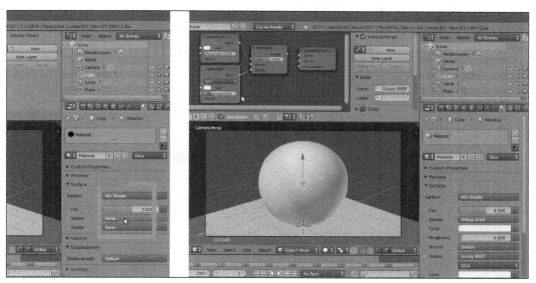

Preparing a basic average material with the Diffuse and the Glossy components

17. Set the **Camera** view mode to **Rendered** by clicking on the **Viewport Shading** button on the window toolbar and selecting the top item or by pressing *Shift + Z* with the mouse cursor inside the 3D view.

18. Go to the **Render** window under the **Properties** panel on the right, and under the **Sampling** subpanel, set both **Clamp Direct** and **Clamp Indirect** to 1.00, and both **Render** and **Preview** to 50 samples.

19. Under the **Light Paths** subpanel, set **Filter Glossy** to 1.00.

20. Go to the **Outliner** window and select the **Lamp** item. Go to the **Object data** window under the **Properties** panel and click on the **Use Nodes** button under the **Nodes** subpanel. Increase the **Strength** value to 300.000.

Now the output will look like what is shown in this screenshot:

Setting the Camera view to Rendered and increasing the Lamp strength

21. Go back to the **Render** window under the **Properties** panel and set the **Percentage** scale for render resolution under **Dimensions** to 25% to have smaller but faster rendering.

22. Under the **Performance** subpanel, set **Viewport BVH Type** to **Static BVH** and check **Use Spatial Splits**, **Cache BVH**, and **Persistent Images** (these are probably not really useful for a simple Spheroid, but they are useful if you want to render a more complex object).

23. Go to the **World** window and click on the **Use Nodes** button under the **Surface** subpanel. Click on the **Color** slot, set the **RGB** values to 0.100, and set the **Strength** value to 0.100.

24. Set the **Factor** value for the **Ambient Occlusion** subpanel to 0.05 but let it remain disabled. You can enable the **Ambient Occlusion** subpanel or not, depending on your preferences, but remember that it adds light to the rendered image. I would say that it's usually better not to have the **Ambient Occlusion** subpanel activated by default but enabled only if really needed. In this case, the very low value can compensate a bit for the darkened background of the World, which is shown in the following screenshot for your reference:

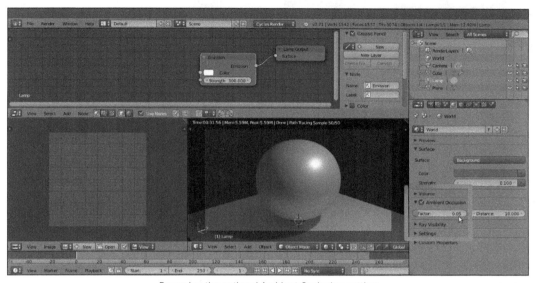

Preparing the optional Ambient Occlusion setting

Optionally, other things that you can do include scaling the floor Plane bigger. In the **Outliner** window, set the mode to **Visible Layers** and click on the arrow icon to the side of the **Plane** item to make it nonselectable. Substitute **Lamp**, the default **Point** item, with a different type (**Sun** or **Spot**) or with a mesh-light plane.

25. Go back to the **Material** window. If you want to save this setting as the user default, press *Ctrl + U* (**Save Startup File**), or save the file with a meaningful name. Among the files provided with this book, you will find this file by the name of `9931OS_02_interface.blend`. The 3D view now looks like what is shown in the following screenshot:

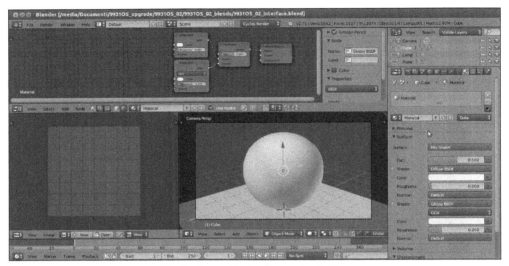

The final overall look of the customization

How it works...

We set a very low World global illumination, keeping its color within the gray scale in order not to affect the color of the material. The floor plane is meant to have light bouncing on the shadowed parts of the object, and this can eventually be helped by the low **Ambient Occlusion** subpanel as well.

We prepared the **Rendered** view port as a **Camera** view to get better feedback for the final rendered image, which will show at 25 percent of the established size in the **UV/Image Editor** window on the bottom-left side of the screen.

By setting the **Clamp** values to `1.00`, we reduced the fireflies produced by the glossy shader, and by increasing the render and preview samples to `50`, we reduced the noise, at the same time keeping the rendering times reasonable, even with a not-very-powerful workstation.

The **Viewport BVH Type** is set to **Static BVH**, and the **Use Spatial Splits**, **Cache BVH**, and **Persistent Images** options are useful to reduce the calculation time for the bounding volume hierarchy of the mesh, which Cycles has to calculate every time it starts rendering. Anyway, these options are useful only if the mesh doesn't get any internal modification between renderings.

There's more...

From now on, every time we start Blender, the layout and the settings we just saved as default will be seen first.

But maybe we don't want to have this Cycles material interface every time we start, and we prefer to have it only as an option to be used if needed. Actually, in the previous steps, we modified the **Default** screen, but it's also possible to create new screens while keeping the original screen available. Here is the way to do this:

1. Start Blender with the factory settings (click on the **File** menu on the top main header and navigate to **Load Factory Setting**) and look at the top of the screen, in the main header on the side of the **Blender Render** button. There are two more buttons labeled **Default** and **Scene**.

2. By clicking on the **Default** button, we can set a different interface layout (there are already nine, each of which is studied for a different task, and their names are perfectly explicative). Clicking on **Scene** shows just the current scene.

3. By clicking on the **+** icon on the side of the **Default** button, we add a new screen layout named `Default.001`. Rename it `Materials`.

4. Then click on the **+** icon on the side of the **Scene** button, and by choosing the **Full Copy** item, add a new scene to the **Scene.001** file. Rename the file as something like `Cycles_Materials`. This new scene is a full copy of the default scene, coexisting but independent.

At this point, we can start with all the instructions already seen in the *How to do it* section of this recipe: switching to **Cycles Render**, splitting the 3D window, assigning the **Subdivision Surface** modifier to the default Cube, and so on.

When done, just click on the screens button, switch back to **Default**, and then save the user preferences (*Ctrl + U*). Now our material creation interface is saved as a screen option in a different scene. Every time we need to access it, it's enough to select the layout **Materials** from the screens button.

Naming materials and textures

It is well known that one of the most important things to do when working in every workflow with every 3D package is to give proper and explicative names to all the assets, that is, to the materials and the textures in our case.

Getting ready

Start Blender, go to the **File** menu in the top-left corner, and choose **Load Factory Setting** (this is just to be sure to start with the default Blender / Cycles settings).

Now, if you are in Blender Internal mode, switch to **Cycles Render**.

How to do it...

Now let's see the way material and texture naming works in Cycles.

Materials:

Adding and renaming materials in the **Material** window is done by performing the following steps:

1. Select the default Cube. Go to the **Material** window in the **Properties** panel. The default Cube already has a material assigned. This material has already been named Material by Blender, as shown in the following screenshot:

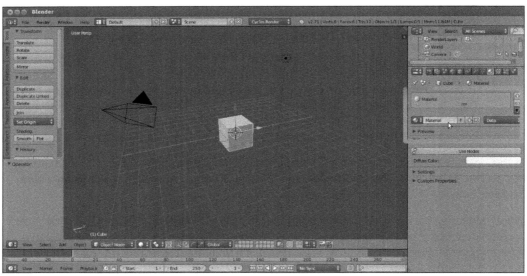

The material name datablock under the Material window

2. When you create a new material, for example, by clicking on the **+** symbol on the side of the material data block (add a new material) under the **Properties** panel, Blender automatically assigns a new name to this material, which is usually something like Material.001, Material.002, Material.003, and so on.

Having an automatic nomenclature can be handy in most cases, but it can become really confusing as a scene grows in complexity or if you have to reuse some of the materials in other situations. In such cases, we'd better rename all our materials with significant names.

To rename a material, it's enough to click with the left mouse button on the material name data block, type a new name, and then press *Enter* to confirm. This can be done in both the **Properties** panel and in the **Material** datablock button on the toolbar of the **Node Editor** window, as shown in the following screenshot:

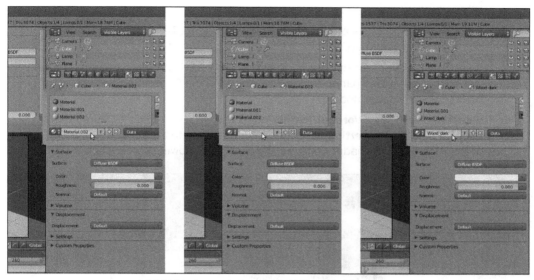

Adding and renaming materials in the Material window

Textures:

Things are a little different for textures. In Cycles, textures are no more data blocks but nodes, so every time we add a **Texture** node to a material network, it automatically gets named according to the kind of texture we added. This means that if we add a **Voronoi Texture**, the texture node is automatically named **Voronoi Texture**. What if we want to rename it to avoid confusion among three or four **Voronoi Texture** nodes? To rename the texture, perform the following steps:

1. Open the 9931OS_02_interface.blend file.

2. Go to the **Node Editor** window and press *Shift* + *A* to add a **Voronoi Texture** node to the material (press *Shift* + *A* and navigate to **Texture | Voronoi Texture**).

   On the right side of the **Node Editor** window, there is a **Properties** panel with several subpanels (press the *N* key if it's not already present). What interests us now is the **Node** subpanel with its two slots, **Name** and **Label**.

As you can see, the name of the node (**Voronoi Texture**) is already present in the **Name** slot. By clicking on the name, it's possible to change it, but at the moment, this seems useful to identify the node in the **Properties** panel.

The **Label** slot, which is empty by default, can be used to label a node in the **Node Editor** window.

3. Press *Shift + D* to duplicate the **Voronoi Texture** node. The duplicated node is automatically named `Voronoi Texture.001`.

4. Select the first **Voronoi Texture** node and write `Voronoi_Diffuse` in the **Label** slot of the **Properties** panel. Connect this node to the **Color** input socket of the **Diffuse BSDF** shader node.

5. Select the duplicated **Voronoi Texture** node and write `Voronoi_Glossy` in the **Label** slot of the **Properties** panel. Connect this node to the **Color** input socket of the **Glossy BSDF** shader node, as shown in the following screenshot:

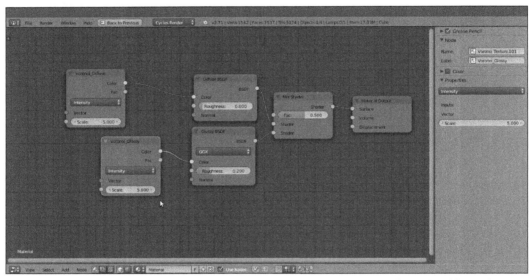

The labeling of the nodes through the Active Node subpanel in the Node Editor Properties side-panel

There's more...

Even though this is not strictly related to renaming, let's quickly see one more option. Right below the **Node** subpanel, there is the **Color** subpanel. Once enabled, this subpanel permits us to assign a color to the selected node to further increase the readability in the **Node Editor** window, as shown in this screenshot:

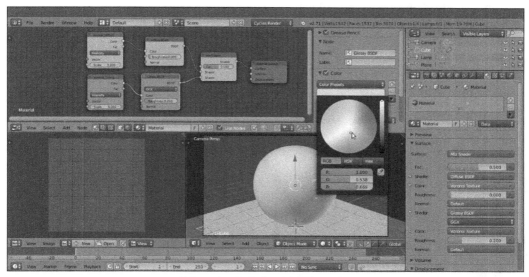

Using colors to further label the nodes

Creating node groups

Single nodes (shaders, textures, input, or whatever) can be grouped together, and this is probably one of the best ways to organize our workflow.

Thanks to node groups, it's easy to store complex materials in ready-to-use libraries. It's possible to share or reuse them in other files, and they can also be used to build handy shader interfaces for easier tweaking of material properties.

Getting ready

Start Blender and open the `9931OS_02_interface.blend` file.

How to do it...

Let's go to the **Node Editor** window directly:

1. Now box-select (place the mouse cursor in the **Node Editor** window, press *B*, and click and drag a box to include the nodes you want to select) the **Diffuse BSDF** and the **Glossy BSDF** nodes, as shown in this screenshot:

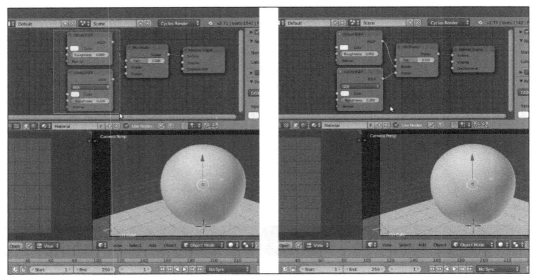

Box-selecting two nodes

2. Press *Ctrl + G* on the keyboard. The background of **Node Editor** changes, showing that now we are in **Edit Mode** inside a group. In fact, there are two selected nodes with a **Group Input** node and a **Group Output** node. Also, the **Surface** subpanel under the **Material** window has changed, and in the **Node Editor** in the **Properties** panel, a new **Interface** tab has appeared, as shown in the following screenshot:

The appearance of the just created and open for editing node group inside the Node Editor window

3. Because the two shaders were already connected to **Mix Shader** (which, in this case, we left out of the group on purpose), both the **Diffuse BSDF** and the **Glossy BSDF** outputs are now connected to two **BSDF** sockets automatically created on the **Group Output** node.

4. As for every **Edit Mode** in Blender, by pressing the *Tab* key, we go out of **Edit Mode**, closing the node group, as shown in this screenshot:

The closed node group

The node group is still showing the two **BSDF** outputs (actually connected to the input sockets of the **Mix Shader** node), the name data block, and the *fake user* button (**F**). This last one is the same as in Blender Internal. It prevents the user count from ever becoming zero, and therefore prevents the deletion of any non-assigned material. When you save the file and/or close Blender by assigning the *fake user* to a non-assigned material, you are sure that it will not be deleted. This is particularly handy when you are building a material library.

5. Now click on the name data block of the node group and change the default name, NodeGroup, to something else. I wrote BasicShader.

6. Press *Tab* and go to **Edit Mode** again. Click on the only empty socket in the **Group Input** node and drag a link to the **Color** input socket of the **Diffuse BSDF** node. The empty socket now connected to the **Diffuse BSDF** node has changed and is now indicated as **Color**. Moreover, a new empty socket has appeared on the **Group Input** node, as shown in the following screenshot:

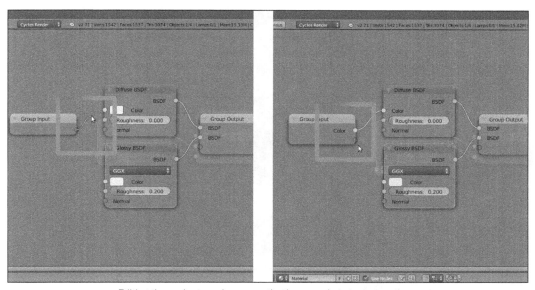

Editing the node group by connecting inner sockets to expose them

7. Repeat the previous step for the new empty input socket and connect it to the **Color** input socket of the **Glossy BSDF** node. Again, a new empty socket has appeared, ready to be connected to something else.

8. Now look at the **Properties** panel to the right. The **Interface** subpanel is reflecting what we are doing in the **Node Editor**. In fact, in the little **Input** window, there are two **Color** sockets, and we can double-click to rename them (Color1 and Color2 in our case). To remove a socket, just click on the name in the **Properties** panel, and then click on the **X** icon in the bottom **Name** slot, as shown in this screenshot:

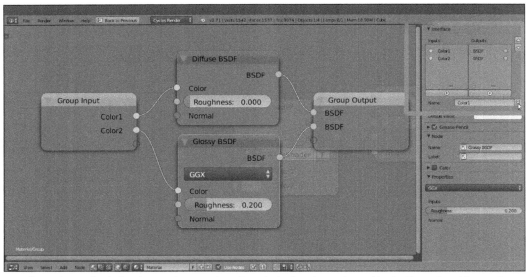

Renaming and ordering the new input sockets through the Interface subpanel in the Properties side-panel

9. Repeat the process to create input sockets for other properties of the **Diffuse BSDF** and **Glossy BSDF** nodes. Then press *Tab* to exit Edit Mode, which is also shown in the following screenshot for your reference:

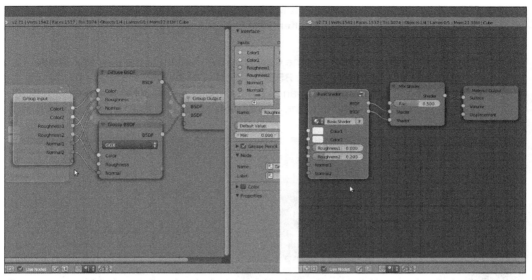

The appearance of the inner connections in the open node group and as exposed input sockets in the closed node group

Here, we get a simple interface for the **BasicShader** node group, and as you can see in the following screenshot, the exposed values can be tweaked. Also, the properties are driven by textures exactly as in other nodes:

The BasicShader node group put to use

10. Press *Tab* again to go back to **Edit Mode**. Move the mouse cursor into the node and press *Shift + A* to add a **Mix Shader** node to the group (press *Shift + A* and navigate to **Shader | Mix Shader**).

11. Connect the **Diffuse BSDF** and the **Glossy BSDF** shaders to the new **Mix Shader** node and its output to one of the **BSDF** sockets. Delete the other node by clicking on the **X** icon in the **Properties** panel. Connect the empty socket of the **Group Input** node to the **Fac** input socket of the **Mix Shader** node, as shown in this screenshot:

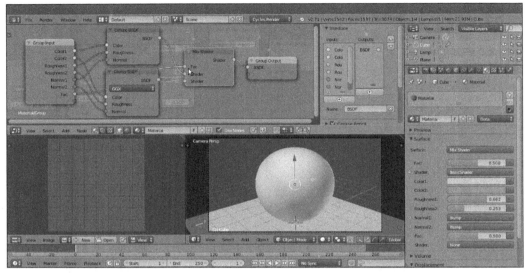

Adding a Mix Shader node inside the node group and one more exposed socket

12. Exit **Edit Mode** and select the outer **Mix Shader** node. Press *Alt + D* (this shortcut removes a node from a network, leaving the connection untouched) to disconnect it and then delete it, or simply press *Ctrl + X* to delete it, leaving the connection untouched. This is shown in the following screenshot:

The final interface of the BasicShader node group

How it works...

I think you get the picture. Basically, almost any input or output socket of the nodes wrapped inside a group can be connected to the outside of the node group to be tweaked.

The good thing about a node group is that you can make instances of that node (by pressing *Shift + D*). Note that when you modify the inner structure of a node group, the modifications get reflected in all the group instances, but the outer (exposed) values on the node group interface are local for each instance and can be individually tweaked.

Every newly created node group is available in both the **Add** menu (press *Shift + A*) and in the slots in the **Material** window of the **Properties** panel, under the item **Group**, to be added on the fly to the network.

To remove a node group, select it and press *Alt + G*. This will break the node envelope but keep the content intact and still connected.

Grouping nodes under frames for easier reading

The shaders we have seen so far are quite simple and easily readable in the **Node Editor** window, but for several materials we'll see in this Cookbook, the node connections will be a lot more complex and confusing. One more aid we can use to improve the readability of these nodes are the frames. We can use them to visually organize the shaders' network.

Getting ready

Start Blender and open the `9931OS_02_interface.blend` file.

How to do it...

Let's see the use of a frame with a simple shader that we already know:

1. Go to the **Node Editor** window and press *Shift + A* to add a **Frame** (press Shift + A and navigate to Layout | Frame). Move the mouse to place its arrow over the nodes, and notice that it always appears to be below them, as shown in the following screenshot:

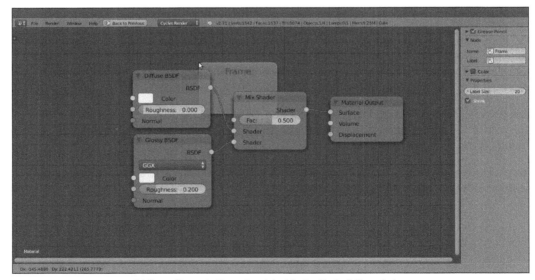

Adding a Frame to the network inside the Node Editor window

2. Move the mouse cursor to a corner of the frame. It turns into a cross, which means that you can click and drag to resize the corners and the sides of the frame to include the desired nodes as shown in the following screenshot:

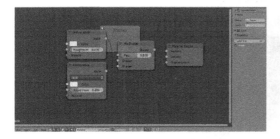 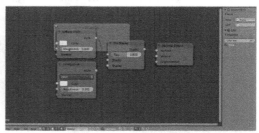

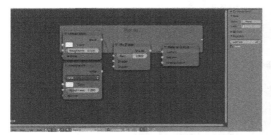 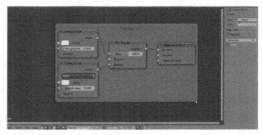

Resizing the Frame to comprise all the nodes

3. Box-select the nodes you want to arrange with the frame (in our case, all of them), then press *Shift*, and select the frame (or just press *A* to deselect the frame and box-select everything so that the frame is selected again as the active object). Press *Ctrl + P* to parent them.

    Now that the nodes are parented to the frame, we can select and move it, and all the contained nodes will follow it as a single object.

    It's still possible to select the single nodes inside the frames and arrange their individual position and connections. To add a new node to the network, we will do as usual (press *Shift + A | ...*) and then parent it to the frame as well.

4. With the frame still selected, go to the **Properties** panel to the right of the **Node Editor** window (Press *N* if not already present). Just like the case of single nodes, in the **Node** subpanel, we can change the **Name** of the frame, assign a **Label** name visible in the **Node Editor** window (I wrote `BasicShader`), and also assign a color.

5. In the **Properties** subpanel right below the **Color** subpanel, we can change the size of the label name, which is set to `20` by default, and by unchecking the **Shrink** item, we can freely resize the frame bigger, which otherwise encloses the nodes with a fixed boundary (the default setting), which is shown in the following screenshot for your reference:

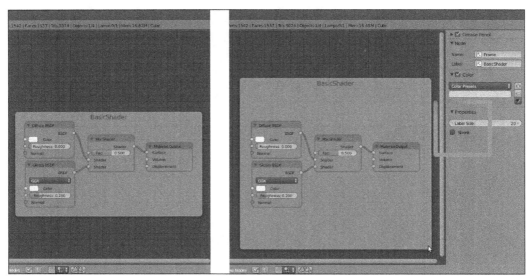

The Frame with label and color

Linking materials and node groups

Similar to Blender Internal, Cycles materials can be linked from libraries. Every blend file containing linkable assets can be a library.

Linking materials is really useful practice. Let's say you have 20 different blend files with objects using an `iron` shader, and at a certain point of your workflow, you need to modify this `iron` material in all the files. By having this material linked in all the 20 files from a single blend, it is possible to update all of them at once by modifying just one shader in the library file (as you know, a linked material reflects the properties of the library material and cannot be edited, differently from an appended material that is local to the file where it has been imported from the library file).

How to do it...

Start Blender, go to the **File** menu in the left part of the main header, and select **Link**, or press *Ctrl + Alt + O*. Then perform the following steps:

1. Browse to the directory where you store your library files. Select the blend file you want to link the material from; for example, try the provided 99310S_02_library. blend file.

2. Browse inside the blend structure, where the linkable assets are divided into subdirectories, shown as folders named Scene, Mesh, Material, NodeTree, Object, and so on. Note that the various folders appear only if the corresponding asset to be linked actually exists inside the blend file.

3. Click on the Material subdirectory. Once inside it, select the material you want to link (for example, Brainy_blue) and press *Enter* to confirm (or click on the **Link/Append from Library** button in the top-right corner), as shown in the following screenshot:

Linking assets through the Blender interface

4. Now click on the **Material datablock** button on the toolbar of the **Node Editor** window and select the name of the linked material—the material labeled with a **LF** prefix; L is for linked and F is for *fake user*.

5. This is because, in the library file, we assigned the *fake user* to the material by clicking on the **F** icon on the side of the material name data block. If not assigned to any *fake user*, the prefix of the linked material would have been **L0**, that is, linked and zero fake users inside the blend file (for example, Plane is simply assigned to the object and has no *fake user*).

    The name of the material is grayed to show that it is a linked material. On the side of the name, a new icon has appeared (a little arrow), and the number of users has been updated to **2** (the *fake user* and the object we assigned the linked material to).

From now on, every modification we make to the material in the library will be reflected in the linked material the moment we load the file.

Not only whole materials but also single node groups can be linked. In this case, instead of the `Material` subdirectory to link from, choose the `NodeTree` subdirectory and then select one or more node groups you want to link.

The data block name of a linked node group is grayed as well. You can modify the exposed values and colors, and you can also enter **Edit Mode**, but that's all. You can't modify the connection or the nodes inside the linked node group. To do this, you have to click on the little arrow icon to the side of the grayed name to make it local and no longer linked from the library file. This would mean that from now on, you have a new independent node group, and that editing the node group in the library won't have any effect on it any more.

There's more...

A very useful add-on to help in node management is the **Node Wrangler** add-on. It allows for effects such as quick material visualization, node switching, UV layer assignment, frame assignments, node arrangements, and so on. To find out more about this add-on, go to `http://wiki.blender.org/index.php/Extensions:2.6/Py/Scripts/Nodes/Node_Wrangler`.

To enable it, just call the **Blender User Preferences** panel (press *Ctrl + Alt + U*) and click on the **Node** tab under the **Categories** item. Enable the **Node Wrangler (aka Node Efficiency Tools)** add-on by clicking on the checkbox to the right. Then click on the **Save User Settings** button to the bottom-left corner of the panel.

3
Creating Natural Materials in Cycles

In this chapter, we will cover the following recipes:

- ▶ Creating a rock material using image maps
- ▶ Creating a rock material using procedural textures
- ▶ Creating a sand material using procedural textures
- ▶ Creating a simple ground material using procedural textures
- ▶ Creating a snow material using procedural textures
- ▶ Creating an ice material using procedural textures

Introduction

Replicating nature can be difficult. Natural materials are usually the most difficult to recreate in a satisfying way using computers, mainly because the chaos of nature is not the best fit for the orderly logic of an electronic machine.

Too often, we even see cubes that look obviously computer-generated because of the neatness and regularity of their shapes or surfaces. Actually, in reproducing true to life a natural object (or material as well), we have to start from the absolute regularity of the computer simulation, and then blemish it step by step in a controlled way to reach a more natural look.

Creating a rock material using image maps

In this recipe, we will create a realistic rock material that looks like the samples shown in the following screenshot, using an image map. We'll see a material made with procedurals in the this recipe.

The image-based rock material as it appears in the final rendering

Image maps are particularly useful for several reasons: they already have the necessary color information of a natural surface ready to be used; they can be easily edited in any image editor to obtain different kinds of information, for example, high levels for the bump maps; and they are processed faster than procedurals by the software (procedural textures must be calculated every time). Moreover, they can nowadays be found easily on the Web for free, in several sizes and resolutions.

For our recipe, we'll use the `rockcolor_tileable_low.png` image map, which you can find in the `textures` folder provided with this cookbook. This is just a low-resolution texture image provided for the sake of this exercise. Obviously, you can use any other different image with a bigger resolution. Here is a screenshot of the tileable rock image texture for your reference:

The tileable rock image texture provided with this cookbook

In any case, for any image you are going to use, just remember to make it tileable in your preferred image editor. In GIMP, this task can be automatically done by a plugin that can be found by navigating to **Filter | Map | Make Tileable**.

Getting ready

Start Blender and load the `99310S_02_interface.blend` file, which saw in the previous chapter. Remember that all the blend files and the textures needed for the exercises of this book can be downloaded from the support page on the Packt Publishing website.

Now, we'll create a new file named `99310S_start.blend`, and we'll be using it as the starting point for the most of our recipes. To do so, perform the following steps:

1. Select the Spheroid and (just for the purpose of this exercise) delete it by pressing *X*.

2. Ensure that the 3D cursor is at the center of the scene (*Shift + C*), and with the mouse pointer in the 3D window, press *Shift + A* to pop up the **Add** menu. Then add a new Cube primitive (press *Shift + A* and navigate to **Mesh | Cube**).

3. Press *Tab* to go out of **Edit Mode** if needed (this depends on whether you are using Blender with the factory settings or not), and move the cube 2 units up on the *z* axis.

4. Go to the **Outliner** and select the **Lamp** item, in the **Object data** window under the **Properties** panel, switch the **Type of Lamp** to **Sun**. Then set the **Strength** to `2.000` and the color values to `1.000` for **R**, `0.872` for **G**, and `0.737` for **B**.

5. Reselect the Cube, go to the **Material** window under the **Properties** panel, and save the file as `99310S_start.blend`.

How to do it...

Now carry out the following steps to create the rock material:

1. Click on the **New** button in the **Material** window under the **Properties** panel, or in the toolbar of the **Node Editor** window.

2. Rename `Material.001` as `Rock_01` (the numbering is because I assume that you are going to experiment with several values, especially colors, producing more and different kind of rock materials) and save the file as `99310S_03_Rock_imagemap.blend`.

3. Put the mouse on the **Node Editor** window and add an **Image Texture** node (press *Shift + A* and navigate to **Texture | Image Texture**). Then add a **Mapping** node (press *Shift + A* and navigate to **Vector | Mapping**), and a **Texture Coordinate** node (press *Shift + A* and navigate to **Input | Texture Coordinate**).

4. Connect the **Generated** output socket of the **Texture Coordinate** node to the **Vector** input socket of the **Mapping** node, and its **Vector** output to the **Vector** input of the **Image Texture** node. Also connect the **Color** output of the **Image Texture** node to the **Color** input of the **Diffuse BSDF** shader node.

5. Set the **Viewport Shading** mode of the **Camera** view to **Rendered** by pressing *Shift + Z* with the mouse cursor in the 3D window. The rendered Cube turns pink because there is no image texture loaded yet, as shown in the following screenshot:

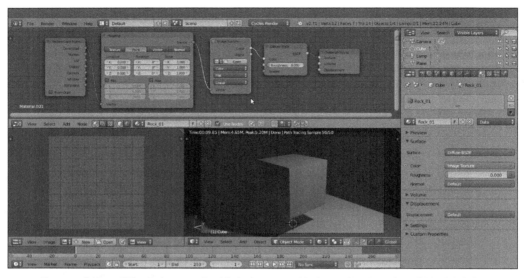

The overall view of Blender's customized Default screen with the rendered preview of the pink Cube

6. Click on the **Open** button in the **Image Texture** node, browse to the `textures` folder, and select the `rockcolor_tileable_low.png` image.

7. As we selected **Generated** as the mapping mode, the image is mapped flat on the Cube from the *z* axis and appears stretched on the sides. Disconnect the **Generated** output of the **Texture Coordinate** node and connect the **Object** node instead. Then click on the **Flat** button on the **Image Texture** node to select the **Box** item. The texture looks now correctly mapped on each face of the Cube, as shown in this screenshot:

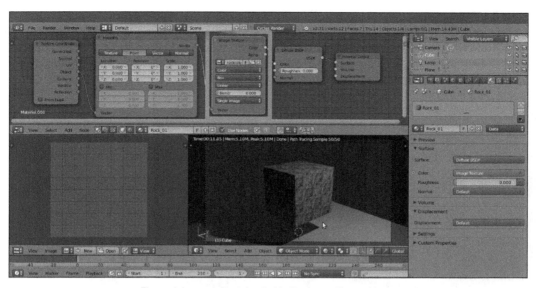

The rock image texture loaded in the Image Texture node

8. Go to the **Object modifiers** window and assign a **Subdivision Surface** modifier to the Cube. Set the **Subdivisions** levels to 4 both for **View** and **Render**. Then check the **Optimal Display** item.

9. Press *Shift + Z* to go out of the viewport's **Rendered** mode. Then press *Tab* to go to **Edit Mode** and scale all the vertices to double (press *Tab*, then press *S*, enter the digit *2*, and finally, press *Enter*). Now, go out of **Edit Mode**.

10. Press *T* to make the **Tool Shelf** panel appear in the **Camera** view, and click on the **Smooth** button under the **Tools** tab. Press *T* again.

11. Go to the **Mapping** node in the **Node Editor** window and set the **Scale** values for **X**, **Y**, and **Z** to 0.250.

12. Although the image map we used is tileable, there are visible seams at the corners of the subdivided Cube. In the **Image Texture** node, set **Blend factor** to 0.200 to soften the seams (this factor is used to blend the edges of the faces of the Cube that, remember, is still a six-faced solid at its lower level, though looks like a Spheroid as of now). The output of blurring effect of the Blend factor is shown in the following screenshot:

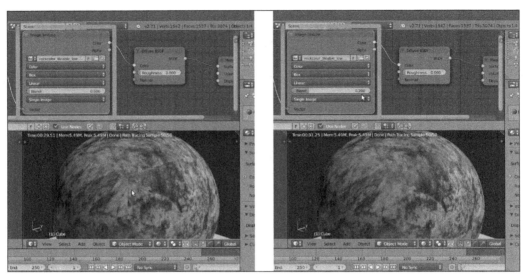

The edges seams visible on the surface of the subdivided Cube, and the blurring effect of the Blend factor

13. Now add a **ColorRamp** node (press *Shift + A* and navigate to **Converter | ColorRamp**) between the **Image Texture** node and the **Diffuse BSDF** shader. Set the interpolation to **B-Spline**, move the marker of the black color to position (**Pos:**) 0.495 and the white marker to position 0.235, as shown in this screenshot:

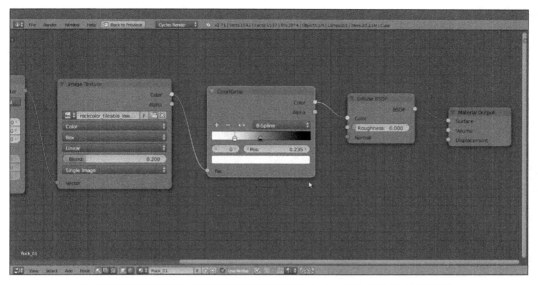

The ColorRamp node pasted between the Image Texture and the Diffuse BSDF nodes

14. Add a **Bump** node (press *Shift + A* and navigate to **Vector | Bump**). Connect the **Color** output of the **ColorRamp** to the **Height** input of the **Bump** node, and the **Normal** output of the latter to the **Normal** input of the **Diffuse BSDF** shader. Detach the **Color** link from the **Color** input of the **Diffuse BSDF** node and leave the **Bump** node's **Strength** value to 1.000, as shown in the following screenshot:

The Bump node pasted between the ColorRamp and Diffuse BSDF nodes

15. Add a **Mix Shader** node and a **Glossy BSDF** shader, and connect them to be mixed with the **Diffuse BSDF** shader. Set the **Glossy BSDF** node's **Roughness** value to 0.150 and the **Mix Shader** node's **Fac** value to 0.300. Connect the **Normal** output of the **Bump** node to the **Normal** input socket of the **Glossy BSDF** shader, as shown in this screenshot:

Adding the Mix Shader and the Glossy BSDF nodes

16. Add an **RGB** node (press *Shift + A* and navigate to **Input | RGB**) and a **MixRGB** node (press *Shift + A* and navigate to **Color | MixRGB**). Connect both the **Color** outputs of the **RGB** and **Image Texture** nodes to the **Color1** and **Color2** input sockets of the **MixRGB** node. Connect the **Color** output of the **MixRGB** node to the **Color** input sockets of the **Diffuse BSDF** and **Glossy BSDF** shaders.

17. Set the **Fac** value of the **MixRGB** node to 0.800. Click on the color slider of the **RGB** node and set the values to 0.407 for **R**, 0.323 for **G**, and 0.293 for **B**, as shown in the following screenshot:

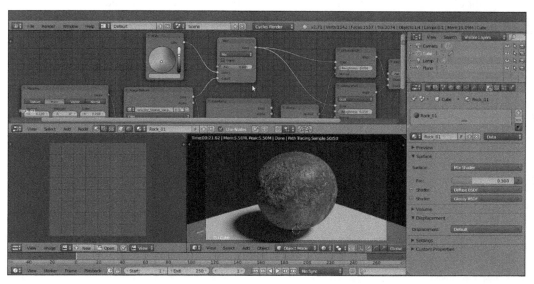

Setting the color for the material

18. Add a new **MixRGB** node (press *Shift + A* and navigate to **Color | MixRGB**). Drag it to be pasted between the first **MixRGB** node and the **Diffuse BSDF** shader, and set **Blend Type** to **Add**.

19. Connect the **Color** output of the second **MixRGB** node (which we can call the **Add-MixRGB** node) to the **Color** input socket of the **Glossy BSDF** shader node, and set its **Fac** value to 1.000.

20. Connect the **Color** output of the **Image Texture** node to the **Color1** input socket of the **Add-MixRGB** node so that the preceding connection coming from the first **MixRGB** node (which we can call **Mix-MixRGB**) switches automatically to the **Color2** input socket of the **Add-MixRGB** node, as shown in this screenshot:

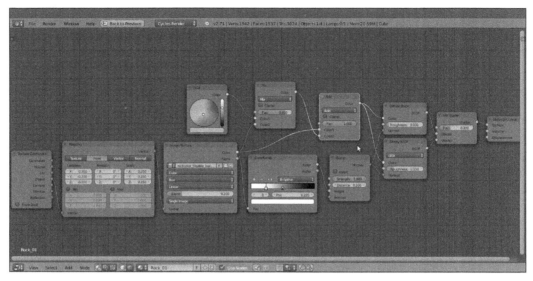

Adding more variations to the rock color

21. If you wish, model a very quick rock mesh by sculpting or deforming the subdivided Cube in proportional **Edit Mode**, and assign to it the Rock_01 material as shown in the following screenshot:

How it works...

We mapped a colored image of a rock with the **Box** option available in the **Image Texture** node (developed by the Project Mango team for open movie production of *Tears of Steel* to quickly map objects without the need to unwrap them), and set the **Blend** factor to 0.200 to have smooth transitions at the corners. Although we had a tileable image texture, this has been necessary because we set the **Scale** values for the three axes in the **Mapping** node to 0.250.

First, by connecting the **MixRGB** node's **Color** output directly to the **Color** input of the **Diffuse BSDF** shader node, we had a quick visual feedback of the image mapping, and thanks to the **ColorRamp** node, we achieved the following goals:

- ▶ We converted the colored image to a gray-scale image to be used for the bump.
- ▶ By moving the color markers, we remapped the values of the **ColorRamp** node's position values to reverse and increase the contrast (we could have obtained the same result by processing the color map in GIMP, for example, by desaturating it and playing with the curve tool). In any case, it's possible to visualize the **ColorRamp** node itself on the object by temporarily connecting it to the **Color** input socket of the **Diffuse BSDF** shader or an **Emission** shader node connected to the **Material Output** node.

This contrasted result has been applied as a bump map to both the **Diffuse BSDF** and **Glossy BSDF** shaders.

Then we mixed a brownish color (the **RGB** node) with the **Color** output of the image of the rock, and the result was added to the **Image Texture** node's output.

There's more...

We can improve the rocky effect by adding displacement to the geometry. Unlike bump or normal effects on the mesh surface, which are just optical illusions giving an impression of perturbing the mesh surface, displacement is an actual deformation of the mesh based on the gray-scale values of a texture.

At least in this case, there is no need for precise correspondence between the already textured surface and the displacement because it would be barely noticeable. Therefore, we can use object modifiers to obtain a fast but effective result, by performing the following steps:

1. Starting from the Rock_imagemap.blend file we just created, select the Cube and go to the **Object modifiers** window under the **Properties** panel. In the **Subdivision Surface** modifier already assigned, lower the **Subdivisions** levels for both **View** and **Render** to 3.

2. Add a new **Subdivision Surface** modifier and set the levels to 4.

3. Now add a **Displace** modifier. Click on the **Show textures in texture tab** button, the last button on the right of the **Texture** slot. This switches to the **Texture** window, where we can click on the **New** button and then change the default **Clouds** texture to a **Voronoi** texture node. Set the **Size** value to 2.00 and leave the rest of the values unchanged. Go back to the **Object modifiers** window and set the modifier's **Strength** value to 0.800.

4. Add a new **Displace** modifier. Switch to the **Texture** window and assign a new **Voronoi Texture** node. Change the **Size** value to 1.20. Back in the modifier, set the **Strength** value to 0.300.

5. Add one more **Displace** modifier. This time, we are going to use the default **Clouds** texture as it is. Just go to the **Object modifiers** window and set the **Strength** value to 0.150, as shown in this screenshot:

A different rock model, thanks to displacement

Of course, these are just basic values. You can change them and also play with different kinds of procedural textures to obtain several rock shapes.

Creating a rock material using procedural textures

In this recipe, we will try to reach a result similar to the rock material we made through image maps in the previous recipe, but using only procedural textures. The output will look like what is shown in the following screenshot:

The procedural rock material as it appears in the final rendering

Getting ready

Start Blender and load the 9931OS_start.blend file.

1. Select the Cube, go to the **Object modifiers** window, and assign a **Subdivision Surface** modifier. Set the **Subdivisions** levels for **View** and **Render** to 4. Go back to the **Material** window.

2. Press *T* and in the **Tool Shelf**, click on the **Smooth** button under the **Shading** subpanel. Press *T* again to get rid of the **Tool Shelf**.

3. Press *Tab* to go to **Edit Mode**. If necessary, select all the vertices by pressing the *A* key and scale everything to double the current size (press *S*, enter the digit *2*, and press *Enter*). Go out of **Edit Mode**.

4. Save the file as `99310S_start_smoothed.blend`. The customized Default screen will now look as shown in the following screenshot:

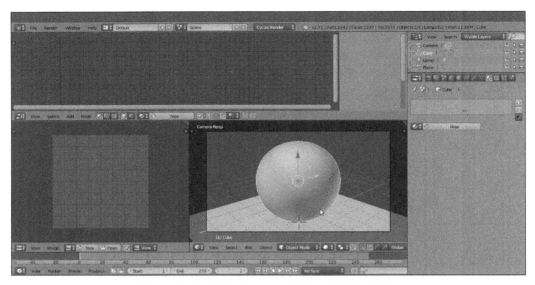

The customized Default screen with the subdivided Cube

How to do it...

Now we are going to create the rock material by performing the following steps:

1. Select the Spheroid (the smoothed Cube) and click on **New** in the **Material** window under the **Properties** panel or in the **Node Editor** toolbar. Rename the material `Rock_proc_01`.

2. In the **Node Editor** window, add a **Noise Texture** node (press *Shift + A* and navigate to **Texture | Noise Texture**). Then press *Shift + D* to duplicate it three times. Adjust the four **Noise Texture** nodes in a column, and in the **Properties** panel to the right (press *N* key if it is not already present), label them `Noise Texture01`, `Noise Texture02`, `Noise Texture03`, and `Noise Texture04`.

3. Add a **Texture Coordinate** node (press *Shift + A* and navigate to **Input | Texture Coordinate**) and a **Mapping** node (press *Shift + A* and navigate to **Vector | Mapping**). Connect the **Object** output of the **Texture Coordinate** node to the blue **Vector** input of the **Mapping** node. Then connect the **Mapping** node's **Vector** output to the **Vector** input sockets of the four texture nodes. Set the **Mapping** node's **Location** values to `0.100` for **X** and `-0.100` for **Y** and **Z**, as shown in the following screenshot:

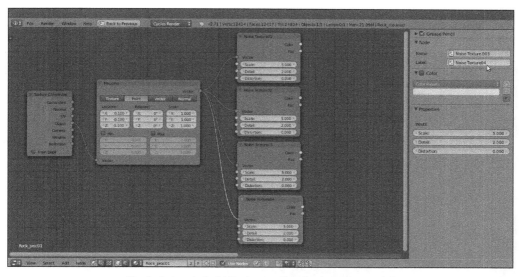

The first steps to build the bump effect for the rock material

4. Add a **MixRGB** node (press *Shift + A* and navigate to **Color | MixRGB**). Connect the first two **Noise Texture** nodes' **Color** output to the **Color1** and **Color2** input of the **MixRGB** node. Set **Blend Type** to **Overlay** and the **Fac** value to 1.000.

5. Connect the **Overlay-MixRGB** node's output to the **Color** input socket of the **Diffuse BSDF** shader node.

6. Put the mouse cursor in the **Camera** view and press *Shift + Z* to set it to **Rendered** mode.

7. Go to the **Noise Texture01** node and set **Scale** to 4.000 and the **Distortion** value to 1.400. Then go to the **Noise Texture02** node and set **Scale** to 6.000, **Detail** to 1.000, and the **Distortion** value to 0.700.

8. Press *Shift + D* to duplicate the **MixRGB** node, and paste it between the **Overlay-MixRGB** and the **Diffuse BSDF** nodes. Connect the **Color** output of the **Noise Texture03** node to the **Color2** input socket and set the **Blend Type** to **Darken**. Go to the **Noise Texture03** node, and set **Scale** to 15.000 and **Detail** to 3.000.

9. Add a **ColorRamp** node (press *Shift + A* and navigate to **Converter | ColorRamp**) and paste it between the **Darken-MixRGB** and the **Diffuse BSDF** nodes. Label it ColorRamp01 and set **Interpolation** to **Ease**, the black cursor's position to 0.364, and the white cursor's position to 0.632.

10. Press *Shift + D* to duplicate the **ColorRamp** node, and move it close to the **Noise Texture04** node. Label the duplicated node ColorRamp02 and set the white cursor's position to 0.340 and the black cursor's position to 0.400.

11. Set the **Noise Texture04** node's **Scale** value to 45.000, **Detail** value to 0.100, and **Distortion** to 1.000, as shown in the following screenshot:

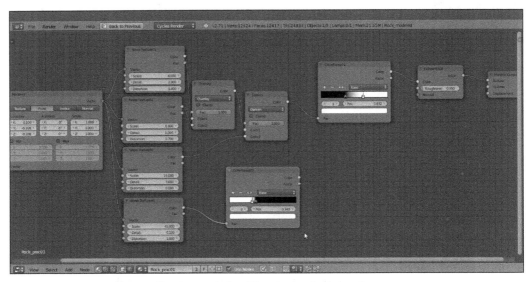

Starting to mix the different procedurals together

12. Connect the **Color** output of the **Noise Texture04** node to the **Fac** input socket of the **ColorRamp02** node. Then add a **MixRGB** node (press *Shift + A* and navigate to **Color | MixRGB**) and label it Mix01.

13. Paste the **Mix01** node after the **ColorRamp01** node. Then connect the **Color** output of the **ColorRamp02** node to the **Color2** input socket of the **Mix01** node. Also connect the **Fac** output of the **Noise Texture01** node to the **Fac** input socket of the **Mix01** node.

14. Add a new **MixRGB** node (press *Shift + A* and navigate to **Color | MixRGB**) and label it Mix02. Paste it between the **ColorRamp02** and the **Mix01** nodes.

15. Add a **Bump** node (press *Shift + A* and navigate to **Vector | Bump**) and connect the **Color** output of the **Mix01** node to the **Height** input socket of the **Bump** node. Connect the **Normal** output of the **Bump** node to the **Normal** input socket of the **Diffuse BSDF** shader node. Click on the **Invert** item checkbox.

The steps that are detailed after this screenshot will result in the bump effect:

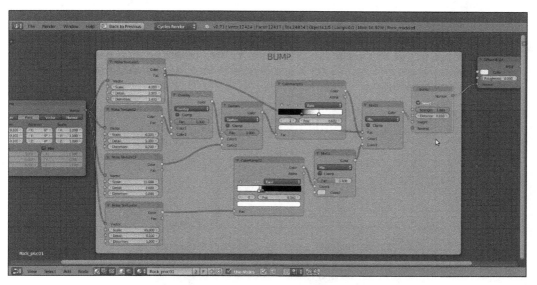

The BUMP frame containing the nodes to build the bump effect

16. Add a **Glossy BSDF** shader node (press *Shift + A* and navigate to **Shader | Glossy BSDF**) and a **Mix Shader** node (press *Shift + A* and navigate to **Shader | Mix Shader**). Paste the **Mix Shader** node between the **Diffuse BSDF** and the **Material Output** nodes, and connect the **Glossy BSDF** output to the second **Shader** input socket.

17. Connect the **Normal** output of the **Bump** node to the **Normal** input socket of the **Glossy BSDF** shader. Set the **Glossy BSDF** shader's **Roughness** to 0.150 and the **Fac** value of the **Mix Shader** node to 0.300.

18. Add an **RGB** node (press *Shift + A* and navigate to **Input | RGB**) and connect it to the **Color** input socket of the **Diffuse BSDF** shader node. Set the color values to 0.407 for **R**, 0.323 for **G**, and 0.293 for **B**.

19. Add a **MixRGB** node, label it Mix03, and paste it between the **RGB** and the **Diffuse BSDF** nodes. Connect the **Color** output of the **Darken-MixRGB** node to the **Color2** input socket of the **Mix03** node.

20. Add a new **MixRGB** node. Set **Blend Type** to **Add** and the **Fac** value to 0.800. Connect the **Color** output of the **ColorRamp01** node to the **Color1** input socket, and the output of the **Mix03** node to the **Color2** input socket of the **MixRGB** node. Connect the **Color** output of the **Add-MixRGB** node to the **Color** input socket of the **Diffuse BSDF** node.

21. Add an **RGB Curves** node (press *Shift + A* and navigate to **Color | RGB Curves**) and paste it between the **Add-MixRGB** and the **Diffuse BSDF** nodes. Connect its output to the **Color** input socket of the **Glossy BSDF** shader node.

22. Click on the **RGB Curves** node's little window to create a new point. Set its position values to 0.24545 for **X** and 0.38125 for **Y**. Then create another point and set the position values to 0.74545 for **X** and 0.51875 for **Y**, as shown in the following screenshot:

Screenshot of the COLOR frame connected to the Diffuse and Glossy shaders

How it works...

Even if this material looks a bit complex at first sight, you must note that we just mixed four procedural noise textures with different settings and iterations to build the bump effect and create the color pattern to some extent:

▶ In the first stage, from steps 2 to 15, we built the bump pattern by mixing the output of the noise textures (the **Overlay**, **Darken**, **Mix01**, and **Mix02** nodes converging to the input socket of the **Bump** node) through **MixRGB** nodes, and in some cases also edited their levels using the **ColorRamp** nodes to obtain a more random, natural look (**ColorRamp1** and **ColorRamp2**, all the nodes inside the **BUMP** frame).

▶ In the second stage, from steps 18 to 22, we built the color pattern by mixing a simple color output with the output of some of the **Noise Texture** nodes, and then edited the result using an **RGB Curves** node (nodes inside the **COLOR** frame).

► The results of both the bump and the color patterns were then piped into the appropriate sockets of the nodes inside the **SHADER** frame, that is, the **Diffuse BSDF** node was mixed with the **Glossy BSDF** node to add specularity (steps 16 and 17). The overall material network in the **Node Editor** window is shown in the following screenshot:

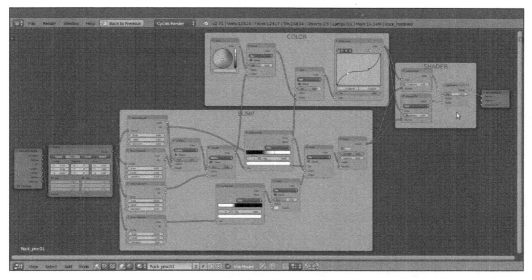

The overall vision of the material network

Creating a sand material using procedural textures

In this recipe, we will create a sand material that looks like what is shown in the following screenshot, which is good for both close and distant objects:

The sand material as it appears in the final rendering

Getting ready

Start Blender and switch to the **Cycles Render** engine. Then perform the following steps:

1. Delete the default Cube and add a Plane (press *Shift + A* and navigate to **Mesh | Plane**).

2. Press *Tab* to go to **Edit Mode** and scale it nine times bigger, with 18 units per side (press *S*, enter the digit 9, and press *Enter*). Go out of **Edit Mode**.

3. Go to the **World** window and click on the **Use Nodes** button under the **Surface** subpanel in the **Properties** panel to the right of the screen. Then click on the little square with a dot on the right side of the **Color** slot. Select the **Sky Texture** item from the pop-up menu. Set the **Strength** value to 1.900.

4. Select the **Lamp**, go to the **Object data** window, and click on the **Use Nodes** button. Then change the **Type of Lamp** to **Sun** and set **Strength** to 3.000. Change the color values to 1.000 for **R**, 0.935 for **G**, and 0.810 for **B**. In orthogonal top view, rotate the **Sun** lamp by 45°, as shown in the following screenshot:

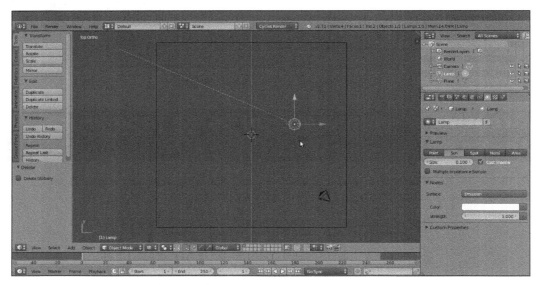

The scene from the top with the Sun Lamp selected

5. Add a Cube and a UV Sphere to the scene and place them leaning on the Plane.

6. Select the Cube and click on the **Smooth** button in the **Shading** subpanel under the **Tools** tab to the left of the 3D window (press the *T* key to make it appear if it is not present).

7. Select the UV Sphere and perform the same actions as given in step 6.

8. Select the Cube, and in the **Object modifiers** window, add a **Bevel** modifier. Set **Width** to 0.1000, **Segments** to 2, and **Profile** to 0.15. Assign a **Subdivision Surface** modifier, set both the **Subdivisions** levels to 4, and check the **Optimal Display** item. Assign a **Smooth** modifier and set **Factor** to 1.000 and **Repeat** to 15.

9. Select the UV Sphere and assign a **Subdivision Surface** modifier with **Subdivisions** levels set to 2 and the usual **Optimal Display** item checked.

10. Select the Plane, click on the **Smooth** button, and then go to **Edit Mode** and press *W*. In the **Specials** pop-up menu, select the **Subdivide** item. Press the *F6* key to call the **Options** pop-up menu (or go to the panel at the bottom of the **Tool Shelf** tabs) and set **Number of Cuts** to 10.

11. Go out of **Edit Mode**, go to the **Object modifiers** window, and assign a **Subdivision Surface** modifier. Switch to the **Simple** subdivision algorithm and set both **Subdivisions** to 3. Check the **Optimal Display** item.

12. Assign a **Displace** modifier and then click on the **Show texture in texture tab** button to the side of the **New** button. In the **Texture** window, click on the **New** button and switch the default **Clouds** texture with the **Voronoi** texture. Set the **Size** value to 5.00.

13. Assign a new **Displace** modifier, click on the **Show texture in texture tab** button, and load a **Voronoi** texture again. Leave the **Size** value at 0.25.

14. Assign a **Smooth** modifier and set **Factor** to 1.000 and the **Repeat** value to 5.

15. Place the Camera to have a nice angle on the Plane and switch from the 3D view to a Camera view (by pressing the *0* key on the numeric keypad).

16. Split the 3D window into two horizontal rows and change the upper row to a **Node Editor** window. Put the mouse cursor in the 3D view and press *Shift + Z* to set the **Camera** view mode to **Rendered**.

17. Go to the **Render** window. Under the **Sampling** subpanel, set both the **Clamp Direct** and **Clamp Indirect** values to 1.000. Go to the **Light Path** subpanel and set the **Filter Glossy** value to 1.000.

18. Set the **Render** samples to 25. The **Rendered** preview is shown in the following screenshot for your reference:

The prepared scene as it appears in the Rendered preview, with the rendering settings to the right

How to do it...

We have prepared the scene. Now let's start with the creation of the sand material using the following steps:

1. Select the Plane and click on the **New** button in the **Material** window under the **Properties** panel or in the **Node Editor** toolbar. Rename the material Sand_01.

2. Keeping the *Shift* key pressed, select the UV Sphere, the Cube, and for last one, the Plane (that is the active object of the multi-selection) by right-clicking on them. Press *Ctrl + L*, and in the **Make Links** pop-up menu, select the **Material** item to assign the same material to the other two objects. The Sand_01 material is now assigned to all three objects.

3. In the **Material** window under the **Properties** panel to the right, switch the **Diffuse BSDF** shader with a **Mix Shader** node. In both the **Shader** slots, assign a **Diffuse BSDF** shader.

4. In the **Node Editor**, add an **RGB** node (press *Shift + A* and navigate to **Input | RGB**) and an **RGB Curves** node (press *Shift + A* and navigate to **Color | RGB Curves**). Connect the output of the **RGB** node to the **Color** input socket of the first **Diffuse BSDF** shader and to the **Color** input socket of the **RGB Curves** node. Then connect the output of the **RGB Curves** node to the **Color** input socket of the second **Diffuse BSDF** shader node.

5. Change the color values of the **RGB** node to `0.500` for **R**, `0.331` for **G**, and `0.143` for **B**. Click on the **RGB Curves** node window to create a new point, and set the coordinates to `0.48182` for **X** and `0.56875` for **Y**.

6. Add a **Noise Texture** node (press *Shift + A* and navigate to **Texture | Noise Texture**), a **Texture Coordinate** node (press *Shift + A* and navigate to **Input | Texture Coordinate**), and a **Mapping** node (press *Shift + A* and navigate to **Vector | Mapping**).

7. Connect the **Object** output of the **Texture Coordinate** node to the **Vector** input of the **Mapping** node, and then connect the **Vector** output to the **Vector** input of the **Noise Texture** node.

8. Connect the **Fac** output of the **Noise Texture** node to the **Fac** input of the **Mix Shader** node. Increase the **Detail** value of the texture to `5.000`.

9. Press *Shift + D* to duplicate the **Mix Shader** node and paste it between the first **Mix Shader** node and the **Material Output** node. Add a **Glossy BSDF** shader node (press *Shift + A* and navigate to **Shader | Glossy BSDF**), set its **Roughness** to `0.700`, and connect its output to the second **Shader** input socket of the second **Mix Shader** node. Set the **Fac** value to `0.100`.

10. Connect the **Color** output of the **RGB** node to the **Color** input socket of the **Glossy BSDF** shader node.

11. Add a **Frame** (press *Shift + A* and navigate to **Layout | Frame**), press *Shift* and multi-select the **RGB** node, the **RGB Curves** node, the **Noise Texture** node, the two **Diffuse BSDF** nodes, the **Glossy BSDF** shader, the two **Mix Shader** nodes, and the **Frame**, and press *Ctrl + P* to parent them. In the **Properties** panel (press *N* key in the **Node Editor** window), label the **Frame** as `SAND COLOR`, as shown in the following screenshot:

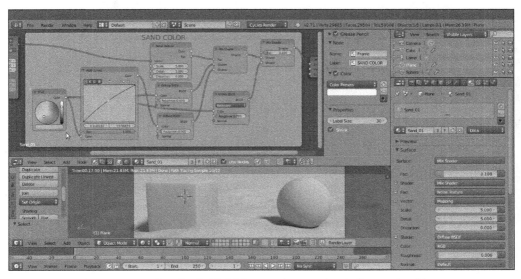

The total vision of the SAND COLOR frame and the rendered effect on the objects

12. Add a new **Noise Texture** node and a **Wave Texture** node (press *Shift + A* and navigate to **Texture | ...**). Select both and press *Shift + D* to duplicate them. Label them `Wave Texture01`, `Wave Texture02`, `Noise Texture01`, and `Noise Texture02`.

13. Arrange the four texture nodes in a column like this: **Wave Texture01**, **Noise Texture01**, **Noise Texture02**, and **Wave Texture02**. Connect the **Mapping** output to the texture nodes' **Vector** input.

14. Set the **Scale** value of **Wave Texture01** to `3.000`, **Distortion** to `25.000`, and **Detail** to `10.000`. Set the **Detail** value of **Noise Texture01** to `10.000` and **Distortion** to `0.500`. Set the **Detail** value of **Noise Texture02** to `10.000` as well. Finally, set the **Wave Texture02** node's **Scale** value to `25.000`, **Distortion** to `15.000`, and **Detail Scale** value to `5.000`.

15. Add a **MixRGB** node (press *Shift + A* and **Color | MixRGB**) and label it `Mix01`. Connect the **Wave Texture01** node's **Color** output to the **Color1** input and the **Noise Texture01** node's **Color** output to the **Color2** input.

16. Select the **MixRGB** node and press *Shift + D* to duplicate it. Label it `Mix02` and connect the **Color** output of the **Mix01** node to the **Color1** input of the **Mix02** node. Then connect the **Wave Texture02** node's **Color** output to its **Color2** input.

17. Connect the **Color** output of the **Noise Texture02** node to the **Fac** input socket of the **Mix02** node. Now the **Node Editor** window looks like what is shown in the following screenshot:

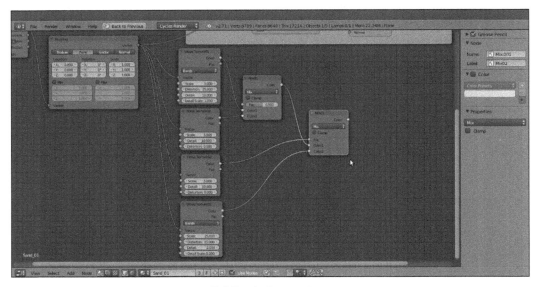

Building the bump pattern

18. Add a **Math** node (press *Shift + A* and navigate to **Converter | Math**) and label it `Bump_Strength`. Change **Operation** to **Multiply** and connect the output of the **Mix02** node to the first **Value** input socket. Set the second **Value** input socket's value to `1.000` and connect the node output to the **Displacement** input socket of the **Material Output** node, as shown in this screenshot:

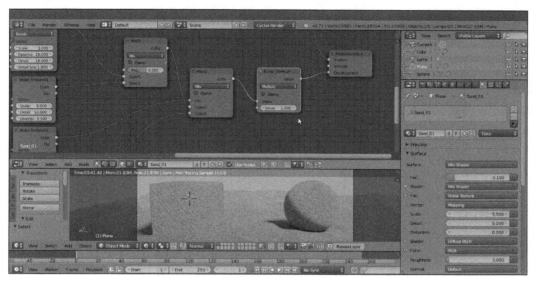

The effect of the total output of the bump nodes connected to the Displacement input of the Material Output node

19. Add a **Hue/Saturation** node (press *Shift + A* and navigate to **Color | Hue/Saturation**), label it `Hue Saturation Value01`, and drag it onto the link connecting the **Noise Texture01** node to the **Mix01** node to paste it in between. Set **Value** to `10.000`.

20. Press *Shift + D* to duplicate the **Hue/Saturation** node, label the duplicate `Hue Saturation Value02`, and drag it onto the link connecting the **Wave Texture02** node to the **Mix02** node. Set **Value** to `0.100`.

21. Press *Shift + D* to duplicate it again, name the duplicate `Hue Saturation Value03`, and drag it between the **Mix02** node and the **Bump Strength** node. Set **Value** to `0.350`. The following screenshot shows the effect of adding variation to the bump:

Adding variation to the bump pattern

22. Add a **Bright/Contrast** node (press *Shift + A* and navigate to **Color | Bright Contrast**). Drag it so that it's pasted between the **Noise Texture02** node and the **Mix02** factor input. Set the **Bright** value to `-0.250` and the **Contrast** value to `1.000`.

23. Add a **Frame**, press *Shift* (or box-select (press *B* key) these 11 nodes and then the **Frame**), and press *Ctrl + P* to parent them. Label the **Frame** SAND BUMP, as shown in the following screenshot:

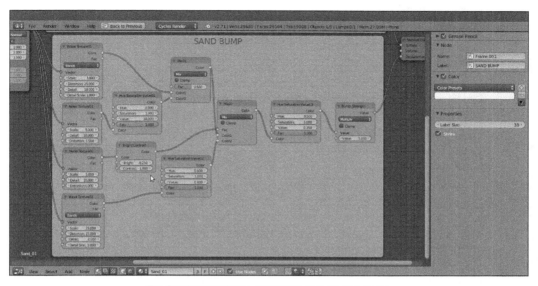

The SAND BUMP frame containing all the bump nodes

24. Select the **Wave Texture02** node and press *Shift + D* to duplicate it twice (if the node is still parented to the **SAND BUMP** frame after duplication, press *Alt + P* to unparent it). Label them Wave Texture03 and Wave Texture04. Then duplicate the **Bright/Contrast** node twice and name the duplicates Bright/Contrast02 and Bright/Contrast03.

25. Select one of the **MixRGB** nodes and press *Shift + D* to duplicate it. Set **Blend Type** (and the label) to **Divide** and the **Factor** to 1.000.

26. Connect the **Mapping** vector output to the **Vector** input sockets of the two new wave textures.

27. Connect each **Color** output of the two new wave textures to the respective **Color** input of the **Bright/Contrast02** nodes. Then connect their color output to the **Color1** and **Color2** input of the **Divide** node.

28. In the **Wave Texture03** node, set **Scale** to 0.500, **Distortion** to 25.000, **Detail** to 10.000, and **Detail Scale** to 1.000. In the **Bright/Contrast02** node, set the **Bright** value to 0.000 and the **Contrast** value to -0.800.

29. In the **Wave Texture04** node, set **Scale** to 1.000, **Distortion** to 10.000, **Detail** to 5.000, and **Detail Scale** to 1.000. In the respective **Bright/Contrast03** node, set the **Bright** value to 0.000 and the **Contrast** value to -0.800.

30. Add a **Math** node (press *Shift + A* and navigate to **Converter | Math**). Set **Operation** to **Multiply**, label it Multiply01, and leave the first **Value** as it is—the same as the **Scale** value of the **Wave Texture03** node (0.500). Set the second **Value** to 1.000. Connect the **Value** output to the **Scale** input socket of the **Wave Texture03** node.

31. Press *Shift + D* to duplicate the **Math** node (label it Multiply02). Move it to the side of the **Wave Texture04** node and set the first **Value** to be the same as the **Scale** value of the texture node (1.000). Set the second **Value** to 1.000 as well, and connect the **Value** output to the **Scale** input of the **Wave Texture04** node.

32. Add a **Value** node (press *Shift + A* and navigate to **Input | Value**). Connect the output to the second **Value** input sockets of both the **Multiply-Math** nodes. Label it Waves_ size and set the input value to 1.000.

33. Add a **Frame**, parent the last added nodes, and label it `BIG WAVES`, as shown in the following screenshot:

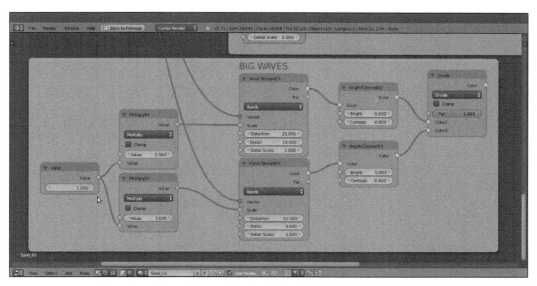

A new frame containing a new bump effect to be added to the previous one

34. Duplicate the **Bump_Strength** node, unparent it from the **SAND BUMP** node, and set the **Operation** to **Add**. Drag it onto the link between the **Bump_Strength** node and the **Material Output** node, and label it `Add_Bump01`.

35. Connect the **Divide** node output of **BIG WAVES** to the second **Value** input socket of the **Add_Bump01** node, as shown in this screenshot:

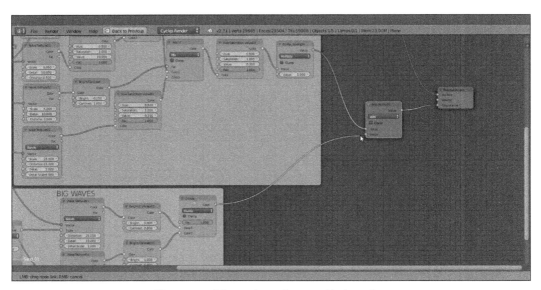

The output of the two bump frames added together

36. Duplicate a **Noise Texture** node (label it `Noise Texture03`), a **Bright/Contrast** node (label it `Bright/Contrast04`), and a **Math** node (label it `Grain_Strength`). Connect the **Mapping** output to the **Vector** input of the texture node. Then connect the **Noise Texture** node's **Color** output to the **Bright/Contrast04** node's **Color** input and its output to the first **Value** input socket of the **Grain_Strength** node. Set its operation to **Multiply** and the second **Value** to `0.250`.

37. Set the texture **Scale** to `200.000`, **Detail** to `1.000`, and **Distortion** to `0.000`. Set the **Bright/Contrast04** node's **Bright** value to `0.000` and **Contrast** to `0.200`.

38. Add a **Frame**, parent the three nodes to it, and label it **GRANULARITY**, as shown in the following screenshot:

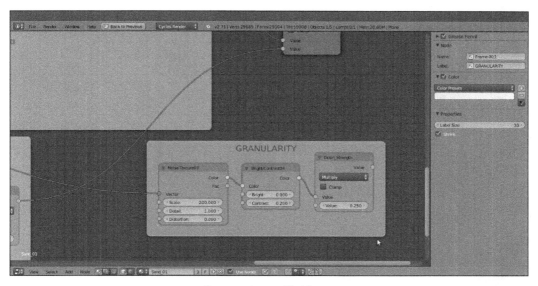

One more bump effect frame

39. Duplicate the **Add_Bump01** node, and label it Add_Bump02, and paste it between the **Add_Bump01** node and the **Material Output** node. Connect the **Grain_Strength** output of the **GRANULARITY** frame to the second **Value** input socket of the **Add_Bump02** node.

40. Duplicate the **Add_Bump02** node and paste it just before the **Material Output** node. label it **TOTAL BUMP STRENGTH**, set the node **Operation** to **Multiply**, and set the second **Value** to 0.500, as shown in this screenshot:

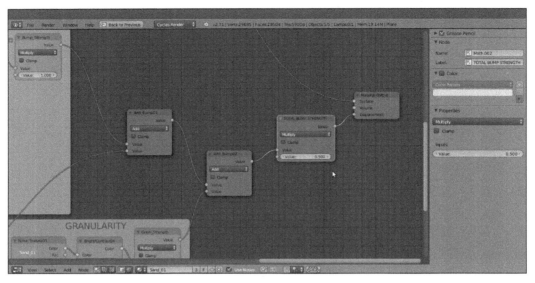

The GRANULARITY frame output added to the previous bump ones

So here we are now—the sand shader is complete, and this is how the nodes' network looks in the **Node Editor** window:

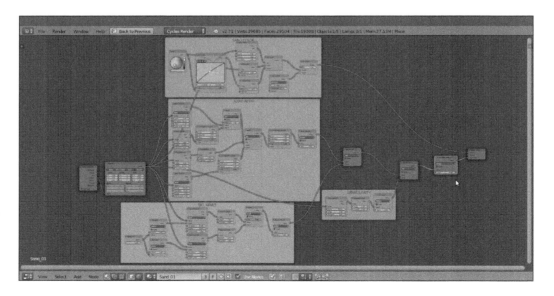

To obtain the image shown at the beginning of this recipe, we also added a few elements to the scene:

▶ A new Cube primitive, with a simple diffuse pure white material, added just for reference to light intensity.

▶ An Ico Sphere primitive, set as invisible and disabled for the rendering in **Outliner**. It works as target **Object** for a Boolean modifier assigned to the sand Cube and is placed in the stack between the **Subdivision Surface** and **Smooth** modifiers, as shown in the following screenshot:

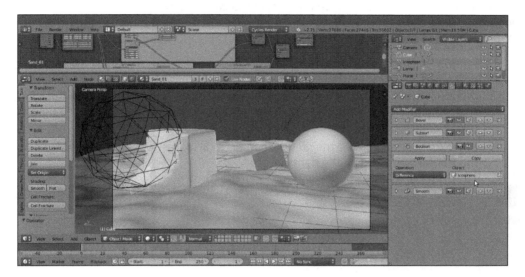

How it works...

The concept behind the structure of this material is basically the same as that for the procedural rock, and it can be subdivided into stages as well:

▶ From step 1 to step 10, we built the color part of the shader, blending two differently colored **Diffuse BSDF** nodes on the ground of a **Noise Texture** factor, and building a basic shader with the **Glossy BSDF** component.

▶ From step 12 to step 22, we built the main bump effect, this time piped directly as whole in the **Displacement** input of the **Material Output** node rather than to the **Normal** input sockets per shader.

▶ From step 24 to step 32, we built a supplementary bump effect, this time to simulate the big waves you usually see on a desert's sand dunes. This effect was left apart from the main bump to be easily reduced or eliminated if required. Then we added two **Math** nodes set to **Multiply** and driven by a **Value** node to automatically set the size of the big sand waves. Actually, this is more a repeating effect, and the bigger the value, the smaller and closer the waves.

> ▸ In steps 36 and 37, we built a last bump effect to add the sand grain if necessary, for example, for objects very close to the camera. In steps 39 and 40, we summed all the bump effects, to be driven by the last **Math** node value.

Every stage has been framed and properly labeled to make it more easily readable in the **Node Editor** window.

There's more...

One more thing we can do to improve this material is combine everything into a handy group node, at the same time leaving the fundamental values to be tweaked exposed on the node group interface. To do this follow these steps:

1. Put the mouse cursor in the **Node Editor** window and press the *B* key. Two horizontal and a vertical lines appear at the location of the mouse cursor. Click and drag the mouse to encompass the framed nodes, leaving outside only the **Texture Coordinate** node, the **Mapping** node, and the **Material Output** nodes. After the mouse button is released, everything you encompassed is selected.

2. Press *Ctrl + G* and create the group. Then press *N* in the **Node Editor** window to call the **Properties** panel on the right side.

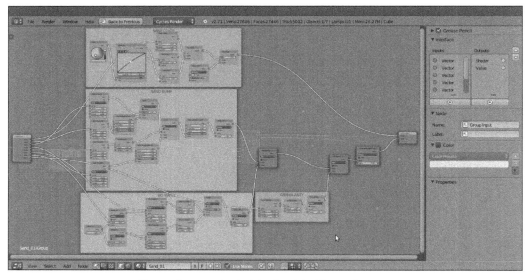

The previous sand material network inside a node group

3. Press *Tab* to go out of **Edit Mode**. Then click on the little window on the interface to change the name from `NodeGroup` to `Sand_Group`.

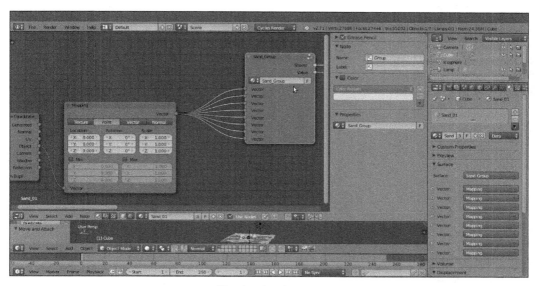

The closed node group

As you can see, inside the group, the **Group Input** node collects all the **Vector** sockets from which the various texture nodes take their mapping coordinates, so we now have eight **Vector** sockets in the outer interface, all connected to the same **Object** output of the **Mapping** node. However, we need only one **Vector** input to map all the textures inside the group, so let's perform the following steps:

1. Press *Tab* to go to **Edit Mode** again and deselect everything by pressing the *A* key.

2. Select the first bottom **Vector** output by clicking on the list of names in the little **Inputs** window under the **Properties/Interface** panel. Delete the corresponding **Vector** socket from the **Group Input** node by clicking on the **X** icon to the side of the newly appeared **Name** slot. Then click on the **X** icon again, and go on like this to delete all the **Vector** sockets except the last socket at the top of the list as shown in the following screenshot:

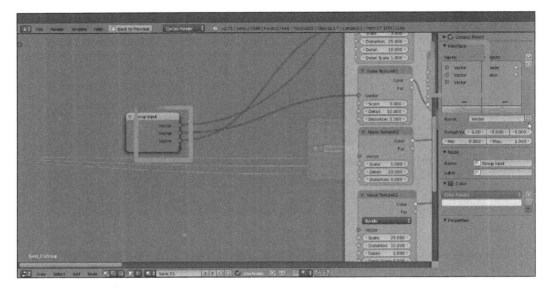

3. Now press *Shift*, select the **Group Input** node and the first texture node, and press *F* to automatically connect them.

4. Repeat to connect all the eight texture nodes to the **Vector** socket of the **Group Input** node.

Now we need to expose some of the values to modify the material from the interface, so let's perform the following steps:

1. From the second **Value** socket of the **Bump_Strength** node inside the **SAND BUMP** frame, click and drag a link to the bottom free socket in the **Group Input** node. In the **Input** window under the **Properties** panel, double-click on the newly appeared input socket name, **Value**, and write Sand_strength.

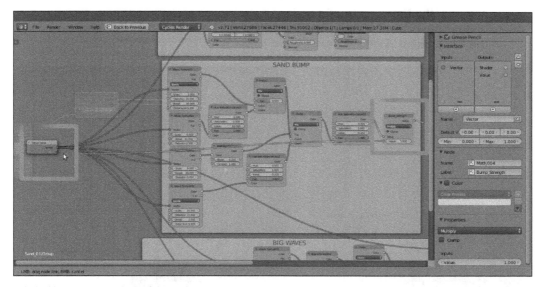

All the Vector input sockets of the nodes are connected to a single socket on the Group Input node, and the Bump Strength value is exposed by a new connection

2. Repeat step 1 for the second **Value** socket of the **Waves_Strength** and the **Grain_Strength** nodes, and rename the respective input as Waves_strength and Granularity.

3. Now click on the **Waves_size** node inside the **BIG WAVES** frame and delete it. Click and drag the second **Value** socket of the **Multiply01** node to the **Group Input** node, and rename the new socket Waves_size. Click and drag a link from the second **Value** socket of the **Multiply02** node, and connect it to the **Waves_size** socket as well.

4. We also need to expose the second **Value** socket of the **TOTAL BUMP STRENGTH** frame. Rename the new socket on the interface as `Total strength`. This is in fact the value for the overall bump of the material.

5. After this, we can do the following: expose the color input by deleting the **RGB** node in the **SAND COLOR** frame and connecting the **Color** input sockets of the **Diffuse BSDF**, **RGB Curves**, and **Glossy BSDF** shader node's to the **Color** socket on the **Group Input** node; expose the sand's grain size value, connecting the **Scale** input socket of the **Noise Texture03** node to a **Grain_size** socket; and finally, by clicking on the arrows in the **Properties** panel, order the position of the input sockets on the **Group Input** node as shown in this screenshot:

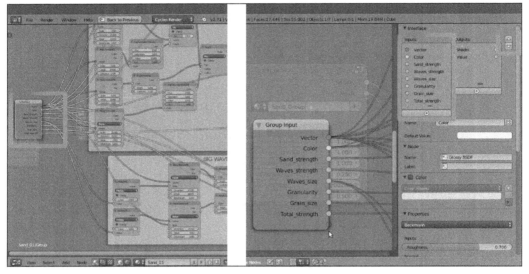

The sockets created on the Group Input node and reflected in the Interface subpanel

6. Press *Tab* to close the group. On the interface, we now have the controls to increase or decrease the overall bump effect, the sand color and grain, the wave strength, and scale/repetition, as we can see in the following screenshot:

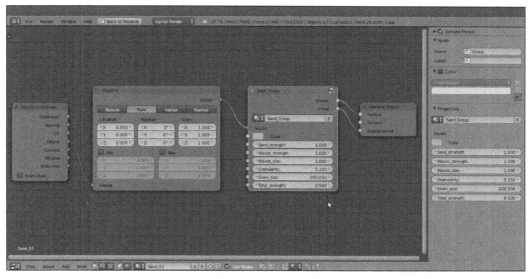

The final Sand_Group node with all the exposed input on its interface

The group is now available under the **Add** menu, and its shortcut involves pressing *Shift + A* and navigating to **Group | Sand_Group**. It can be reused for other materials in the same scene and also with different interface values, or linked/appended from a library in other blend files.

Creating a simple ground material using procedural textures

In this recipe, we will create a basic, raw ground material as shown in this screenshot:

The ground material as it appears in the final rendering

Getting ready

Start Blender and switch to **Cycles Render**. Then perform the following steps:

1. Delete the default Cube and add a Plane. Go to **Edit Mode** and scale it 15 times bigger (30 units per side; press *Tab*, then press *S*, enter the digit *15*, and press *Enter*). Go out of **Edit Mode**.

2. Go to the **Object modifiers** window and assign a **Subdivision Surface** modifier to the Plane. Switch from **Catmull-Clark** to **Simple**, and set the levels of **Subdivisions** for both **View** and **Render** to 4. Check the **Optimal Display** item.

3. Assign a second **Subdivision Surface** modifier. Again, switch to **Simple**, set the levels of **Subdivisions** for both **View** and **Render** to 4, and check the **Optimal Display** item.

4. Assign a **Displace** modifier. Click on the **Show texture in texture tab** button to the side of the **New** button. In the **Texture** window, click on the **New** button, select **Voronoi** texture, and increase the **Size** value to 1.80. Go back to the **Object modifiers** window and set the displacement **Strength** to 0.100.

5. Assign a second **Displace** modifier and select the default **Clouds** texture. Set the **Size** value to 0.75, the **Depth** value to 5, and the displacement **Strength** value to 0.150.

6. Assign a third **Displace** modifier. Again, select the default **Clouds** texture and increase the **Size** value to 4.00 (the slider arrives at a maximum of 2.00, but you can click on the value and enter higher values) and the **Depth** value to 4. Then switch **Noise** from **Soft** to **Hard** and click on the **Basis** button to change **Noise Basis** from **Blender Original** to **Voronoi F4**. Go to the **Colors** subpanel above the **Clouds** subpanel, and adjust the **Brightness** value to 0.900 and the **Contrast** value to 1.500. Set the displacement strength to 0.500.

7. In the **Shading** subpanel (which is accessible from the **Transform** menu), under the **Tool Shelf** tabs to the left of the 3D view, click on the **Smooth** button.

8. Go to the **World** window and click on the **Use Nodes** button in the **Surface** subpanel under the **Properties** panel. Then click on the little square with a dot on the right side of the **Color** slot. From the menu, select **Sky Texture**. Set the **Strength** value to 1.400.

9. Go to the **Outliner** and select the **Lamp** item. Go to the **Object data** window and click on **Use Nodes**. Then change **Type of Lamp** to **Sun** and set the **Strength** value to 1.400. Change the light color values to 1.000 for **R**, 0.935 for **G**, and 0.810 for **B**. In the orthogonal top view (press the 7 and 5 keys in the numeric keypad), rotate the Sun Lamp by 90°.

10. Place the **Camera** to have a nice angle on the Plane (you can also use the **Lock Camera to View** item in the (press *N*) **Properties** side panel), and switch from the 3D view to the **Camera** view (by pressing *0* from the numeric keypad).

11. Split the 3D window into two horizontal rows. Change the upper row to a **Node Editor** window.

12. Go to the **Render** window, and under the **Sampling** subpanel, set both the **Clamp Direct** and **Clamp Indirect** values to 1.000. Go to the **Light Path** subpanel and set the **Filter Glossy** value to 1.000.

13. Reselect the **Plane** and go to the **Material** window under the **Properties** panel. Disable the transformation widget by clicking on the icon in the 3D window toolbar or by pressing *Ctrl* and the spacebar, as shown in the following screenshot:

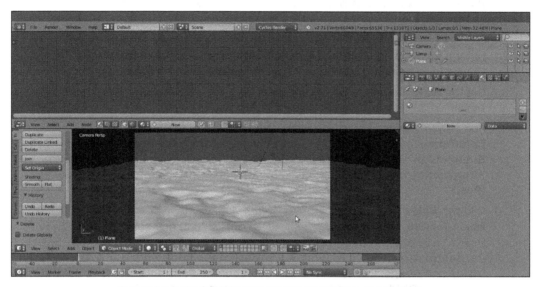

Screenshot in the Solid viewport shading mode of the ground scene

In the final scene, I added three UV Spheres with simple diffuse colors, just for lighting reference. Obviously, you can skip this step.

How to do it...

Let's now start with the ground material:

1. Put the mouse cursor in the **Camera** view and press *Shift + Z* to switch the **Viewport Shading** mode to **Rendered**.

2. Click on the **New** button in the **Material** window or in the **Node Editor** toolbar. Rename the material Ground_01.

3. In the **Node Editor** window, add a **Texture Coordinate** node (press *Shift + A* and navigate to **Input | Texture Coordinate**), a **Mapping** node (press *Shift + A* and navigate to **Vector | Mapping**), and a **Musgrave Texture** node (press *Shift + A* and navigate to **Texture | Musgrave Texture**).

4. Connect the **Object** output of the **Texture Coordinate** node to the **Vector** input of the **Mapping** node and the **Vector** output of this node to the **Vector** input of the **Musgrave Texture** node.

5. Connect the **Color** output of the **Musgrave Texture** node to the **Color** input of the **Diffuse BSDF** shader. In the **Properties** panel, label the **Diffuse BSDF** shader as Diffuse01. Set the **Scale** value of the **Musgrave Texture** node to 0.500.

6. Add a **Wave Texture** node (press *Shift + A* and navigate to **Texture | Wave Texture**) and a **MixRGB** node (press *Shift + A* and navigate to **Color | MixRGB**). Paste the **MixRGB** node between the **Musgrave Texture** node and the **Diffuse01** shader node, and connect the **Wave Texture** node's color output to the **Color2** input socket of the **MixRGB** node.

7. Set the **MixRGB** node's **Blend Type** to **Subtract** and label it Subtract01. Connect the **Mapping** output to the **Wave Texture** node's **Vector** input.

8. Set the **Wave Texture** node's **Scale** value to 0.200, **Distortion** to 20.000, **Detail** to 16.000, and **Detail Scale** to 5.000.

9. Add a **ColorRamp** node (press *Shift + A* and navigate to **Converter | ColorRamp**) and drag it onto the link connecting the **Wave Texture** node to the **Subtract01** node to paste it between them. Label it ColorRamp01, change the **Interpolation** mode to **B-Spline**, and move the black stop to the 0.230 position (**Pos:**).

10. Add two **Noise Texture** nodes (press *Shift + A*, navigate to **Texture | Noise Texture**, and then press *Shift + D* to duplicate it) and name them Noise Texture01 and Noise Texture02. Connect the **Mapping** node to them. Select the **Subtract01** node, press *Shift + D* to duplicate it twice, and change **Blend Type** to **Divide** and **Dodge**. Connect the **Color** output of the **Subtract01** node to the **Color1** input of the **Divide** node, and connect the **Color** output of the **Noise Texture01** node to the **Color2** input of the **Divide** node.

11. Then connect the **Color** output of the **Divide** node to the **Color1** input of the **Dodge** node, and the **Color** output of the **Noise Texture02** node to the **Color2** input of the **Dodge** node.

12. Label the **Dodge** node `Dodge01` and connect its output to the **Color** input of the **Diffuse01** shader. Set the **Noise Texture01** scale to `10.000`, **Detail** to `5.000`, and **Distortion** to `0.300`. For **Noise Texture02**, set **Scale** to `35.000`, **Detail** to `5.000`, and **Distortion** to `1.000`, as shown in the following screenshot:

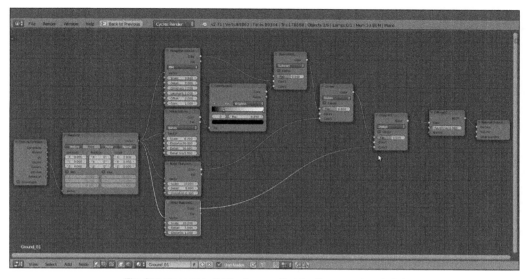

The first steps to build the bump effect for the ground material

13. Add two **Voronoi Texture** nodes (press *Shift + A*, navigate to **Texture | Voronoi Texture**, and rename the nodes `Voronoi Texture01` and `Voronoi Texture02`) and a new **MixRGB** node (press *Shift + A* and navigate to **Color | MixRGB**). Set the **Blend Type** to **Subtract** and label it `Subtract02`. Connect the color output of the **Voronoi Texture01** node to the **Color1** input socket, and the color output of the **Voronoi Texture02** node to the **Color2** input socket.

14. Set the **Subtract02** node's **Fac** value to `1.000`, and then go to the **Voronoi Texture01** node. Set **Coloring** to **Cells** and **Scale** to `18.100`. Go to the **Voronoi Texture02** node, leave **Coloring** as **Intensity**, and set the **Scale** value to `18.000`.

15. Select the two **Voronoi Texture** nodes and the **Subtract02** node, and press *Shift + D* to duplicate them. Label the texture nodes as `Voronoi Texture03` and `Voronoi Texture04`, and the **MixRGB** node as `Subtract03`.

16. Connect the **Mapping** node output to the **Vector** input sockets of the four **Voronoi Texture** nodes.

17. Change the **Coloring** of the **Voronoi Texture03** node back to **Intensity**, and set the **Scale** value to 18.500. Set the **Scale** value of **Voronoi Texture04** to 6.500.

18. Add a new **MixRGB** node (press *Shift + A* and navigate to **Color | MixRGB**) and change the **Blend Type** to Dodge. Label it Dodge02 and set the **Fac** value to 1.000. Connect the output of the **Subtract02** node to the **Color1** input socket and the output of the **Subtract03** node to the **Color2** input socket.

19. Add a **MixRGB** node again (press *Shift + A* and navigate to **Color | MixRGB**). Change the **Blend Type** to **Add** and paste it between the **Dodge01** node and the **Diffuse01** shader node. Then connect the output of the **Dodge02** node to the **Color2** input socket.

20. Disconnect the link between the **Add** output and the **Color** input socket of the **Diffuse01** shader node, and add a **Bump** node (press *Shift + A* and navigate to **Vector | Bump**). Connect the output of the **Add** node to the **Height** input socket of the **Bump** node. Then connect the **Normal** output of the **Bump** node to the **Normal** input socket of the **Diffuse01** shader. Set the **Add** node's **Fac** value to 0.280 and the **Bump** node's **Strength** value to 0.800.

21. Add a **ColorRamp** node (press *Shift + A* and navigate to **Converter | ColorRamp**) and label it ColorRamp02. Paste it between the **Dodge02** and the **Add** nodes. Set **Interpolation** to **B-Spline** and move the black color slider and stop at position 0.330.

22. Add a **RGB to BW** node (press *Shift + A* and navigate to **Converter | RGB to BW**) and paste it between the **Add** and the **Bump** nodes.

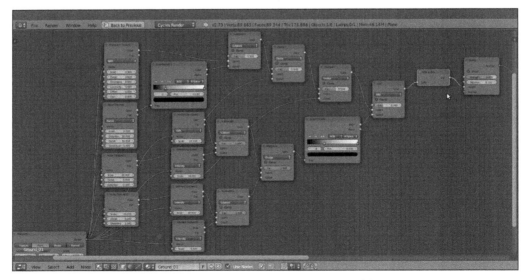

The total BUMP network for the ground material

23. Parent the nodes to a **Frame** (press *Shift + A* and navigate to **Layout | Frame**) and label it BUMP, as shown in the following screenshot:

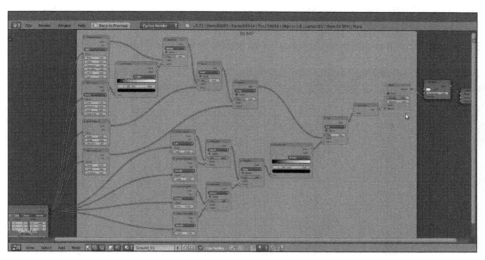

The BUMP frame

24. Add a **Mix Shader** node (press *Shift + A* and navigate to **Shader | Mix Shader**) and a second **Diffuse BSDF** shader (press *Shift + A* and navigate to **Shader | Diffuse BSDF**). Name them Mix Shader01 and Diffuse02, respectively. Then paste the **Mix Shader01** node between the **Diffuse01** and the **Material Output** nodes, and connect the **Diffuse02** node to the second **Shader** input socket of the **Mix Shader01** node.

25. Once again, add a **Mix Shader** node (press *Shift + A* and navigate to **Shader | Mix Shader**) and a **Diffuse BSDF** shader (press *Shift + A* and navigate to **Shader | Diffuse BSDF**). Label them Mix Shader02 and Diffuse03. Then paste the **Mix Shader02** node between the **Mix Shader01** node and the **Material Output** node, and connect the **Diffuse03** node to the second **Shader** input socket.

26. Connect the **Bump** node output to the **Normal** input of the **Diffuse02** and **Diffuse03** shader nodes.

27. Change the **Diffuse01** color values to 0.593 for **R**, 0.460 for **G**, and 0.198 for **B**; the **Diffuse02** color values to 0.423 for **R**, 0.234 for **G**, and 0.092 for **B**; and the **Diffuse03** color values to 0.700 for **R**, 0.620 for **G**, and 0.329 for **B**.

28. Once more, add a **Mix Shader** node (press *Shift + A* and navigate to **Shader | Mix Shader**) and a **Glossy BSDF** shader (press *Shift + A* and navigate to **Shader | Glossy BSDF**). Label the first node Mix Shader03 and paste it between the **Mix Shader02** and the **Material Output** nodes. Connect the **Glossy BSDF** shader to the second **Shader** input socket of the **Mix Shader03** node, and set its **Roughness** value to 0.300 and the color values to 0.593 for R, 0.460 for **G**, and 0.198 for **B**, just like the **Diffuse01** color.

29. Connect the **Bump** node output to the **Normal** input socket of the **Glossy BSDF** node.

30. Add a **Layer Weight** node (press *Shift + A* and navigate to **Input | Layer Weight**), connect the **Fresnel** output to the **Fac** input socket of the **Mix Shader03** node, and set the **Blend** value to 0.300.

31. Parent these recently added nodes to a new **Frame** and label it COLOR.

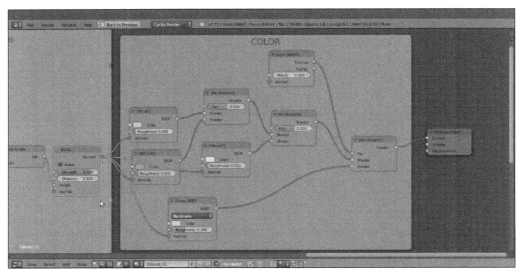

The COLOR frame

32. Add one more **Noise Texture** node (press *Shift + A* and navigate to **Texture | Noise Texture**) and a new **ColorRamp** node (press *Shift + A* and navigate to **Converter | ColorRamp**). Connect the **Mapping** node output to the **Noise Texture** node's **Vector** input (label it Noise Texture03) and the **Fac** output of **Noise Texture** to the **Fac** input of the **ColorRamp** node (label it ColorRamp03).

33. For the last time, add a **MixRGB** node and set the **Blend Type** to **Difference**. Then connect the **Color** output of the **ColorRamp03** node to the **Color1** input socket of the **Difference** node, and the **Color** output of the **Difference** node to the **Fac** input socket of the **Mix Shader01** node. Set the **Fac** value of the **Difference** node to 0.255.

34. Set the **Noise Texture03** node's scale to 1.000 and the **Detail** value to 5.000. Switch the **ColorRamp03** node's **Interpolation** to **B-Spline**, move the **0** value of **color stop** to position 0.285, move the **1** color stop to position 0.740, and click on the **+** icon to add a new color stop. Set its color to black and move it to position 0.320.

35. Connect the output of the **Dodge01** node inside the **BUMP** frame to the **Color2** input socket of the **Difference** node. Connect the **Color** output of the **ColorRamp02** node inside the **BUMP** frame to the **Fac** input socket of the **Mix Shader02** node inside the **COLOR** frame.

And we're done! Here is a screenshot of what the Blender UI will now look like:

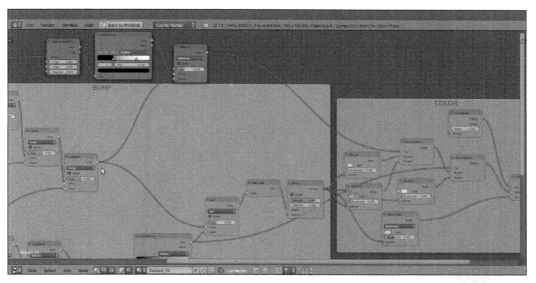

Part of the bump output is connected to the COLOR frame by the three upper nodes and the bottom ColorRamp node

How it works...

The way this material works is very similar to the sand material of the previous recipe, although a lot simpler:

> ▸ We mixed two slightly different colors using the values of a **Noise Texture** node as the stencil factor, then mixed a third, similar color on the ground of the bump output to obtain the whitish, pebble-like effect you see in the rendered image. We created the ground roughness using an ensemble of procedural textures mixed in several ways, whose total sum was then connected to the **Normal** input sockets of the three **Diffuse BSDF** nodes and of the **Glossy BSDF** shader, as shown in the following screenshot:

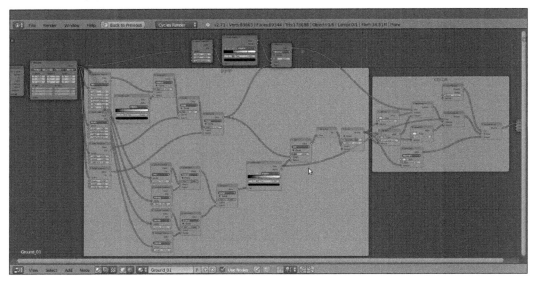

The overall vision of the ground material network

Creating a snow material using procedural textures

In this recipe, we will create a snow material, as shown in the following screenshot, and also fake a slight and cheap Subsurface Scattering effect:

The snow material as it appears in the final rendering

Getting ready

Start Blender and open the 99310S_Snow_start.blend file.

In this file, there is a prepared scene with a Spheroid (the usual Cube with a four-level **Subdivision Surface** modifier), a Suzanne (press *Shift + A* and navigate to **Add | Mesh | Monkey**) with a **Subdivision Surface** modifier as well, and the famous Stanford bunny (http://en.wikipedia.org/wiki/Stanford_bunny), leaning on a subdivided, displaced, and smoothed Plane renamed Snow_ground. Suzanne is Blender's mascot and an alternative to free test models such as the Stanford bunny itself. By the way, I thought of grouping them in the same scene to have different shapes to test the material.

In the file, there is also a Plane working as mesh-light and a Spot pointing in the opposite direction to try to enhance the translucency of the snow.

How to do it...

Let's start creating the snow material:

1. Go to the **World** window and click on the **New** button. Then click on the little square with a dot on the right side of the **Color** slot. From the menu, select **Sky Texture**.

2. Go to the **Material** window and select the **Snow_ground** item in the **Outliner**. Click on the **New** button in the **Material** window under the **Properties** panel or in the **Node Editor** toolbar. Rename the material as Snow_01.

3. Press *Shift* and select the Spheroid, Suzanne, and the Stanford bunny. Then select the Plane to have it as the active object. Press *Ctrl + L* and go to **Materials**.

4. Put the mouse cursor in the **Camera** view and press *Shift + Z* to set the **Viewport Shading** mode to **Rendered**.

5. In the **Material** window under the **Properties** panel to the right, under the **Surface** subpanel, switch the **Diffuse BSDF** shader with a **Mix Shader** node. In the first **Shader** slot, select a **Diffuse BSDF** shader, and in the second slot, select a **Glossy BSDF** shader.

6. Set the **Roughness** value of the **Glossy BSDF** shader to 0.300.

7. Add a **Fresnel** node (press *Shift + A* and navigate to **Input | Fresnel**) and a **Math** node (press *Shift + A* and navigate to **Converter | Math**). Set the **IOR** (short for **Index Of Refraction**) value of the **Fresnel** node to 1.300. Then connect its **Fac** output to the first **Value** socket of the **Math** node. Set the second **Value** to 10.000 and the operation mode to **Divide**. Finally, connect its **Value** output to the **Fac** input socket of the **Mix Shader** node.

8. Add a **Translucent BSDF** node (press *Shift + A* and navigate to **Shader | Translucent BSDF**). Set its color values to 0.598 for **R**, 0.721 for **G**, and 1.000 for **B**.

9. Select the **Mix Shader** node, press *Shift + D* to duplicate it, and paste it between the first **Mix Shader** node and the **Material Output** node. Connect the **Translucent BSDF** node's output to the second input socket. Set the **Fac** value of the second **Mix Shader** node to 0.300. Here is a screenshot of the basic shader for your reference:

The basic shader for the snow material

10. Add a **Noise Texture** node (press *Shift + A* and navigate to **Texture | Noise Texture**) and press *Shift + D* to duplicate it. In the **Properties** panel of the **Node Editor** window (press the *N* key to make this appear if necessary), label them Noise Texture01 and Noise Texture02.

11. Add a **Texture Coordinate** node (press *Shift + A* and navigate to **Input | Texture Coordinate**) and a **Mapping** node (press *Shift + A* and navigate to **Vector | Mapping**). Connect the **Object** output of the **Texture Coordinate** node to the **Vector** input of the **Mapping** node. Then connect the **Vector** output of the **Mapping** node to both the **Vector** input sockets of the **Noise Texture** nodes.

12. Add a **Math** node (press *Shift + A* and navigate to **Converter | Math**) and press *Shift + D* to duplicate it three times so that you obtain four **Math** nodes. Label them `Math01`, `Math02`, `Math03`, and `Math04`.

13. Connect the **Noise Texture01** node's **Fac** output (the gray one) to the first **Value** input of the **Math01** node and set the second **Value** to `2.000`. Set the **Operation** to **Multiply**.

14. Connect the **Fac** output of the **Noise Texture02** node to the first **Value** input of the **Math02** node and let its second **Value** be the default, which is `0.500`. Set the **Operation** to **Multiply**.

15. Now connect both the output of the two previous **Math** nodes to the input **Value** sockets of the **Math03** node. Set the **Operation** to **Add**.

16. Connect the output of the **Math03** node to the first **Value** input of the **Math04** node. Set its **Operation** to **Multiply** and let the second **Value** be the default, which is `0.500`.

17. Connect the **Math04** node output to the **Displacement** input socket of the **Material Output** node.

18. Now go to the **Noise Texture02** node and change the **Scale** value to `15.000`. Leave the other values (also for the **Noise Texture01** node) as they are (that is, `5.000` for **Scale**, `2.000` for **Detail**, and `0.000` for **Distortion**).

19. Go to the **Mapping** node and set the **Scale** value to `0.500` for all three axes. Now the Blender UI will look like what is shown in this screenshot:

The bump pattern

20. Add two **Frames**, label them SNOW COLOR and SNOW BUMP, and parent the appropriate nodes to them as shown in the following screenshot:

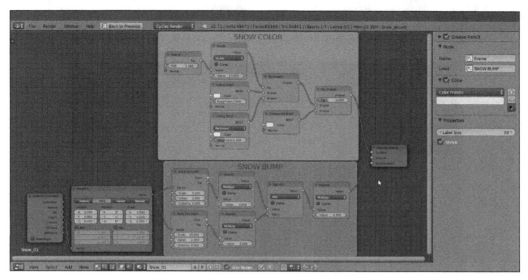

The overall vision of the snow material network

How it works...

As usual, to understand the creation of this material more easily, we will divide it into two stages: the first stage for the general color and consistency of the snow, and the second stage to add bumpiness to the surface. These stages are explained in detail as follows:

▶ **First stage**: We just made a basic shader by mixing the **Diffuse BSDF** and the **Glossy BSDF** shaders by the **IOR** value of the **Fresnel** node. The **Fresnel** output value is divided by the **Math-Divide** node to obtain a softer transition (try to change the second value from 10.000 to 1.000 to see a totally different effect). Then we also mixed a bluish **Translucent** shader but gave predominance to the basic shader by setting the factor value in the second **Mix Shader** node to 0.300. The **Translucent** shader gives the appearance of light seeping through snow and showing in the shadowed areas of the object, working as a very fast and cheap Subsurface Scattering effect.

▶ **Second stage**: We added two **Noise Texture** nodes with different scale values to simulate the bumpiness of soft snow. The first two **Multiply-Math** nodes set the influence of each noise separately. These values were merged by the **Add-Math** node and piped in one more **Math** node, set to **Multiply** as well, to establish the overall weight of the bump effect that, being directly connected to the **Displacement** input in the **Material Output** node, affects all the shaders in the network.

Creating an ice material using procedural textures

In this recipe, we will create a semi-transparent ice material that will look like this:

The ice material as it appears in the final rendering

Getting ready

Start Blender, load the 99310S_start.blend file, and perform the following steps:

1. Delete the **UV/Image Editor** window by joining it with the 3D view.

2. Select the **Plane** item, go to **Edit Mode**, and scale it eight times bigger (press *Tab*, then press S, enter the digit 8, and press *Enter*). Go out of **Edit Mode** and move the Plane 1 unit upward (press *Tab*, then press G, enter the digit 1, press Z, and finally, press *Enter*).

3. Select the **Cube** and press *N* to make the **Properties** panel visible. Go to the **View** subpanel and check the **Lock Camera to View** item. The borders of the **Camera** view turn red, which mean that you can directly use the mouse to move, zoom in, and adjust the position of the Camera around the selected object (the Cube in this case) to obtain a view similar what is shown in the right half of this screenshot:

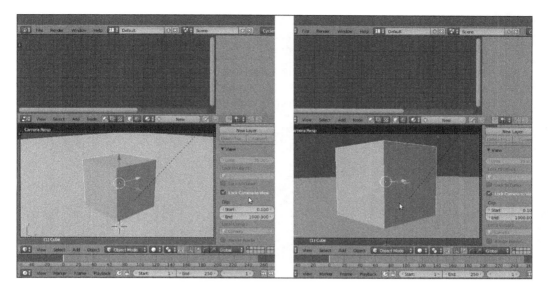

4. Next, uncheck the **Lock Camera to View** item.

5. Go to the **World** window and set **Color** to black.

6. Select **Sun Lamp** in the **Outliner**, and in the **Object data** window, set the **Strength** value to 3.000, **Size** to 1.000, and the **Color** values to 0.900 for **R**, 0.872 for **G**, and 0.737 for **B**.

7. Select the **Cube**, go to **Edit Mode**, and press the *W* key. In the **Specials** pop-up menu, select **Subdivide**. Press the *F6* key, and in the **Subdivide** pop-up panel under the 3D Cursor position, set **Number of Cuts** to 2. Go out of **Edit Mode**.

8. Go to the **Object modifier** window and assign a **Subdivision Surface** modifier to the Cube. Switch from **Catmull-Clark** to **Simple**. Set the **Subdivisions** levels to 5 for both **View** and **Render**. Check the **Optimal Display** item.

9. Assign a **Displace** modifier, and in the **Textures** window, click on **New** and select the **Voronoi** texture. Set the **Size** value to 1.20. Back in the **Object modifiers** window, set the displacement **Strength** to 0.050.

10. Assign a new **Displace** modifier and select **Voronoi** texture again, but this time, set the **Size** value to 0.80. Set the displacement **Strength** value to 0.075.

11. Assign a third **Displace** modifier, select the **Voronoi** texture, and leave the default size (0.25) as it is. Set the displacement **Strength** value to 0.020. Here is a screenshot of the displaced Cube primitive for your reference:

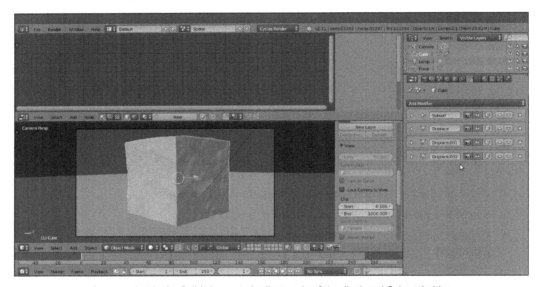

A screenshot in the Solid viewport shading mode of the displaced Cube primitive

12. Switch the Camera's **Viewport Shading** to the **Rendered** mode.

How to do it...

After preparing the scene, we are going to create the material:

1. Select the **Cube** and click on **New** in the **Material** window under the **Properties** panel or in the **Node Editor** toolbar. Rename the material Ice_01.

2. In the **Material** window to the right of the screen, under the **Surface** subpanel, switch the **Diffuse BSDF** shader with a **Mix Shader** node. In the first **Shader** slot, select a **Glass BSDF** shader, and in the second slot, select a **Transparent BSDF** shader.

3. Set the **Glass BSDF** shader's color totally white and the **IOR** value to `1.309`. Set the **Transparent BSDF** shader's color values to `0.448` for **R**, `0.813` for **G**, and `1.000` for **B**.

4. Add a **Fresnel** node (press *Shift + A* and navigate to **Input | Fresnel**) and connect it to the **Fac** input socket of the **Mix Shader** node. Then set the **IOR** value to `1.309`.

5. Add a **Glossy BSDF** shader (press *Shift + A* and navigate to **Shader | Glossy BSDF**). Set the color to pure white and the **Roughness** value to `0.050`.

6. Select the **Mix Shader** node and press *Shift + D* to duplicate it. Connect the output of the first `Mix Shader` node to the first `Shader` input socket of the duplicated one, and the **Glossy BSDF** shader output to the second **Shader** input socket. Add a **Layer Weight** node (press *Shift + A* and navigate to **Input | Layer Weight**) and connect the **Facing** output to the **Fac** socket of the second **Mix Shader** node.

7. Add a **Voronoi Texture** node (press *Shift + A* and navigate to **Texture | Voronoi Texture**). Set **Coloring** to **Cells** and the **Scale** value to `25.000`.

8. Add a **Noise Texture** node (press *Shift + A* and navigate to **Texture | Noise Texture**) and set only the **Scale** value to `25.000`.

9. Add a **Math** node (press *Shift + A* and navigate to **Converter | Math**) and set **Operation** to **Maximum**. Connect the **Fac** output of the **Voronoi Texture** and **Noise Texture** nodes to the first and the second **Value** input of the **Math** node.

10. Add a **Bump** node (press *Shift + A* and navigate to **Vector | Bump**). Connect the **Maximum-Math** node output to the **Height** input of the **Bump** node, and its **Normal** output to the **Normal** input sockets of the **Glass BSDF** and **Glossy BSDF** shaders.

11. Set the **Strength** value of the **Bump** node to `0.250`.

12. Add an **RGB Curves** node (press *Shift + A* and navigate to **Color | RGB Curves**) and paste it between the **Maximum-Math** and the **Bump** nodes. Set the point in the little window of the node interface at these coordinates: `0.25455` for **X** and `0.28125` for **Y**. Click on the little window to create a new point and set its coordinates to `0.74091` for **X** and `0.26250` for **Y**.

13. Add a **Texture Coordinate** node (press *Shift + A* and navigate to **Input| Texture Coordinate**) and a **Mapping** node (press *Shift + A* and navigate to **Vector | Mapping**). Connect the **Object** output of the **Texture Coordinate** node to the **Vector** input of the **Mapping** node. Then connect the **Vector** output of the **Mapping** node to the **Vector** input sockets of both the **Voronoi Texture** and **Noise Texture** nodes, as shown in the following screenshot:

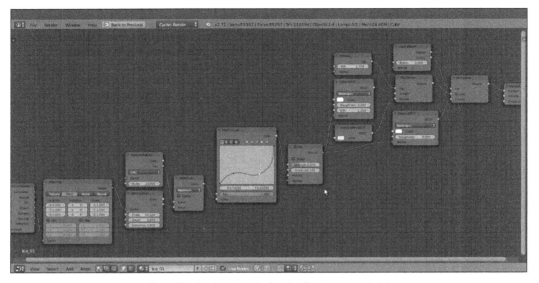

The quite simple network of nodes for the ice material

How it works...

This time, we started by mixing a **Glass BSDF** shader and a **Transparent** shader node, modulated by a **Fresnel** node, and we set the **IOR** values of both the **Fresnel** and the **Glass BSDF** to the refraction value of ice. We also added a **Glossy BSDF** shader to provide specularity, mixed by a **Layer Weight** node set on **Facing** (because the more a mesh normal faces the point of view, the more evident the specular effect is).

Then, using mixed procedural textures, we created the bump effect to perturb the surface of the object (note that the bump also affects the material's refraction).

See also

Here are some links to lists of IOR values that can be used in mixing the **Diffuse BSDF** component with the **Glossy BSDF** component through a **Fresnel** node:

- `http://blenderartists.org/forum/showthread.php?71202-Material-IOR-Value-reference`

- `http://blenderartists.org/forum/showthread.php?117271-The-IOR-of-diferent-materials`

The following is a computational and scientific search engine that allows you to quickly research the IOR of a given substance by typing its name:

- `http://www.wolframalpha.com/`

4
Creating Man-made Materials in Cycles

In this chapter, we will cover the following recipes:

- ▶ Creating a generic plastic material
- ▶ Creating a Bakelite material
- ▶ Creating an expanded polystyrene material
- ▶ Creating a clear (glassy) polystyrene material
- ▶ Creating a rubber material
- ▶ Creating an antique bronze material with procedurals
- ▶ Creating a multipurpose metal node group
- ▶ Creating a rusty metal material with procedurals
- ▶ Creating a wood material with procedurals

Introduction

On most occasions, artificial materials are quite easy to recreate in Cycles.

In the previous chapters we discussed the mechanics of building materials through procedural textures using the Cycles render engine. In this chapter, we'll discuss some artificial materials. Starting with one or two examples of simple materials, such as plastic, we will progress to more complex materials. We'll also take a look at the decayed material shaders and treat them as worn or rusty metals.

Note that in Cycles, it's not actually necessary to add the nodes for the texture mapping coordinates to any shader network. This is because, by default and if not otherwise specified, Cycles automatically uses the **Generated** mapping coordinates for procedural textures and any existing UV coordinate layer for the image textures.

Anyway, I think it's a good habit to add both the **Texture Coordinate** and the **Mapping** nodes to all the materials to permit easy reutilization of the shaders on different objects with different mapping options, scales, and locations.

Creating a generic plastic material

In this recipe, we will create a generic plastic shader and add slight granularity (optional) to the surface, as shown in the following screenshot:

The generic plastic material as it appears in the final rendering

Getting ready...

Start Blender and load the `9931OS_Suzanne_start.blend` file. This is a prepared scene, with Suzanne (the monkey head primitive that is Blender's mascot) leaning on a white Plane, a Camera, a mesh-light emitting slightly yellowish light, and a low-intensity gray World.

 We'll use a lot this file as starting point for several of our recipes.

How to do it...

Now we will go straight to creation of the material, so follow these steps:

1. Select **Suzanne** and click on **New** in the **Material** window under the **Properties** panel or in the **Node Editor** toolbar. Rename the material `Plastic_Green_Soft`.

2. Set the **Viewport Shading** mode of the **Camera** view to **Rendered** by moving the mouse into the 3D view and pressing *Shift + Z*.

3. In the **Material** window under the **Properties** panel, switch the **Diffuse BSDF** shader with a **Mix Shader** node, and in the first **Shader** slot, select a **Diffuse BSDF** shader. In the second **Shader** slot, select a **Glossy BSDF** node.

4. Change the **Diffuse BSDF** color to bright green (change the values of **R** to 0.040, **G** to 0.800, and **B** to 0.190) and the **Glossy BSDF** shader's **Roughness** value to 0.300.

5. Press *Shift + D* to duplicate the **Mix Shader** node, and paste it between the first **Mix Shader** node and the **Material Output** node. Set the **Fac** value to 0.100.

6. Duplicate the **Glossy BSDF** node and connect its output to the second input socket of the second **Mix Shader** node. Set its **Roughness** value to 0.500, as shown in the following screenshot:

A screenshot of the entire Blender interface with the basic shader nodes in the Node Editor window at the top

7. Add a **Noise Texture** node (press *Shift + A* and navigate to **Texture | Noise Texture**), a **Texture Coordinate** node (press *Shift + A* and navigate to **Input | Texture Coordinate**), and a **Mapping** node (press *Shift + A* and navigate to **Vector | Mapping**).

8. Connect the **Object** output of the **Texture Coordinate** node to the **Vector** input of the **Mapping** node, and the output of this node to the input of the **Noise Texture** node.

9. Set the **Noise Texture** node's **Scale** value to 50.000. Add a **Math** node (press *Shift + A* and navigate to **Converter | Math**). Connect the **Noise Texture** node's **Fac** output to the first **Value** input of the **Math** node. Set the **Math** node's **Operation** to **Multiply** and second **Value** to 0.050. Connect its **Value** output to the **Displacement** input socket of the **Material Output** node, as shown in the following screenshot:

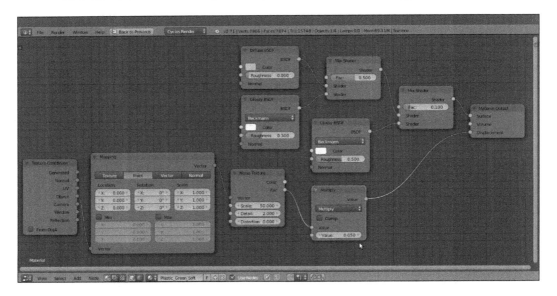

The very simple bump effect added to the shader nodes by connecting the output of the Noise Texture node to the Displacement input socket of the Material Output node

10. Save the file as Plastic_soft.blend.

How it works...

This is one of the simplest materials you can build in Cycles. It consists of a colored **Diffuse BSDF** component mixed at 50 percent with a white **Glossy BSDF** shader and another low **Glossy BSDF** shader to make the specular effect more diffused. A tiny **Noise Texture** node, connected directly to the **Displacement** input of the **Material Output** node, adds a slightly dotted bump effect to the whole material, as if it is some kind of industrial plastic used for toys.

Creating a Bakelite material

Bakelite is a very common type of plastic and can be found in a lot of different colors and patterns. In this recipe, we will create the black type (which was once really common), as shown in this screenshot:

The black Bakelite material as it appears in the final rendering

Getting ready...

Start Blender and load the `99310S_Suzanne_start.blend` file again:

1. With the mouse arrow in the **Camera** view, press the *T* key. Select the **Suzanne** mesh. Go to the **Tools** tab under the **Tool Shelf** panel on the left. Select **Flat** under **Shading**. Press *T* again to close the **Tool Shelf** panel.

2. Go to the **Object modifiers** window in the **Properties** panel. Expand the **Subdivision Surface** modifier panel and set the levels both for **View** and **Render** to 1.

How to do it...

Now we are going to create the material by performing the following steps:

1. Go to the **Material** window and click on **New** (or do this as usual, in the **Node Editor** toolbar). Rename the material `Plastic_Bakelite_Black`.

2. Set the **Viewport Shading** mode of the **Camera** view to **Rendered**.

3. Switch the **Diffuse BSDF** shader with a **Mix Shader** node, and in the first **Shader** slot, select a **Diffuse BSDF** shader. In the second **Shader** slot, select a **Glossy BSDF** node.

4. Change the **Diffuse BSDF** color to pure black and the **Glossy BSDF** shader color to light gray (**RGB** to `0.253`). Set the **Roughness** value of the **Glossy BSDF** shader to `0.100` and the **Fac** value of the **Mix Shader** node to `0.800`.

5. Press *Shift + D* to duplicate the **Mix Shader** node, and paste it between the **Glossy BSDF** shader and the first **Mix Shader** node.

6. With the mouse arrow in the **Node Editor** window, press *N*. Select the first **Mix Shader** node, and in the **Label** slot in the **Active Node** panel on the right, write `Mix Shader1`. Select the second **Mix Shader** node, and in the **Label** slot, write `Mix Shader2`.

7. Add an **Anisotropic BSDF** shader (press *Shift + A* and navigate to **Shader | Anisotropic BSDF**) and connect its output to the second input socket of the **Mix Shader2** node.

8. Set the **Mix Shader2** node's **Fac** value to `0.500`. Set the **Anisotropic BSDF** node's color to light gray, and set the same color for the **Glossy BSDF** shader (that is, **RGB** to `0.253`). Set the **Glossy BSDF** shader's **Roughness** value to `0.100` and **Rotation** to `0.500` as shown in the following screenshot:

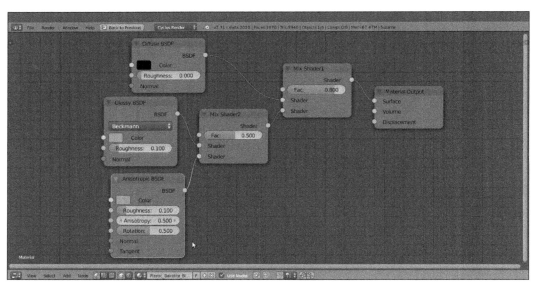

The simple shader network for the basic Bakelite material

9. Save the file as `Plastic_Bakelite.blend`.

How it works...

Basically, we made the same kind of material as the green plastic material, but this time, we enhanced the reflectivity (mirror) by lowering the **Roughness** value. We also added an **Anisotropic BSDF** specularity effect with the same roughness and color as those for the **Glossy BSDF** shader. The **Rotation** value of the **Anisotropic BSDF** shader sets the flow of the highlights on the mesh. The direction of the specularity rotates as this value increases from 0.000 to 1.000.

Anisotropy is a method of enhancing image quality of textures on surfaces that are far away and steeply angled with respect to the point of view. An anisotropic surface will change in appearance as it rotates about its geometric normal.

There's more...

Starting from the black material, let's now try to make a differently processed Bakelite material, as shown in the following screenshot:

A different type of Bakelite

First, we'll make a node group of the Bakelite material by performing the following steps:

1. Click on the material name and rename it `Plastic_Bakelite2`. Then save the file as `Plastic_Bakelite2.blend`.

2. Select the **Diffuse BSDF**, **Glossy BSDF**, **Anisotropic BSDF**, and two **Mix Shader** nodes and press *Ctrl + G* to make a group.

3. Click and drag the **Diffuse BSDF** node's **Color** socket into the empty socket of the **Group Input** node. Drag the **Fac** socket of the **Mix Shader2** node, and in the **Interface** subpanel of the **Properties** panel of the **Node Editor** window, rename it `Aniso`. This will drive the influence of the anisotropic shader on the glossy shader. Click and drag the **Fac** socket of the **Mix Shader1** node to the empty socket of **Group Input** node. Rename it `Spec`. This will drive the amount of final specularity of the shader.

Here is a screenshot of the creation of the Bakelite node group for your reference:

The creation of the Bakelite node group

4. Press *Tab* to close the group. Rename it `Bakelite`.

Now we'll add the nodes needed to create the differently colored material that we decided at the beginning of this section:

1. In the **Node Editor** window, add the following nodes in linear sequence from left to right: a **Texture Coordinate** node (press *Shift + A* and navigate to **Input | Texture Coordinate**), a **Mapping** node (press *Shift + A* and navigate to **Vector | Mapping**), a **Noise Texture** node (press *Shift + A* and navigate to **Texture | Noise Texture**), a **ColorRamp** node (press *Shift + A* and navigate to **Converter | ColorRamp**), and a **MixRGB** node (press *Shift + A* and navigate to **Color | MixRGB**).

2. Connect the **Object** output of the **Texture Coordinate** node to the **Vector** input of the **Mapping** node, and the output of this node to the input of the **Noise Texture** node. Connect the **Color** output of the **Noise Texture** node to the **ColorRamp** input socket, and the **Color** output of the **ColorRamp** node to the **Color1** input socket of the **MixRGB** node. Connect the **Color** output of the **MixRGB** node to the **Color** input of the **Bakelite** node group.

3. Set the **Noise Texture** node's **Scale** to 4.000, **Detail** to 4.200, and **Distortion** to 1.700.

4. Set the **ColorRamp** node's **Interpolation** to **B-Spline**. Move the black color marker to position 0.277 and the white color marker to 0.686.

5. Set **MixRGB** node's **Blend Type** to **Divide** (but remember to experiment with the other types as well) and the **Fac** value to 0.600. Change the **Color2** values of **R** to 0.799, **G** to 0.442, and **B** to 0.220.

6. In the **Bakelite** node group interface, set the **Spec** value to 0.300, as shown in the following screenshot:

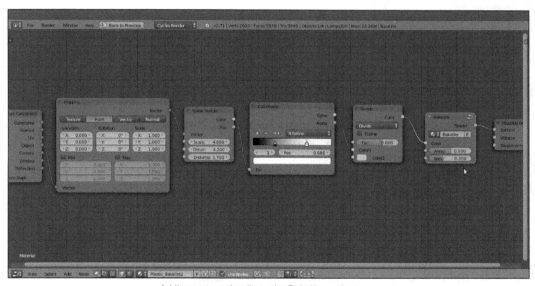

Adding texture details to the Bakelite node group

7. You can also smooth the **Suzanne** mesh in the **Tool Shelf** panel (press *T*) and increase the **Subdivision** levels of the **Subdivision Surface** modifier to 2.

8. Save the file.

Creating an expanded polystyrene material

In this recipe, we will create a classic white expanded polystyrene material, as shown in this screenshot:

The white expanded polystyrene material as it appears in the final rendering

Getting ready...

First, let's prepare the scene:

1. Start Blender and load the `99310S_Suzanne_start.blend` file. Add a Cube primitive to the scene and place it leaning on the Plane, close to Suzanne. Move it upwards by 1 Blender unit.

2. With the mouse arrow in the **Camera** view, press *Shift + F* to enter **Walk Mode** (in this mode, you can press the *W* key to go forward, press *S* to go back, move the mouse to decide the direction, and click or press *Enter* to confirm). Adjust the **Camera** position so as to center the two objects in the frame.

3. Select the **Cube** object and go to the **Object modifiers** window. Assign a **Boolean** modifier.

4. Press *Shift + D* to duplicate the Cube, and move it a bit upward (press *G*, then press *Z*, enter *.4*, and press *Enter*). Reselect the first **Cube**, and in the **Object** field of the **Boolean** modifier panel, select the second Cube (**Cube.001**). Set **Operation** to **Difference**. Go to **Edit Mode** and scale all the vertices a bit larger on the *x* and *y* axes (press *S*, then press *Shift + Z*, enter *1.200*, and press *Enter*).

5. Exit **Edit Mode** and reselect **Cube.001**. Move it a bit on the *x* axis (press *G*, then press *X*, enter *.4*, and press *Enter*).

6. Go to the **Object** window and set **Maximum Draw Type** to **Wire**. Then go to the **Ray Visibility** subpanel (usually at the bottom) and uncheck all the items. This way, **Cube.001** becomes visible in the 3D view, but is not yet rendered in the preview.

7. Just to be sure that the second cube is not visible (the previous step should be enough for the final rendering), go to **Outliner** and click on the camera icon to the right of the **Cube.001** item.

8. Select the first **Cube** and assign a **Bevel** modifier. Set the **Width** value to 0.0200. Move it higher in the stack of modifiers and place it before the **Boolean** modifier.

9. Assign a **Subdivision Surface** modifier and set both the **Subdivisions** levels to 2. Check the **Optimal Display** item and move it higher in the stack. Place it before the **Boolean** modifier but after the **Bevel** modifier.

10. Press *T* to call the **Tool Shelf** panel. Set the **Cube** shading to **Smooth**.

11. Press *Shift*, select both **Cube** and the **Cube.001** objects, and rotate them on *z* axis towards the **Camera** (press *R*, then press *Z*, enter *-40*, and then press *Enter*).

12. Press *T* to close the **Tool Shelf** panel. The following screenshot shows the process of building the box object:

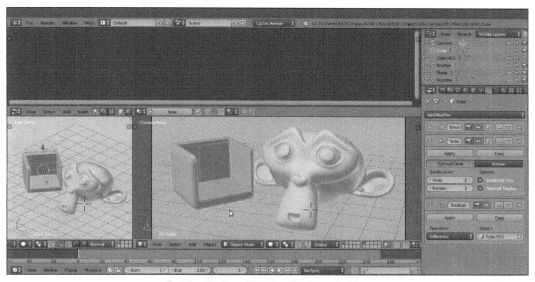

Building the box object by a Boolean modifier

13. Select the **Plane** object, and in the **Material** window, switch the **Diffuse BSDF** shader with a **Mix Shader** node. Then, in the **Shader** slots, select a **Diffuse BSDF** node and a **Glossy BSDF** shader node. Add a **Layer Weight** node (press *Shift + A* and navigate to **Input | Layer Weight**) and connect the **Facing** output to the **Fac** input socket of the **Mix Shader** node. Set the color of the **Diffuse BSDF** node as follows: **R** to 0.530, **G** to 0.800, and **B** to 0.800.

How to do it...

Now we are going to create the material by performing the following steps:

1. Select **Suzanne** and click on **New** in the **Material** window under the **Properties** panel or in the **Node Editor** toolbar. Rename the material `Plastic_expanded_polystyrene`.

2. Switch the **Diffuse BSDF** shader with a **Mix Shader** node, and in the first **Shader** slot, select a **Diffuse BSDF** shader. In the second **Shader** slot, select a **Glossy BSDF** node.

3. Set the **Diffuse BSDF** shader color and the **Glossy** shader color to pure white. Set the **Roughness** value of the **Glossy BSDF** shader to 0.600. Add a **Fresnel** node (press *Shift + A* and navigate to **Input | Fresnel**). Connect its output to the **Fac** input socket of the **Mix Shader** node. Set the **IOR** value to 1.550.

4. Add a **Voronoi Texture** node (press *Shift + A* and navigate to **Texture | Voronoi Texture**), a **Texture Coordinate** node (press *Shift + A* and navigate to **Input | Texture Coordinate**), and a **Mapping** node (press *Shift + A* and navigate to **Vector | Mapping**).

5. Connect the **Object** output of the **Texture Coordinate** node to the **Vector** input of the **Mapping** node, and the output of this node to the **Vector** input of the **Voronoi Texture** node.

6. Set the **Voronoi Texture** node's **Scale** value to 25.000. Add a **Bump** node (press *Shift + A* and navigate to **Vector | Bump**). Connect the **Fac** output of the **Voronoi Texture** node to the **Height** input socket of the **Bump** node, and the output of this node to the **Normal** input sockets of the **Diffuse BSDF** and **Glossy BSDF** shader nodes.

7. Check the **Invert** item on the **Bump** node and set the **Strength** value to 0.500, as shown in the following screenshot:

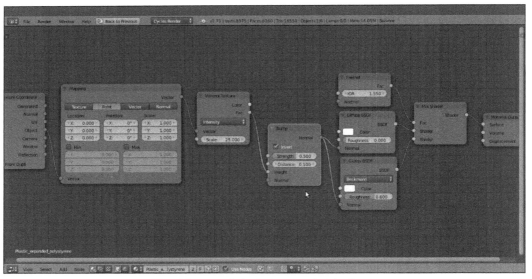

The white expanded polystyrene material network

8. Press *Shift* and select the **Cube** object and **Suzanne**. Then press *Ctrl + L*, and in the **Make Links** pop-up menu, select the **Material** item to assign the material of the active object to the other object.

9. Save the file as `Plastic_expanded_polystyrene.blend`.

How it works...

You have probably noticed that this recipe is simply a variation of the generic plastic shader. We changed the color to white, and instead of **Noise Texture**, we used a **Voronoi Texture** node with a different scale to add the typical polystyrene pattern. Then, by increasing the **Roughness** value of the **Glossy BSDF** shader, we made the specularity more diffused.

Creating a clear (glassy) polystyrene material

In this recipe, we will create a glassy polystyrene material (which you find on the body of ballpoint pens), as shown in the following screenshot:

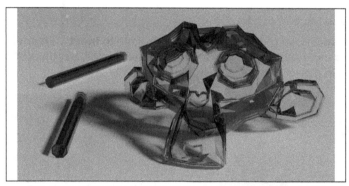

The glassy polystyrene material as it appears in the final rendering

Getting ready...

First, we need the usual preparation:

1. Start Blender and load the 9931OS_Suzanne_start.blend file.

2. Select the **Suzanne** mesh and press *T*. In the **Tool Shelf** panel on the left side, select **Flat** under **Shading**. Press *T* again to close the **Tool Shelf** panel.

3. Go to the **Object modifiers** window in the **Properties** panel and delete the **Subdivision Surface** modifier. Add a **Solidify** modifier and set the **Thickness** value to 0.0350. Add a **Bevel** modifier and set the **Width** value to 0.0050. Uncheck the **Clamp Overlap** item.

How to do it...

Now we are going to create the material by performing the following steps:

1. Go to the **Material** window and click on **New** (or as usual, go to the **Node Editor** toolbar). Rename the material `Plastic_clear_polystyrene`.

2. Set the **Viewport Shading** mode of the **Camera** view to **Rendered**.

3. Switch the **Diffuse BSDF** shader with a **Mix Shader** node, and in the first **Shader** slot, select a **Mix Shader** node again. In the second **Shader** slot, select a **Glass BSDF** node. Set its **IOR** value to `1.460`. Change the values of **R** to `0.688`, **G** to `0.758`, and **B** to `0.758`.

4. Go to the second **Mix Shader** node, and in its first **Shader** slot, select a **Transparent BSDF**. In the second **Shader** slot, select a **Glossy BSDF** node. Change the **Glossy BSDF** node color values for **R** to `0.688`, **G** to `0.758`, and **B** to `0.758`. Change the **Roughness** value to `0.010`.

5. Add a **Fresnel** node (press *Shift + A* and navigate to **Input | Fresnel**) and connect it to the **Fac** input sockets of both the **Mix Shader** nodes. Set the **IOR** value to `1.460`, as shown in the following screenshot:

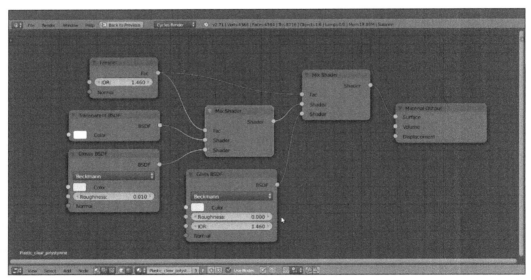

The completed network for the glassy polystyrene material

6. Save the file as `Plastic_clear_polystyrene.blend`.

Creating a rubber material

In this recipe, we will create a generic rubber shader, as shown in this screenshot:

The rubber material as it appears in the final rendering

Getting ready...

Start Blender and load the `9931OS_Suzanne_start.blend` file.

How to do it...

Now we are going to create the material by performing the following steps:

1. Click on **New** in the **Material** window under the **Properties** panel or in the **Node Editor** toolbar. Rename the material `Rubber`.

2. With the mouse arrow in the **Camera** view, press *Shift + Z* to set it to **Rendered** mode.

3. Switch the **Diffuse BSDF** shader with a **Mix Shader** node, and in the second **Shader** slot, select a **Glossy BSDF** node. In the first **Shader** slot, select a new **Mix Shader** node. Set the **Glossy BSDF** node's **Roughness** value to `0.350`.

4. Go to the second **Mix Shader** node, and in the first **Shader** slot, select a **Diffuse BSDF** node. In the second **Shader** slot, select a **Velvet BSDF** node. Set the **Velvet BSDF** shader node's **Sigma** value to `0.600`.

5. Add a **Fresnel** node (press *Shift + A* and navigate to **Input | Fresnel**) and connect it to the **Fac** input of both the **Mix Shader** nodes. Set the **IOR** value to 1.519, as shown in the following screenshot:

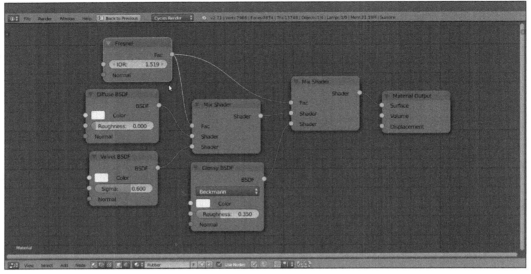

The basic shader network

6. Add a **Texture Coordinate** node (press *Shift + A* and navigate to **Input | Texture Coordinate**), a **Mapping** node (press *Shift + A* and navigate to **Vector | Mapping**), a **Voronoi Texture** node, and a **Noise Texture** node (press *Shift + A* and navigate to **Texture | Voronoi Texture**, do the same to add **Noise Texture** node).

7. Connect the **Object** output of the **Texture Coordinate** node to the **Vector** input of the **Mapping** node, and the latter's output to the **Vector** input sockets of the two texture nodes.

8. Set the **Voronoi Texture** node's **Coloring** to **Cells** and the **Scale** value to 350.000. Set the **Noise Texture** node's **Scale** value to 450.000 and **Detail** to 5.000.

9. Add two **Math** nodes (press *Shift + A* and navigate to **Converter | Math**). Set the **Operation** of the second node to **Multiply**. Connect the **Fac** output of the **Voronoi Texture** node to the first **Value** input socket of the **Add-Math** node. Connect the **Fac** output of the **Noise Texture** node to the second **Value** input socket of the **Add-Math** node.

10. Connect the **Add-Math** node output to the first **Value** input socket of the **Multiply-Math** node. Set second **Value** to 0.060 and connect the output to the **Displacement** input socket of the **Material Output** node, as shown in the following screenshot:

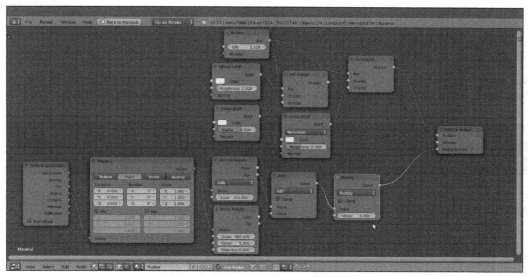

The slight bump effect added to the network

11. Add a **MixRGB** node (press *Shift + A* and navigate to **Color | MixRGB**) and move it close to the **Voronoi Texture** node. Set the **Blend Type** to **Multiply**. Connect the **Voronoi Texture** node's **Color** output to the **Color2** input socket of the **Multiply-MixRGB** node. Then connect the **Color** output of this node to the **Color** input sockets of the **Diffuse BSDF**, **Velvet BSDF**, and **Glossy BSDF** shaders.

12. Add an **RGB** node (press *Shift + A* and navigate to **Input | RGB**) and connect it to the **Color1** input socket of the **Multiply-MixRGB** node, as shown in this screenshot:

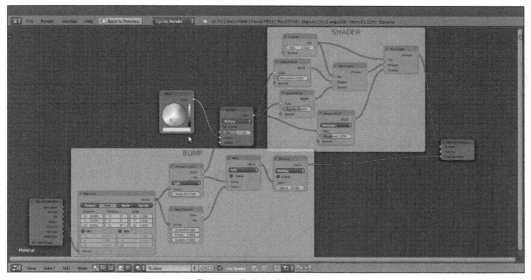

The overall view of the network

13. Save the file as `Rubber.blend`.

How it works...

We built the shader in steps 1 to 5. We added a slight bump effect in steps 6 to 10. In the last two steps, we just added the **RGB** node, a control used to set the color of the material.

Creating an antique bronze material with procedurals

In this recipe, we will create a bronze shader that looks similar to a ruined, corroded, and antique statue, as shown in the following screenshot:

The antique bronze material as it appears in the final rendering when assigned to the poor Suzanne mesh!

Getting ready...

Start Blender and load the `99310S_Suzanne_start.blend` file. Then perform the following steps:

1. With **Suzanne** selected, click on the **Object Mode** button in the **Camera** view toolbar. Choose **Vertex Paint**.

2. Click on the **Paint** item in the toolbar and select **Dirty Vertex Colors**, the first option at the top. Then press *T*, and in the **Option** panel at the bottom of the **Tool Shelf** panel, set **Blur Strength** to 0.01 and **Dirt Angle** to 90. Check the **Dirt Only** item, as shown in this screenshot:

The Dirty Vertex Colors setting and the effect on the Suzanne mesh

3. Go to the **Object data** window under the **Properties** panel. Double-click on the **Col** item in the **Vertex Colors** subpanel and rename it V_col.

4. Return in **Object Mode** and press *T* to close the **Tool Shelf** tabs.

5. Save the file as 99310S_Suzanne_vcol.blend. We will use this file for other recipes.

How to do it...

Now we are going to create the material by performing the following steps:

1. First, save the file as Bronze_antique.blend.

2. Click on **New** in the **Material** window under the **Properties** panel or in the **Node Editor** toolbar. Rename the material Bronze_antique.

3. In the **Material** window, switch the **Diffuse BSDF** shader with a **Mix Shader** node, and in the first **Shader** slot, select a **Diffuse BSDF** shader. In the second **Shader** slot, select a **Glossy BSDF** node. Set the **Diffuse BSDF** shader node's **Roughness** value to 1.000 and the **Glossy BSDF** node's **Roughness** value to 0.300.

4. Now add a **Layer Weight** node (press *Shift + A* and navigate to **Input | Layer Weight**), a **ColorRamp** node (press *Shift + A* and navigate to **Converter | ColorRamp**), and a **MixRGB** node (press *Shift + A* and navigate to **Color | MixRGB**). In the **Properties** panel of the **Node Editor** window (press *N* to make it appear), label the **ColorRamp** node as ColorRamp1. Set its **Interpolation** mode to B-Spline.

5. Connect the **Facing** output of the **Layer Weight** node to the **Fac** input of the **ColorRamp1** node, and its **Color** output to the **Fac** input socket of the **MixRGB** node.

6. Set the **Color1** value of the **MixRGB** node as **R** to 0.771, **G** to 1.000, and **B** to 0.848. Set the **Color2** values as **R** to 0.222, **G** to 0.013, and **B** to 0.000.

7. Add an **Invert** node (press *Shift + A* and navigate to **Color | Invert**). Paste it between the **ColorRamp1** and the **MixRGB** nodes'.

8. Press *Shift + D* to duplicate the **MixRGB** node, and set **Blend Type** to **Burn**. Set the **Fac** value to 0.090. Connect the **Mix-MixRGB** node's **Color** output to the **Color1** input socket of the **Burn-MixRGB** node.

9. Press *Shift + D* to duplicate the **MixRGB** node again. Set the **Blend Type** to **Overlay** and the **Fac** value to 0.200. Connect its **Color** output to both the **Color** input sockets of the **Diffuse BSDF** and **Glossy BSDF** shaders. Now connect the **Color** output of the **Burn-MixRGB** node to the **Color1** input socket of the **Overlay-MixRGB** node, as shown in the following screenshot:

The shader part of the material

10. Add an **Attribute** node (press *Shift + A* and navigate to **Input | Attribute**). Select and press *Shift + D* to duplicate the **ColorRamp** and the **Invert** nodes. Label them as ColorRamp2 and Invert2, respectively, and move them close to the **Attribute** node.

11. Write the name of the Vertex Color layer, V_col, in the **Name** slot of the **Attribute** node. Then connect its **Color** output to the **Fac** input of the **ColorRamp2** node. Move the white color stop to position 0.485.

12. Connect the **Color** output of the **ColorRamp** node to the Color input of the **Invert2** node, then connect the **Color** output of the **Invert2** node to the **Fac** input socket of the **Mix Shader** node, as shown in the following screenshot:

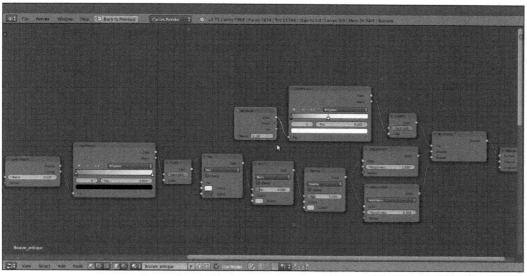

The shader modulated by the Dirty Vertex Colors output

13. Add a **Texture Coordinate** node (press *Shift + A* and navigate to **Input | Texture Coordinate**), a **Mapping** node (press *Shift + A* and navigate to **Vector | Mapping**), four **Noise Texture** nodes (press *Shift + A*, navigate to **Textures | Noise Texture**, and press *Shift + D* to duplicate them), and a **Musgrave Texture** node (press *Shift + A* and navigate to **Textures | Musgrave Texture**).

14. Label the four **Noise Texture** nodes as Noise Texture1, Noise Texture2, Noise Texture3, and Noise Texture4.

15. Connect the **Object** output of the **Texture Coordinate** node to the **Vector** input of the **Mapping** node. Connect the **Vector** output of this node to the **Vector** input sockets of all the five texture nodes.

16. For the **Noise Texture1** node, set **Scale** to 1.000 and **Detail** to 5.800. For the **Noise Texture2** node, set **Scale** to 30.000 and **Detail** to 0.300. For the **Noise Texture3** node, set **Scale** to 18.500 and **Detail** to 0.300. Finally, for the **Noise Texture4** node, set **Scale** to 65.000 and **Detail** to 0.300.

17. For the **Musgrave Texture** node, set **Type** to **Multifractal**, **Scale** to 15.000, **Detail** to 2.600, **Dimension** to 0.800, and **Lacunarity** to 0.400.

18. Add a **MixRGB** node (press *Shift + A* and navigate to **Color | MixRGB**), set **Blend Type** to **Difference**, and label it as Difference1. Press *Shift + D* to duplicate it. Label the duplicate as Difference2.

19. Connect the **Color** output of the **Noise Texture1** node to the **Color1** input socket of the **Difference1** node, and set the **Fac** output of this node to 1.000. Connect the **Color** output of the **Musgrave Texture** node to the **Color2** input socket of the **Difference1** node.

20. Connect the **Color** output of the **Noise Texture2** node to the **Color1** input socket of the **Difference2** node, and the **Color** output of the **Noise Texture3** node to the **Color2** input socket of the **Difference1** node.

21. Press *Shift + D* to duplicate the **Difference1** node, and set the **Blend Type** to **Divide**. Connect the **Color** output of the **Difference1** node to the **Color1** input socket of the **Divide** node, and the **Color** output of the **Difference2** node to the **Color2** input socket.

22. Add a **Math** node (press *Shift + A* and navigate to **Converter | Math**). Connect the output of the **Divide** node to the first **Value** input socket, and the **Color** output of the **Noise Texture4** node to the second **Value** socket.

23. Press *Shift + D* to duplicate the **Math** node, and set the **Operation** to **Multiply**. Connect the **Value** output of the **Add-Math** node to the first input socket of the **Multiply-Math** node. Set second **Value** to -0.050.

24. Add a **ColorRamp** node (press *Shift + A* and navigate to **Converter | ColorRamp**), paste it between the **Noise Texture1** node and the **Difference1** node, and label it as ColorRamp3. Set **Interpolation** to **Ease**. Move the black color stop to the 0.318 position and the white color stop to the 0.686 position.

25. Connect the output of the **Multiply-Math** node to the **Displacement** input socket of the **Material Output** node, as shown in the following screenshot:

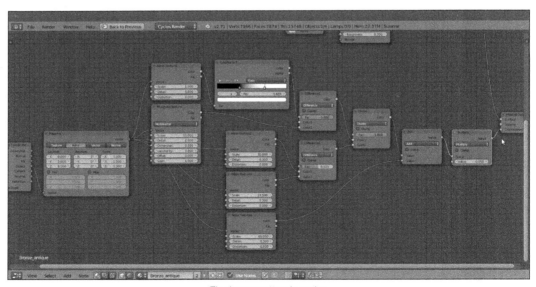

The bump pattern's nodes

26. Add two new **ColorRamp** nodes (press *Shift + A* and navigate to **Converter |
    ColorRamp**). Label them as ColorRamp4 and ColorRamp5.

27. Connect the **Fac** output of the **Noise Texture3** node to the **ColorRamp4** node.
    Set the color black stop to the 0.479 position and the white stop to the
    0.493 position.

28. Connect the **Color** output of the **ColorRamp4** node to the **ColorRamp5** node's
    input socket, and the **Color** output of this node to the **Color2** input sockets
    of the **Burn** and **Overlay** nodes.

29. Click on the **+** icon on the **ColorRamp5** node to add a new color stop in the
    middle of the color slider. Set the black stop color (index 0) for **R** to 0.216,
    G to 0.027, and **B** to 0.007; the middle stop color (index 1) for **R** to 0.539,
    G to 0.261, and **B** to 0.000; and the white color stop color (index 2) for **R** to
    0.515, **G** to 0.433, and **B** to 0.088, as shown in the following screenshot:

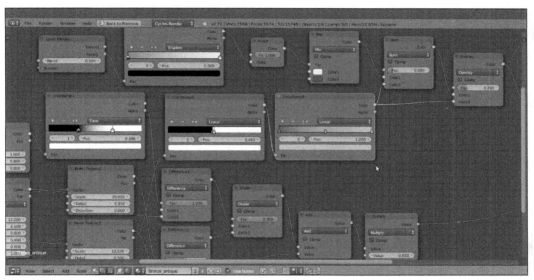

Adding color details to the ground of the bump textures

How it works...

We use the Vertex Color layer set in the *Getting ready* section as a stencil map to distribute
both the colored **Diffuse BSDF** and the **Glossy BSDF** shaders, driven by the **Facing** option
of the **Layer Weight** input node.

Most of the bump effect is created by the **Noise Texture** and **Musgrave Texture** nodes, which are mixed and clamped in several ways by the **ColorRamp** nodes. Here is a screenshot of the entire material network:

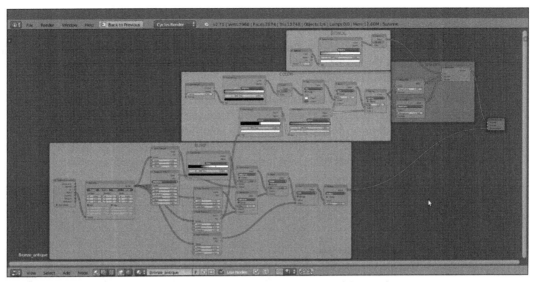

The overall view of the antique bronze material network

As usual, the last **Math** node, which is set to **Multiply**, establishes the strength of the bump.

Creating a multipurpose metal node group

All the metal materials you can see in the following screenshot (pewter, gold, silver, chromium, and aluminum) were obtained from a single shader node group linked and applied to each Suzanne with different interface settings.

To take a look at the scene, open the `9931OS_04_metals.blend` file. In this recipe, we will build the generic **Metal** node group shader. You can find it in the `9931OS_04_metal_group.blend` file, as shown in the following screenshot:

Some examples of different metal materials created by the same node group

Getting ready...

Start Blender and load the `9931OS_Suzanne_start.blend` file.

How to do it...

Now we are going to create the node group by performing the following steps:

1. Click on **New** in the **Material** window under the **Properties** panel or in the **Node Editor** toolbar.

2. In the **Material** window, switch the **Diffuse BSDF** shader with a **Mix Shader** node, and in the first **Shader** slot, select a **Glossy BSDF** shader. In the second **Shader** slot, select an **Anisotropic BSDF** node.

3. Press *Shift + D* to duplicate the **Mix Shader** node, and paste it just after the first **Mix Shader** node. Add a **Diffuse BSDF** shader (press *Shift + A* and navigate to **Shader | Diffuse BSDF**) and connect it to the second **Shader** input of the second **Mix Shader** node, as shown in the following screenshot:

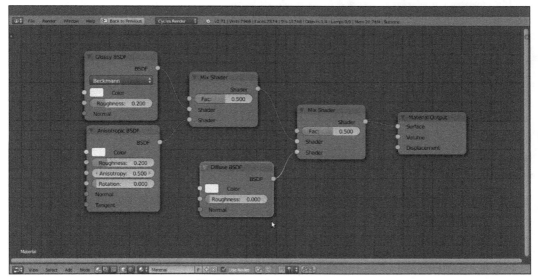

The basic metal shader network

4. Add a **Fresnel** node (press *Shift + A* and navigate to **Input | Fresnel**) and connect it to the **Fac** input of the second **Mix Shader** node.

5. Add a **Bright Contrast** node (press *Shift + A* and navigate to **Color | Bright Contrast**). Connect its **Color** output to the **Color** input sockets of the **Glossy BSDF** and **Anisotropic BSDF** shader nodes.

6. Add a **Bump** node (press *Shift + A* and navigate to **Vector | Bump**). Connect its **Normal** output to the **Normal** input sockets of the **Fresnel**, **Diffuse BSDF**, **Glossy BSDF**, and **Anisotropic BSDF** shader nodes.

7. Select all the nodes except the **Material Output** node, and press *Ctrl + G* to create a group, as shown in the following screenshot:

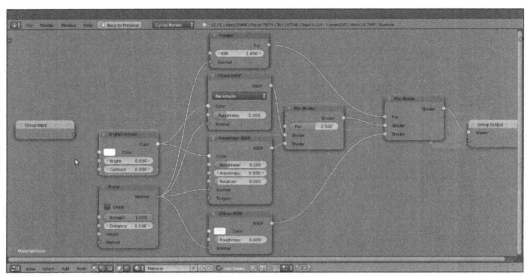

The nodes inside the node group

Now we must expose all the values necessary to tweak the node group for the different types of metal:

1. Click and drag the **IOR** input socket of the **Fresnel** node into the empty socket of the **Group Input** node.

2. Repeat step 1 with the **Color** input socket of the **Diffuse BSDF** shader node. Then drag the **Color** socket of the **Bright/Contrast** node and connect it to the same **Color** socket on the **Group Input** node, as shown in this screenshot:

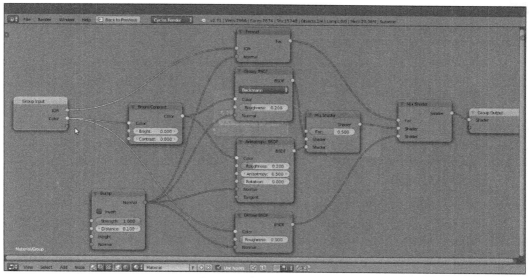

Creating the exposed sockets

3. Add a **Math** node (press *Shift + A* and navigate to **Converter | Math**). Set **Operation** to **Subtract** and first **Value** to 1.000. Drag its second **Value** input socket to the **Group Input** node, label the new socket as Coated, and then connect the **Value** output to the **Bright** input socket of the **Bright/Contrast** node. In the **Interface** subpanel under the **Properties** panel, set the **Max** value for the **Coated** socket to 1.200, as shown in the following screenshot:

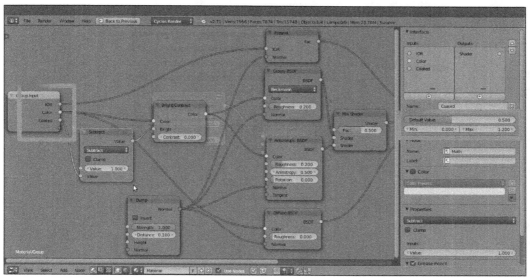

The setting of the Min and Max values through to the Interface subpanel

4. Drag the **Roughness** input socket of the **Glossy BSDF** shader. Then drag the **Roughness** socket of the **Anisotropic BSDF** shader and connect it to the same socket on the **Group Input** node.

5. Click and drag the **Fac** socket of the first **Mix Shader** node into a new, empty socket. Rename it `Aniso_Amount`. Click and drag the **Anisotropy** socket of the **Anisotropic BSDF** shader node into a new, empty socket. Repeat this step for the **Rotation** input socket.

6. Now click and drag the **Height** socket of the **Bump** node into a new, empty socket. Rename it `Bump`. Repeat this step for the **Distance** and the **Strength** sockets, and rename the sockets `Bump_Distance` and `Bump_Strength`, respectively.

7. Also repeat for the **Normal** socket of the **Bump** node.

8. Finally, click and drag the **Tangent** input socket of the **Anisotropic BSDF** shader.

9. Use the arrows in the top-right corner of the **Interface** subpanel to order the sockets in the **Group Input** node (the same order should be used for the

10. **Group Output** node), as shown in the following screenshot:

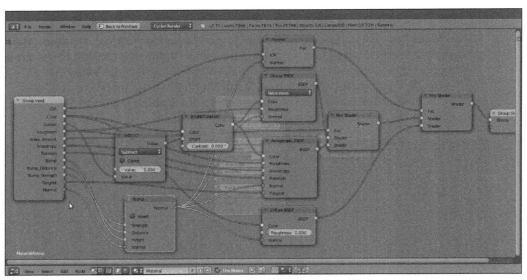

The final layout of the completed node group in Edit Mode

11. Exit **Edit Mode** by pressing *Tab*. Rename the group `Metal`. Although this is not "strictly necessary here, you can also click on the **F** icon on the interface to activate the *fake user* for the node group.

12. Save the file as `Metal_group.blend`.

How it works...

The effect of this node group is mainly based on the IOR value (the refractive index of a material is a number that describes how light propagates through that material or gets reflected on its surface). This value can be quite different for each kind of metal. In the node, the exposed **IOR** value drives the amount of blending of the Diffuse component with the Mirror component made by the **Glossy BSDF** and **Anisotropic BSDF** shader nodes combined, but that can also be mutually blended accordingly to the **Aniso_Amount** value.

The **Anisotropy** and **Rotation** values of the **Anisotropic BSDF** shader are exposed as well. and the same for the **Tangent** input if a particular mapping option must be used (for example, a layer of UV coordinates).

Textures must be connected to the **Bump** input socket on the **Bump** node. The **Bump_Strength** socket establishes the amount of bump influence. The **Bump_Distance** socket is a multiplier for the strength of influence. The **Bump** node output is piped to all the **Normal** input of the **Fresnel**, **Diffuse BSDF**, **Glossy BSDF**, and **Anisotropic BSDF** nodes to keep a consistent effect among all the components. Similarly, both the **Glossy BSDF** and **Anisotropic BSDF** nodes' **Roughness** values are driven by a single-interface input.

Finally, let's discuss the color of the metal. The color that arrives at the **Diffuse BSDF** shader by passing through the **Bright/Contrast** node gets modified by a **Coated** value larger than `0.000`. The result is a different input for the mirror component. The **Subtract-Math** node simply inverts the effect of the numeric input of the **Coated** socket.

Besides the links provided at the end of the previous chapter, for a list of IORs, you can take a look at these links:

- `http://refractiveindex.info/`
- `http://www.robinwood.com/Catalog/Technical/Gen3DTuts/Gen3DPages/RefractionIndexList.html`
- `http://forums.cgsociety.org/archive/index.php/t-513458.html`

 Note that for some materials (especially metals), different lists report different IOR values.

Creating a rusty metal material with procedurals

In this recipe, we will create a rusty shader that will be mixed with the metal shader by a stencil factor, as shown in the following screenshot:

The rusty metal material as it appears in the final rendering

Getting ready...

Start Blender and load the `99310S_Suzanne_vcol.blend` file. Then perform the following steps:

1. Go to the **World** window. Click on the dotted little box to the right of the **Color** slot under the **Surface** subpanel. In the pop-up menu, select the **Environment Texture** item.

2. Click on the **Open** button and browse to the `textures` folder to load the `Barce_Rooftop_C_3K.hdr` image.

3. Set the **Strength** value to `0.200`. Then go back to the **Material** window.

How to do it...

Now we are going to create the shader by performing the following steps:

1. Click on the **File** item in the upper main header. Select the **Link** item. If necessary, browse to the folder where you stored all the blend files. Select the `99310S_04_metal_group.blend` file. From there, click on the **NodeTree** entry and then select the **Metal** item. Click on the **Link/Append from Library** button to link the node group.

2. Click on **New** in the **Material** window under the **Properties** panel or in the **Node Editor** toolbar. Rename the material `Rusty_metal`.

3. In the **Material** window, switch the **Diffuse BSDF** shader with a **Mix Shader** node, and in the first **Shader** slot, select a **Diffuse BSDF** shader. In the second **Shader** slot, under **Group** in the pop-up menu, load the linked **Metal** node group, as shown in the following screenshot:

The Properties pop-up menu used to select different nodes

4. Add **Frame** (press *Shift + A* and navigate to **Layout | Frame**). Select the **Diffuse BSDF** shader, the **Metal** node group, the **Mix Shader** node, and then the **Frame**. Press *Ctrl + P* to parent them. In the **Properties** panel of the **Node Editor** window (press the *N* key to make it appear), label the **Frame** as SHADERS.

5. In the **Metal** group, set the **IOR** value to 1.370. Change the Color values for **R** to 0.229, **G** to 0.307, and **B** to 0.299. Set the **Roughness** value to 0.200, **Aniso_Amount** to 0.200, and **Anisotropy** to 0.600.

6. Add a **Texture Coordinate** node (press *Shift + A* and navigate to **Input | Texture Coordinate**) and two **Mapping** nodes (press *Shift + A* and navigate to **Vector | Mapping**). Connect the **Object** output of the **Texture Coordinate** node to the **Vector** input of both the **Mapping** nodes. Label them as `Mapping1` and `Mapping2`.

7. Now add a **Musgrave Texture** node (press *Shift + A* and navigate to **Texture |
    Musgrave Texture**) and label it as `Musgrave Texture1`. Add a **Noise Texture**
    node (press *Shift + A* and navigate to **Texture | Noise Texture**), label it as `Noise
    Texture1`, and add a **ColorRamp** node (press *Shift + A* and navigate to **Converter |
    ColorRamp**). Label this node as `ColorRamp1`.

8. Set the **Musgrave Texture** node's **Scale** value to `6.000` and **Detail** to `1.300`. Press
    Shift + D to duplicate it, and label the duplicate as `Musgrave Texture2`. Set the
    Noise Texture node's **Scale** value to `7.800`, **Detail** to `8.000`, and **Distortion** to `2.000`.

9. Connect the **Vector** output of the **Mapping1** node to the **Vector** input sockets of the
    Musgrave Texture1 and **Noise Texture1** nodes. Then connect the **Vector** output of
    the **Mapping2** node to the **Vector** input sockets of the **Musgrave Texture2** node. In
    the **Mapping2** node, set the **Location** value to `0.100` and **Scale** to `0.600` for the
    three axes. Then change the **Rotation** value of **X** to `7` and **Y** to `-5`.

10. Connect the **Fac** output of the **Noise Texture** node to the **Fac** input of the
    ColorRamp1 node. Set its **Interpolation** to **Ease**. Move the black color
    stop to the `0.321` position and the white color stop to the `0.600` position.

11. Add a **MixRGB** node (press *Shift + A* and navigate to **Color | MixRGB**). Set the
    Fac value to `1.000` and **Blend Type** to **Add**. Then connect the color output of the
    Musgrave Texture1 node to the **Color1** input socket and the **Color** output of the
    Musgrave Texture2 node to the **Color2** input socket of the **Add-MixRGB** node.

12. Press *Shift + D* to duplicate the **Add-MixRGB** node. Set **Blend Type** to **Divide** and
    the **Fac** value to `0.309`. Connect the **Fac** output of the **Noise Texture1** node to the
    Color1 input socket and the output of the **Add-MixRGB** node to the **Color2** input
    socket of the **Divide-MixRGB** node.

13. Connect the output of the **Divide-MixRGB** node to the **Fac** input socket of
    the **ColorRamp1** node. Press *Shift + D* to duplicate the **Divide-MixRGB** node,
    and change the **Blend Type** to **Multiply**. Set the **Fac** value to `1.000` and connect
    the output of the **ColorRamp1** node to the **Color1** input socket.

14. Add an **Attribute** node (press *Shift + A* and navigate to **Input | Attribute**)
    and connect its **Color** output to the **Color2** input socket of the **Multiply-MixRGB**
    node. In its **Name** slot, write the name of the Vertex Color layer, (`Col_vp`).

15. Add **Frame** (press *Shift + A* and navigate to **Layout | Frame**). Select the
    Musgrave Texture node, the **Noise Texture** node, the **ColorRamp1** node, the
    three **MixRGB** nodes, the **Attribute** node, and then the **Frame**. Press *Ctrl + P*
    to parent them. Label the frame as `STENCIL`.

16. Connect the output of the **Multiply-MixRGB** node under the **STENCIL** frame
    to the **Fac** input socket of the **Mix Shader** node under the **SHADERS** frame,
    as shown in the following screenshot:

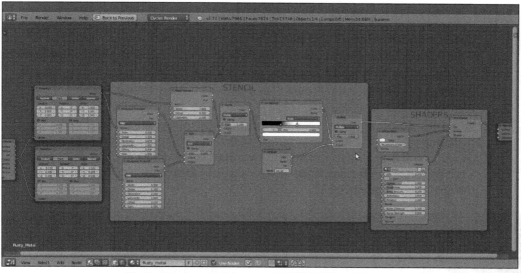

The first two frames of the material, SHADERS and STENCIL

17. Add two **Voronoi Texture** nodes (press *Shift + A*, navigate to **Texture | Voronoi Texture**, and label them as Voronoi Texture1 and Voronoi Texture2) and a **Wave Texture** node (press *Shift + A* and navigate to **Texture | Wave Texture**). In the **Voronoi Texture1** node, set the **Coloring** to **Cells** and the **Scale** value to 20.000. In the **Voronoi Texture2** node, set the **Scale** value to 19.000. Set the **Wave Texture** node's **Scale** value to 1.000.

18. Connect the **Vector** output of the **Mapping1** node to the **Vector** input sockets of these three new texture nodes.

19. Add a **MixRGB** node (press *Shift + A* and navigate to **Color | MixRGB**), set the **Blend Type** to **Difference**, and label it as Difference1. Set the **Fac** value to 1.000. Then connect the **Voronoi Texture1** node's **Color** output to the **Color1** input socket and the second **Voronoi Texture2** node's **Color** output to the **Color2** input socket.

20. Press *Shift + D* to duplicate the **Difference1** node, and label the duplicate as Difference2. Connect the **Color** output of the **Difference1** node to the **Color1** input socket of the **Difference2** node. Then connect the **Color** output of the **Wave Texture** node to the **Color2** input socket.

21. Add two **ColorRamp** nodes (press *Shift + A* and navigate to **Converter | ColorRamp**), label them as ColorRamp2 and ColorRamp3, and connect the output of the **Difference2** node to their **Fac** input socket. Set the **ColorRamp2** node's **Interpolation** to **Ease** and move the black color stop to the 0.486 position. Set the **ColorRamp3** node's **Interpolation** to **B-Spline** and move the black color stop to the 0.304 position.

22. Press *Shift + D* to duplicate the **Difference2** node, and label the duplicate as `Difference3`. Place it after the **ColorRamp2** node and **ColorRamp3** nodes. Connect the **ColorRamp2** node's **Color** output to the **Color1** input socket and the **ColorRamp3** node's **Color** output to the **Color2** input socket of the **Difference3** node.

23. Add **Frame** (press *Shift + A* and navigate to **Layout | Frame**). Select these lastly added nodes and then the **Frame**. Press *Ctrl + P* to parent them. Rename the frame `RUST_BUMP`.

24. Select the **SHADERS** frame and add a **Bump** node (press *Shift + A* and navigate to **Vector | Bump**). Connect the **Difference3** node's output to the **Height** input socket of the **Bump** node. Connect the **Normal** output of this node to the **Normal** input socket of the **Diffuse BSDF** node inside the **SHADERS** frame, as shown in the following screenshot:

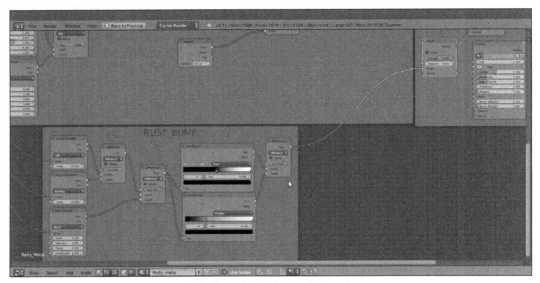

The frame for the bump of the rust

25. Select the **STENCIL** frame and add a **MixRGB** node (press *Shift + A* and navigate to **Color | MixRGB**) and a **Bright/Contrast** node (press *Shift + A* and navigate to **Color | Bright Contrast**). Paste the **MixRGB** node right after the **Multiply-MixRGB** node. Set **Blend Type** to **Difference** and then connect the output of the **Difference3** node inside the **RUST_BUMP** frame to the **Color2** input socket. Paste the **Bright/Contrast** node right after this last **Difference** node. Set the **Bright** value to 0.500 and the **Contrast** value to 1.000, as shown in the following screenshot:

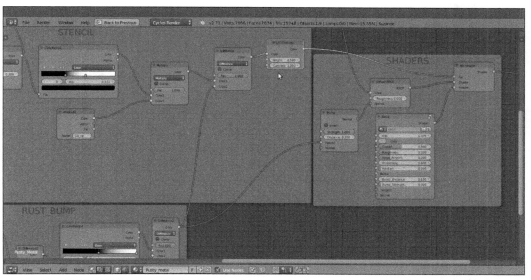

The RUST_BUMP output added to the stencil to separate the metal surface from the rusty surface

26. Add an **RGB Curves** node (press *Shift + A* and navigate to **Color | RGB Curves**), two **ColorRamp** nodes (press *Shift + A*, navigate to **Converter | ColorRamp**, and label them as ColorRamp4 and ColorRamp5), a **Noise Texture** node (press *Shift + A*, navigate to **Texture | Noise Texture**, and label it as Noise Texture2), and a **MixRGB** node (press *Shift + A* and navigate to **Color | MixRGB**).

27. In the **RGB Curves** node's interface, click on the diagonal line to add a control point. In the **X** and **Y** slots at the bottom, set the values to 0.50000 and 0.26000, respectively. Click again to add a new control point, and set **X** to 0.51000 and **Y** to 0.75000.

28. Connect the **Color** output of the **RGB Curves** node to the **Fac** input of the **ColorRamp5** node.

29. Go to the **ColorRamp4** node. Select the black color stop and change the color values of **R** to 0.991, **G** to 0.591, and **B** to 0.084. Select the white color stop and change the color values of **R** to 0.105, **G** to 0.013, and **B** to 0.010.

30. Click four times on the **+** icon on the **ColorRamp4** node interface to add four new color stops. Select **4** as the index number and move it to the 0.889 position. Change the color values of **R** to 0.930, **G** to 0.456, and **B** to 0.105. For index **3**, set **Pos** to 0.754, **R** to 0.624, **G** to 0.250, and **B** to 0.053. For index **2**, set **Pos** to 0.521, **R** to 0.418, **G** to 0.159, and **B** to 0.068. Finally, for index **1**, set **Pos** to 0.286, **R** to 0.246, **G** to 0.098, and **B** to 0.034.

31. With the mouse arrow inside the colorband on the **ColorRamp4** node, press *Ctrl + C* to copy it. Move the mouse arrow to the colorband of the **ColorRamp5** node. Press *Ctrl + V* to paste the colors and the stops. Set the **ColorRamp5** node's **Interpolation** to **Constant**.

32. Connect the **Color** output of both the **ColorRamp4** and **ColorRamp5** nodes to the **Color1** and **Color2** input sockets of the **MixRGB** node, respectively. Set the **MixRGB** node's **Blend Type** to **Dodge** and the **Fac** value to 1.000.

33. Press *Shift + D* to duplicate the **Dodge-MixRGB** node, set the **Blend Type** to **Multiply**, and label it as Multiply2. Lower the **Fac** value to 0.500. Connect the **Dodge-MixRGB** node's output to the **Color1** input of the **Multiply2** node and the **Color** output of the **Noise Texture2** node to the **Color2** input.

34. Set the **Noise Texture2** node's **Scale** value to 16.000, **Detail** to 2.500, and **Distortion** to 1.000. Connect the **Object** output of the **Mapping1** node to the **Vector** input of the **Noise Texture2** node.

35. Add a **Hue Saturation Value** node (press *Shift + A* and navigate to **Color | Hue Saturation Value**). Place it right after the **Multiply2** node. Connect the **Multiply2** output to the **Color** input socket of the **Hue Saturation Value** node. Then set the **Hue** value to 0.465 and the **Saturation** value to 1.050.

36. Press *Shift + D* to duplicate the **Multiply2** node, and place the duplicate close to the **Noise Texture2** node. Set the **Blend Type** to **Overlay** and the **Fac** value to 0.250. Connect the **Fac** output of the **Noise Texture2** node to the **Color1** input socket of the **Overlay-MixRGB** node, and change **Color2** to pure white. Connect the **Overlay-MixRGB** node's output to the **Value** input socket of the **Hue Saturation Value** node.

37. Add **Frame** (press *Shift + A* and navigate to **Layout | Frame**). Select these recently added nodes and then the **Frame**. Press *Ctrl + P* to parent them. Rename the frame RUST_COLOR.

38. Connect the output of the **Hue Saturation Value** node inside the **RUST_COLOR** frame to the **Color** input socket of the **Diffuse BSDF** shader node inside the **SHADERS** frame. Then connect the **Color** output of the **Divide** node inside the **STENCIL** frame to the **Color** input of the **RGB Curves** node inside the **RUST_COLOR** frame, as shown in the following screenshot:

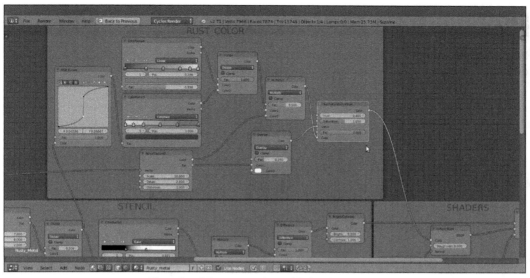

The color of the rusty surface added to the network

39. Save the file as `Metal_rusty.blend`.

How it works...

From step 2 to step 4, we built the basic shader arrangement. From step 6 to step 15, we made the **STENCIL** frame to separate the rust material from the polished metal.

From step 17 to step 23, we built the bump effect for the rust, and from step 26 to step 37, we added the rust color.

There's more...

We used the **Dirty Vertex Colors** layer named `Col_vp` again, this time to give a denser pattern to certain areas of Suzanne compared to other areas. Remember that a Vertex Colors layer can be modified and improved by manual vertex painting on the mesh in **Vertex Paint** mode. We can also use a gray-scale image map, painted in GIMP or in Blender itself and then UV-mapped on the mesh to obtain more precise and localized effects.

Creating a wood material with procedurals

In this recipe, we will create a generic wood material—a shader that can be easily adapted to different situations—as shown in the following screenshot:

The procedural wood material as it appears in the final rendering

Getting ready...

Start Blender and load the `99310S_Suzanne_start.blend` file. Then perform these steps:

1. Go to the **World** window and click on the button with a dot icon to the right of the **Color** slot under the **Surface** subpanel. In the pop-up menu, select the **Environment Texture** item.

2. Click on the **Open** button and browse to the `textures` folder to load the `Barce_Rooftop_C_3K.hdr` image.

3. Set the **Strength** value to `0.300`. Then go back to the **Material** window.

4. Go to the **Camera** view and add a **Cube** primitive to the scene. Place it leaning on the Plane, to the right of Suzanne. Move it up by 1 Blender unit.

5. With the mouse arrow in the **Camera** view, press *Shift + F* to enter **Walk Mode**. Adjust the Camera position to center the two objects in the frame.

6. Select the **Cube**, go to **Edit Mode**, and scale it to at least twice its current size. Exit **Edit Mode**, and using the 3D manipulator widget (which can be enabled in the 3D view toolbar), move the Cube upwards to stay nicely on the Plane. Press *N*, and in the **Properties** panel, select the **Lock Camera to View** item. Then adjust the Camera position framing the two objects.

7. Assign a **Bevel** modifier to the Cube, set **Width** to `0.0450`, and set the **Segments** value to `4`.

8. Press *T* to call the **Tool Shelf** panel. Set the Cube shading to **Smooth**.

9. Select **Suzanne** and rotate it a bit towards the left on the *z* axis.

10. Press *T* to close the **Tool Shelf** panel.

Setting up the scene

How to do it...

Now we are going to create the material by performing the following steps:

1. Click on **New** in the **Material** window under the **Properties** panel or in the **Node Editor** toolbar. Rename the material Wood.

2. Switch the **Diffuse BSDF** shader with a **Mix Shader** node, and in the first **Shader** slot, select a **Diffuse BSDF** shader. In the second **Shader** slot, select a **Glossy BSDF** node. Set the **Glossy BSDF** node's **Roughness** value to 0.300.

3. Add a **Fresnel** node (press *Shift + A* and navigate to **Input | Fresnel**) and a **MixRGB** node (press *Shift + A* and navigate to **Color | MixRGB**). Set the **IOR** value of the **Fresnel** node to 2.000. Connect its output to the **Color1** input socket of the **MixRGB** node. Set the **MixRGB** node's **Blend Type** to **Multiply**, label it as Multiply1, and set the **Fac** value to 0.900. Connect the **Multiply1** node's output to the **Fac** input socket of the **Mix Shader** node.

4. Add **Frame** (press *Shift + A* and navigate to **Layout | Frame**). Select the **Diffuse BSDF**, **Glossy BSDF**, **Mix Shader**, **Multiply1**, and **Fresnel** nodes. Then select the **Frame** and press *Ctrl + P* to parent them. Label the frame as SHADERS.

5. Add one **Texture Coordinate** node (press *Shift + A* and navigate to **Input | Texture Coordinate**) and three **Mapping** nodes (press *Shift + A*; navigate to **Vector | Mapping**; add the first node; duplicate the other nodes; and then label them as Mapping1, Mapping2, and Mapping3). Connect the **Object** output of the **Texture Coordinate** node to the **Vector** input of the three **Mapping** nodes.

6. Set the **Scale** value of the **Mapping1** node to 2.000 for all the three axes. Set the **Scale** value only for the *x* axis of the **Mapping2** node to 20.000. Then set the **Scale** value only for the *x* axis of the **Mapping3** node to 15.000.

7. Add a **Noise Texture** node (press *Shift + A* and navigate to **Texture | Noise Texture**) and two **Wave Texture** nodes (press *Shift + A* and navigate to **Texture | Wave Texture**). Label them as Noise Texture1, Wave Texture1, and Wave Texture2.

8. Set the **Scale** of the Noise Texture1 node to 6.000 and **Detail** to 0.000. Connect the **Mapping1** node's output to the **Noise Texture** node's **Vector** input socket.

9. Connect the **Mapping2** node's output to the **Vector** input of the **Wave Texture1** node. Set the **Wave Texture1** node's **Scale** value to 0.200 and **Distortion** to 20.000.

10. Connect the **Mapping3** node output to the **Wave Texture2** node's **Vector** input socket. Set **Wave Type** to **Rings**, the **Scale** value to 0.070, and the **Distortion** value to 44.000.

11. Add a **MixRGB** node (press *Shift + A* and navigate to **Color | MixRGB**). Set the **Blend Type** to **Multiply** (label it as Multiply1) and the **Fac** value to 1.000. Connect the **Noise Texture** node's **Color** output to the **Color1** input socket and the **Wave Texture1** node's **Color** output to the **Color2** input socket.

12. Connect the **Multiply1** node's output to the **Color** input of the **Diffuse BSDF** shader. Press *Shift + D* to duplicate it, change the **Blend Type** to **Add**, and paste it between the **Multiply1** node and the **Diffuse BSDF** shader node. Connect the **Wave Texture2** node's **Color** output to the **Color2** input socket of this **Add-MixRGB** node (labelled as Add1).

13. Add a **ColorRamp** node (press *Shift + A* and navigate to **Converter | ColorRamp**), label it as ColorRamp1, and paste it right after the **Noise Texture1** node. Set **Interpolation** to **B-Spline** and move the black color stop to the 0.345 position.

14. Press *Shift + D* to duplicate the **ColorRamp1** node, paste it right after the **Wave Texture1** node, and label it as `ColorRamp2`. Move the black color stop to the `0.505` position and the white color stop to the `0.975` position.

15. Press *Shift + D* to duplicate the **ColorRamp2**, label it as `ColorRamp3`, and paste it right after the **Wave Texture2** node. Move the black color stop to the `0.495` position and the white color stop to the left end of the slider, and set **Pos** as `0.000`, as shown in the following screenshot:

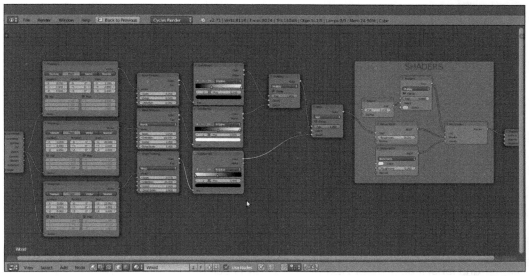

The textures required to draw the wood effect summed and connected to the shader part of the material

16. Now add a **MixRGB** node (press *Shift + A* and navigate to **Color | MixRGB**) and connect the **Add1** node's **Color** output to its **Fac** input socket. Set the **Color1** values of **R** to `1.000`, **G** to `0.500`, and **B** to `0.150`. Set the **Color2** values of **R** to `0.694`, **G** to `0.205`, and **B** to `0.027`.

17. Press *Shift + D* to duplicate the **MixRGB** node. Paste the duplicate right after the original node. Connect the **MixRGB** node's output to the **Color2** input socket, change **Blend Type** to **Multiply**, and label it as `Multiply3`.

18. Add a **Frame** (press *Shift* + *A* and navigate to **Layout | Frame**). Press *Shift* and select the three texture nodes, the three **ColorRamp** nodes, the four **MixRGB** nodes, and then the **Frame**. Press *Ctrl* + *P* to parent them. Label the frame as COLOR, as shown in the following screenshot:

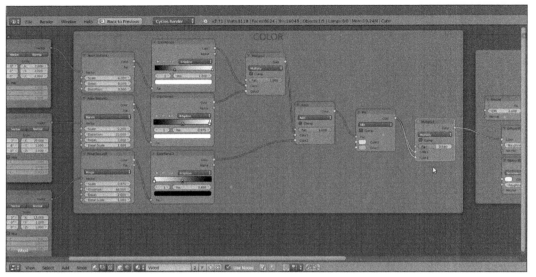

Adding more color to the veining

19. Add a new **Noise Texture** node (press *Shift* + *A*, navigate to **Texture | Noise Texture**, and label it as Noise Texture2), a **Math** node (press *Shift* + *A* and navigate to **Converter | Math**), and a **Bump** node (press *Shift* + *A* and navigate to **Vector | Bump**).

20. Connect the **Mapping3** node's output to the **Vector** input socket of the **Noise Texture2** node. Then connect the **Color** output of this node to the second **Value** input of the **Math** node. Set its **Operation** to **Add**, label it as Add2, and connect its output to the **Height** input socket of the **Bump** node.

21. Set the **Bump** node's **Strength** value to 0.200. Connect the **Normal** output of the **Bump** node to the **Normal** input of the **Fresnel**, **Diffuse BSDF**, and **Glossy BSDF** nodes inside the **SHADERS** frame. Set the **Noise Texture2** node's **Scale** value to 43.000 and **Detail** to 16.000.

22. Go to the **Add1** node inside the **COLOR** frame, click on the output node, and drag it so that it is connected to the first **Value** input socket of the **Add2-Math** node.

23. Add a **Frame** (press *Shift* + *A* and navigate to **Layout | Frame**). Select the three nodes and then the **Frame**. Press *Ctrl* + *P* to parent them. Label the frame as BUMP, as shown in the following screenshot:

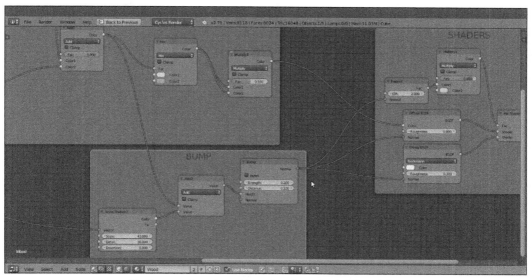

The bump pattern, based in part on the output of the veining

24. Save the file as `Wood.blend`.

How it works...

From steps 1 to 4, we built the basic shader using the usual **Diffuse BSDF** and **Glossy BSDF** nodes, mixed by a **Fresnel** value and multiplied by the values of a medium gray color.

From steps 5 to 18, we built the color of the wood's veins, adding three procedurals to be used as splitting factors for the two wood colors set in the penultimate **MixRGB** node. Using the last **Multiply3** node, we made the color more saturated (actually, we multiplied the values by themselves).

From steps 19 to 23, we built the bump using a noise grain summed to the veins' values by the **Add2-Math** node. We set a low value for the bump's **Strength** value, but you can use higher values (together with higher roughness values) to obtain less polished surfaces, which can give you different kinds of wood in the output.

5
Creating Complex Natural Materials in Cycles

In this chapter, we will cover the following recipes:

- ▶ Creating an ocean material using procedural textures
- ▶ Creating underwater environment materials
- ▶ Creating a snowy mountain landscape with procedurals
- ▶ Creating a realistic earth as seen from space

Introduction

In *Chapter 3*, *Creating Natural Materials in Cycles*, we saw some of the simpler natural materials that are possible to build in Cycles, keeping them out of any landscape context to make them more easily understandable.

Now it's time to deal with more elaborate natural materials. In this chapter, we will examine the way to mix different basic shaders to mimic the look of complex natural objects and their environments (very often, these two things fit together neatly).

Creating an ocean material using procedural textures

In this recipe, we will build an ocean surface material, using the **Ocean** modifier and procedural textures to create the foam, and establish a set of nodes to locate it on the higher parts of the waves:

The final look of the ocean material, with three simple and brightly colored objects to be reflected by the surface

Getting ready

Before we start with creating the shaders, let's prepare the ocean scene:

1. Start Blender and switch to the Cycles rendering engine. Select the default **Cube**, delete it (press *X*), and add a **Plane** (with the mouse arrow in the 3D window, press *Shift + A* and navigate to **Mesh | Plane**). In **Object Mode**, scale the plane smaller to 0.300. Don't apply a size.

2. Go to the **Object modifiers** window and assign an **Ocean** modifier. Set these values of **Geometry** to **Generate**, **Repeat X** and **Repeat Y** to 4, **Spatial Size** to 20, and **Resolution** to 12.

3. Press the *N* key, and in the **Transform** panel, set these values for the Plane in **Location** for **X** as -6.90000, **Y** as -7.00000, and **Z** as 0.00000.

4. Make sure that you are at frame 1, and with the mouse arrow in the modifier's **Time** slot, press *I* to add a key for the animation. Go to frame 25, change the **Time** value from 1.00 to 2.00, and press the *I* key again to set a second key.

5. In the **Choose Screen layout** button at the top, switch from **Default** to **Animation**. In the **Graph Editor** window, press *T*. In the **Set Keyframe Interpolation** pop-up menu, select the **Linear** item under **Interpolation**. Then press *Shift + E*, and in the **Set Keyframe Extrapolation** pop-up menu, select the **Linear Extrapolation** item to make the ocean animation constant and continuous.

6. Go back to the **Default** screen and rename the **Plane** as `Ocean_surface`. Have a look at the following screenshot:

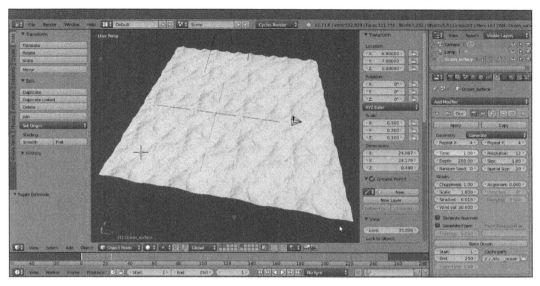

The Plane with the assigned Ocean modifier, and the settings to the right

7. Place the **Camera** to have a nice angle on the ocean, and then go to the **Camera** view (press *0* on the numeric keypad).

8. Add a **Cube** in the middle of the scene and, if you want, a UV Sphere in the foreground. Place these so that they float in the air. Their only purpose is to get reflected by the ocean surface during the shader setup.

9. Go to the **World** window and click on the **Use Nodes** button under the **Surface** subpanel. Then click on the little square with a dot on the right side of the color slot. From the pop-up menu, navigate to **Texture | Sky Texture**.

10. Select the **Lamp**, go to the **Object data** window, and click on the **Use Nodes** button under the **Nodes** subpanel. Set a yellowish color for the light (change the value of **R** to `1.000`, **G** to `0.989`, and **B** to `0.700`). Turn it to **Sun**, set the **Size** value to `0.010`, and set the **Strength** value to `2.500`.

11. Go to the **Render** window, and under the **Sampling** subpanel, set both the **Clamp Direct** and **Clamp Indirect** values to 1.00. Set the samples to 100 for **Render** and 50 for **Preview** (you can obviously change these values according to the power of your machine).

   Now, because the shader we are going to build is largely transparent, we need to simulate the water body as seen from above the surface.

12. Add a new **Plane** in **Edit Mode** and scale it 10 times bigger (20 Blender units per side; press *Tab*, then press *S*, enter digit 10, and press *Enter*). Exit **Edit Mode** and move the Plane so that it is centered on the ocean Plane location, then move it 1 unit down on the *z* axis. You can do it like this: go to the **Top** view and move the new Plane of 7 Blender units first along the *x* axis and then along the *y* axis. Then press *G*, press *Z*, enter digit -1, and press *Enter*.

13. In **Edit Mode**, press *W* to subdivide it by the **Specials** menu. Then press *T* to open the **Tool Shelf** panel on the left, and under **Number of Cuts** in the **Operator** panel at the bottom, and select **3**.

14. Go to the **Vertex Paint** mode and paint a very simple gray-scale gradient, changing from black at the vertices close to the Camera location to a plain white color on the opposite side.

   There are five rows of vertices on the Plane (ideally, all the rows are along the global *x* axis), so you can paint the first row with **RGB** value as 0.000, second with **RGB** value as 0.250, third with **RGB** value as 0.500, fourth with **RGB** value as 0.750, and fifth with **RGB** value as 1.000 to have a perfect gray-scale gradient.

15. In the **Object data** window, under the **Vertex Colors** tab, rename the Vertex Color layer as Col_emit. Have a look at the following screenshot:

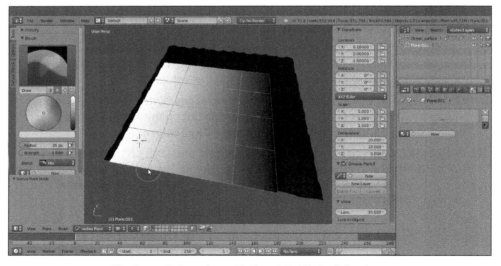

The Ocean_Bottom plane with the painted Vertex Colors layer

16. Exit **Vertex Paint** mode and rename this second Plane `Ocean_bottom`.

17. Split the 3D window into two horizontal rows. Change the upper row to a **Node Editor** window.

18. Assign very simple colored materials to the Cube and the UV Sphere; plain **Diffuse BSDF** shaders are enough.

How to do it...

We will be performing this in four parts:

  ▸   Creating the water surface and the bottom shaders

  ▸   Creating the foam shader

  ▸   Creating the stencil material for the location of foam

  ▸   Putting everything together

Let's start!

Creating the water surface and the bottom shaders

Let's now create the water surface and the bottom shaders:

1. Select the **Ocean_bottom** object. Click on the **New** button in the **Material** window under the **Properties** panel or in the **Node Editor** toolbar. Rename the new material as `Ocean_bottom` as well.

2. Switch the **Diffuse BSDF** shader with a **Mix Shader** node. In the first and the second slots, load two **Emission** shaders.

3. Add an **Attribute** node (press *Shift + A* and navigate to **Input | Attribute**) and connect the **Color** output to the **Fac** input of the **Mix Shader** node. In the **Name** slot of the **Attribute** node, write `Col_emit`, which is the name of the **Vertex Color** layer.

4. Change the color of the first **Emission** node for **R** to `0.178`, **G** to `0.150`, and **B** to `0.085`. Set the **Strength** value to `1.000`.

5. Change the color values of the second **Emission** node for **R** to `0.213`, **G** to `0.284`, and **B** to `0.380`. Set the **Strength** value to `2.000`.

The **Ocean_bottom** material is ready. Have look at the following screenshot:

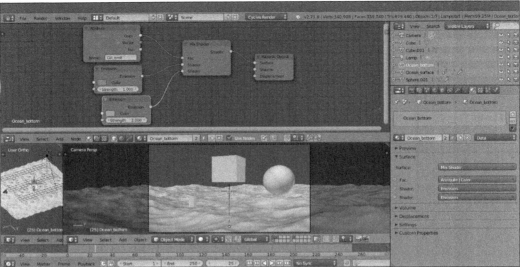

The Ocean_bottom material and the scene visible in the Solid viewport shading mode through the Camera view

6. Now select **Ocean_surface** and click on **New** in the **Material** window under the **Properties** panel or in the **Node Editor** toolbar. Rename this material as Ocean_surface.

7. Replace the **Diffuse BSDF** node with a **Mix Shader** node, and in the first **Shader** slot, assign a **Transparent BSDF** node. In the second slot, assign a **Glass BSDF** shader. In the **Properties** panel of the **Node Editor** window, label the **Mix Shader** node as Mix Shader01.

8. Change the **Transparent BSDF** nodes **Color** values for **R** to 0.055, **G** to 0.124, and **B** to 0.042 (you can also do this by connecting an **RGB** node to the **Color** input socket, as shown in the example blend file provided). Set the **Glass BSDF** shader node's **Roughness** value to 0.900 and the **IOR** value to 1.333.

9. Add a **Layer Weight** node (press *Shift + A* and navigate to **Input | Layer Weight**), connect the **Facing** output to the **Fac** input of the **Mix Shader01** node, and set the **Blend** value to 0.050.

10. Select the **Mix Shader01** node and press *Shift + D* to duplicate it. Add a **Glossy BSDF** shader (press *Shift + A* and navigate to **Shader | Glossy BSDF**) and connect it to the second **Shader** input socket of the **Mix Shader02** node. Connect the output of the **Mix Shader01** node to the first **Shader** input socket of the **Mix Shader02** node, and the output of this node to the **Surface** input of the **Material Output** node.

11. Add a **Fresnel** node (press *Shift + A* and navigate to **Input | Fresnel**). Connect this to the **Fac** input of the **Mix Shader02** node. Set the **IOR** value to 1.333 as shown in the following screenshot:

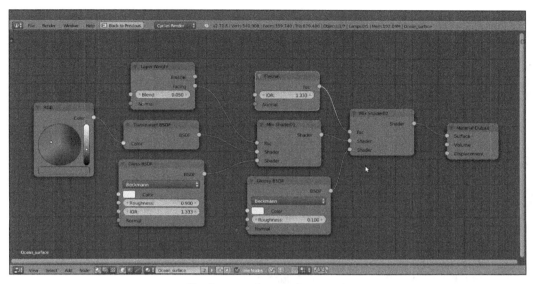

The Ocean_surface shader network

12. Now select all the nodes except the **Material Output** node, and press *Ctrl + G* to make a group. Select and delete the **Group Input** node to the left (press the *X* key), and drag the **Mix Shader02** node's output to the empty socket of the **Group Output** node.

13. Press *Tab* to close the node group, and rename it as Ocean_water.

Creating the foam shader

Let's now create the shader for the foam:

1. Add a **Noise Texture** node (press *Shift + A* and navigate to **Texture | Noise Texture**) and a **Voronoi Texture** node (press *Shift + A* and navigate to **Texture | Voronoi Texture**) nodes. Select them and press *Shift + D* to duplicate them. Label them as Noise Texture01, Noise Texture02, Voronoi Texture01, and Voronoi Texture02.

2. Add four **ColorRamp** nodes (press *Shift + A* and navigate to **Converter | ColorRamp**, then press *Shift + D* to duplicate them). Label them as ColorRamp01, ColorRamp02, ColorRamp03, and ColorRamp04. Place the four texture nodes in a vertical column and arrange the **ColorRamp** nodes to their side. Connect the **Color** output of each texture node to the **Fac** input of the respective **ColorRamp** node.

3. Set **Interpolation** of the **ColorRamp01** node to **B-Spline**, **ColorRamp02** and **ColorRamp03** to **Ease**, and **ColorRamp04** to **B-Spline** again.

4. Go to the **ColorRamp01** node. Move the black color stop to position 0.345 and the white color stop to position 0.633.

5. Go to the **ColorRamp02** and **ColorRamp03** nodes. Move the black color stop to position 0.159 and the white color stop to position 0.938 for both nodes. Leave the **ColorRamp04** color stops as they are.

6. Set the **Scale** value of the **Noise Texture01** node to 500.000, the **Noise Texture02** node to 100.000, the **Voronoi Texture01** node to 100.000, and the **Voronoi Texture02** node to 90.000.

7. Add a **Texture Coordinate** node (press *Shift + A* and navigate to **Input | Texture Coordinate**) and a **Mapping** node (press *Shift + A* and navigate to **Vector | Mapping**). Connect the **UV** output of the **Texture Coordinate** node to the **Vector** input socket of the **Mapping** node. Then connect the **Vector** output of this node to the **Vector** input sockets of the four texture nodes.

8. Add a **MixRGB** node (press *Shift + A* and navigate to **Color | MixRGB**), set the **Blend Type** to **Subtract**, and label it as Subtract01. Set the **Fac** value to 1.000. Connect the **Color** outputs of the **ColorRamp01** and **ColorRamp02** nodes to the **Color1** and **Color2** input sockets of the **Subtract01** node.

9. Select the **Subtract01** node, press *Shift + D* to duplicate it, and set the **Blend Type** to **Multiply**. Label it as Multiply and connect the **Color** outputs of the **ColorRamp03** and **ColorRamp04** nodes to its **Color1** and **Color2** input sockets.

10. Duplicate a **MixRGB** node again, set the **Blend Type** to **Difference**, and name it Difference as well. Then connect the **Color** outputs of the **ColorRamp03** and **ColorRamp04** nodes to the **Color1** and **Color2** input sockets of this **Difference** node.

11. Duplicate one of the **MixRGB** nodes one more time. Set the **Blend Type** to **Lighten** and label it as Lighten. Lower the **Fac** value to 0.500. Connect the **Color** output of the **Multiply** node to the **Color1** input of the **Lighten** node, and the **Color** output of the **Difference** node to the **Color2** input socket.

12. Add an **Invert** node (press *Shift + A* and navigate to **Color | Invert**) and move it on the link connecting the **Difference** and the **Lighten** nodes to be automatically pasted in between.

13. Add a new **ColorRamp** node, label it as ColorRamp05, and connect the **Lighten** node output to its **Fac** input. Then move the black color stop to position 0.298 and the white color stop to position 0.486.

14. Add a new **MixRGB** node (press *Shift + A* and navigate to **Color | MixRGB**), set the **Blend Type** to **Subtract**, and label it as Subtract02. Set the **Fac** value to 1.000. Connect the **ColorRamp05** node's **Color** output to the **Color1** input of **Subtract02** node and the output of the **Subtract01** node to the **Color2** input socket.

15. Add an **RGB to BW** node (press *Shift + A* and navigate to **Converter | RGB to BW**), a **Bump** node (press *Shift + A* and navigate to **Vector | Bump**), and a **Diffuse BSDF** shader (press *Shift + A* and navigate to **Shader | Diffuse BSDF**).

16. Connect the **Subtract02** node's output to the **RGB to BW** node, the output of this node to the **Height** input socket of the **Bump** node, and the **Normal** output of the **Bump** node to the **Normal** input of the **Diffuse BSDF** shader. Set the **Bump** node's **Strength** value to 1.000 as shown in the following screenshot:

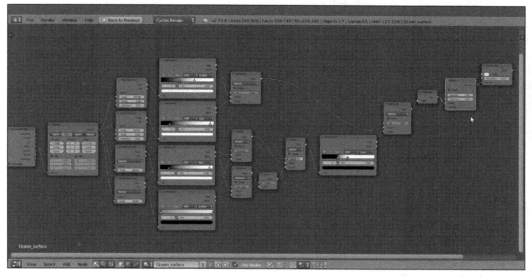

The network for the foam shader

17. Select all of these nodes and press *Ctrl + G*. Delete the **Group Input** node on the left.

18. Drag the **BSDF** output of the **Diffuse BSDF** shader onto the right side, to the empty socket of the **Group Output** node. Repeat this for the **Color** output of the **Subtract02** node.

19. Press *Tab* to close the group. Rename it as Foam.

Creating the stencil material for the foam location

What we need now is a way to limit both the amount and the presence of the foam in the upper parts of the waves:

1. Add **Gradient** (press *Shift + A* and navigate to **Texture | Gradient Texture**) and **Voronoi Texture** (press *Shift + A* and navigate to **Texture | Voronoi Texture**) texture nodes, select them, and press *Shift + D* to duplicate them. Label them as Gradient Texture01, Gradient Texture02, Voronoi Texture03, and Voronoi Texture04.

2. Set the **Gradient Types** to **Easing** for both the nodes, the **Scale** value of the **Voronoi Texture03** node to 250.000, and the Scale value of the **Voronoi Texture04** node to 50.000.

3. Add three **Mapping** nodes (press *Shift + A* and navigate to **Vector | Mapping**, then press *Shift + D* to duplicate them). Label them as `Mapping01`, `Mapping02`, and `Mapping03`.

4. Add a **Texture Coordinate** node (press *Shift + A* and navigate to **Input | Texture Coordinate**) and a **Geometry** node (press *Shift + A* and navigate to **Input | Geometry**).

5. Connect the **Normal** output of the **Geometry** node to the **Vector** input of the **Mapping01** node. Next, connect the **Position** output of the **Geometry** node to the **Vector** input of the **Mapping02** node. Then connect the **UV** output of the **Texture Coordinate** node to the **Vector** input of the **Mapping03** node.

6. In the **Mapping02** node, change the **Location** value of **X** to `0.500` and the **Rotation** value of **Y** to `90°`.

7. Connect the output of the **Mapping01** to the input of the **Gradient Texture01**, the output of the **Mapping02** to the input of the **Gradient Texture02**, and the output of the **Mapping03** to both the **Vector** inputs of the last two **Voronoi Texture** nodes.

8. Add a **ColorRamp** node (press *Shift + A* and navigate to **Converter | ColorRamp**), label it as `ColorRamp06`, and connect the **Color** output of the **Voronoi Texture04** node to its **Fac** input. Set **Interpolation** to **B-Spline**. On the **ColorRamp06** node, click on the little **+** icon to add a new color stop (medium gray) in the middle of the slider. Change its color to total black and move it to position `0.068`.

9. Add a **Math** node (press *Shift + A* and navigate to **Converter | Math**), set the **Operation** to **Multiply**, and label it as `Multiply02`. Connect the **Color** output of the **Gradient Texture02** node to the first **Value** input socket of the **Multiply02** node.

10. Add a **MixRGB** node (press *Shift + A* and navigate to **Color | MixRGB**), set the **Blend Type** to **Difference**, and label it as `Difference02`. Set the **Fac** value to `1.000`. Connect the **Color** output of the **Gradient Texture01** to the **Color1** input socket, and the **Value** output of the **Multiply02** node to the **Color2** input socket of the **Difference02** node.

11. Press *Shift + D* to duplicate the **MixRGB** node, set the **Blend Type** to **Subtract**, and label it as `Subtract03`. Connect the **ColorRamp06** node's **Color** output to both the **Color2** and to the **Fac** input sockets. Then connect the **Color** output of the **Voronoi Texture03** node to the **Color1** input socket.

12. Add a new **ColorRamp** node (press *Shift + A* and navigate to **Converter | ColorRamp**), label it as `ColorRamp07`, and connect the output of the **Difference02** node to the **Fac** input. Then move the white color stop to position `0.344`.

13. Duplicate one of the **MixRGB** nodes, set the **Blend Type** to **Burn**, and label it as `Burn` as well. Connect the **Color** output of the **ColorRamp07** node to the Color1 input of the **Burn** node. Then connect the output of the **Subtract03** node to the **Color2** input socket of the **Burn** node as shown in the following screenshot:

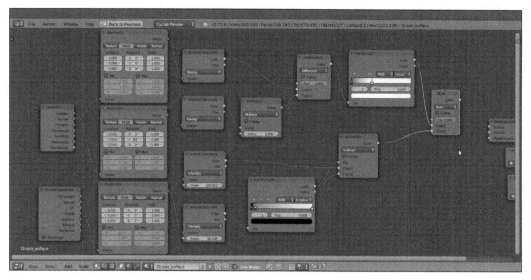

The stencil network

14. Now select all of these nodes, press *Ctrl + G*, and drag the **Burn** node output on the right to connect it to the empty socket of the **Group Output** node. Press *Tab* to close the group. Rename it as `Foam_location`.

Putting everything together

What is left now is just to connect these three groups to build the final shader:

1. Add a **Mix Shader** node (press *Shift + A* and navigate to **Shader | Mix Shader**). Label it as `Mix Shader03` and connect its output to the **Surface** input socket of the **Material Output** node.

2. Connect the **Shader** output of the **Ocean_water** group to the first **Shader** input of the **Mix Shader03**. Then connect the **BSDF** output of the **Foam** group to the second **Shader** input.

3. Add two **MixRGB** nodes (press *Shift + A* and navigate to **Color | MixRGB**). Set the **Blend Type** of the first node to **Multiply** and the **Fac** value to 0.550. Then label it as `Multiply03`. Set the second node **Blend Type** to **Burn** and the **Fac** to 0.200. Then label it as `Burn02`.

4. Connect the **Color** output of the **Foam_location** group to the **Color1** input of the **Multiply03** node, and the **Color** output of the **Foam** group to the two **Color2** inputs of both the **Multiply03** and **Burn02** nodes.

5. Connect the **Multiply03** node's output to the **Color1** input of the **Burn02** node. Connect the output of the **Burn02** node to the **Fac** input of the **Mix Shader03** node as shown in the following screenshot:

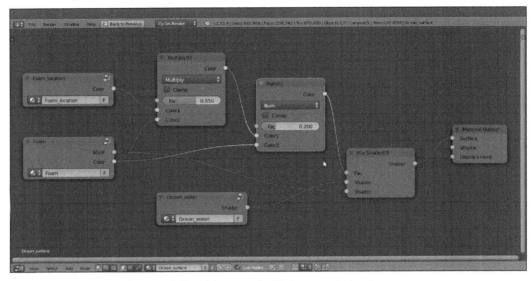

The overall view of the network with the connected node groups

How it works...

This material, which looks quite complex, is actually easily understandable by splitting the entire process in three stages corresponding to the three group nodes:

▶ In the first stage, we created the basic ocean water shader by mixing a **Glass** node with a **Transparent BSDF** shader on the ground of the **Facing** value of the **Layer Weight** node and then also with a **Glossy BSDF** shader driven by the index of refraction of water (the **IOR** value of the **Fresnel** node, which is 1.333 for water at 20°C). In other words, the ocean surface nicely reflects the environment but for the faces looking towards the Camera (the **Facing** factor), it is transparent. Very important is the **Bottom_ocean** Plane, which is used to mimic the volume of the water and the underwater perspective and also emitting light to enhance the effect of the sun bouncing from the ocean surface to any floating object. The result of this first stage is shown in the following rendering:

Only the water shader rendered

▶ In the second stage, we created the material for the foam—a simple, white **Diffuse BSDF** shader. In fact, the peculiarity of the foam shader is mostly in the frothy bumpiness (and in the lacy-shaped outline cut by the procedural textures of the **Foam_location** shader). Have a look at the rendered foam shader:

Only the foam shader rendered

▶ In the third stage, this group of nodes establishes the location of the foam that is mainly formed in the higher parts of waves in the real world, behaving as a gray-scale stencil map. Basically, a gradient texture is mapped on the **Position** (vertices) and multiplied for the **Normal** coordinates of the ocean mesh that, being created by the **Ocean** modifier, is constantly changing. So, only as the waves rise do they show foam at the top. This effect has been lessened and made a bit random to show some foam scattered around the rest of the surface as well. This works not only for stills but also in animation.

In the following screenshot, you can see the rendering of the resulting black-and-white mask that we used as a stencil for foam location (the image obtained by simply connecting the mask output to an **Emission** shader node to get a quick rendering and preview):

The only stencil material rendered

See also

The Blender **Ocean** modifier is able to create its own foam effect, generated as Vertex Colors and baked to a series of images (frames) saved in a directory. These images are then automatically mapped on the surface. They can be used as stencil masks instead of the **Foam_location** group node.

To know more about the **Ocean** modifier, you can take a look at the wiki documentation at `http://wiki.blender.org/index.php/Doc:2.6/Manual/Modifiers/ Simulate/Ocean`.

Creating underwater environment materials

In this recipe, we will create an underwater environment as shown in the following screenshot, looking especially at a fake caustic effect projected by the water's wavy surface and from an atmospheric perspective, obtained by a per material dedicated node group:

The underwater environment in the final rendering

 Note that this atmospheric perspective effect is actually a fake and it is not obtained by a volume material. Volumetric shaders will be explained in *Chapter 9*, *Special Materials*, of this Cookbook.

Getting ready

Let's start by preparing the scene:

1. Start Blender and switch to the Cycles rendering engine. Select the **Cube** and go to **Edit Mode**. Scale it 21 times bigger (Press *A* to select all the vertices, then press *S*, enter digit *21*, and finally press *Enter*). Then scale it on the *z* axis of 0.230 (press *S*, then press *Z*, enter .23, and press *Enter*).

2. Go to the **Top** view (press *7* on the numeric keypad) and press *Ctrl + R* to add three edge loops along the global *x* axis. Then press *Ctrl + R* again to add three edge loops along the *y* global axis. The Cube is now subdivided into 16 equal parts.

3. Select all the faces, go to the **Shading** tab under the **Tool Shelf** panel to the left, and click on the **Flip Direction** button to invert the normals (which must look inwards).

4. Exit **Edit Mode**, switch to the **Objects modifiers** window, and assign a **Subdivision Surface** modifier. Set the type of subdivision to **Simple** and the **Subdivisions** to 4 both for the **View** and the **Render** levels.

5. Assign a second **Subdivision Surface** modifier. Again, set the type of subdivision to **Simple** but the **Subdivisions** to 2 for both the **View** and the **Render** levels.

6. Now assign an **Ocean** modifier. Set the values of **Geometry** to **Displace**, **Spatial Size** to 20, and **Resolution** to 12.

7. Go to the **Tool Shelf** again, and in the **Edit** subpanel under the **Tools** tab, click on the **Smooth** button below the **Shading** item.

8. Go to the **Object data** window and click on the **+** icon under the **UV Maps** subpanel to add a set of UV coordinates. There is no need to unwrap the Cube. Check the **Double Sided** item in the **Normals** subpanel at the top.

9. Make sure you are at frame **1**, go to the **Object modifiers** window, and move the mouse over the **Ocean** modifier **Time** slot. Press the *I* key to add a key for the animation. Go to frame **25**, change the **Time** value from 1.00 to 2.00, and press *I* again to set a second key.

10. In the **Choose Screen** layout button at the top, switch from **Default** to **Animation**. In the **Graph Editor** window, press *T*, and in the **Set Keyframe Interpolation** pop-up menu, select the **Linear** item under **Interpolation**. Then press *Shift + E*, and in the **Set Keyframe Extrapolation** pop-up menu, select the **Linear Extrapolation** item to make the ocean animation constant and continuous.

11. Rename the Cube as Ocean_surface as shown in the following screenshot:

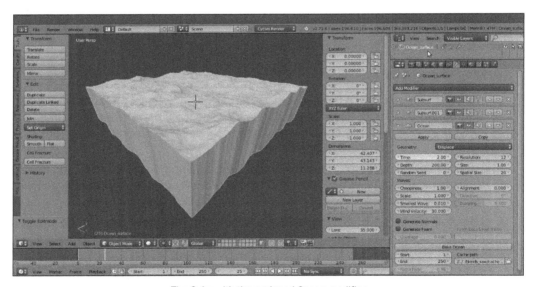

The Cube with the assigned Ocean modifier

12. Move the Camera to a place below the ocean surface Set the **Location** value of **X** to 16.80000, **Y** to -2.64000, and **Z** to 0.95000. Then set the **Rotation** value of **X** to 92°, **Y** to 0°, and **Z** to 90°. Next, go to the **Camera** view (press *0* on the numeric keypad).

13. Add a **Cube**, a **UV Sphere,** and whatever other objects you want to add floating under the ocean surface. Assign them very simple and colored **Diffuse BSDF** materials. Add a big **Cylinder** to the background, close to the far side of the **Ocean_surface** object. Immerse half of it in water (and half will be in the air). Assign a simple **Diffuse BSDF** material to this item too. Smooth the Cylinder and the UV Sphere. If you wish, assign a **Subdivision Surface** modifier to the UV Sphere.

14. Now add a **Plane**. Place it at **Location** values of **X** as -3.22600, **Y** as -2.79600, and **Z** as -2.24463. Enter **Edit Mode** and scale it 30 times bigger (press A to select all of the geometry, then press S, enter *30* and press *Enter*). Using the **Specials** menu (press W) divide the Plane five or six times. Activate the **PET** (**Proportional Editing Tool**), randomly select vertices, and move them up to model the dunes of the ocean bed. Exit **Edit Mode**, smooth it by the **Tools** tab under the **Tool Shelf** panel, and assign a **Subdivision Surface** modifier at level 2. Disable the modifier visibility in the viewport by clicking on the eye icon. Rename it as Ocean_bed.

15. Add a **Cube**. In **Edit Mode**, divide it a couple of times (press W, and **Subdivide Smooth**), in **Proportional Editing** mode and by selecting vertices quickly model a big round rock. Replicate it three or four times by rotating and scaling the copies. Place them in a scattered manner on the **Ocean_bed**. Smooth it and assign a **Subdivision Surface** modifier. Disable the modifier visibility in the viewport.

16. Go to the **World** window and click on **Use Nodes**. Then click on the little square with a dot on the right side of the color slot. From the menu, select **Sky Texture**. Click on the **Sky Type** button above the little window and switch to the **Preetham** type.

17. Select the **Lamp**. In the **Object data** window, click on the **Use Nodes** button and set a yellowish color for the light (set the values for **R** to 1.000, **G** to 0.989, and **B** to 0.700). Change it to a **Sun**. Set the **Size** value to 0.010 and the **Strength** value to 2.500. Then set the **Rotation** values of **X** to 22°, **Y** to -7°, and **Z** to 144°. You might know that for a Sun Lamp, the location doesn't matter.

18. Go to the **Render** window. Under the **Sampling** subpanel, set the **Clamp Direct** and the **Clamp Indirect** values to 1.00. Then set the **Samples** to 25 for both **Preview** and **Render**. Under the **Light Paths** subpanel, disable both the **Reflective Caustics** and **Refractive Caustics** items.

As an alternative, just open the 9931OS_05_underwater_start.blend file and use the prepared scene.

How to do it...

First, let's perform the easy steps by appending the materials that are already made so that we can reuse them:

1. From the 9931OS_03_Rock_procedurals.blend file, append the Rock_proc01 material. Select the **Rocks** object and assign the newly appended material.

2. From the 9931OS_03_Ground.blend file, append the Ground_01 material. Select the **Ocean_bed** object and assign the material.

Now let's move on to the more complex steps:

1. From the `99310S_05_Ocean.blend` file, append the `Ocean_surface` object, material. Select the **Ocean_surface** object and assign the material. Rename it as `Ocean_surface_under`.

2. With the **Ocean_surface** object still selected, enter **Edit Mode**. Go to the **Face** selection mode and select only the upper faces. Then press *Ctrl + I* to invert the selection. In the **Material** window under the **Properties** panel, click on the **+** icon on the right (Add a new material slot), rename the new material as `Null`, and click on the **Assign** button. Now the **Ocean_surface** object has two different materials: the transparent water surface and the opaque sides and bottom (a simple white **Diffuse BSDF** material). Exit **Edit Mode**.

3. In the **Material** window, click on the **Ocean_surface_under** material to select it. In the **Node Editor** window, delete the **Foam** and the **Foam_location** node groups. Also delete the two **MixRGB** nodes. Just leave the **Ocean_water** node group connected to the second **Shader** input socket of the **Mix Shader** node, which in turn is connected to the **Material Output** node.

4. Add a **Texture Coordinate** node (press *Shift + A* and navigate to **Input | Texture Coordinate**), a **Mapping** node (press *Shift + A* and navigate **Vector | Mapping**), and an **Image Texture** node (press *Shift + A* and navigate to **Texture | Image Texture**). Connect the **UV** output of the **Texture Coordinate** node to the **Vector** input of the **Mapping** node, and the **Vector** output of this node to the **Vector** input socket of the **Image Texture** node.

5. In the **Image Texture** node, load the `caustics_tileable_low.png` texture and set the **Color Space** to **Non-Color Data**.

6. Add a **Diffuse BSDF**, a **Transparent BSDF**, and a **Mix Shader** node (press *Shift + A* and navigate to **Shader | Diffuse BSDF**, and repeat the same for the other two nodes). Label them as `Diffuse_Caustics`, `Transparent_Caustics`, and `Mix Shader_Caustics`.

7. Connect the **Diffuse_Caustics** node's output to the first **Shader** input socket of the **Mix Shader_Caustics** node, and the **Transparent_Caustics** output to the second **Shader** input socket. Then connect the **Color** output of the **Image Texture** node to the **Color** input socket of the **Transparent_Caustics** shader node, and the **Alpha** output of the **Image Texture** node to the **Fac** input of the **Mix Shader_Caustics** node.

8. Now connect the output of the **Mix Shader_Caustics** node to the first (and still empty) **Shader** input socket of the first **Mix Shader** node.

9. Add a **Light Path** node (press *Shift + A* and navigate to **Input | Light Path**). Connect the **Is Camera Ray** output to the **Fac** input of the first **Mix Shader** node. Add **Frame** (press *Shift + A* and navigate to **Layout | Frame**) and parent these last nodes to it. Then label it as `FAKE_CAUSTICS` as shown in the following screenshot:

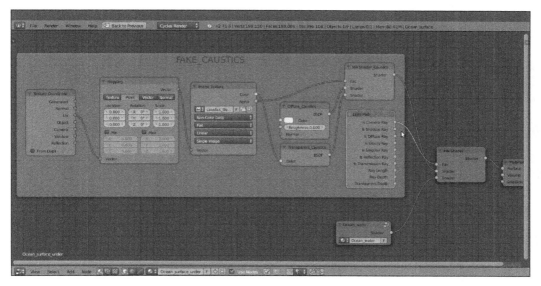

The FAKE_CAUSTICS frame mixed with the Ocean_Water node group on the ground of the Is Camera Ray output of the Light Path node

The following screenshot shows where we are so far:

The point where we are so far

What is missing now is the underwater atmospheric perspective effect. There are several ways to obtain this, for example, by compositing a Mist pass rendered in Blender Internal or by using a volumetric shader. However, we are going to do this with a simple node group added to every one of the different materials:

10. Add a **Camera Data** node (press *Shift + A* and navigate to **Input | Camera Data**), a **Math** node (press *Shift + A* and navigate to **Converter | Math**), an **Emission** node (press *Shift + A* and navigate to **Shader | Emission**), and a **Mix Shader** node (press *Shift + A* and navigate to **Shader | Mix Shader**). Label the **Mix Shader** node as Mix Shader_Fog.

11. Connect the **View Z Depth** output of the **Camera Data** node to the first **Value** input of the **Math** node. Set the **Math** node's **Operation** to **Multiply** and the second **Value** to 0.030. Check the **Clamp** option. Connect the **Multiply** node output to the **Fac** input socket of the **Mix Shader_Fog** node.

12. Connect the **Emission** output to the second **Shader** input of the **Mix Shader_Fog** node. Set the **Color** values for **R** to 0.040, **G** to 0.117, and **B** to 0.124.

13. Select all the new nodes and press *Ctrl + G* to make a group. Click and drag the first **Shader** input socket of the **Mix Shader_Fog** node into the empty socket of the **Group Input** node on the left and repeat this step by connecting the **Shader** output socket on the right. Press *Tab* to close the group. Then rename it as Fog_underwater as shown in the following screenshot:

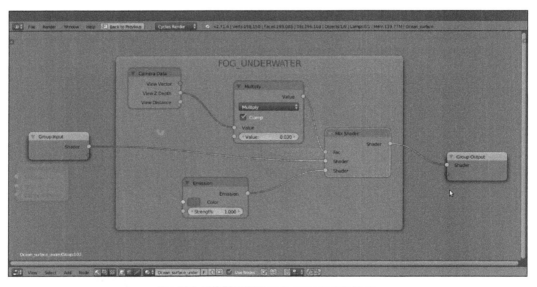

The FOG_UNDERWATER node group in Edit Mode

14. Add and paste the **Fog_underwater** node (press *Shift + A* and navigate to **Group | Fog_underwater**) just before the **Material Output** node of every material (in our scene, the **Fog_underwater** node will show eight users if the *fake user* button is selected) as shown in the following screenshot:

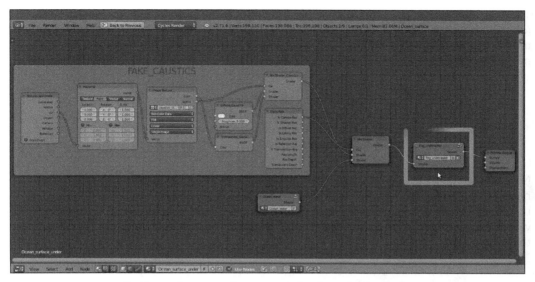

The Fog_underwater node group pasted at the end of the shader

How it works...

First of all, why should we choose a Cube for the ocean surface instead of the simpler Plane?

The reason is very simple: in Cycles, the World emits light, and the only way to avoid this is to set the color to pitch black (or by a combination of a **Light Path** node with the **World** materials, but this is another story). In our scene, the World is set to a bright blue sky color, and with a Plane, the underwater objects and the ocean bed would have been lit too much from the sides and the bottom the result look natural. A Cube, on the other hand, envelops all the underwater elements, limiting the lighting to the Sun Lamp passing through the surface, and projecting the image textured caustics. This gives a more natural-looking result.

The image texture we assigned to the water material is used to obtain a textured transparency effect. Right now, the water surface is actually opaque and transparent according to the black and white values of the textures, so as to allow the Sun Lamp light to pass through and project the caustics.

Thanks to the **Is Camera Ray** output of the **Light Path** node, the caustics image texture is not directly renderable on the ocean surface, but it nevertheless has some effect on the other materials. Because the value of **Is Camera Ray** is 1, the rays starting from the Camera and directly hitting the ocean surface can render only the clean water material plugged into the second input socket of the **Mix Shader** node, while the transmitted caustics (plugged in the first **Shader** socket = 0) get rendered.

The **Fog_underwater** node group is simply an emitter material serving as the background (deep green in this case) and mapped on every underwater material according to the *z* depth of the Camera (it also works with the Camera frame, in the viewport). The density of the fog is set by the **Multiply** node's second **Value**. For the ocean body, a value of 0.030 is good enough.

 The Camera *z* axis must not be confused with the global coordinate *z* axis, which is the vertical blue line visible in the 3D view. The Camera *z* axis, on the other hand, is the ideal line connecting the starting point of view to any visible element in the scene.

Note that we didn't expose the values of the nodes in the **Fog_underwater** group. This is because in **Edit Mode**, we can tweak the internal values of just one node to automatically update all the fog group instances assigned to the other materials. Besides, we know that the values exposed on the group interface would overwrite the internal settings and work only for that single node instance.

The final underwater environment rendered from a different point of view

Creating a snowy mountain landscape with procedurals

In this recipe, we will make a snowy mountain landscape by reusing existing shaders—the Rock_procedural and the Snow materials. We will improve these materials by grouping them and exposing the useful values. Then we will create a new group node that will work as a stencil to depict snow in a more customizable and natural way on the rocks as shown in the following screenshot:

The snowy mountain landscape as it appears in the final rendering

Getting ready

As usual, let's start with the preparation of the scene. In this case, we start with an almost ready blend file:

1. Start Blender and open the `99310S_05_RockSnow_start.blend` file, where there is a scene with a placed Camera—a simply modeled **Mountain** object and a **Plane** set as **Emitter**.

2. Select the **Mountain** object, go to the **Object modifiers** window, and assign a **Subdivision Surface** modifier. Set the levels to 2 for both **View** and **Render**.

3. Assign a second **Subdivision Surface** modifier. Set the levels to 1 for both **View** and **Render**.

4. Assign a **Displace** modifier. Click on the **Show texture in texture** tab to the extreme right of the **Texture** name slot to go to the **Textures** window. Assign a **Voronoi** procedural texture. Set the **Size** to 1.00. Go back to the **Displace** modifier and set the **Strength** to -0.200.

5. Assign a second **Displace** modifier. In the **Texture** window, assign a new **Voronoi Texture** and set **Distance Metric** to **Manhattan** and **Size** to 0.50. Back in the **Displace** modifier panel, set the **Strength** to -0.050.

6. Assign a third **Displace** modifier, select a **Clouds** texture, and set **Noise** to **Hard** and the **Displace** modifier's **Strength** to 0.040.

7. Assign a fourth **Displace** modifier. In the **Texture** window, assign a **Musgrave** procedural texture. Set the **Type** to **Hetero Terrain**, **Dimension** to 0.650, **Lacunarity** to 2.000, **Octaves** to 0.500, **Offset** to 0.250, **Basis** to **Voronoi F1**, and **Size** to 2.00. Back in the **Displace** modifier panel, set the **Strength** to 0.300.

8. Assign a fifth **Displace** modifier. In the **Texture** window, assign a **Distorted Noise** texture. Set the **Noise Distortion** to **Voronoi F1**, Basis to **Improved Perlin**, **Distortion** to 2.000, and **Size** to 3.30. Back in the **Displace** modifier panel, set the **Strength** to 0.100 as shown in the following screenshot:

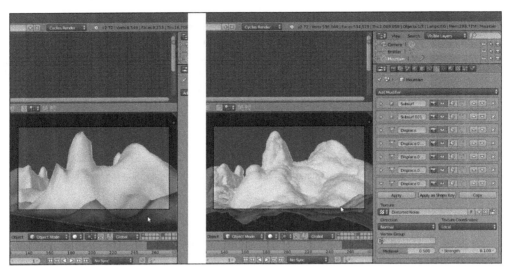

The mountain object obtained using different settings—without and with the several modifiers

9. Now disable the **Display** modifier in viewport button (the eye icon) of each modifier.

10. Go to the **World** window and click on the **Use Nodes** button. Then click on the little square with a dot on the right side of the **Color** slot. From the pop-up menu, select **Sky Texture**. On the **Background** node, set the **Strength** value to 1.200.

11. Add a **Mix Shader** node (press *Shift + A* and navigate to **Shader | Mix Shader**) and paste it between the **Background** and the **World Output** nodes. Switch the link of the **Background** node with the second input socket.

12. Add a **Texture Coordinate** node (press *Shift + A* and navigate to **Input | Texture Coordinate**), a **Mapping** node (press *Shift + A* and navigate to **Vector | Mapping**), an **Environment Texture** node (press *Shift + A* and navigate to **Texture | Environment Texture**), and a new **Background** node (press *Shift + A* and navigate to **Shader | Background**).

13. Connect the **Generated** output of the **Texture Coordinate** node to the **Vector** input socket of the **Mapping** node, and the output of this node to the **Vector** input socket of the **Environment Texture** node. Connect the **Color** output of this node to the **Color** input socket of the second **Background** node.

14. Connect the output of the second **Background** node to the first input socket of the **Mix Shader** node, and set its **Strength** to 0.250. Add a **Light Path** node (press *Shift + A* and navigate to **Input | Light Path**). Connect the **Is Camera Ray** output to the **Fac** input socket of the **Mix Shader** node.

15. Go to the **Environment Texture** node and click on the **Open** button. Browse to the `texture` folder and load the `WinterForest_Env.hdr` image (it's a free, high-dynamic-range image downloaded from the sIBL Archive at `http://www.hdrlabs.com/sibl/archive.html`, and licensed under the Creative Commons Attribution-NonCommercial-ShareAlike 3.0 License).

16. Go to the **Mapping** node and set the **Rotation** value of Z to `19°` as shown in the following screenshot:

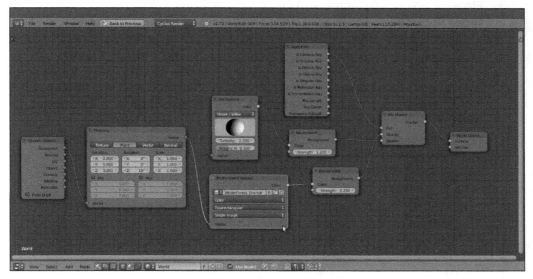

The World network setting

17. Go to the **Render** window, and under the **Sampling** subpanel, set both the **Clamp Direct** and **Clamp Indirect** values to `1.00`. Set the **Samples** to `10` for **Preview** and `25` for **Render**. Under the **Light Paths** subpanel, disable both the **Reflective Caustics** and **Refractive Caustics** items and set the **Filter Glossy** to `1.00`.

How to do it...

We are going to create the scene and materials by dividing the process into four stages:

▸ Appending and grouping rock and snow shaders

▸ Mixing the material groups

▸ Creating a stencil shader

▸ Adding an atmospheric perspective

So, let's start with the first stage.

Appending and grouping the rock and the snow shader

Let's append the required (and previously made) materials, and group them for convenience:

1. From the `99310S_03_snow.blend` file, append the `Snow_01` material, and for now, assign it to the **Mountain** object.

2. In the **Node Editor** window, select all the nodes except **Texture Coordinates** and **Material Output**, and press *Ctrl + G* to group them.

3. Place the **SNOW_COLOR** frame to the right of the **SNOW_BUMP** frame. Select the **Group Output** node, and in the (press N) **Properties** panel of the **Node Editor** window, delete the **Value** output.

4. Add a **Bump** node (press *Shift + A* and navigate to **Vector | Bump**). Connect the **Value** output of the **Math04** node inside the **SNOW_BUMP** frame to the **Height** input socket of the **Bump** node. Then connect the **Normal** output of the **Bump** node to the **Normal** input sockets of the **Diffuse BSDF**, **Glossy BSDF**, and **Translucent BSDF** shaders inside the **SNOW_COLOR** frame.

5. Click on the **Strength** socket of the **Bump** node and drag it into the empty socket on the **Group Input** node. Rename the socket (automatically named Strength) as `Bump_Strength`. Repeat this step for the **Distance** socket and rename it as `Bump_Distance`.

6. Drag the **Color** input socket of the **Diffuse BSDF** node into the empty socket of the **Group Input** node. Move the new socket to the top of the list and rename it as `Snow_Color`. Drag the **Color** input of the **Glossy BSDF** shader node and connect it to the same **Snow_Color** socket.

7. Drag the **Color** input socket of the **Translucent BSDF** node into the empty socket of the **Group Input** node. Move the new socket upwards, just below the **Snow_Color** socket, and rename it as `Transl_Color`.

8. Move the **Vector** socket on the **Group Input** node to the bottom of the list, and close the group. Rename it as `Snow_02` and check the *fake user* option. Click on the **Bump_Strength** slider and type `1.500` as shown in the following screenshot:

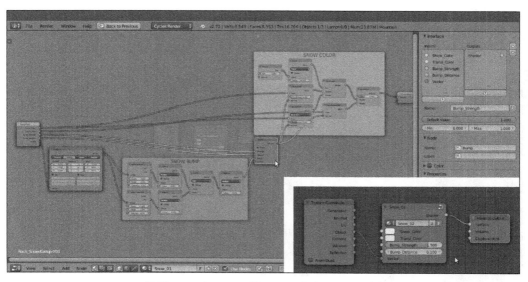

Making a node group of the appended snow material

9. From the `99310S_03_Rock_procedurals.blend` file, append the `Rock_proc01` material. Go to the **Material** datablock button on the **Node Editor** toolbar and assign it to the **Mountain** object.

10. In the **Node Editor** window, select all the nodes except the **Texture Coordinates** and the **Material Output** nodes. Press *Ctrl + G* to group them. Set the **Location** values in the **Mapping** node to `0.000` for all the three axes.

11. Add a **Math** node (press *Shift + A* and navigate to **Converter | Math**). Set the **Operation** to **Multiply** and the first **Value** to `1.000`. Press *Shift + D* to duplicate it, and do this three times. Connect the **Value** outputs of each of the four **Multiply-Math** nodes to the **Scale** input sockets of the four **Noise Texture** nodes inside the **BUMP** frame.

12. Now, in the second **Value** slot of each **Multiply-Math** node, set `10.000` for **Noise Texture01**, `15.000` for **Noise Texture02**, `37.500` for **Noise Texture03**, and `112.500` for **Noise Texture04**.

13. Add a **Voronoi Texture** node (press *Shift + A* and navigate to **Texture | Voronoi Texture**), switch the **Coloring** to **Cells**, and connect its **Fac** output to the first **Value** input socket (the socket with value of `1.000`) of each of the four **Multiply-Math** nodes.

14. Connect the **Voronoi Texture** node's **Vector** input socket to the **Vector** output of the **Mapping** node and drag the link from its **Scale** input socket to the empty socket of the **Group Input** node. Rename the new socket as `Rock_Scale` as shown in the following screenshot:

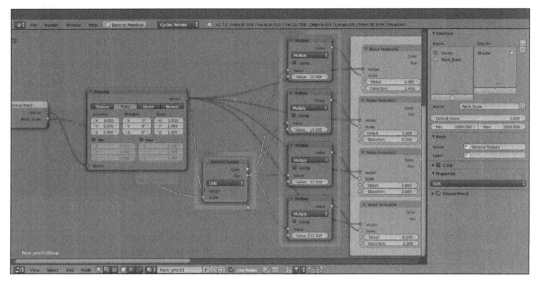

Adding Math nodes to tweak the exposed scale values of the textures for the procedural rock material

15. Now go to the **COLOR** frame and delete the **RGB** node. Then select the **Mix03** node and press *Ctrl + X* to delete it, maintaining the connection of the **Darken** node to the **Color2** socket of the **Add** node.

16. Add a **MixRGB** node (press *Shift + A* and navigate to **Color | MixRGB**), label it as `Mix03` again, and paste it between the **RGB Curves** node and the **Diffuse BSDF** shader. Set the **Blend Type** to **Color** and connect its output to the **Color** input socket of the **Glossy BSDF** shader.

17. Press *Shift + D* to duplicate the **Mix03** node. Label the duplicate as `Mix04` and paste it between the **RGB Curves** and the **Mix03** nodes. Set its **Blend Type** to **Multiply** and the **Color2** to pure black. Then select both the **Mix03** and **Mix04** nodes and parent them to the **COLOR** frame as shown in the following screenshot:

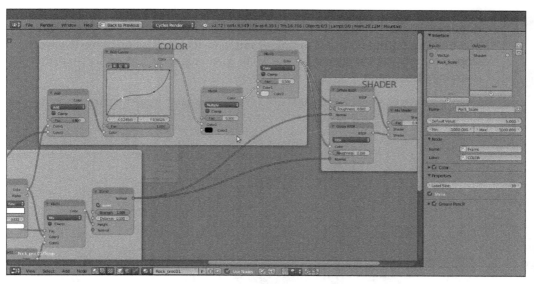

Adding color variations to the rock material

18. Click on the **Color2** input socket of the **Mix03** node. Drag it to the empty socket of the **Group Input** node. Move the new socket to the top of the list and rename it as `Rock_Color`.

19. Repeat the preceding step with the **Fac** socket of the **Mix04** node, and rename the new socket as `Rock_Darkness`. Move the **Vector** socket on the **Group Input** node to the bottom of the list.

20. Add a new **MixRGB** node (press *Shift + A* and navigate to **Color | MixRGB**) and a **ColorRamp** node (press *Shift + A* and navigate to **Converter | ColorRamp**). Connect the **Color** output of the **Mix03** node to the **Color1** input socket of the new **MixRGB** node, and the **Color** output of **Mix01** to the **Color2** input socket.

21. Connect the **Color** output of the new **MixRGB** node to the **Fac** input socket of the **ColorRamp** node. Then connect the **Color** output of this node to the empty socket of the **Group Output** node. Go to **ColorRamp** and set the position of the black color stop to `0.500` and the position of the white color stop to `0.545` as shown in the following screenshot:

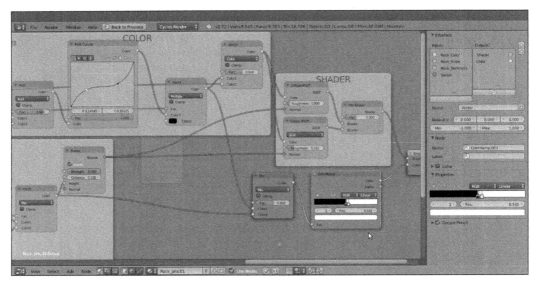

Creating a Color output in the node group to be used later to detail the stencil effect

22. Drag the **Strength** and the **Distance** sockets of the **Bump** node to the **Group Input** node, and rename them as `Bump_Strength` and `Bump_Distance`, respectively. Move the **Vector** socket to the bottom. Press *Tab* to exit **Edit Mode**.

23. Rename the group as `Rock_proc_02`, and enable the *fake user*. Set the **Rock_Color** values for **R** `0.078`, **G** to `0.067`, and **B** to `0.056`; the **Rock_Scale** to `0.600`; and the **Rock_Darkness** to `0.469` as shown in the following screenshot:

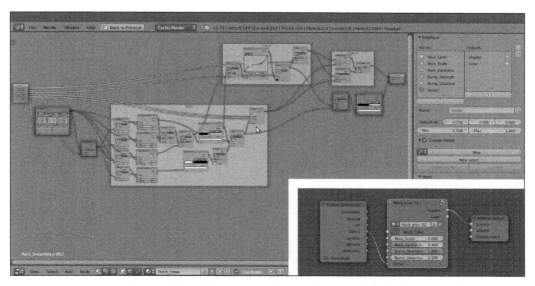

The overall view of the procedural rock node group in Edit Mode

Mixing the material groups

Now we can start to build the real shader by mixing the procedural rock and snow materials:

1. Press *Shift + A* with the mouse in the **Node Editor** window and add the **Snow_02** group node (press *Shift + A* and navigate to **Group | Snow_02**). Then rename the material as Rock_Snow in the **Node Editor** toolbar.

2. Add a **Mix Shader** node (press *Shift + A* and navigate to **Shader | Mix Shader**) and paste it between the **Rock_proc_02** group node and the **Material Output** node. Connect the **Shader** output of the **Snow_02** group node to the second **Shader** input socket of the **Mix Shader** node.

3. Connect the **Object** output of the **Texture Coordinate** node to the **Vector** input socket of the **Snow_02** group node as shown in the following screenshot:

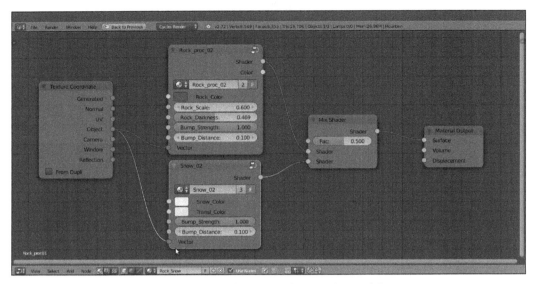

Starting to build the snowy rock mountain material

Creating the stencil shader

At this point, both the materials are assigned to the **Mountain** object, but if you render the preview now, they will appear on the whole mesh surface as a mixture of rock and snow. We must build a separator to establish where the surface will show only the rock and where it will show only the snow:

1. Add a **Geometry** node (press *Shift + A* and navigate to **Input | Geometry**), two **Mapping** nodes (press *Shift + A* and navigate to **Vector | Mapping**), two **Gradient Texture** nodes (press *Shift + A* and navigate to **Texture | Gradient Texture**), and a **ColorRamp** node (press *Shift + A* and navigate to **Converter | ColorRamp**).

2. In the **Properties** panel of the **Node Editor**, label these four nodes as follows: Mapping01, Mapping02, Gradient Texture01, Gradient Texture02, and ColorRamp01. Connect the **Normal** output of the **Geometry** node to the **Vector** input socket of the **Mapping01** node and the **Position** output to the **Mapping02** node. Then connect the **Mapping01** node to the **Gradient Texture01** node and the **Mapping02** node to the **Gradient Texture02** node.

3. Leave the **Gradient Type** of the **Gradient Texture01** node as **Linear** and set the **Gradient Type** of the **Gradient Texture02** to **Quadratic**. In the **Mapping01** node, set the **Location** value of **X** as -0.210 and the **Rotation** value of **Y** as 90°. In the **Mapping02** node, set only the **Rotation** value of **Y** as 90°.

4. Add three **MixRGB** nodes (press *Shift + A* and navigate to **Color | MixRGB**). Set the **Fac** of the first one to 0.000 and label it as Add01. Then connect the **Color** outputs of both the **Gradient Texture** nodes to the **Color1** and to the **Color2** input sockets.

5. Connect the output of the **Add01** node to the **Fac** input socket of the **ColorRamp01** node. Then set its **Interpolation** to **B-Spline** and move the black color stop to 0.600 position. Add a new color stop, set the color to pure black, and move it to the 0.700 position. Then move the position of the white color stop to 0.800.

6. Label the other two **MixRGB** nodes as **Burn01** and **Burn02**. Connect the **Color** output of the **ColorRamp01** node to the **Color1** input socket of the **Burn01** node, and the **Color** output of this node to the **Color1** input of the **Burn02** node. Set the **Blend Type** for both the nodes to **Burn**.

7. Add a **Frame** (press *Shift + A* and navigate to **Layout | Frame**) and parent all of these nodes to it. Label the frame as SLOPE as shown in the following screenshot:

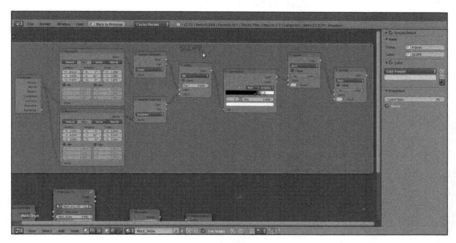

The SLOPE frame

8. Now press *Shift + D* to duplicate one of the **Mapping** nodes (press *Alt + P* to unparent it from the frame), and move it to under the **SLOPE** frame. Label it as Mapping03 and change the **Location** value of **X** to -0.600.

9. Add a **Noise Texture**, a **Voronoi Texture**, and a **Musgrave Texture** node (press *Shift + A* and navigate to **Texture | Noise Texture**, repeat the same for all other nodes) and place them in a column next to the **Mapping03** node. Set the **Noise Texture** node's **Scale** value to 4.600. Set the **Voronoi Texture** node's **Coloring** to **Cell** and the **Scale** to 28.700. Set the **Musgrave Texture** node's type to **Ridged Multifractal**, the **Scale** to 3.500, **Detail** to 16.000, **Dimension** to 0.900, **Lacunarity** to 0.600, **Offset** to 0.500, and **Gain** to 5.000.

10. Connect the **Vector** output of the **Mapping03** node to the **Vector** inputs of the three textures. Then add a **MixRGB** node (press *Shift + A* and navigate to **Color | MixRGB**), set the **Blend Type** to **Burn**, and label it as `Burn03`.

11. Connect the **Fac** outputs of the **Noise Texture** and **Voronoi Texture** nodes to the **Color1** and **Color2** input sockets of the **Burn03** node. Press *Shift + D* to duplicate the **Burn03** node, label it as `Burn04`, and set its **Fac** value to `1.000`. Connect the **Color** output of the **Burn03** node to the **Color1** input socket of the **Burn04** node. Then connect the **Fac** output of the **Musgrave Texture** node to its **Color2** input socket.

12. Add a **ColorRamp** node (press *Shift + A* and navigate to **Converter | ColorRamp**), label it as `ColorRamp02`, and paste it between the **Burn03** and the **Burn04** nodes. Set **Interpolation** to **Ease** and move the white color marker to the `0.487` position.

13. Add a **Frame** (press *Shift + A* and navigate to **Layout | Frame**), select all of these nodes and then the frame, and press *Ctrl + P* to parent them. Label the frame as `DENSITY` as shown in the following screenshot:

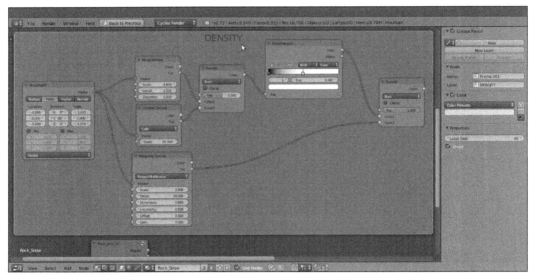

The DENSITY frame

14. Box-select the two frames (with all the nodes inside) and press *Ctrl + G* to create a group. Add a **MixRGB** node (press *Shift + A* and navigate to **Color | MixRGB**), set the **Blend Type** to **Soft Light**, and set the **Fac** value to `1.000`. Connect the **Color** output of the **Burn02** node inside the **SLOPE** frame to the **Color1** input socket. Then connect the **Color** output of the last **Burn04** node inside the **DENSITY** frame to the **Color2** input socket.

15. Drag the **Color** output of the **Soft Light** node into the empty socket of the **Group Output** node to create a new **Color** output on the interface. Then add a new **ColorRamp** (press *Shift + A* and navigate to **Converter | ColorRamp**), label it as `ColorRamp04`, and paste it between the **Soft Light** and the **Group Output** nodes. Set **Interpolation** to **Ease**, the black color stop to the `0.500` position, and the white color stop to the `0.600` position.

16. Go to the **SLOPE** frame. Click and drag the **Fac** socket of the **Add01** node to the empty socket of the **Input Group** node. Rename the new input as `Snow_amount`.

17. Go to the **DENSITY** frame and attach the **Vector** input of the **Mapping03** node to the empty socket of the **Input Group** node. Move it up by clicking on the little arrow icon in the **Properties** panel, and press *Tab* to close the group. Rename it as `Separator` as shown in the following screenshot:

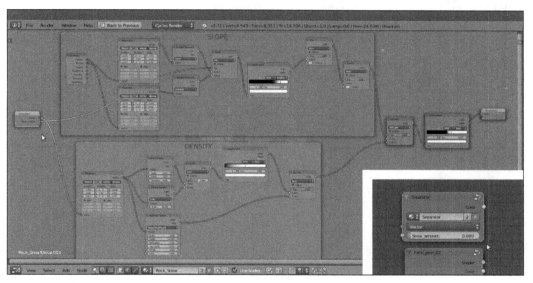

The outputs of the SLOPE and DENSITY frames added inside the Separator node group

18. Connect the **Object** output of the **Texture Coordinate** node to the **Vector** input socket of the **Separator** node group. For the rendering of the image at the beginning of this recipe, I've set the **Snow_amount** value to `0.724`.

19. Add one more **MixRGB** node (press *Shift + A* and navigate to **Color | MixRGB**), set the **Blend Type** to **Add**, and connect the **Color** output of the **Separator** group node to the **Color1** input socket. Then connect the **Color** output of the **Rock_proc_02** group node to the **Color2** input socket. Set the **Fac** value to `1.000` and connect the **Color** output to the **Fac** input socket of the **Mix Shader** node.

Adding the atmospheric perspective

The final step we can do to improve our material is to append the **Fog_underwater** node group, from the `9931OS_05_underwater_final.blend` file located in **Nodetree**. Rename this node `Atmos_persp` and paste it just before the **Material Output** node. Then press *Tab* to open the group by entering **Edit Mode**. Set the **Multiply** node value to `0.010` and the color values of the **Emission** shader for **R** to `0.078`, **G** to `0.133`, and **B** to `0.250` as shown in the following screenshot:

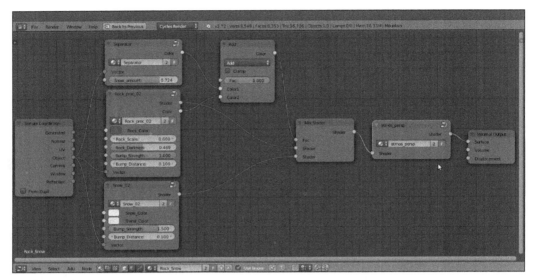

The overall network and the atmospheric perspective node group added at the end of the shader. Note the Color output of the Rock material added to the output of the Separator to work as stencil or blending factor.

How it works...

Now let's see how this material actually works, by dividing the creation's process into three parts:

> ► Firstly, we appended the `Snow` material and made a group, exposing the required properties and changing the way the bump works. In other words, we deleted the output to the **Displacement** input of the **Material Output** node and implemented a per shader bump.
>
> This doesn't really make a big difference in the final rendering. Just be aware that a bump piped in the **Displacement** socket can react to Ambient Occlusion (which we didn't use in the scene, by the way), but this is not true with the per shader bump.

► Secondly, we appended the `Rock_procedural` material and made a group of it as well. Again, all the necessary values were exposed, and although we kept the material unaltered in this scene, the group could now be easily reused for different kinds of rock in other projects or on different objects.

We added a **Math** node set to **Multiply** for every texture **Scale** value that needed to be driven by one single exposed input. The first **Value** of the **Math** node, set to the original scale value, gets multiplied by the driven second **Value**, thus increasing or decreasing (for values smaller than 1.000) the final scale value.

► Thirdly, we built `Separator`, a node group outputting gray-scale values that are connected to the **Fac** input of the **Mix Shader** node, which works as a stencil map, separating the two different materials on the mesh surface accordingly to black and white values. The two gradient textures in the **SLOPE** frame, mapped on the position and the normals of the mesh and then blended together by the **Burn** nodes, make the snow material (the white color value of the stencil map) appear more on the mesh's faces that have more a horizontal trend than a vertical one. Thanks to the **Add01** node, mixing the gradients driven by the exposed input **Snow_amount** and influencing the gradient of the **ColorRamp01** node, it's also possible to set the quantity of snow (the white color in the stencil) on the whole object. The mixed textures in the **DENSITY** frame make the separation line between black and white more frayed and realistic, and so also the **Color** output of the **Separator** group that is added to a **Color** output of the **Rock** shader just before being connected to the **Fac** input of the **Mix Shader**. Have a look at the following screenshot:

The only mask and the Rendered versions of three different values of the Snow_amount slider

In the preceding set of screenshots, you can see the different effects of the 0.000, 0.700, and 1.000 values of the **Snow_amount** slider. The black-and-white mask works as a separator between the rock and the snow materials.

Creating a realistic Earth as seen from space

In this recipe, we will create a realistic Earth as shown in the following screenshot, using both image textures from the Web and some procedurals:

The Earth as it appears in the final rendering

Getting ready

The image textures provided with this Cookbook have generally been heavily down-scaled and are good for demonstration purposes only (in this case, for a very distant Earth render). For better results with this recipe, replace these low-resolution images with high-resolution versions that you can find at these addresses:

- http://www.shadedrelief.com/natural3/pages/textures.html
- http://www.shadedrelief.com/natural3/pages/clouds.html
- http://celestia.h-schmidt.net/earth-vt/
- http://www.celestiamotherlode.net/catalog/earth.php

Before you download anything, always take a look at the license of the images provided by any site you can find to ensure that they are released as freely usable, especially if you are going to use them for commercial work. All the preceding links should be okay, but on the Internet, things can change quite quickly, so double-check!

You will need at least five image maps for this recipe: Earth-color, the color of the land or sea in daylight; Earth-night, the color of the land or sea at night (usually provided with superimposed city lights); Earth-bump, a gray-scale, high map of the continents; Earth-spec, an outline with the continents in black and the water masses perfectly white; and Clouds, a gray-scale map of the clouds as shown in the following screenshot:

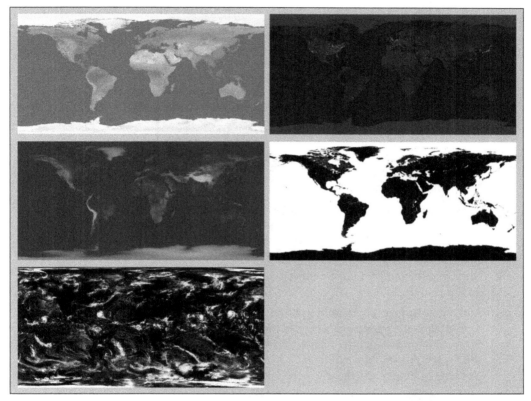

The five image textures

Actually, Cycles can handle very big textures pretty well, even 16 K images (that is, images made by 16.000 pixels for the longest side), so you can use them at the best resolution you can find. Be aware that the bigger the resolution of the textures, the longer the rendering times, especially if they are used as bump maps.

Now perform the following steps:

1. Start Blender and switch to the Cycles Render engine.

2. Delete the default **Cube** and add a **UV Sphere** (with the mouse arrow in the 3D view, press *Shift + A* and navigate to **Mesh | UV Sphere**). In the **Outliner**, rename it as `Earth_Surface`.

3. With the mouse arrow in the **Camera** view, press the *1* key on the numeric keypad to go to the **Front** view. Then press the *5* key to switch to **Orthogonal**. Next, press *Tab* to enter **Edit Mode**, followed by *A* to select all the vertices. Finally, press *U*. In the **UV Mapping** pop-up menu, select **Sphere Projection**. Then exit **Edit Mode**.

4. Make sure you place the 3D Cursor at the center of the **UV Sphere**. Then add an **Empty** (press *Shift + A* and navigate to **Empty | Arrows**). In the **Object data** window, set its **Size** to 2.00 and rename it as Empty_terminator. Go to the **Object Constraints** window and assign a **Damped Track** constraint to the **Empty_terminator**. In the **Target** field, select the **Sun** item (the Lamp), and in the **To** field, click on the **X** button.

5. Reselect the **UV Sphere** and go to the **UV Maps** subpanel under the **Object data** window. Click on the **+** icon button to add a new UV coordinates layer. Rename it as UVMap_terminator.

6. Go to the **Object modifiers** window and assign a **Subdivision Surface** modifier first, followed by a **UVProject** modifier. For this modifier, in the **UV Map** field, select the **UVMap_terminator** item. In the **Object to use as projector transform** field, select the **Empty_terminator**.

7. Press *Shift + D* and press *Enter* to duplicate the **Earth_Surface** object. In the **Transform** subpanel under the **Properties** panel to the right (press *N* if this is not activated), set the **Scale** value for **X**, **Y**, and **Z** to 1.001. Rename it as Earth_Clouds.

8. Duplicate it again, set the **Scale** value to 1.002, and rename it as Earth_Atmosphere.

9. Add a new **Empty** (press *Shift + A* and navigate to **Empty | Plain Axes**) and rename it as Empty_Earth. In the **Object data** window, set its **Size** to 2.00. Press *Shift* and select the **Earth_Surface**, **Earth_Clouds**, **Earth_Atmosphere**, and the **Empty_Earth** objects. Press *Ctrl + P* and click on **Object** to parent the three UV Spheres to **Empty_Earth**.

10. Select **Empty_Earth**, and in the **Transform** panel, set the **Rotation** values of **X** to 18.387°, **Y** to 0.925°, and **Z** to -4.122° (you can obviously rotate the **Empty_Earth** as you wish, but this helps provide a nice point of view on the specular effect showing on the oceans).

11. Select the **Camera**, and in the **Transform** panel, set the **Location** values of **X** to -0.64000, **Y** to -4.70000, and **Z** to 0.12000. Then set the **Rotation** values of **X** to 89°, **Y** to 0°, and **Z** to -9°. Go to the **Object data** window and change the **Focal Length** to 60.000 (millimeters). Press the *0* key on the numeric keypad to go to the **Camera** view.

12. Go to the **World** window and change the background **Color** to pure black.

13. Select the **Lamp** and change it to a **Sun**. Set the **Size** to 0.050 and the **Strength** to 10.000. Set the **Color** values for **R** to 1.000, **G** to 0.902, and **B** to 0.679. In the **Transform** panel, set the **Location** values of **X** to 158.00000, **Y** to -27.00000, and **Z** to 107.00000. For **Rotation**, set **X** to 1.5°, **Y** to 56°, and **Z** to -8° (Sun lamps don't need a location, but in this case, we need it to establish a target for a later-to-come day/night terminator trick).

14. Go to the **Render** window. Under the **Sampling** subpanel, set the **Clamp Direct** and **Clamp Indirect** values to 1.00, the **Preview** samples to 20, and the **Render** samples to 50.

15. Go to the **Scene** window. In the **Color Management** subpanel, click on the **Use Curves** item. Set the **Exposure** value to 1.000. Then click inside the curve window to add a new point, and place it at position **X** as 0.61149 and **Y** as 0.71250. Then set the value of the **B** channel for the **White Level** between 0.800 and 0.850.

How to do it...

After the creation of the 3D scene and the setting of the lighting, let's go for the materials, starting with the planet's surface.

The planet surface

In the **Outliner** (just temporarily), hide the **Earth_Clouds** and **Earth_Atmosphere** objects by clicking on the little eye icons to the right side of the names. This is to see only the **Earth_Surface** in the viewport, rendered and updated in real time as we work on the material:

1. Select the **Earth_Surface** object. Click on the **New** button in the **Material** window under the **Properties** panel or in the **Node Editor** toolbar. Rename the material as Surface.

2. In the **Material** window under the main **Properties** panel, switch the **Diffuse BSDF** shader with a **Mix Shader** node. In the first **Shader** slot, load a new **Diffuse BSDF** shader and set its **Roughness** value to 1.000. In the second **Shader** slot, load a **Glossy BSDF** node. Then set its **Roughness** value to 0.700 and **Distribution** to **Beckmann**. Set the **Fac** value of the **Mix Shader** to 0.100.

3. Press *N* in the **Node Editor** window to open the **Active Node** panel. Label the shaders as Diffuse_Lands and Glossy_Lands and the **Mix Shader** as Mix Shader_Lands.

4. Add an **Image Texture** node (press *Shift + A* and navigate to **Texture | Image Texture**) and connect its **Color** output to both the **Color** input sockets of the **Diffuse_Lands** and **Glossy_Lands** shaders. Click on the **Open** button on the **Image Texture** node, browse to your textures directory, and load the Earth-col_low.png image (or a high-resolution version, if available). Label the image node as Color_Day.

5. Add a new **Image Texture** node (press *Shift + A* and navigate to **Texture | Image Texture**) and a **Bump** node (press *Shift + A* and navigate to **Vector | Bump**). Connect the **Color** output of this **Image Texture** node to the **Height** input socket of the **Bump** node. Then connect the **Normal** output of the **Bump** node to the **Normal** input sockets of both the **Diffuse_Lands** and the **Glossy_Lands** nodes.

6. Label the second **Image Texture** node as Bump. Then click on its **Open** button and load the Earth-bump_low.png image. Set the **Color Space** to **Non-Color Data**. Label the **Bump** node as Bump_Lands and set the **Strength** value to 0.020.

7. Add a **MixRGB** node (press *Shift + A* and navigate to **Color | MixRGB**) and paste it between the **Color_Day** and the **Diffuse_Lands** nodes. Set the **Blend Type** to **Color**, the **Fac** value to 0.300, and the **Color2** value for **R** to 0.072, **G** to 0.127, and **B** to 0.578.

8. Add a **Frame** (press *Shift + A* and navigate to **Layout | Frame**). Press *Shift* and select the two image texture nodes (**Color_Day** and **Bump**), the **Color** node, **Bump_Lands** node, **Diffuse_Lands** and **Glossy_Lands** shaders, and then the **Frame**. Press *Ctrl + P* to parent them. Label the **Frame** as LANDS as shown in the following screenshot:

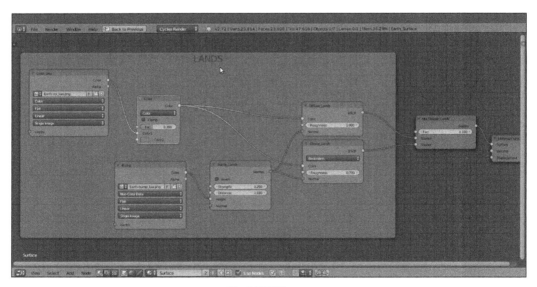

The LANDS frame

9. Now add a **Noise Texture** node (press *Shift + A* and navigate to **Texture | Noise Texture**), a **Bump** node (press *Shift + A* and navigate to **Vector | Bump**), a **Diffuse BSDF** shader (press *Shift + A* and navgiate to **Shader | Diffuse BSDF**), and a **Glossy BSDF** shader (press *Shift + A* and navigate to **Shader | Glossy BSDF**).

10. Set the **Noise Texture** node's **Scale** value to `1000.000` and connect its **Color** output to the **Height** input socket of the **Bump** node. Label this node as `Bump_Seas`, set the **Strength** value to `0.015`, and connect its **Normal** output to the **Normal** input sockets of the new **Diffuse BSDF** and **Glossy BSDF** shaders. Label them as `Diffuse_Seas` and `Glossy_Seas` and set the **Glossy BSDF** node's **Roughness** value to `0.150`.

11. Add a **Frame** (press *Shift + A* and navigate to **Layout | Frame**). Press *Shift* and select the new nodes and then the **Frame**. Press *Ctrl + P* to parent them. Rename the frame as `SEAS`.

12. Add a **Mix Shader** node (press *Shift + A* and navigate to **Shader | Mix Shader**), label it as `Mix Shader_Seas`, and place it just under the **Mix Shader_ Lands** node. Set the **Fac** value to `0.100`. Connect the output of the **Diffuse_Seas** node to the first **Shader** input, and the output of the **Glossy_Seas** node to the second **Shader** input socket.

13. Press *Shift + D* to duplicate the **Mix Shader_Seas** node and paste it between the **Mix Shader_Lands** and the **Material Output** nodes. Label it as `Mix Shader_ Surface`. Connect the output of the **Mix Shader_Seas** node to its second **Shader** input socket.

14. Add a new **Image Texture** node (press *Shift + A* and navigate to **Texture | Image Texture**) and rename it as `Spec/mask`. Connect its **Color** output to the **Fac** input socket of the **Mix Shader_Surface** node. Click on the **Open** button to load the `Earth-spec_low.png` image. Set the **Color Space** to **Non-Color Data**.

15. Add a **Frame** (press *Shift + A* and navigate to **Layout | Frame**). Press *Shift* and select the **Spec/mask** node and then the **Frame**. Press *Ctrl + P* to parent them. Rename the frame as `SEPARATOR LANDS/SEAS`.

16. Now click on the **Color** output of the **Color_Day** image texture inside the **LANDS** frame, and drag it so that it is connected to the **Color** input of the **Diffuse_ Seas shader** node inside the **SEAS** frame.

17. Add a **MixRGB** node (press *Shift + A* and navigate to **Color | MixRGB**) to the **SEAS** frame (just add it and parent it to the frame). Paste it just before the **Diffuse_ Seas** shader. Switch the **Color1** connection to the **Color2** input socket. Then set the **Color1** values for **R** to `0.002`, **G** to `0.002`, and **B** to `0.022`.

18. Add a **ColorRamp** node (press *Shift + A* and navigate to **Converter | ColorRamp**) to the **SEAS** frame and label it as `ColorRamp01`. Connect the **Color** output to the **Color** input of the **Glossy_Seas** shader. Set **Interpolation** to **B-Spline**. Change the black color stop (index **0**) to pure white and the white color stop values (index **1**) for **R** to `0.072`, **G** to `0.127`, and **B** to `0.578`, with **Alpha** value set to `0.000`. Move it to `0.150` position. Click on the **+** icon button to add a new color stop. Change its **Color** values for **R** to `0.965`, **G** to `0.462`, **B** to `0.223`, and **Alpha** to `1.000`. Move it to `0.075` position.

19. Add a **Layer Weight** node (press *Shift + A* and navigate to **Input | Layer Weight**) to the **SEAS** frame. Connect the **Facing** output to the **Fac** input socket of the **ColorRamp01** node and the **Fac** input socket of the **MixRGB** node. Set the **Blend** factor to 0.200 as shown in the following screenshot:

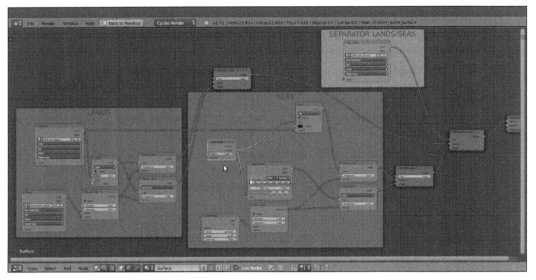

The LANDS and the SEAS frames connected and separated by the simple SEPARATOR LANDS/SEAS

20. Add an **Image Texture** node (press *Shift + A* and navigate to **Texture | Image Texture**), a **ColorRamp** node (press *Shift + A* and navigate to **Converter | ColorRamp**), a **MixRGB** node (press *Shift + A* and navigate to **Color | MixRGB**), and an **Emission** shader (press *Shift + A* and navigate to **Shader | Emission**). Label the **Image Texture** node as Color_Night and the **ColorRamp** as ColorRamp02.

21. Connect the **Color_Night** node's **Color** output to the **Fac** input socket of the **ColorRamp02** node, and the **Color** output of this node to the **Color1** input socket of the **MixRGB** node. Then connect the **MixRGB** node's output to the **Color** input of the **Emission** node.

22. In the **Color_Night** image texture node, load the Earth-night_low.png image. Set the **ColorRamp02** node's **Interpolation** to **B-Spline** and move the black color stop to 0.250 position. Then move the white color stop to the 0.495 position. Set the **MixRGB** node's **Blend Type** to **Multiply**, the **Fac** value to 0.700 and the **Color2** values for **R** to 1.000, **G** to 0.257, and **B** to 0.090. Set the **Emission** node's **Strength** value to 1.000.

23. Add a **Frame** (press *Shift + A* and navigate to **Layout | Frame**). Press *Shift* to select these new nodes and then the **Frame**. Press *Ctrl + P* to parent them. Rename the frame as NIGHT. This is shown in the the following screenshot:

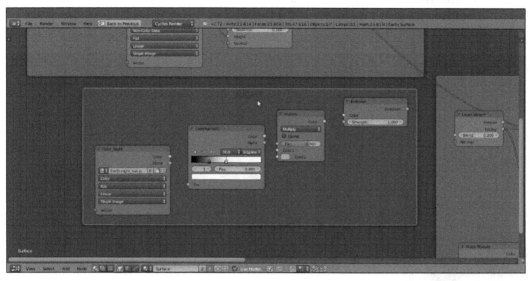

The NIGHT frame

24. Add an **Attribute** node (press *Shift + A* and navigate to **Input | Attribute**), a **Gradient Texture** node (press *Shift + A* and navigate to **Texture | Gradient Texture**) and a **ColorRamp** node (press *Shift + A* and navigate to **Converter | ColorRamp**). Connect the **Vector** output socket of the **Attribute** node to the **Vector** input socket of the **Gradient Texture** node, and the **Color** output of this node to the **Fac** input socket of the **ColorRamp** node.

25. In the **Name** slot of the **Attribute** node, write UVMap_terminator. Set the **ColorRamp** node's **Interpolation** to **B-Spline**. Then move the black color stop to 0.500 and the white color stop to the 0.000 position. Click on the **+** icon button to add a new color stop. Set its color to pure black as well.

26. Add a **Frame** (press *Shift + A* and navigate to **Layout | Frame**). Press *Shift* to select these three nodes and then the frame. Press *Ctrl + P* to parent them. Rename the frame as TERMINATOR.

27. Add a **Mix Shader** node (press *Shift + A* and navigate to **Shader | Mix Shader**), label it as Mix Shader_Terminator, and paste it just between the **Mix Shader_Lands** and the **Mix Shader_Surface** nodes. Connect the output of the **Emission** node inside the **NIGHT** frame to its second **Shader** input socket, and the **Color** output of the **ColorRamp** inside the **TERMINATOR** frame to its **Fac** input socket as shown in the following screenshot:

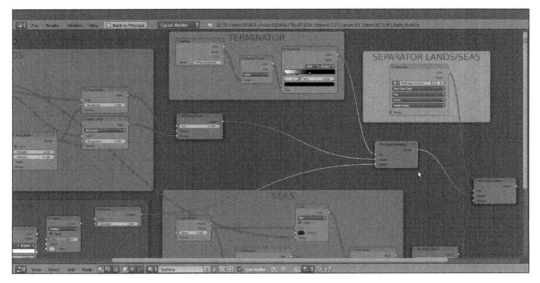

The TERMINATOR frame added to the surface material network

The clouds

As second planet material, let's go with the clouds by performing the following steps:

1. Now go to **Outliner**, unhide the **Earth_Clouds** sphere, and select it. Click on **New** in the **Material** window under the main **Properties** panel or in the **Node Editor** toolbar. Rename the material as Clouds.

2. In the **Material** window under the main **Properties** panel, switch the **Diffuse BSDF** shader with a **Mix Shader** node. Label it as Mix Shader_Clouds, and in the first **Shader** slot, load a **Transparent BSDF** shader. In the second **Shader** slot, load a new **Diffuse BSDF** shader. Set the color of both the shaders to pure white.

3. Add an **Image Texture** node (press *Shift + A* and navigate to **Texture | Image Texture**) and a **Bump** node (press *Shift + A* and navigate to **Vector | Bump**).

4. Label the **Image Texture** node as Clouds and the **Bump** node as Bump_Clouds. Connect the **Bump** node's output to the **Normal** input of the **Diffuse_Clouds** node. Set the **Strength** value to 0.020.

5. Click on the **Open** button of the **Clouds** image texture node and load the Clouds_low.png image. Set the **Color Space** to **Non-Color Data**.

6. Press *Shift + D* to duplicate the **Clouds** image node. Then add a **Texture Coordinate** node (press *Shift + A* and navigate to **Input | Texture Coordinate**) and a **Mapping** node (press *Shift + A* and navigate to **Vector | Mapping**). Connect the **UV** output of the **Texture Coordinate** node to the **Mapping** node, and the output of this node to the **Vector** input socket of the duplicated **Clouds** image texture node.

7. Add a **MixRGB** node (press *Shift + A* and navigate to **Color | MixRGB**) and connect the output of both the two **Clouds** image texture nodes to the **Color1** and **Color2** input sockets. Set the **Blend Type** to **Add** and the **Fac** value to 1.000. Connect the **Color** output to the **Height** input socket of the **Bump_Clouds** node and to the **Fac** input socket of the **Mix Shader_Clouds** node.

8. In the **Mapping** node, set the **Rotation** values of **X** to 32°, **Y** to 17°, and **Z** to 5°.

9. Add a **Frame** (press *Shift + A* and navigate to **Layout | Frame**). Press *Shift* to select the nodes and then the **Frame**. Then press *Ctrl + P* to parent them. Rename the frame as CLOUDS. This is shown in the screenshot:

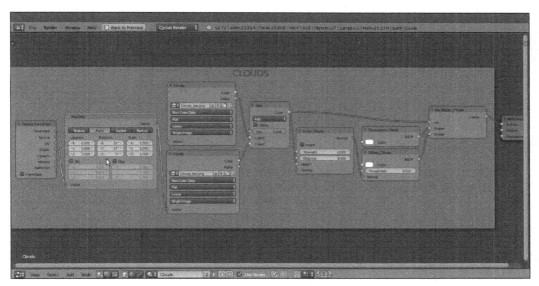

The CLOUDS material

The atmosphere

The third planet material is the atmosphere layer:

1. In **Outliner**, unhide the **Earth_Atmosphere** sphere and select it. Click on **New** in the **Material** window under the main **Properties** panel or in the **Node Editor** toolbar. Rename the new material as Atmosphere.

2. In the **Material** window on the right, under the main **Properties** panel, switch the **Diffuse BSDF** shader with a **Mix Shader** node. Label it as `Mix Shader_ Atmos1`, and in the first **Shader** slot, load a **Transparent BSDF** shader (label it `Transparent_Atmos1`). In the second **Shader** slot, load a **Diffuse BSDF** shader (label it `Diffuse_Atmos1`).

3. Add a **Layer Weight** node (press *Shift + A* and navigate to **Input | Layer Weight**) and a **ColorRamp** node (press *Shift + A* and navigate to **Converter | ColorRamp**). Connect the **Facing** output of the **Layer Weight** node to the **Fac** input of the **ColorRamp** (label it `ColorRamp03`). Set the **ColorRamp03** node's **Interpolation** to **B-Spline**, move the black color stop to the `0.395` position, and set the **Alpha** value to `0.000`. Set the color of the white color stop (index **1**) for **R** to `0.072`, **G** to `0.127`, and **B** to `0.578`.

4. Connect the **Color** output of the **ColorRamp03** node to the **Color** input socket of the **Diffuse_Atmos1** node, and the **Alpha** output to the **Fac** input of the **Mix Shader_Atmos1** node. Set the **Layer Weight** node's blend factor to `0.500`.

5. Add a **Frame** (press *Shift + A* and navigate to **Layout | Frame**). Press *Shift* to select these nodes and then the **Frame**. Then press *Ctrl + P* to parent them. Rename the frame as `ATMOSPHERE`.

6. Add an **Attribute** node (press *Shift + A* and navigate to **Input | Attribute**), a **Gradient Texture** node (press *Shift + A* and navigate to **Texture | Gradient Texture**), and a **ColorRamp** node (press *Shift + A* and navigate to **Converter | ColorRamp**). Connect the **Vector** output socket of the **Attribute** node to the **Vector** input socket of the **Gradient Texture** node, and then the **Color** output of this node to the **Fac** input socket of the **ColorRamp** (label it `ColorRamp04`).

7. In the **Name** slot of the **Attribute** node, type `UVMap_terminator`. Set the **ColorRamp04** node's **Interpolation** to **B-Spline**. Then move the black color stop to the `0.400` position and the white color stop to the `0.600` position, but change this stop's color to black as well. Click on the **+** icon button to add a new color stop. Set its color to pure black and move it to the `0.450` position. Click on the **+** icon button again to add a new color stop. Set its color to pure black and move it to the `0.550` position. Set the **Alpha** of all the four black color stops to the `0.000`. Click once more on the **+** icon button to add a new color stop. Set its color values for **R** to `1.000`, **G** to `0.047`, and **B** to `0.005`. Set **Alpha** value to `0.100` and move it to the `0.500` position.

8. Add a **Mix Shader** node (press *Shift + A* and navigate to **Shader | Mix Shader**), a **Transparent BSDF** node (press *Shift + A* and navigate to **Shader | Transparent BSDF**), and an **Emission** node (press *Shift + A* and navigate to **Shader | Emission**). Label them as `Mix Shader_Atmos2`, `Transparent_Atmos2`, and `Diffuse_Atmos2`.

9. Connect the **Transparent_Atmos2** node's output to the first **Shader** input socket of the **Mix Shader_Atmos2** and the **Diffuse_Atmos2** output to the second **Shader** input. Then connect the **Color** output of the **ColorRamp04** node to the **Color** input socket of the **Diffuse_Atmos2** node and the **Alpha** output to the **Fac** input socket of the **Mix Shader_Atmos2** node.

10. Add a **Frame** (press *Shift + A* and navigate to **Layout | Frame**). Press *Shift* to select these nodes and then the **Frame**. Then press *Ctrl + P* to parent them. Rename the frame as RED_TERMINATOR.

11. Add a final **Mix Shader** node (press *Shift + A* and navigate to **Shader | Mix Shader**), label it as Mix Shader_Atmos3, and set the **Fac** value to 0.950. Connect the output of the **RED_TERMINATOR** frame to the first **Shader** input socket and the output of the **ATMOSPHERE** frame to the second **Shader** input socket. Then connect the output of the **Mix Shader_Atmos3** node to the **Surface** input socket of the **Material Output** node as shown in the following screenshot:

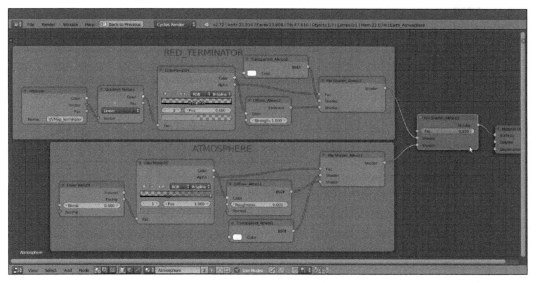

The RED_TERMINATOR and the ATMOSPHERE frames

How it works...

The three overlapping UV Spheres technique is quite old, and (at least for what relates to Blender) dates back to almost 2004—more precisely to the *How to make a realistic planet in Blender(2004)* tutorial I wrote at that time for Blender version 2.23/2.30 (http://www.enricovalenza.com/rlpl.html). That tutorial is now outdated, but the technique and basic concepts still work, even in Cycles. Hence, we get the planet surface on the smaller of the spheres, a clouds layer on a slightly bigger sphere, and the enveloping atmospheric Fresnel effect on the biggest sphere.

We divided the material creation process into the three stages, corresponding to the three layers/spheres. First, we built the more complex of all the three shaders that is the Surface material:

▸ From step 1 to step 8, we built the shader for the continents—simple image textures connected as color factors to a **Diffuse BSDF** and **Glossy BSDF** shaders. From step 9 to step 13, we made the basic shader for the oceans.

▸ In steps 14 and 15, we split the continents component from the oceans using the `Earth-spec` map, a black-and-white image working as a stencil for the factor input of the **Mix Shader_Surface** node. We also connected the `Earth-color` map to the **SEAS** diffuse shader to bring color back to the oceans.

▸ From step 16 to step 19, we added a **ColorRamp** node to the **SEAS** frame, driven by a **Facing** fresnel node. This was done to enhance the color of the water's specularity (according to what NASA's satellite photos often show). A deep blue color was mixed with the color image map by a **MixRGB** node. Thanks to the **Facing** fresnel node, the blue color was mapped on the mesh faces perpendicular to the point of view, resulting in darker water masses towards the center of the Earth sphere.

▸ From step 20 to step 23, we built the night shader. The Earth-night image was clamped (contrasted) by a **ColorRamp** node, and the resulting brightness values were multiplied by a reddish color in the **MixRGB** node. All of this was then assigned to an **Emission** shader. The night side of the Earth surface shows only in the shadow part of the sphere thanks to the **Empty_terminator** trick.

▸ From step 24 to step 27, we built the day/night terminator stencil.

▸ Then, from step 28 to step 36, we built the `Clouds` layer on the second sphere. We added more variety to the single `Clouds_low.png` image by superimposing and offsetting (the mapping rotation of) a copy of the same cloud image.

▸ From step 37 to step 47, we built the `Atmosphere` layer on the third (bigger) sphere, with the Fresnel atmospheric effect and the reddish terminator.

As you have probably noticed, we didn't use any **Texture Coordinate** or **Mapping** nodes to map the image maps. This is because the UV Spheres had been unwrapped with **Image Texture** nodes. The existing UV coordinate layer was automatically taken into account by Cycles for the mapping.

For the ocean bump, which was obtained by the **Noise** procedural, the Generated mapping option was automatically used.

Thanks to the Damped Track constraints, which were targeted to the position of the Sun lamp, we could use the **Empty_terminator** object as a UV coordinates projector for the day/night division on the planet surface and for the red colored transition zone (the red terminator) in the `Atmosphere` layer.

6
Creating More Complex Man-made Materials

In this chapter, we will cover the following recipes:

- ▶ Creating cloth materials with procedurals
- ▶ Creating a leather material with procedurals
- ▶ Creating a synthetic sponge material with procedurals
- ▶ Creating a spaceship hull shader

Introduction

In this chapter, we will see some more complex artificial materials, starting with the relatively simpler materials. Remember that the procedure is basically the same as that for all the materials we have seen so far—the generic shader followed by the color pattern or the bump effect (one or more), depending on the preponderance of the different components.

The only difference is the level of complexity they can reach (for example, look at the *Creating a spaceship hull shade* recipe at the end of this chapter).

Creating cloth materials with procedurals

In this recipe, we will create a generic cloth material, as shown in the following screenshot:

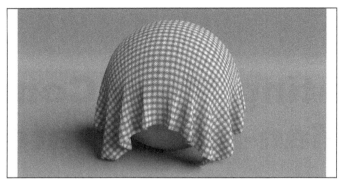

The cloth material as it appears in the final rendering

Getting ready

Before we start creating the material, let's set up the scene by performing the following steps:

1. Start Blender and load the `9931OS_cloth_start.blend` file. In the scene, there is already a cloth simulation.

2. Click on the **Play animation** button in the **Timeline** toolbar (or press *Alt + A*) to see the simulation running and being cached in real time. It consists of a Plane (our fabric) draped on a UV Sphere leaning on a bigger Plane (the floor).

3. After the simulation has been totally cached (a total of 100 frames), in the **Physics** window (the last tab to the right) under the **Cloth Cache** tab, press the **Current Cache to Bake** button to save the simulation. The 100-frame simulation is now cached and saved inside a folder (unless differently specified), named as a blend file, and stored on your hard drive in the same directory as the blend file.

From now on, there is no need to perform calculations about the simulation anymore. Blender will read the simulation data from that cache folder, so it will be possible to quickly scroll through the **Timeline** bar and immediately reach any frame inside the cached range.

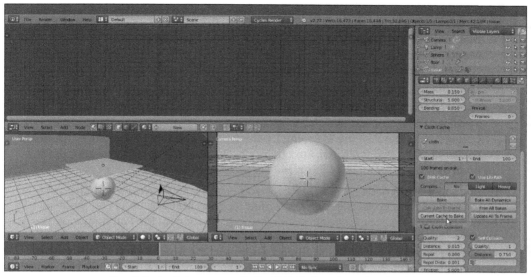

The cloth simulation scene with the Cloth Cache subpanel to the right

How to do it...

Now we are going to create the material on the fabric Plane, which has been first unwrapped by assigning a basic UV layer (**Object data | UV Maps**) and later subdivided by the **Specials** menu. This is done before the cloth simulation by performing the following steps:

1. Go to the **100** frame.

2. Make sure you have the **fabric** Plane selected. Click on **New** in the **Material** window under the main **Properties** panel or in the **Node Editor** window. Rename the new material cloth_generic.

3. In the **Material** window, switch the **Diffuse BSDF** node with a **Mix Shader** node. In the first **Shader** slot, select a **Diffuse BSDF** node, and in the second **Shader** slot, select a **Glossy BSDF** shader node.

4. Set the **Diffuse BSDF** node's **Roughness** value to 1.000. Set the **Glossy BSDF** node's **Roughness** value to 0.500. Change the **Glossy BSDF** node's **Color** values of **R** to 0.800, **G** to 0.730, and **B** to 0.369. Set the **Fac** value of the **Mix Shader** node to 0.160.

5. Add one **Texture Coordinate** node (press *Shift + A* and navigate to **Input | Texture Coordinate**) and two **Mapping** nodes (press *Shift + A* and navigate to **Vector | Mapping**). In the **Properties** panel (press *N*) of the **Node Editor** window, label the two **Mapping** nodes as Mapping1 and Mapping2. Then connect the UV output of the **Texture Coordinate** node to the **Vector** input sockets of both the **Mapping** nodes.

6. Now add two **Wave Texture** nodes (press *Shift + A* and navigate to **Texture | Wave Texture**) and a **Noise Texture** node (press *Shift + A* and navigate to **Texture | Noise Texture**). Label the first two nodes as Wave Texture1 and Wave Texture2. Connect the output of the **Mapping1** node to the **Vector** input sockets of the **Wave Texture1** node and the **Noise Texture** node. Connect the output of the **Mapping2** node to the **Vector** input of the **Wave Texture2** node.

7. Add three **Math** nodes (press *Shift + A* and navigate to **Converter | Math**), one for each texture node. Set their **Operation** mode to **Multiply** and label them as Multiply1, Multiply2 and Multiply3. Then connect the **Fac** output of the **Wave Texture1** node to the first **Value** input socket of the **Multiply1** node, the **Wave Texture2** node to the **Multiply2** node, and the **Noise Texture** node to the **Multiply3** node. Set the second **Value** input socket of the **Multiply1** and **Multiply2** nodes to 1.000, and leave the **Multiply3** node as 0.500.

8. Go to the **Mapping2** node and set the **Rotation** value of **Y** to 90°. Go to the **Wave Texture** nodes, and for both of them, set the **Scale** value to 100.000, **Distortion** to 2.000, and **Detail Scale** to 2.000. For the **Noise Texture** node, set the **Scale** value to 80.000 and the **Distortion** value to 5.000.

9. Add a new **Math** node (press *Shift + A* and navigate to **Converter | Math**) and set **Operation** to **Subtract**. Connect the output of the **Multiply1** and **Multiply2** nodes to the first and the second **Value** input sockets, respectively.

10. Press *Shift + D* to duplicate the last **Math** node. Set the **Operation** mode to **Add**. Connect the output of the **Subtract** node to its first **Value** socket and the output of the **Multiply3** node to the second **Value** input socket.

11. Press *Shift + D* to duplicate a **Multiply** node, label it as Multiply4, and connect the output of the **Add** node to the first **Value** input socket. Set the second **Value** input socket to 0.050. Connect the last **Multiply** node's output to the **Displacement** input socket of the **Material Output** node.

12. Add a **Frame** (press *Shift + A* and navigate to **Layout | Frame**). Press *Shift* and select the two **Mapping** nodes, the three textures, all the **Math** nodes, and then the **Frame**. Press *Ctrl + P* to parent them. Label the frame as BUMP, as shown in the following screenshot:

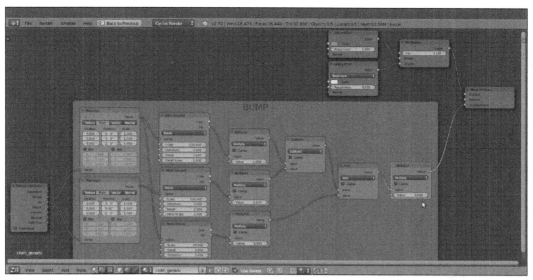

The shader and the network for the fabric bump pattern

13. Add two new **Mapping** nodes (press *Shift + A* and navigate to **Vector | Mapping**). Label them as Mapping3 and Mapping4. Then add two **Wave Texture** nodes (press *Shift + A* and navigate to **Texture | Wave Texture**). Label them as Wave Texture3 and Wave Texture4. As before, connect the **UV** output of the **Texture Coordinate** node to both the **Mapping3** and **Mapping4** nodes, and the output sockets of the latter to the new **Wave Texture** nodes.

14. Go to the **Mapping3** node. Set the **Rotation** value of **Z** to -45° and the **Scale** value of **Y** to 2.000. In the **Mapping4** node, set the **Rotation** value of **Z** to 45° and the **Scale** value of **X** to 2.000. Go to the two **Wave Texture** nodes to set the **Scale** value to 10.900 and the **Detail** value to 0.000.

15. Add two **ColorRamp** nodes (press *Shift + A* and navigate to **Converter | ColorRamp**) and label them as ColorRamp1 and ColorRamp2. Connect the **Fac** output of the **Wave Texture3** to the **Fac** input socket of the **ColorRamp1** node, and the **Fac** output of the **Wave Texture4** node to the **Fac** input socket of the **ColorRamp2** node.

16. Add a **MixRGB** node (press *Shift + A* and navigate to **Color | MixRGB**). Connect the **Color** output of the two **ColorRamp** nodes to the **Color1** and **Color2** input sockets of the **MixRGB** node. Set **Blend Type** to **Multiply** and the **Fac** value to 1.000.

17. Connect the **Color** output of the **Multiply-MixRGB** node to the **Color** input socket of the **Diffuse BSDF** shader node.

18. Add a **Frame** (press *Shift + A* and navigate to **Layout | Frame**). Press *Shift* and select the new nodes and then the **Frame**. Press *Ctrl + P* to parent them. Rename the **Frame** COLOR, as shown in the following screenshot:

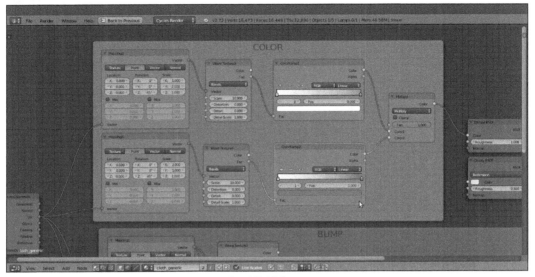

The COLOR frame

19. At this point, we can change the colors inside the two **ColorRamp** gradients to obtain colored patterns. In my example, I set the **ColorRamp1** colors ranging from pure white going to a light blue, and violet for the **ColorRamp2** node.

How it works...

▸ From steps 1 to 3, we just made the basic shader by mixing a rough **Diffues BSDF** shader (**Roughness** to 1.000) with a light glossy shader (the low **Fac** value of the **Mix Shader** node shows a lot more of the diffuse component than the glossy component)

▸ From steps 4 to 10, we built the bump texture of the fabric by mixing two **Wave Texture** nodes in different orientations and by adding a bit of noise

▸ From steps 11 to 18, we built a simple cross-color pattern

There's more...

A lot of variations can be obtained by setting different values for the bump and using different texture nodes and combinations for the color pattern, as shown in the following screenshot:

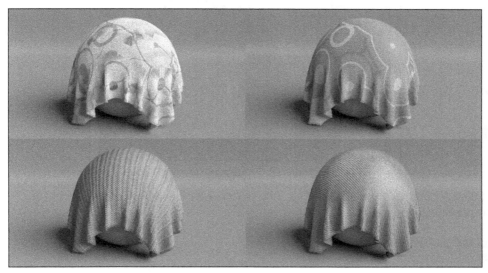

Different color patterns of the cloth material

 All of these examples are included in the `9931OS_06_cloth.blend` file provided with this book.

See also

To learn more about Blender cloth simulation, you can take a look at the online Blender documentation at `http://wiki.blender.org/index.php/Doc:2.6/Manual/Physics/Cloth`.

Creating a leather material with procedurals

In this recipe, we will create a leather-like material, as shown in the following screenshot:

The leather-like material assigned to Suzanne and three wallet-like, simple objects

Start Blender and load the `99310S_06_start.blend` file, where there is already an unwrapped Suzanne mesh.

How to do it...

Now we are going to create the material by performing the following steps:

1. Click on **New** in the **Material** window under the main **Properties** panel or in the **Node Editor** toolbar. Rename the new material `Leather_dark`.

2. In the **Material** window, switch the **Diffuse BSDF** node with a **Mix Shader** node (label it as `Mix Shader2`). In its first **Shader** slot, select a **Mix Shader** node again (label it as `Mix Shader1`), and in the second slot, load an **Anisotropic BSDF** shader node.

3. Add a **Fresnel** node (press *Shift + A* and navigate to **Input | Fresnel**) and connect it to the **Fac** input sockets of both the **Mix Shader** nodes. Set the **IOR** value to `1.490`.

4. Set the **Anisotropic BSDF** node's color to pure white and the **Roughness** value to `0.100`. Add a **Tangent** node (press *Shift + A* and navigate to **Input | Tangent**). Connect it to the **Tangent** input socket of the **Anisotropic BSDF** shader, and in its **Method to use for the Tangent** slot, select the **UV Map** item. Optionally, click on the blank slot to the right to select the name of the UV layer to be used (this is useful if the mesh has two or more UV layers).

5. Add a **Diffuse BSDF** shader (press *Shift + A* and navigate to **Shader | Diffuse BSDF**) and a **Glossy BSDF** shader node (press *Shift + A* and navigate to **Shader | Glossy BSDF**). Connect the **Diffuse BSDF** node to the first **Shader** input socket of the **Mix Shader1** node and the **Glossy BSDF** node to the second **Shader** input socket. Set the **Diffuse BSDF** node's **Roughness** value to 0.800. Set the **Glossy BSDF** distribution to **Beckmann**, **Color** to pure white, and its **Roughness** value to 0.300.

6. Add an **RGB** node (press *Shift + A* and navigate to **Input | RGB**) and connect its **Color** output to the **Color** input socket of the **Diffuse BSDF** node. Change the **Color** values of **R** to 0.100, **G** to 0.080, and **B** to 0.058, as shown in the following screenshot:

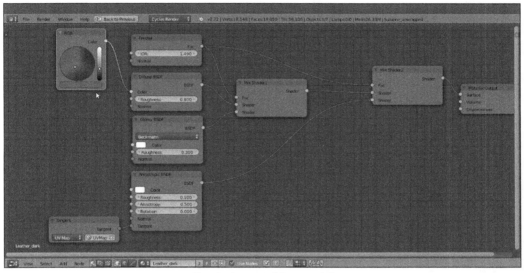

The shader part of the material

7. Add a **Texture Coordinate** node (press *Shift + A* and navigate to **Input | Texture Coordinate**) and two **Mapping** nodes (press *Shift + A* and navigate to **Vector | Mapping**). Connect the **Object** output of the **Texture Coordinate** node to the **Vector** input sockets of both the **Mapping** nodes (label them as Mapping1 and Mapping2). Then in the **Mapping2** node, change the **Rotation** value of **Y** value to 90°.

8. Add two **Voronoi Texture** nodes (press *Shift + A* and navigate to **Texture | Voronoi Texture**) and two **Wave Texture** nodes (press *Shift + A* and navigate to **Texture | Wave Texture**). Place them in a column next to the **Mapping** nodes in this order from top to bottom: **Voronoi Texture1**, **Wave Texture1**, **Voronoi Texture2**, and **Wave Texture2**.

9. Set the **Voronoi Texture1** node's **Coloring** to **Cells** and the **Scale** value to 60.000. Go to the **Wave Texture1** node and set the **Scale** value to 10.000, the **Distortion** value to 10.000, **Detail** to 16.000, and **Detail Scale** to 0.300. Set the **Scale** value of the **Voronoi Texture2** node to 10.000, and copy and paste the values from the **Wave Texture1** node to the **Wave Texture2** node.

10. Now connect the **Mapping1** node output to the **Vector** input sockets of the two **Voronoi Texture** nodes and the **Wave Texture1** node. Connect the output of the **Mapping2** node to the **Vector** input socket of the **Wave Texture2** node.

11. Add a **MixRGB** node (press *Shift + A* and navigate to **Color | MixRGB**). Set the **Blend Type** to **Difference** and the **Fac** value to 1.000. Connect the **Color** output of the **Wave Texture1** node to the **Color2** input socket of the **Difference** node, and the **Color** output of the second **Voronoi Texture2** node to its **Color1** input socket.

12. Label the **Difference** node as **Difference1**. Then press *Shift + D* to duplicate it. Label the duplicate as Difference2 and connect the **Color** output of the **Voronoi Texture2** node to its **Color2** input socket. Connect the **Color** output of the **Wave Texture2** node to the **Color1** input socket of the **Difference2** node.

13. Press *Shift + D* to duplicate the **Difference** node again, change its **Blend Type** to **Multiply** and label it as Multiply1. Connect the output of the **Difference1** node to the **Color1** input socket of the **Multiply1** node. Then connect the output of the **Difference2** node to the **Color2** input socket of the **Multiply1** node.

14. Add a **Math** node (press *Shift + A* and navigate to **Converter | Math**), label it as **Multiply3**, and connect the output of the **Multiply1** node to the first **Value** input socket. Set the second **Value** input socket to 0.100.

15. Press *Shift + D* to duplicate the **Multiply3** node, label it as Multiply2, and connect the **Color** output of the **Voronoi Texture1** node to the first **Value** input socket. Set the second **Value** input socket to -0.200.

16. Press *Shift + D* to duplicate the **Multiply2** node, label it as Add, and change **Operation** to **Add** as well. Connect the output of the **Multiply2** and **Multiply3** nodes to the two **Value** input sockets.

17. Add two **Bump** nodes (press *Shift + A* and navigate to **Vector | Bump**). Label them as Bump1 and Bump2. Then connect the **Bump1** to the **Normal** input sockets of both the **Diffuse BSDF** and **Glossy BSDF** shader nodes. Connect the **Bump2** node to the **Normal** input of the **Anisotropic BSDF** shader. Set the **Strength** value of the **Bump1** node to 0.500 and the **Strength** value of the **Bump2** node to 0.250. Connect the output of the **Add** node to the **Height** input sockets of both the **Bump** nodes.

18. Add a **ColorRamp** node (press *Shift + A* and navigate to **Converter | ColorRamp**). Paste it between the first **Difference1** node and the **Multiply1** node. Set **Interpolation** to **B-Spline** and move the white color stop to the 0.255 position. Label it as ColorRamp1.

19. Press *Shift + D* to duplicate the **ColorRamp1** node, label it as `ColorRamp2`, and paste it between the **Difference2** node and the **Multiply1** node, as shown in the following screenshot:

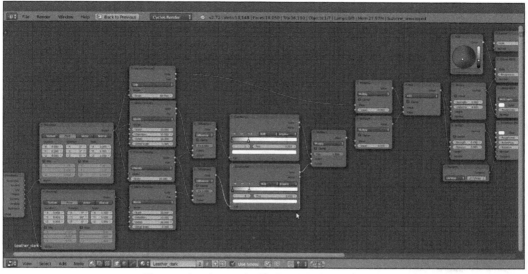

The completed network with the added bump pattern

How it works...

▶ From steps 1 to 6, we built the basic shader for the leather material.

▶ From steps 7 to 19, we built the bump pattern for the leather. We used two different **Bump** nodes with different values for the **Diffuse BSDF** and **Glossy BSDF** nodes and for the **Anisotropic BSDF** shader, to have slightly different light reflections on the surface.

Note that we used the **UV Map** layer information of the mesh for the **Tangent** node to be connected to the **Anisotropic BSDF** shader, and the **Object** mapping node for the bump textures instead.

Actually, we could have used the **UV** mapping output for the texture nodes too, because the mesh had already been unwrapped. However, the scale values for all the nodes in that case would have been double and the flow of the textures on the polygons would have been different (based on the flow of the unwrapped faces in the **UV** window).

Creating a synthetic sponge material with procedurals

In this recipe, we will create a polyurethane sponge material (the type that you usually find in kitchens), as shown in the following screenshot:

The synthetic sponge material when rendered

Getting ready

Follow these steps to create a synthetic sponge material with procedurals:

1. Start Blender and switch to the **Cycles Render** engine.

2. Select the default Cube, and in the **Transform** subpanel to the right of the 3D viewport (under **Dimensions**), change the values of **X** to 0.350, **Y** to 0.235, and **Z** to 0.116. Press *Ctrl + A* to apply the scale.

3. With the mouse arrow in the 3D viewport, add a Plane to the scene (press *Shift + A* and navigate to **Mesh | Plane**). Exit **Edit Mode**, and in the **Transform** subpanel (the **Dimensions** item), set the values of **X** to 20.000 and **Y** to 20.000. Press *Ctrl + A* to apply the scale. Move the Plane down (press *G*, then press *Z*, enter -0.05958, and then press *Enter*) to act as the floor for the sponge.

4. Select the **Lamp** item. In the **Object data** window, click on the **Use Nodes** button and change the type to **Sun**. Set the **Size** to 0.500, **Color** to pure white, and the **Strength** value to 5.000. In the **Transform** panel, set the values of **Rotation** value of **X** to 15°, **Y** to 0°, and **Z** to 76°.

5. Select the **Camera** item, and in the **Object data** window under the **Lens** subpanel, change the **Focal Length** value to 60.000. In the **Transform** subpanel, set the values of the **Location** value of **X** to 0.82385, **Y** to -0.64613, and **Z** to 0.39382. Change the **Rotation** values of **X** to 68°, **Y** to 0°, and **Z** to 51°.

6. Go to the **World** window and click on the **Use Nodes** button under the **Surface** subpanel. Click on the little square with a dot on the right side of the color slot, and from the menu, select **Sky Texture**. Change **Sky Type** to **Preetham** and set the **Strength** value to 0.100.

7. Go to the **Render** window, and under the **Sampling** subpanel, set the **Clamp Direct** and **Clamp Indirect** values to 1.00. Set **Samples** for **Render** and **Preview** to 50.

8. Split the 3D viewport into two rows. Convert the upper row to a **Node Editor** window. Split the bottom view into two parts and convert the left part to another 3D viewport. With the mouse arrow in the left 3D view, press 0 on the numeric keypad to go to the **Camera** view.

9. Select the **Cube**, and with the mouse arrow in the **Camera** view, press *Shift + S*. Navigate to **Cursor to Selected** to place the cursor on the pivot of the Cube (if it's elsewhere). Add **Lattice** to the scene (press *Shift + A* and select **Lattice**). Press *Tab* to exit **Edit Mode**. In the **Transform** subpanel, under **Scale**, set the values of **X** to 0.396, **Y** to 0.264, and **Z** to 0.129. Go to the **Object data** window, and in the **Lattice** subpanel set the **U**, **V**, and **W** values to 3.

10. Reselect the **Cube** and go to the **Object modifiers** window. Assign a **Subdivision Surface** modifier, switch the type of subdivision algorithm from **Catmull-Clark** to **Simple**, and set the **Subdivisions** value to 2 for both **View** and **Render**.

11. Assign a **Bevel** modifier and set the **Width** value to 0.0010. Assign a **Lattice** modifier, and in the empty **Object** field, select the **Lattice** name. Reselect the **Lattice** object and press *Tab* to enter **Edit Mode**. Select the **Lattice** vertices that are indicated in the following screenshot:

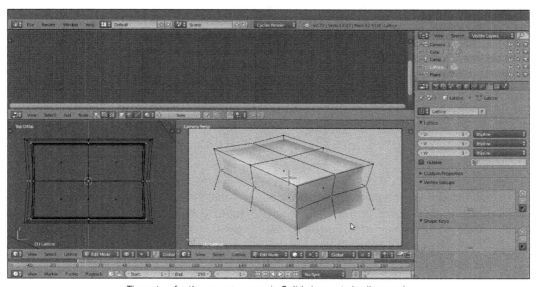

The setup for the sponge scene in Solid viewport shading mode

12. Scale the selected vertices on the *x* and *y* axes to slightly smaller values (press *S*, then press *Shift + Z*, enter digit *.9*, and press *Enter*). Then scale only the upper vertices to slightly smaller values, and similarly scale other vertices to obtain a shape similar to a kitchen sponge. Then exit **Edit Mode** (press *Tab*).

13. Reselect the **Cube**, navigate to **Tool Shelf | Tools | Shading**, and select **Smooth**. With the mouse arrow in the 3D view, press *N* and *T* to close the **Transform** and **Tool Shelf** panels. Go to the **Material** window.

How to do it...

Now let's create the material by performing the following steps:

1. First, select the **Plane** and click on **New** in the **Material** window under the main **Properties** panel or in the **Node Editor** toolbar. In the **Material** window, switch the **Diffuse BSDF** node with a **Mix Shader** node. In the first **Shader** slot, select a **Diffuse BSDF** node, and in the second **Shader** slot, select a **Glossy BSDF** shader node. Set **Distribution** of the **Glossy BSDF** shader to **Beckmann**, the **Fac** value of the **Mix Shader** to 0.400, and the **Diffuse BSDF** node's **Color** to a shade of blue (in my case, **R** to 0.110, **G** to 0.147, and **B** to 0.209).

2. Now select the **Cube** object and click on **Use Nodes** in the **Material** window under the main **Properties** panel or in the **Node Editor** window's toolbar. Rename the new material sponge_polyurethane.

3. In the **Material** window, switch the **Diffuse BSDF** node with a **Mix Shader** node. In the **Label** slot in the **Node** subpanel under the **Properties** panel of the **Node Editor** window (if this is not present, press the *N* key to make it appear), label it as Mix Shader1. Go to the **Material** window, and in the **Mix Shader1** node's first **Shader** slot, select a **Mix Shader** node again. Label it as Mix Shader2. In the second **Shader** slot, select an **Add Shader** node.

4. In the first **Shader** slot of the **Mix Shader2** node, select a **Diffuse BSDF** shader node, and in the second slot, a **Velvet BSDF** node. Set the **Diffuse BSDF** node's **Roughness** value to 1.000 and the **Velvet** node's **Sigma** value to 0.600.

5. Connect the output of the **Velvet** shader to the first **Shader** input of the **Add Shader** node. In its second **Shader** input, load a **Glossy BSDF** shader and set the **Roughness** value to 0.350.

6. Add a **Fresnel** node (press *Shift + A* and navigate to **Input | Fresnel**) and connect it to the **Fac** input socket of the **Mix Shader1** node. Set the **IOR** value to 1.496. Add an **RGB** node (press *Shift + A* and navigate to **Input | RGB**) and connect its output to the **Color** input sockets of the **Diffuse BSDF**, **Velvet**, and **Glossy BSDF** shader nodes. Set the **RGB** node's **Color** of **R** to 0.319, **G** to 1.000, and **B** to 0.435 (any other color is also fine), as shown in the following screenshot:

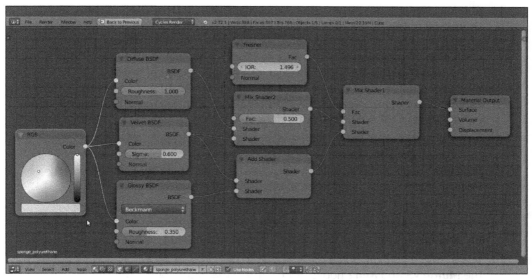

The basic shader component

7. Add a **Texture Coordinate** node (press *Shift + A* and navigate to **Input | Texture Coordinate**), a **Mapping** node (press *Shift + A* and navigate to **Vector | Mapping**), two **Voronoi Texture** nodes (press *Shift + A* and navigate to **Texture | Voronoi Texture**), and two **Noise Texture** nodes (press *Shift + A* and navigate to **Texture | Noise Texture**). Label the textures as `Voronoi Texture1`, `Voronoi Texture2`, `Noise Texture1`, and `Noise Texture2`.

8. Place the four textures in a row. Then connect the **Object** output of the **Texture Coordinate** node to the **Vector** input socket of the **Mapping** node, and the **Vector** output of this node to the **Vector** input sockets of the four texture nodes.

9. Set the **Scale** value of the **Voronoi Texture1** node to `38.000`, the **Voronoi Texture2** node to `62.300`, the **Noise Texture1** node to `300.000`, and the **Noise Texture2** node to `900.000`.

10. Add three **ColorRamp** nodes (press *Shift + A* and navigate to **Converter | ColorRamp**). Label them as `ColorRamp1`, `ColorRamp2`, and `ColorRamp3`. Connect the **Color** output of the **Voronoi Texture1** node to the **Fac** input socket of the **ColorRamp1** node, the **Color** output of the **Voronoi Texture2** node to the **Fac** input socket of the **ColorRamp2** node, and the **Color** output of the **Noise Texture1** node to the **Fac** input socket of the **ColorRamp3** node.

11. Add four **Math** nodes (press *Shift + A* and navigate to **Converter | Math**). Set **Operation** to **Multiply** and label them as `Multiply1`, `Multiply2`, `Multiply3`, and `Multiply4`. Connect the **Color** output of the three **ColorRamp** nodes to the first **Value** input socket of the first three **Multiply-Math** nodes, and the **Color** output of the **Noise Texture2** node to the first **Value** input socket of the **Multiply4** node. Set the second **Value** input socket of the **Multiply1** and **Multiply2** nodes to `1.000`, the second **Value** input socket of the **Multiply3** node to `0.100`, and the second **Value** input socket of the **Multiply4** node to `0.050`.

12. Add a **MixRGB** node (press *Shift + A* and navigate to **Color | MixRGB**). Connect the output of the **Multiply1** node to the **Color1** input socket and the output of the **Multiply2** node to the **Color2** input socket. Change **Blend Type** to **Add** and the **Fac** value to `1.000`. Label the **Add-MixRGB** node as `Add1`.

13. Press *Shift + D* to duplicate the **Add1** node, and label it as `Add2`. Connect the output of the **Add1** node to the **Color1** input socket. Then connect the output of the **Multiply3** node to the **Color2** input socket of the **Add2** node.

14. Press *Shift + D* to duplicate the **Add2** node, and label it as `Add3`. Paste it between the **Multiply3** and **Add2** nodes, and connect the output of the **Multiply4** node to the **Color2** input socket of the **Add3** node.

15. Add a new **Math** node (press *Shift + A* and navigate to **Converter | Math**), set **Operation** to **Multiply**, and label it as `Multiply5`. Connect the output of the **Add2** node to the first **Value** input socket of the **Multiply5** node, and set the second **Value** input socket to `1.000`.

16. Connect the output of the **Multiply5** node to the **Displacement** input socket of the `Material Output` node, as shown in the following screenshot:

The bump pattern

17. Now box-select (press the *B* key and then click and drag the selection to enclose the objects) the **ColorRamp1**, **ColorRamp2**, **Multiply1**, **Multiply2**, **Add1**, **Add2**, and **Multiply5** nodes. Press *G* and move them to the right to make room for new nodes on the left side.

18. Add an **RGB Curves** node (press *Shift + A* and navigate to **Color | RGB Curves**) and paste it between the **Voronoi Texture1** node and the **ColorRamp1** node. Label it as `RGB Curves1`. Click on the curve to add a control point, and in the coordinate slots below the node window, set the **X** value to `0.26111` and the **Y** value to `0.50000`. Click to add a second control point. Set **X** to `0.73889` and **Y** to `0.51111`.

19. Press *Shift + D* to duplicate the **RGB Curves1** node. Paste it between the **Voronoi Texture2** and **ColorRamp2** nodes. Label it as `RGB Curves2`.

20. Go to the **ColorRamp1** node and move the white color stop to the `0.240` position. Then go to the **ColorRamp2** node and repeat this step. Next, go to the **ColorRamp3** node, move the white color stop to the `0.550` position, and set **Interpolation** to **Ease**, as shown in the following screenshot:

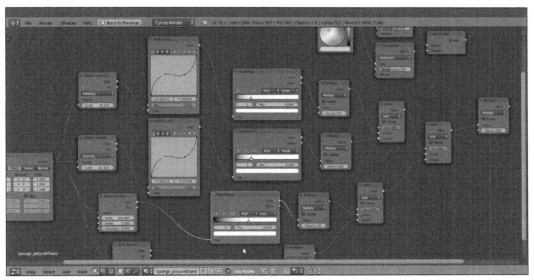

Tweaking the bump pattern

How it works...

▶ From steps 2 to 6, we built the basic shader for the sponge material and the color. As you can see in the **Rendered** camera view, without the bump pattern, there is a visible artifact in the more distant side of the mesh. This is due to the **Smooth** shading we set in step 13 of the *Getting ready* section. Setting the shading to **Flat** again would remove the artifact, but would also show the blocky faces of the deformed sponge mesh. In this case, because of the bump pattern and the fact that the mesh is subdivided, this is not a major issue, and both solutions (smooth but with artifacts or flat but blocky) are fine.

▸ From steps 7 to 20, we built the sponge bump pattern by mixing **Voronoi Texture** nodes at different sizes, with increased contrast due to the **ColorRamp** nodes. Then we add some noise to avoid a highly smoothed surface.

Creating a spaceship hull shader

In this recipe, we will create a spaceship hull material. We will add random, tiny light windows based on the values of procedural textures, and the spaceship's logo as if it were painted in red on the hull, as shown in the following screenshot:

The final, rendered spaceship hull material assigned to a displaced Torus primitive

Getting ready

To start creating this spaceship hull, we need the spaceship and space first. Follow these steps to build a quick and easy model and set up the scene:

1. Start Blender and switch to the **Cycles Render** engine. Select the default **Cube** and delete it.

2. With the mouse arrow in the 3D view, press *Shift + A* and add a **Torus** primitive (press *Shift + A* and navigate to **Mesh | Torus**). In **Edit Mode**, scale it to at least twice its current size (press *A* to select all the vertices, then type *S*, enter *2*, and press *Enter*).

3. Exit **Edit Mode**, and in **Outliner**, select the **Lamp** object. In the **Object data** window, change it to **Sun**. Then set the **Size** value to 0.050. Click on the **Use Nodes** button and set the **Strength** value to 10.000. Change the **Color** value of **RGB** to 0.800.

4. Go to the **World** window and click on the **Use Nodes** button under the **Surface** subpanel. Click on the little square with a dot to the right of the **Color** slot. From the menu, select **Sky Texture**. Set the **Strength** to 0.100.

5. Select the **Camera**, and in the **Transform** panel, set the **Location** values of **X** to 6.10677, **Y** to -0.91141, and **Z** to -2.16840. Set the **Rotation** values of **X** to 112.778°, **Y** to -0.003°, and **Z** to 81.888°.

6. Go to the **Render** window, and under the **Sampling** subpanel, set the **Samples** to 25 for **Preview** and 100 for **Render**. Then set the **Clamp Indirect** value to 1.00, but let the **Clamp Direct** value remain as 0.00. Go to the **Film** subpanel and check the **Transparent** item. Then set the output **File Format** to **RGBA**.

7. Under the **Light Paths** subpanel, disable both the **Reflective** and **Refractive** **Caustics** items. Set **Filter Glossy** value to 1.00. Under the **Performance** subpanel, set the **Viewport BVH Type** to **Static BVH** (this should speed up the rendering a bit, considering the fact that the model is static and doesn't change shape). Check the **Persistent Images** and **Use Spatial Splits** items.

8. Press *N* with the mouse arrow in the 3D view to close the **Properties** panel. Then press *T* to get rid of the **Tool Shelf** panel. Split the 3D view into two rows. Convert the upper row to a **Node Editor** window.

9. Split the bottom window into two parts. Convert the left part to a **UV/Image Editor** window. Select **Torus** and press *Tab* to go to **Edit Mode**. In the window toolbar, change the selection mode to **Face select**. Select only one face on the mesh (whichever you prefer). Press the *A* key twice to select all the faces, and keep the first face selected as the active face. Then press the *U* key. In the **UV Mapping** pop-up menu, select the **Follow Active Quads** item, and then in the next pop-up menu set **Even** as **Edge Length Mode**. Click on the **OK** button.

10. With the mouse arrow in the **UV/Image Editor** window, press *A* to select all the vertices of the UV islands. Then scale them to one-third of their current size (press *S*, enter digit *.3*, and press *Enter*). Press *Tab* to exit **Edit Mode**, and change **UV/Image Editor** to **3D View**. Convert the right 3D viewport to a **Camera** view by pressing the *0* key on the numeric keypad (with the mouse arrow in the 3D view).

11. Go to the **Object modifiers** window and assign a **Subdivision Surface** modifier to **Torus**. Set the **Subdivisions** level to 4 for both **View** and **Render**. Set the **Camera** view mode to **Rendered** and go to the **Material** window.

How to do it...

Now let's start creating the material. The steps to create a basic hull shader are as follows:

1. Click on **New** in the **Material** window under the main **Properties** panel or in the **Node Editor** toolbar. Rename the new material spacehull.

2. In the **Material** window, switch the **Diffuse BSDF** node with a **Mix Shader** node. Label it as `Mix Shader1`. In the first **Shader** slot, select a new **Mix Shader** node (label it as `Mix Shader2`), and in the second slot, select an **Anisotropic BSDF** node.

3. In the first **Shader** slot of the **Mix Shader2** node, select a **Diffuse BSDF** node, and in the second slot, select a **Glossy BSDF** node. Set the **Distribution** of both the **Glossy BSDF** and **Anisotropic BSDF** nodes to **Ashikmin-Shirley**.

4. In the **Anisotropic BSDF** shader node, set the **Rotation** value to `0.250`. In the **Diffuse BSDF** node, set the **Roughness** value to `0.500`.

5. Add a new `Mix Shader` node (press *Shift + A* and navigate to **Shader | Mix Shader**) and paste it between the **Mix Shader1** and the **Material Output** nodes. Label it as `Mix Shader_Spec_Amount` and connect the output of the **Diffuse BSDF** node to the first **Shader** input socket (so that the link from the **Mix Shader2** node automatically switches to the second socket). Set the **Fac** value to `0.300`.

6. Add a **Fresnel** node (press *Shift + A* and navigate to **Input | Fresnel**). Connect its output to the **Fac** input sockets of the **Mix Shader1** and **Mix Shader2** nodes. Set the **IOR** value to `100.000`.

7. Add a **Frame** (press *Shift + A* and navigate to **Layout | Frame**). Press *Shift* and select all the nodes except the **Material Output** node. Then select the **Frame** and press *Ctrl + P* to parent all of them. Label the frame as `SHADER`, as shown in the following screenshot:

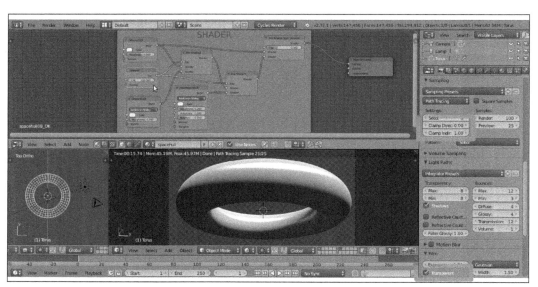

The SHADER frame

The steps to create hull's panels are as follows:

8. Add a **Texture Coordinate** node (press *Shift + A* and navigate to **Input | Texture Coordinate**), a **Mapping** node (press *Shift + A* and navigate to **Vector | Mapping**), two **Image Texture** nodes (press *Shift + A* and navigate to **Texture | Image Texture**), and one **Musgrave Texture** node (press *Shift + A* and navigate to **Texture | Musgrave Texture**).

9. Label the textures as `Image Texture1_Hull`, `Image Texture2_Hull`, and `Musgrave Texture_Hull`. Place them in a column.

10. Press *Shift + D* to duplicate the **Mapping** node twice. Label the nodes as `Mapping1_Hull`, `Mapping2_Hull`, and `Mapping3_Hull`. Place them in a column to the left of the texture nodes. Connect the UV output of the **Texture Coordinate** node to the **Vector** input sockets of the three **Mapping** nodes. Connect the **Vector** output of each of the **Mapping** nodes to the **Vector** input socket of each of the texture nodes.

11. Click on the **Open** button in the **Image Texture1_Hull** node to load image `spacehull.png`. Then click on the little arrows to the left of the **Open** button in the **Image Texture2_Hull** node to select the same image texture. Go to the **Musgrave Texture** node and set the **Scale** value to `115.500`, the **Detail** value to `4.500`, the **Dimension** value to `0.200`, and the **Lacunarity** value to `0.600`.

12. Go to the **Mapping1_Hull** node and set the **Scale** value of **X** to `2.000`, **Y** to `4.000`, and **Z** to `6.000`. Then go to the **Mapping2_Hull** node and set the **Scale** value of **Y** to `2.000` and **Z** to `3.000`. Next, go to the **Mapping3_Hull** node and set the **Scale** value of **Z** to `0.100`.

13. Add a **MixRGB** node (press *Shift + A* and navigate to **Color | MixRGB**). Set **Blend Type** to **Multiply** and the **Fac** value to `1.000`. Label it as `Multiply1_Hull`. Then connect the **Color** output of the **Image Texture1_Hull** node to the **Color1** input socket and the **Color** output of the **Image Texture2_Hull** node to the **Color2** input socket.

14. Press *Shift + D* to duplicate the **Multiply1_Hull** node, change **Blend Type** to **Overlay**, and label it as `Overlay_Hull`. Set the **Fac** value to `0.050`. Connect the output of the **Multiply1_Hull** node to the **Color1** input socket and the **Color** output of the **Musgrave Texture** node to the **Color2** input socket.

15. Add a **ColorRamp** node (press *Shift + A* and navigate to **Converter | ColorRamp**), label it as `ColorRamp_Hull`, and connect the output of the **Overlay_Hull** node to its **Fac** input socket. Move the black color stop to the `0.500` position.

16. Add a **Bump** node (press *Shift + A* and navigate to **Vector | Bump**), label it as `Bump_Hull`, and connect the output of the **Multiply1_Hull** node to the **Height** input socket. Set the **Strength** value to `0.400`.

17. Add a **Frame** (press *Shift + A* and navigate to **Layout | Frame**). Press *Shift* and select the three **Mapping** nodes, the two **Image Texture** nodes, the **Musgrave Texture** node, the **Bump** node, the **ColorRamp** node, the two **MixRGB** nodes, and then the **Frame**. Press *Ctrl + P* to parent them. Label the frame as HULL, as shown in the following screenshot:

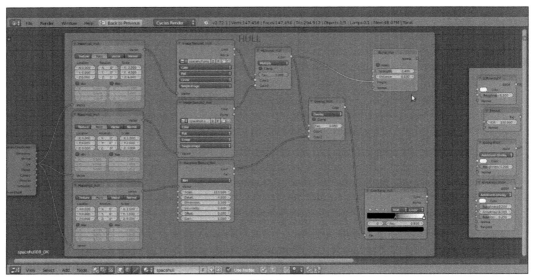

The HULL frame

18. Connect the **Normal** output of the **Bump_Hull** node to the **Normal** input sockets of the **Diffuse BSDF**, **Glossy BSDF**, and **Anisotropic BSDF** nodes inside the **SHADER** frame. Then connect the output of the **Overlay_Hull** node to the **Color** input sockets of the same **Diffuse BSDF**, **Glossy BSDF**, and **Anisotropic BSDF** nodes. Next, connect the **Color** output of the **ColorRamp_Hull** node to the **Roughness** input sockets of the **Glossy BSDF** and **Anisotropic BSDF** shader nodes, as shown in this screenshot:

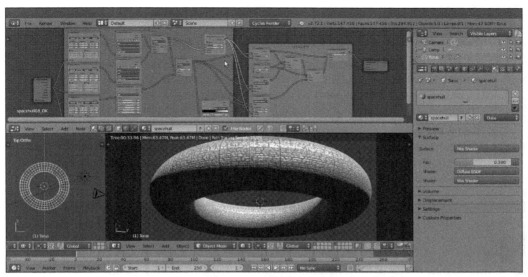

The output of the HULL frame connected to the SHADER frame nodes

The steps to create hull's logo are as follows:

19. Add a new **Mapping** node (press *Shift + A* and navigate to **Vector | Mapping**) and a new **Image Texture** node (press *Shift + A* and navigate to **Texture | Image Texture**). Label them as `Mapping4_Name` and `Image Texture3_Name`, respectively. Connect the UV output of the **Texture Coordinate** node to the **Mapping4_Name** node, and the output of this node to the **Vector** input socket of the **Image Texture_Name** node.

20. Click on the **Open** button of the **Image Texture** node and load the `spacehull_name.png` image, an image texture of the ARGUS logo with a transparent background (alpha channel).

21. Go to the **HULL** frame and add a **MixRGB** node (press *Shift + A* and navigate to **Color | MixRGB**). Label it as `Mix_Hull_Name` and paste it between the **Overlay_Hull** node and the **Diffuse BSDF** shader node. Then connect its **Color** output to the **Color** input socket of the **Glossy BSDF** and **Anisotropic BSDF** shader nodes.

22. Connect the **Color** output of the **Image Texture_Name** node to the **Color2** input socket of the **Mix_Hull_Name** node. Then connect the **Alpha** output of the **Image Texture_Name** node to the **Fac** input socket of the **Mix_Hull_Name** node.

23. Go to the **Mapping4_Name** node and check both the **Min** and **Max** items. Then set the **Location** value of **X** to -3.300 and **Y** to 1.000. Set the **Scale** value of **Y** to 2.500. (These values depend on the scale and location you want for your logo on the spaceship; just experiment looking at the real-time-rendered preview.)

24. Add a **Frame** (press *Shift + A* and navigate to **Layout | Frame**). Press *Shift* and select the **Mapping4_Name** node, the **Image Texture3_Name** node, and then the **Frame**. Press *Ctrl + P* to parent them. Label the frame as NAME, as shown in the following screenshot:

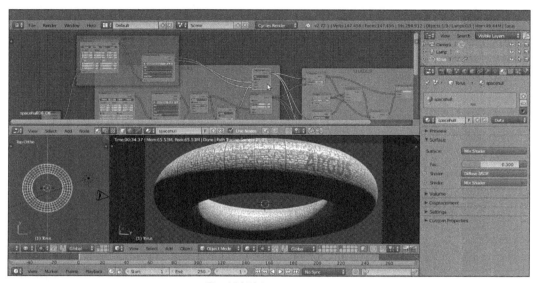

The ARGUS logo on the hull

The steps to create the windows are as follows:

25. Add a new **Mapping** node (press *Shift + A* and navigate to **Vector | Mapping**) and two **Image Texture** nodes (press *Shift + A* and navigate to **Texture | Image Texture**). Label them as Mapping5_Windows, Image Texture4_Windows, and Image Texture5_Windows. Connect the **Texture Coordinate** node's **UV** output and the **Mapping** node's output to the **Image Texture** nodes as usual. Then set the **Mapping** node's **Scale** values to 10.000 for the three axes.

26. Click on the **Open** button of the **Image Texture4_Windows** node and load the spacehull_windows_lights.png image. Then click on the **Open** button of the **Image Texture5_Windows** node and load the spacehull_windows_bump.png image. Set **Color Space** for both the image nodes to **Non-Color Data**.

27. Add two **MixRGB** nodes (press *Shift + A* and navigate to **Color | MixRGB**). Set **Blend Type** to **Multiply** and **Fac** values to `1.000.` for both the nodes Label them as `Multiply2_Windows_Light` and `Multiply2_Windows_Bump`. Connect the output of the **Image Texture4_Windows** node to the **Color1** input socket of the **Multiply2_Windows_Light** node, and the output of the **Image Texture5_Windows** node to the **Color1** input socket of the **Multiply2_Windows_Bump** node.

28. Add a **ColorRamp** node (press *Shift + A* and navigate to **Converter | ColorRamp**), label it as `ColorRamp_Windows`, and move the black color stop to the `0.919` position. Connect the output of the **Multiply2_Windows_Light** node to its **Fac** input socket.

29. Add a new **Bump** node (press *Shift + A* and navigate to **Vector | Bump**), label it as `Bump_Windows`, and connect the output of the **Multiply2_Windows_Bump** node to the **Height** input socket. Set the **Strength** value to `50.000`.

30. Add a **Frame** (press *Shift + A* and navigate to **Layout | Frame**). Press *Shift* and select the **Mapping5_Windows** node, the **Image Texture4_Windows** and **Image Texture5_Windows** nodes, the two **MixRGB** nodes, the **ColorRamp_Windows** and the **Bump_Windows** nodes, and then the **Frame**. Press *Ctrl + P* to parent them. Label the frame as **WINDOWS**, as shown in the following screenshot:

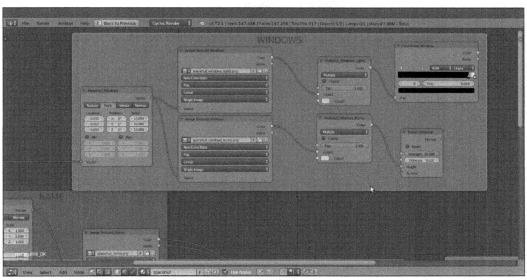

The WINDOWS frame

31. Add a **Vector Math** node (press *Shift + A* and navigate to **Converter | Vector Math**) and set **Operation** to **Average**. Connect the **Normal** output of the **Bump_Windows** node inside the **WINDOWS** frame to the first **Vector** input socket, and the **Normal** output of the **Bump_Hull** node inside the **HULL** frame to the second **Vector** input socket. Then connect the **Normal** output of the **Average Bump_Hull** node to the **Normal** input sockets of the **Diffuse BSDF**, **Glossy BSDF**, and **Anisotropic BSDF** shader nodes, as shown in this screenshot:

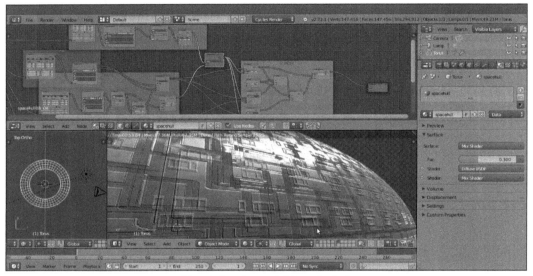

The windows bump visible on the hull

The steps to create the location mask for the windows are as follows:

32. Add one more **Mapping** node (press *Shift + A* and navigate to **Vector | Mapping**) and four **Checker Texture** nodes (press *Shift + A* and navigate to **Texture | Checker Texture**). Connect the **Texture Coordinate** node and the nodes as usual. Then label them as `Mapping6_Mask`, `Checker Texture1_Mask`, `Checker Texture2_Mask`, `Checker Texture3_Mask`, and `Checker Texture4_Mask`. In all, the four **Checker Texture** nodes change **Color2** to pure black.

33. Add a **MixRGB** node (press *Shift + A* and navigate to **Color | MixRGB**), set **Blend Type** to **Screen** and **Fac** value to `1.000`, and label it as `Screen_Mask`. Connect the **Color** output of the **Checker Texture1_Mask** node to the **Color1** input socket of the **Screen_Mask** node, and the **Color** output of the **Checker Texture2_Mask** node to the **Color2** input socket.

34. Press *Shift + D* to duplicate the **MixRGB** node, change the duplicate node's **Blend Type** to **Add**, and label it as `Add_Mask1`. Connect the output of the **Screen_Mask** node to the **Color1** input socket. Then connect the **Color** output of the **Checker Texture3_Mask** node to the **Color2** input socket.

35. Press *Shift + D* to duplicate the **Add_Mask1** node, and label the duplicate as `Add_Mask2`. Connect the output of the **Add_Mask1** node to the **Color1** input socket. Then connect the **Color** output of the **Checker Texture4_Mask** node to the **Color2** input socket.

36. Add a **ColorRamp** node and label it as `ColorRamp_Mask`. Connect the output of the **Add_Mask2** node to its **Fac** input socket. Then move the black color stop to the `0.100` position and the white color stop to the `0.000` position. Set **Alpha** of the black color stop to `0.000`.

37. Go to the **Checker Texture** nodes. Set the **Scale** value for the **Checker Texture1_ Mask** node to `1.600`, the **Checker Texture2_Mask** node to `8.800`, the **Checker Texture3_Mask** node to `3.000`, and the **Checker Texture4_Mask** node to `9.700`. Go to the **Mapping6_Mask** node and set the **Scale** values to `0.500` for all the three axes.

38. Add a **Frame** (press *Shift + A* and navigate to **Layout | Frame**). Press *Shift* to select the recently added nodes and then the **Frame**. Press *Ctrl + P* to parent them. Rename the frame as `MASK WINDOWS` as shown in the following screenshot:

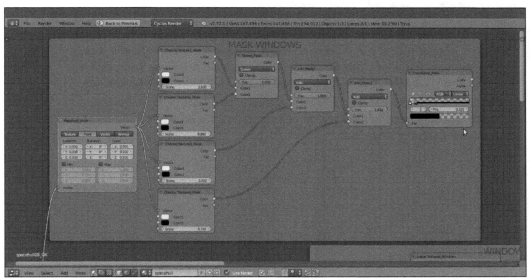

The MASK WINDOWS frame

The steps to create the final connections are as follows:

39. Connect the **Color** output of the **ColorRamp_Mask** node to the **Color2** input sockets of both the **Multiply2_Windows_Lights** and **Multiply2_Windows_Bump** nodes, as shown in this screenshot:

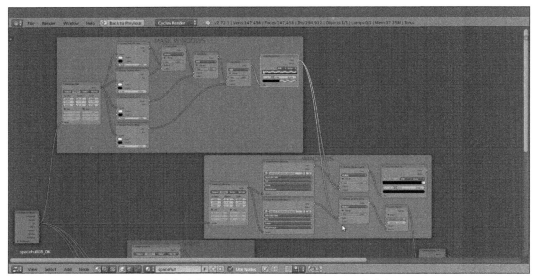

The MASK WINDOWS frame output connected to the WINDOWS frame nodes

40. Go to the **SHADER** frame and add a **Mix Shader** node (press *Shift + A* and navigate to **Shader | Mix Shader**). Label it as `Mix Shader3` and paste it between the **Mix Shader_Spec_Amount** and the **Material Output** nodes.

41. Connect the **Color** output of the **ColorRamp_Windows** node inside the **WINDOWS** frame to the **Fac** input socket of the **Mix Shader3** node, as shown in the following screenshot:

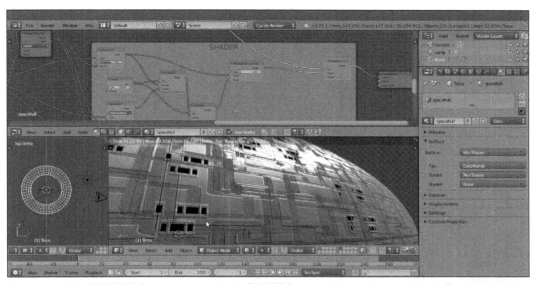

The output of the WINDOWS frame connected to the SHADER frames nodes and the result in the Rendered preview

The steps to create the light emitter for the windows are as follows:

42. Inside the **SHADER** frame, add an **Emission** shader node (press *Shift + A* and navigate to **Shader | Emission**), a **ColorRamp** node (press *Shift + A* and navigate to **Converter | ColorRamp**), and an **Object Info** node (press *Shift + A* and navigate to **Input | Object Info**). Label the **ColorRamp** node as `ColorRamp_Lights_Colors`, change **Interpolation** to **Constant**, and add six more color stops (eight total). Change the color values alternatively of **R** to `0.800`, **G** to `0.517`, **B** to `0.122`; and **R** to `0.800`, **G** to `0.198`, and **B** to `0.040` (or any other color you prefer).

43. Connect the **Random** output of the **Object Info** node to the **Fac** input socket of the **ColorRamp** node, and the output of this node to the **Color** input socket of the **Emission** node.

44. Connect the **Emission** node's output to the second **Shader** input socket of the **Mix Shader3** node. Then set **Strength** to 3.000, as shown in the following screenshot:

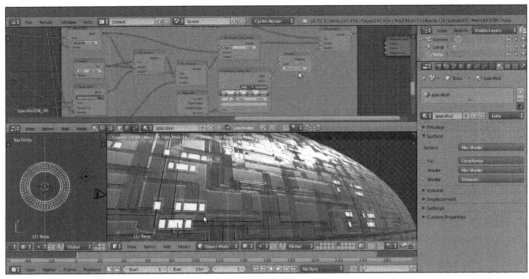

The windows on the hull getting illuminated by the ColorRamp_Lights_Colors node and an Emission node output connected to the SHADER output

How it works...

> From step 1 to step 7, we built the general shader for the metallic hull, which is similar to the metal node group we saw in *Chapter 4, Creating Man-made Materials in Cycles*. This was achieved by mixing **Diffuse BSDF** and **Glossy BSDF** shaders with an **Anisotropic BSDF** node on a ground with a quite high **IOR** value (100.000), and through the usual **Mix Shader** nodes. We added one more **Mix Shader** node (**Mix Shader_Spec_Amount**) to include the possibility of setting more specularity than anisotropy, and vice versa.

▸ From step 8 to step 18, we built the **HULL** frame group by superimposing two differently scaled versions of the same image. Then they could be used for the color, bump, and specular components. These components were obtained by contrasting the paneling through a **ColorRamp** node and then going straight to the **Glossy BSDF** shader's roughness and the **Anisotropic BSDF** shader, to add a metallic look. The mixture of both **Glossy BSDF** and **Anisotropic BSDF** is made on the ground of a **Fresnel** node set to `100.000`. A very high value like this is needed because the specularity is then mixed again with the **Diffuse BSDF** component to the purpose to obtain a slider to tweak the effect.

▸ From step 19 to step 24, we added the red hull's logo, ARGUS, using its own alpha channel to overimpose it on the hull surface's panels..

▸ From step 25 to step 30, we built the **WINDOWS** frame group.

▸ In step 31, we merged (averaged) the bump effect of the windows with the bump effect of the hull's panels.

▸ From step 32 to step 38, we made the masking for the windows to give them a random appearance.

▸ From step 39 to step 41, we simply connected the various frames' output.

▸ From step 42 to step 44, we created the light-emitting material for the windows. Note that the **WINDOWS_ MASK** frame group provides the masking for the windows' positions. The **WINDOW** frame group provides the whiteness values for the windows, the bump, and the last nodes added to the **SHADER** frame the light emission based on the output of the previous frame groups.

There's more...

The appearance of the hull can be improved even further using some displacement to add geometric details to the spaceship surface, which (at the moment) is a bit too smooth:

1. Go to the **Object modifiers** window and assign a second **Subdivision Surface** modifier to **Torus**. Set the **Subdivisions** levels to 2 for both **View** and **Render**.

2. Assign a **Displace** modifier. Then click on the **Show texture in texture tab** button on the right side of the **Texture** slot. In the **Textures** window, click on the **New** button. Then replace the default **Clouds** texture with an **Image or Movie** texture.

3. Click on the **Open** button and load the `spacehull_displ.exr` texture.

4. Go back to the **Object modifiers** window and set the displacement's **Strength** value to `0.200`. In the **Texture Coordinates** slot, select **UV**.

This way, the displacement features get mixed with the hull bump panels of the shader, giving a nice result. The `spacehull_displ.exr` texture is a 32-bit float displacement map created and stored in the **Blender Internal** engine. I modeled the Planes and scaled Cubes a simple **greeble** panel, then I baked the displacement on a different and unwrapped Plane, as shown in the following screenshot:

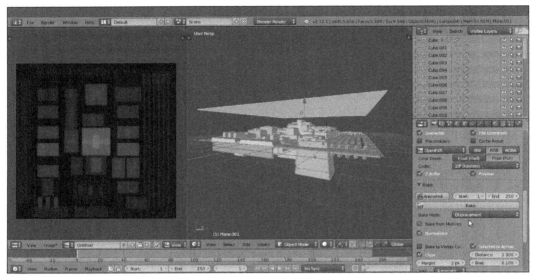

The greeble scene ready for the baking

If you want to take a look at the baking scene, open the `99310S_06_greeble.blend` file.

Finally, we can try to set the first **Subdivision Surface** modifier level to 4 and lower the second **Subdivision Surface** modifier's level to 1. Then, starting from the top one, apply all the modifiers. You will inevitably lose the details but will obtain a much lighter mesh—589,824 faces against the initial 2,359,296—and considering the fact that most of the details come from the texturing, the result looks pretty good (at least from a distance). It also looks good if the shading is set to **Flat** instead of **Smooth**.

The Torus spaceship with the applied modifiers

See also

▸ The displacement technique on the Blender Artists forum, at `http://blenderartists.org/forum/showthread.php?273033-Sculpting-with-UVs-and-displacements`.

7
Subsurface Scattering in Cycles

In this chapter, we will cover the following recipes:

- ▶ Using the Subsurface Scattering shader node
- ▶ Simulating Subsurface Scattering in Cycles using the Translucent shader
- ▶ Simulating Subsurface Scattering in Cycles using the Vertex Color tool
- ▶ Simulating Subsurface Scattering in Cycles using the Ray Length output in the Light Path node
- ▶ Creating a fake Subsurface Scattering node group

Introduction

Subsurface Scattering is the effect of light not getting directly reflected by a surface but penetrating it and bouncing internally before getting absorbed or leaving the surface at a nearby point. In short, light is *scattered*.

The RGB channels of a surface color can have different scattering values, depending on the material; for example, for human skin the red component is more scattered (as a rough approximation, you could say that the values for the three channels are blue = 1, green = 2, and red = 4).

In Cycles, a true Subsurface Scattering node has been introduced in Blender 2.67. Since Version 2.72, it also works with the GPU (only in the Experimental feature set).

But sadly, it still has the common big Cycles problem—it takes a lot of samples to produce a noise-free rendering. In short, it's slow.

Besides the true node, there are other ways to simulate Subsurface Scattering in Cycles. All the recipes in this chapter faking the SSS effect use the **Translucent** shader node to achieve this effect, and shifting of colors is simulated by giving a main color to the translucent component. Keep in mind that even if the scattering effect in the true SSS node could be basically considered a sort of translucency effect, these tricks are not comparable to the real Subsurface Scattering effect. They are just ways to give the impression that light is being scattered through a material surface.

Also, depending on the recipe, you'll see that the effects of Subsurface Scattering can be quite different, and the more suitable method should be used according to the type of material you are going to create. The differences in these recipes are basically in the way translucency mixing is driven by different types of input.

Using the Subsurface Scattering shader node

Let's first see how the true **Subsurface Scattering** node works in Cycles, and an example is given in the following screenshot:

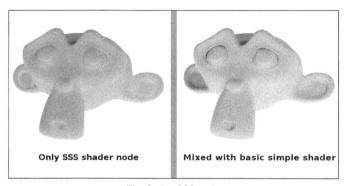

The Cycles SSS node

Getting ready

To see how the true **Subsurface Scattering** node works, let's first use it as the only component of the shader, and later mix it with a basic diffuse-glossy shader.

Let's start by setting the Plane under Suzanne as a light emitter to enhance the backlight effect of the SSS effect:

1. Start Blender and open the 99310S_07_start.blend file, where there is an unwrapped Suzanne mesh leaning on a Plane, with two mesh-light emitters and the Camera as shown in the following screenshot:

Screenshot of the provided 99310S_07_start.blend file

2. Go to **Outliner** and select the **Plane** object. As you can see in the **Node Editor** window, it has an already set material called `Plane`.

3. Go to the **Material** window under the main **Properties** panel, and in the **Surface** subpanel, switch the **Diffuse BSDF** shader with an **Emission** shader as shown in the following screenshot:

Switching the Diffuse BSDF shader with an Emission shader through the Material window

4. Set the **Strength** value to 5.000.

5. With the mouse arrow in the viewport, press *Shift + Z* to go to the **Rendered** view.

How to do it...

Now let's begin creating the SSS material using the following steps:

1. Select **Suzanne** and click on the **New** button in the **Surface** subpanel under the **Material** window in the main **Properties** panel, or in the **Node Editor** window.

2. Using only the **Material** window, replace the **Diffuse BSDF** shader with a **Subsurface Scattering** node as shown in the following screenshot:

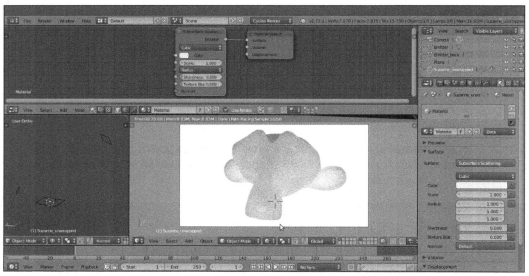

The Rendered preview of Suzanne with the SSS node as the material

As you can see, the scattering effect is clearly visible in the **Rendered** preview, but actually, it's so strong that all the facial features of poor Suzanne are confused and result in a jelly-like, muddish material.

By default, the **Scale** value of the **Subsurface Scattering** node is set to 1.000, evidently a bit too high for an object that is supposed to be 2 meters tall (remember that by default, one Blender unit is supposed to be equal to 1 real world meter).

3. Gradually lower the **Scale** parameter, either in **Node Editor** or in the **Material** window, to select a value in the range of 0.100 to 0.200. In my case, I arrived at 0.150. Now some of Suzanne's facial features are clearly discernible, as shown in the following screenshot:

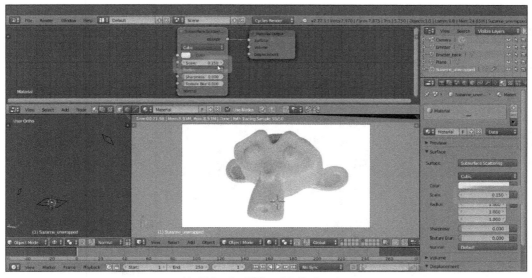

Modifying the SSS node's Scale value

4. Click on the **Radius** button on the node interface in the **Node Editor** window (or directly in the **Material** window), and change the values of **R** to 4.000, **G** to 2.000, and **B** to 1.000 as shown in the following screenshot:

Modifying the SSS node's Radius values

5. Lower the **Scale** value to 0.070; set the **Sharpness** value to 1.000; and click on the **Color** box to set values of **R** to 1.000, **G** to 0.500, and **B** to 0.250.

6. Rename the material SSS_01 and save the file as SSS_material, as shown in the following screenshot:

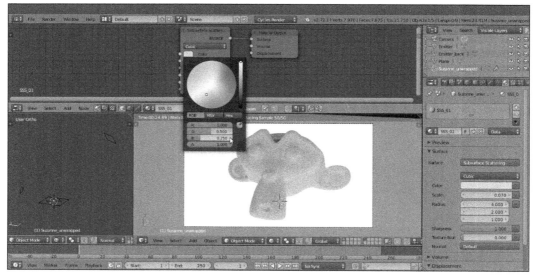

Setting a flesh color for the Suzanne SSS

7. Now click on the **F** icon to the right side of the **Material datablock** name to enable the *fake user*. Then click on the number **2** icon and rename the new material SSS_02. Enable the *fake user* for this material as well.

8. Add an **Add Shader** node (press Shift + A and navigate to **Shader** | **Add Shader**) and paste it between the **SSS** node and the **Material Output** node.

9. Add a **Mix Shader** node (press *Shift + A* and navigate to **Shader** | **Mix Shader**), and connect it to the first **Shader** input socket of the **Add Shader** node so that the previous connection coming from the **SSS** node automatically switch to the second **Shader** input socket.

10. Add a **Diffuse BSDF** node and a **Glossy BSDF** shader node (press *Shift + A* and navigate to **Shader** | **...**), and connect them to the first and to the second **Shader** input sockets of the **Mix Shader** node respectively, as shown in the following screenshot:

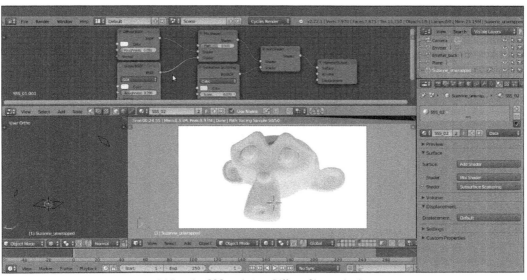

Adding the SSS node to a Diffuse-Glossy shader

11. Add a **Layer Weight** node (press *Shift + A* and navigate to **Input | Layer Weight**) and connect its **Facing** output to the **Fac** input socket of the **Mix Shader** node. Set the **Blend** value to 0.800.

12. Add an **RGB** node (press *Shift + A* and navigate to **Input | RGB**) and connect its output to the **Color** input sockets of the **Diffuse BSDF**, **Glossy BSDF**, and **SSS** nodes. Set the **RGB** node's **Color** values for **R** to 1.000, **G** to 0.500, and **B** to 0.250 as shown in the following screenshot:

Setting the same flesh color for all the shader nodes

13. Save the file.

Let's try now a slightly different setting, with two sliders for the mixture of **SSS** and basic shaders. We will also give distinct colors to the **Diffuse BSDF**, **Glossy BSDF**, and **SSS** components of the shader to highlight their distribution on the mesh.

1. First, select the **Plane** object, and in the **Material** window, switch the **Emission** shader with a **Diffuse BSDF** shader node.

2. Reselect **Suzanne** and click on the number **2** button close to the **Material datablock** name. Rename the new material SSS_03. Then enable the *fake user* for this material as well.

3. Delete the **RGB** node. Then set the **Diffuse BSDF** shader node's **Color** values for **R** to 0.031, **G** to 0.800, and **B** to 0.000 (bright green); and the **Glossy BSDF** node's **Color** values for **R** to 0.646, **G** to 0.800, and **B** to 0.267 (yellow). Set the **Glossy BSDF** node's **Roughness** value to 0.200 and **Distribution** to **Beckmann**. Set the **Subsurface Scattering** shader node's **Color** values for **R** to 0.800, **G** to 0.086, and **B** to 0.317 (a vivid pink). Change **Falloff** from **Cubic** to **Gaussian**.

4. Label the **Mix Shader** node as Mix Shader1, press *Shift + D* to duplicate it, and label the duplicate as Mix Shader2. Paste it between the **Add Shader** and **Material Output** nodes.

5. Connect the **Mix Shader1** node's output to the first **Shader** input socket of the **Mix Shader2** node so that the connection from the **Add Shader** automatically switches to the second **Shader** input socket.

6. Press *Shift + D* to duplicate the **Mix Shader2** node, label the duplicated node as Mix Shader3, and paste it between the **Mix Shader2** and the **Material Output** nodes.

7. Connect the output of the **Subsurface Scattering** node to the second **Shader** input socket of the **Mix Shader3** node as shown in the following screenshot:

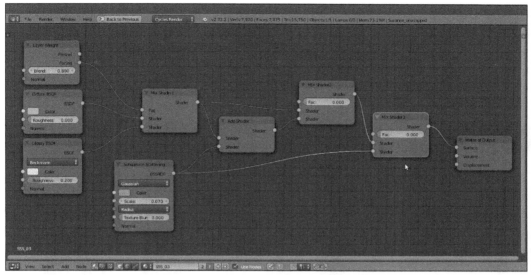

Adding one more Mix Shader node to further tweak the SSS amount

8. Save the file as SSS_material_02.blend.

How it works...

The scattering amount for the three **RGB** color channels is set in the **Radius** item on the node interface, while **Scale** is to set the dimensions the object would have in the real world. Starting with a default value of 1.000, the **Scale** value must usually be proportionally inverse lowered. The bigger the object desired in the real world, the lower the **Scale** value in the node. Otherwise, the scattering effect may become too strong.

The best way to mix the **Subsurface Scattering** node with the rest of any shader is by using the **Add Shader** node. However, with this node, it's not possible to establish the amount of influence of the **SSS** on the shader, so a trick must be performed. The Diffuse-Glossy component of the shader is again mixed with the output of the **Add Shader** node, through a **Mix Shader** node.

In the previously explained SSS_03 material, there are two **Mix Shader** nodes that can be used to tweak the influence of the effect. By raising their **Fac** values, it's also possible to switch from total absence to full scattering effect, as shown in the following compilation of screenshots:

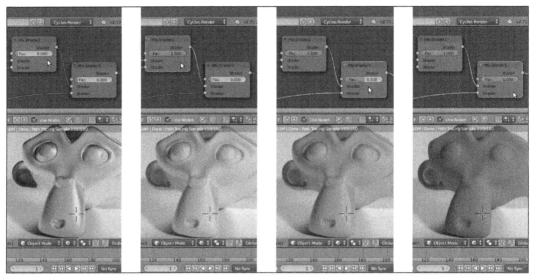

Different effects of different Fac values of the last Mix Shader node

See also

▸   Refer to http://en.wikipedia.org/wiki/Subsurface_scattering

Simulating Subsurface Scattering in Cycles using the Translucent shader

In this recipe, we will create a fake Subsurface Scattering material using the Translucent BSDF shader node as shown in the following screenshot:

The rendered result of the fake SSS of this recipe

As someone suggested, this material could actually be quite good to make candles.

Getting ready

Start Blender and open the 99310S_07_start.blend file:

1. Go to the **Render** window, and in the **Sampling** subpanel, click on the **Method to sample lights and materials** button to switch from **Path Tracing** to **Branched Path Tracing**. Enable the **Square Samples** item, and under **AA Samples**, set the **Render** value to 8. Finally, click on the **Pattern** button to select the **Correlated Multi-Jitter** item.

2. Save the file as 99310S_SSS_translucent.blend.

How to do it...

Let's go ahead and create the material using the following steps:

1. Select the **Suzanne** object and click on the **New** button in the **Node Editor** window toolbar, or in the **Material** window to the right. Rename the material `SSS_translucent`.

2. In the **Material** window, switch the **Diffuse BSDF** shader with a **Mix Shader** node. In the first **Shader** slot, select a **Diffuse BSDF** shader again, and in the second slot, select a **Glossy BSDF** shader node.

3. Set the **Diffuse BSDF** shader node's **Color** values for **R** to `0.031`, **G** to `0.800`, and **B** to `0.000`. Set the **Glossy BSDF** node's **Color** values for **R** to `0.646`, **G** to `0.800`, and **B** to `0.267`. Set the **Glossy BSDF** node's **Roughness** value to `0.200` and **Distribution** to **Beckmann**.

4. Select the **Mix Shader** node and go to the **Properties** side-panel of the **Node Editor** window (if not present, move the mouse to the **Node Editor** window and press the *N* key to make it appear). In the **Label** slot inside the **Node** subpanel, label the **Mix Shader** node as `Mix Shader1`. Then set its **Fac** value to `0.200`.

5. Add a new **Mix Shader** node (press *Shift + A* and navigate to **Shader | Mix Shader**), label it as `Mix Shader2`, and paste it between the **Mix Shader1** node and the **Material Output** node.

6. Add a **Translucent BSDF** node (press *Shift + A* and navigate to **Shader | Translucent BSDF**) and connect it to the second **Shader** input socket of the **Mix Shader2** node. Set the **Color** values of **R** to `0.800`, **G** to `0.086`, and **B** to `0.317`.

7. Add a **Texture Coordinate** node (press *Shift + A* and navigate to **Input | Texture Coordinate**), a **Mapping** node (press *Shift + A* and navigate to **Vector | Mapping**), and a **Noise Texture** node (press *Shift + A* and navigate to **Texture | Noise Texture**).

8. Connect the **UV** output of the **Texture Coordinate** node to the **Vector** input socket of the **Mapping** node, and the output of this node to the **Vector** input socket of the **Noise Texture** node. Set the **Noise Texture** node's **Scale** value to `20.000`.

9. Add a **Bump** node (press *Shift + A* and navigate to **Vector | Bump**) and connect the **Color** output of the **Noise Texture** node to the **Height** input socket of the **Bump** node. Then connect the **Normal** output of this node to the **Normal** input sockets of the **Diffuse BSDF**, **Glossy BSDF**, and **Translucent BSDF** nodes. Leave the **Bump** strength at `1.000`.

10. Add a **Fresnel** node (press *Shift + A* and navigate to **Input | Fresnel**) and connect it to the **Fac** input socket of the **Mix Shader2** node. Set the **IOR** value to 8.000 as shown in the following screenshot:

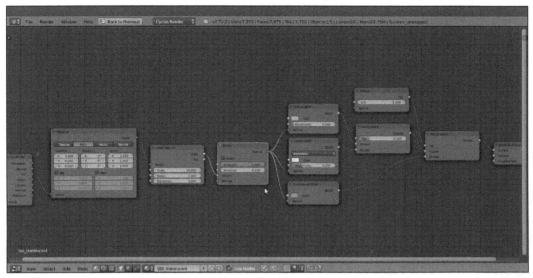

The overall view of the material network

11. Save the file.

How it works...

This is probably the simpler form of the fake Subsurface Scattering effect you can get in Cycles. It is obtained by simply blending a translucent effect with a basic Diffuse-Glossy shader. By varying the amount of the **IOR** value in the **Fresnel** node (set quite high as a starting point), it is possible to establish the amount of translucency on the mesh. We also added a **Noise Texture** bump effect to the material, just to make it appear more jelly-like.

Note that we gave almost complementary colors to the **Diffuse BSDF** and **Translucent BSDF** shaders to show the effect more clearly, but colors similar to each other can work better. Also note that the translucent effect actually follows the direction of the lighting. Try to rotate the **Emitter** and the **Emitter_back** planes around the Suzanne mesh to verify this in real time, through the **Rendered** view as shown in the following screenshot:

A preview of the fake SSS material lit from a different angle

Note that for the three components of the shader (**Diffuse BSDF**, **Glossy BSDF**, and **Translucent BSDF**) we used (and will also use for the following recipes) the same colors of the SSS_03 material. This was done to make an easier comparison between the effects obtained in the recipes.

Simulating Subsurface Scattering in Cycles using the Vertex Color tool

In this recipe, we will create a fake Subsurface Scattering material as shown in the following screenshot, using the Vertex Color tool:

The Rendered result of the vertex color fake SSS material of this recipe

Getting ready

Start Blender and open the 99310S_07_start.blend file.

1. Go to the **Render** window, and in the **Sampling** subpanel, click on the **Method to sample lights and materials** button to switch from **Path Tracing** to **Branched Path Tracing**. Enable the **Square Samples** item, and under **AA Samples**, set the **Render** value to 8. Finally, click on the **Pattern** button to select the **Correlated Multi-Jitter** item.

2. Select the **Suzanne** mesh, click on the **Mode** button in the **Camera** view toolbar, and choose **Vertex Paint** (or just press the *V* key). Now Suzanne goes into **Vertex Paint** mode.

3. Click on the **Paint** item to the left of the **Mode** button and select **Dirty Vertex Colors**. Then press *T*, and in the last operation subpanel (**Dirty Vertex Color**) at the bottom of the **Tool Shelf** panel, set **Blur Strength** to 0.50, **Highlight Angle** to 90°, and **Dirt Angle** to 90°. Enable the **Dirt Only** item as shown in the following screenshot:

A screenshot of Suzanne in Vertex Paint mode and the Dirty Vertex Color values at the bottom of the Tool Shelf

The Suzanne mesh inside the 99310S_07_start.blend file already had a Vertex Color layer named Col. With the previous procedure, we overwrote it.

4. Go to the **Object data** window under the main **Properties** panel to see it in the **Vertex Colors** subpanel. Then go back to **Object Mode** and press *T* to get rid of the **Tool Shelf** panel.

5. Save the file as 99310S_07_SSS_vcol.blend.

How to do it...

After the vertex color preparation, let's go for the material itself by following these steps:

1. Click on the **New** button in the **Node Editor** window toolbar or in the **Material** window under the main **Properties** panel. Rename the material SSS_vcol.

2. In the **Material** window, switch the **Diffuse BSDF** shader with an **Add Shader** node. In the first **Shader** slot, select a **Mix Shader** node. In the second **Shader** slot, select a **Translucent BSDF** shader node. In the **Properties** side panel to the right of the **Node Editor** window, label the **Mix Shader** node as Mix Shader1.

3. Go to the **Mix Shader1** node. In the first **Shader** slot, select a **Diffuse BSDF** shader node. In the second **Shader** slot, select a **Glossy BSDF** shader node. Set the **Glossy BSDF** node's **Roughness** value to 0.450 and **Distribution** to **Beckmann**.

4. Add a **Fresnel** node (press *Shift + A* and navigate to **Input | Fresnel**), connect it to the **Fac** input socket of the **Mix Shader1** node, and set the **IOR** value to 3.850.

5. Set the **Diffuse BSDF** node's **Color** values for **R** to 0.031, **G** to 0.800, and **B** to 0.000 (the same bright green as in the *Simulating Subsurface Scattering in Cycles using the Translucent shader* recipe); and the **Translucent BSDF** node's **Color** values for **R** to 0.800, **G** to 0.086, and **B** to 0.317 (the same pink as in the *Using the Subsurface Scattering shader node* recipe). Set the **Glossy BSDF** node's **Color** values for **R** to 0.646, **G** to 0.800, and **B** to 0.267, again it's the same yellowish color as in the *Using the Subsurface Scattering shader node* recipe).

6. Add a **Texture Coordinate** node (press *Shift + A* and navigate to **Input | Texture Coordinate**), a **Mapping** node (press *Shift + A* and navigate to **Vector | Mapping**), and a **Noise Texture** node (press *Shift + A* and navigate to **Texture | Noise Texture**).

7. Connect the **UV** output of the **Texture Coordinate** node to the **Vector** input socket of the **Mapping** node, and the output of this node to the **Vector** input socket of the **Noise Texture** node. Set the **Noise Texture** node's **Scale** value to 20.000.

8. Add a **Bump** node (press *Shift + A* and navigate to **Vector | Bump**) and connect the **Color** output of the **Noise Texture** node to the **Height** input socket of the **Bump** node. Then connect the **Normal** output of this node to the **Normal** input sockets of the **Diffuse BSDF**, **Glossy BSDF**, and **Translucent BSDF** nodes.

9. Add a new **Mix Shader** node (press *Shift + A* and navigate to **Shader | Mix Shader**), label it as `Mix Shader2`, and paste it between the **Add Shader** and **Material Output** nodes. Then move the connection from the **Add Shader** node to the second **Shader** input socket, and connect the output of the **Mix Shader1** node to the first **Shader** input socket of the **Mix Shader2** node.

10. Add an **Attribute** node (press *Shift + A* and navigate to **Input | Attribute**) and a **ColorRamp** node (press *Shift + A* and navigate to **Converter | ColorRamp**). In the **Name** slot of the **Attribute** node, write the vertex color layer name, that is, `Col`. Then connect the **Color** output of **Attribute** node to the **Fac** input socket of the **ColorRamp** node. In the **ColorRamp** node, move the white color stop to 0.350 position.

11. Add an **RGB Curves** node (press *Shift + A* and navigate to **Color | RGB Curves**) and connect the **Color** output of the **ColorRamp** node to the **Color** input socket of this node. Then connect its **Color** output to the **Fac** input socket of the **Mix Shader2** node.

12. Inside the **RGB Curves** node's interface window, move the first curve control point coordinate values for **X** to 0.00000 and **Y** to 0.88125, and the second point coordinate values for **X** to 1.00000 and **Y** to 1.00000.

13. Save the file. The overall network will be as shown in the following screenshot:

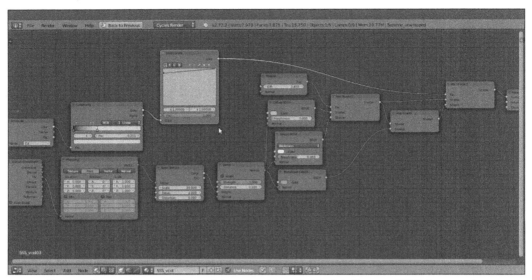

The overall network; note the Vertex Color output intensified by ColorRamp and RGB Curves nodes

How it works...

Compared to the former recipe, in this case, we used information about the Vertex Color, enhanced by the **ColorRamp** node, to drive the mixing of the translucency with the other components of the shader. It's clear that the final result is largely due to vertex painting. We obtained this result quickly through the Dirty Vertex Color tool, but that could also be painted by hands (imagine you're painting a mask for a skull under the face skin).

Simulating Subsurface Scattering in Cycles using the Ray Length output in the Light Path node

In this recipe, we will create a fake Subsurface Scattering material using the **Ray Length** output of the **Light Path** node.

The Rendered result of the fake SSS material of this recipe

Getting ready

Start Blender and open the `99310S_07_start.blend` file.

1. Go to the **Render** window, and in the **Sampling** subpanel, click on the **Method to sample lights and materials** button to switch from **Path Tracing** to **Branched Path Tracing**. Enable the **Square Samples** item, and under **AA Samples**, set the **Render** value to 8. Finally, click on the **Pattern** button to select the **Correlated Multi-Jitter** item.

2. Save the file as `99310S_07_SSS_raylength.blend`.

How to do it...

Let's create the material using the following steps:

1. Select the **Suzanne** object. Click on the **New** button in the **Node Editor** window toolbar or in the **Material** window to the right of the screen. Rename the material `SSS_raylength`.

2. In the **Material** window, switch the **Diffuse BSDF** shader with a **Mix Shader** node. Label it as `Mix Shader1`. In its first **Shader** slot, select a **Diffuse BSDF** shader. In its second **Shader** slot, select a new **Mix Shader** node. Label this node as `Mix Shader2`.

3. Go to the **Mix Shader2** node. In its first **Shader** slot, select a new **Mix Shader** node and label it as `Mix Shader3`. In the second **Shader** slot, select a **Glossy BSDF** node.

4. Add a **Layer Weight** node (press *Shift + A* and navigate to **Input | Layer Weight**) and connect its **Facing** output to the **Fac** input socket of the **Mix Shader1** node. Set the **Blend** value to 0.950.

5. Set the **Fac** value of the **Mix Shader2** node to 0.200 and the **Fac** value of the **Mix Shader3** node to 0.700. Set the **Glossy BSDF** node's **Roughness** to 0.100.

6. Connect the **Diffuse BSDF** node output to the first **Shader** input socket of the **Mix Shader3** node. Add an **Add Shader** node (press *Shift + A* and navigate to **Shader | Add Shader**) and connect it to the second **Shader** input socket of the **Mix Shader3** node.

7. Go to the **Add Shader** node, and in the first **Shader** slot, select the last **Mix Shader** node. Label it as Mix Shader4. In the second **Shader** slot, select a **Translucent BSDF** shader node.

8. Connect the output of the **Diffuse BSDF** node to the first **Shader** input socket of the **Mix Shader4** node, and the output of the **Translucent BSDF** node to the second **Shader** input socket.

9. Set the **Diffuse BSDF** shader node's **Color** values for **R** to 0.031, **G** to 0.800, and **B** to 0.000; the **Glossy BSDF** shader node's **Color** values for **R** to 0.646, **G** to 0.800, and **B** to 0.267; and the **Translucent BSDF** shader node's **Color** values for **R** to 0.800, **G** to 0.086, and **B** to 0.317.

10. Add a **Voronoi Texture** node (press *Shift + A* and navigate to **Texture | Voronoi Texture**) and a **Bump** node (press *Shift + A* and navigate to **Vector | Bump**). Connect the **Color** output of the **Voronoi Texture** node to the **Height** input socket of the **Bump** node and the **Normal** output of this node to the **Normal** input sockets of the **Diffuse BSDF**, **Glossy BSDF**, and **Translucent BSDF** nodes. Set the **Voronoi Texture** node's **Scale** value to 32.600 and the **Bump** node's **Strength** value to 0.100. Then enable the **Invert** item in the **Bump** node.

11. Add a **Light Path** node (press *Shift + A* and navigate to **Input | Light Path**) and a **Math** node (press *Shift + A* and navigate to **Converter | Math**). Set the **Math** node's **Operation** to **Multiply**. Connect the **Ray Length** output of the **Light Path** node to the first **Value** input socket of the **Math** node. Then set the second **Value** input socket to -8.000.

12. Press *Shift + D* to duplicate the **Math** node. Set **Operation** to **Power**. Connect the output of the **Multiply** math node to the first **Value** input socket of this node. Set the second **Value** input socket to 3.000. Enable the **Clamp** item.

13. Press *Shift + D* to duplicate the **Power-Math** node, set **Operation** to **Add**, and connect the output of the **Power** node to its first **Value** input socket. Connect its output to the **Fac** input socket of the **Mix Shader4** node.

14. Connect the **Fac** output of the **Voronoi Texture** node to the second **Value** input socket of the **Add-Math** node.

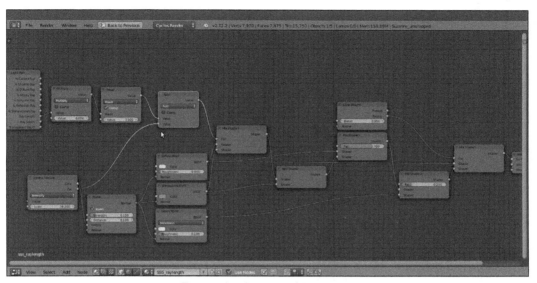

The completed network of the material

15. Save the file.

How it works...

In this recipe, we used the **Ray Length** output of the **Light Path** node to drive the amount of translucency on the mesh. **Ray Length** does exactly what its name suggests. It returns the length of a light ray passing through an object. So basically, it is possible for Cycles to know the thickness of a mesh. On the thicker parts, the translucency will show less or even for nothing, whereas it will be more visible on the thinner parts of the mesh.

 Note that in the shader network, the **Ray Length** output was intensified by a set of **Math** nodes and added to the **Voronoi Texture** node's output. Then it was connected to the factor input of the **Mix Shader** node to drive the blending of the Diffuse and of the Translucent components.

Creating a fake Subsurface Scattering node group

In this recipe, we will create a fake Subsurface Scattering node group that can be mixed with other nodes to add the fake scattering effect to a material. In this screenshot, you can see the effect of the **Subsurface Scattering** node alone on the Suzanne mesh:

The rendered result of the fake SSS node group assigned to Suzanne

In the following screenshot, you can see the effect of the node group added to the usual basic shader material:

Mixed with a Diffuse-Glossy shader

Again, we will use the colors of the previous recipes.

Getting ready

Start Blender and open the `9931OS_07_start.blend` file.

1. Go to the **Render** window, and in the **Sampling** subpanel, click on the **Method to sample lights and materials** button to switch from **Path Tracing** to **Branched Path Tracing**. Enable the **Square Samples** item and under **AA Samples**, set the **Render** value to `8`. Finally, click on the **Pattern** button to select the **Correlated Multi-Jitter** option.

2. Save the file as `9931OS_07_SSS_ngroup.blend`.

How to do it...

Now let's create the material using the following steps:

1. Click on the **New** button in the **Node Editor** window toolbar or in the **Material** window under the main **Properties** panel. In the **Node Editor** window, delete the **Diffuse BSDF** shader node.

2. Add a **Light Path** node (press *Shift + A* and navigate to **Input | Light Path**) and a **Geometry** node (press *Shift + A* and navigate to **Input | Geometry**).

3. Add a **Math** node (press *Shift + A* and navigate to **Converter | Math**). Set **Operation** to **Multiply** and connect the **Ray Length** output of the **Light Path** node to the first **Value** input socket. Set the second **Value** input socket to `-1.500`.

4. Press *Shift + D* to duplicate the **Multiply-Math** node, and set **Operation** to **Power**. Connect the **Multiply-Math** node output to the second **Value** input socket of the **Power** node. Set the first **Value** to `20.000`.

5. Press *Shift + D* to duplicate the **Power** node, and set **Operation** to **Add**. Connect the **Power** node output to the second **Value** input socket of the **Add-Math** node, and the **Is Camera Ray** output of the **Light Path** node to the first **Value** input socket of the **Add-Math** node.

6. Press *Shift + D* to duplicate the **Add** node. Set the **Operation** to **Minimum**. Connect the output of the **Add** node to the first **Value** input socket of the **Minimum** node, and set the second **Value** input socket to `1.000`.

7. Press *Shift + D* to duplicate the **Power** node, and place it after the **Minimum** node. Connect the output of the **Minimum** node to the first **Value** input socket of the duplicated **Power** node.

8. Add a **Value** node (press *Shift + A* and navigate to **Input | Value**), label it as `Contrast`, and connect its output to the second **Value** input socket of the last **Power-Math** node. Set **Value** to `1.200`.

9. Press *Shift + D* to duplicate any of the **Math** nodes, set **Operation** to **Subtract**, and connect the **Backfacing** output of the **Geometry** node to its second **Value** input socket. Set the first **Value** input socket to 1.000.

10. Press *Shift + D* to duplicate the **Subtract** node, set **Operation** to **Add**, and paste it between the first **Add** and **Minimum** nodes. Connect the output of the **Subtract** node to the second **Value** input socket of the last **Add** node.

11. Add a **ColorRamp** node (press *Shift + A* and navigate to **Converter | ColorRamp**) and connect the output of the last **Power-Math** node to its **Fac** input socket. Add a **Translucent BSDF** node (press *Shift + A* and navigate to **Shader | Translucent BSDF**) and connect the **Color** output of the **ColorRamp** node to its **Color** input socket.

12. Set the **ColorRamp** node's **Interpolation** to **B-Spline**. Click on the **Add** button to add a new stop with **Color** values for **R** as 0.500, **G** as 0.500, and **B** as 0.500 at the position of 0.500.

13. Add a **MixRGB** node (press *Shift + A* and navigate to **Color | MixRGB**). Set **Blend Type** to **Overlay** and the **Fac** value to 1.000. Connect the **Color** output of the **ColorRamp** node to the **Color1** input socket. Set **Color2** values for **R** as 0.500, **G** as 0.054, and **B** as 0.077.

14. Connect the **Color** output of the **Overlay** node to the **Color** input socket of the **Translucent BSDF** node. Connect the output of the **Translucent BSDF** node to the **Surface** input socket of the **Material Output** node as shown in the following screenshot:

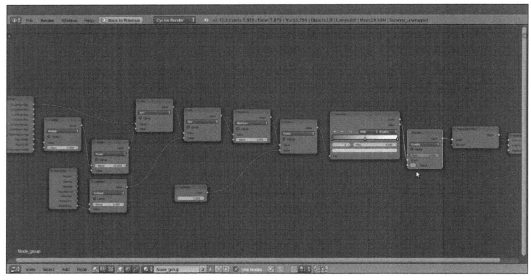

The network to be grouped

15. Now select all the nodes except the **Value** and **Material Output** nodes. Press *Ctrl + G* to create a **Node Group**.

16. Rename the exposed input socket to the left of the node group as `Contrast`, set the value on the group interface, and then delete the original **Value** node.

17. Click and drag the **Color2** socket of the **Overlay** node to the empty socket on the **Group Input** node, and rename the exposed socket as `Subsurface Scattering_color`. Then click and drag the **Normal** socket of the **Translucent BSDF** shader node to the empty socket as shown in the following screenshot:

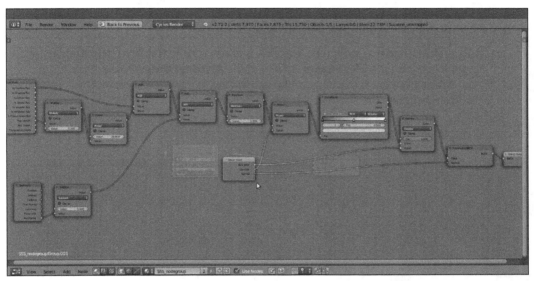

The network inside the open-for-editing node group

18. Press *Tab* to close the node group, and rename it `SSS_group`.

So now, we have made the Subsurface Scattering node group, ready to be mixed with any surface material.

Let's now create a simple material to mix the node group using the following steps:

1. Add a **Mix Shader** node, a **Diffuse BSDF** node, and a **Glossy BSDF** shader node (press *Shift + A* and navigate to **Shader | ...**). Connect the **Diffuse BSDF** node output to the first **Shader** input socket of the **Mix Shader** node and the **Glossy BSDF** shader output to the second **Shader** input socket.

2. Connect the **Mix Shader** output to the **Surface** input socket of the **Material Output** node.

3. Set the **Color** values of the **Diffuse BSDF** shader node for **R** to `0.031`, **G** to `0.800`, and **B** to `0.000`. Set the **Color** values of the **Glossy BSDF** node for **R** to `0.646`, **G** to `0.800`, and **B** to `0.267`.

4. Add a **Voronoi Texture** node (press *Shift + A* and navigate to **Texture | Voronoi Texture**) and a **Bump** node (press *Shift + A* and navigate to **Vector | Bump**). Connect the **Fac** output of the texture node to the **Height** input socket of the **Bump** node, and the **Normal** output of this node to the **Normal** input sockets of the **Diffuse BSDF** and **Glossy BSDF** shaders, and also of the SSS_group node group.

5. Set the **Bump** node's **Strength** to 0.150 and enable the **Invert** item. Set the **Voronoi Texture** node's **Scale** value to 22.500.

6. Add a **Fresnel** node (press *Shift + A* and navigate to **Input | Fresnel**) and connect it to the **Fac** input socket of the **Mix Shader** node. Set the **IOR** value to 3.250.

Now let's simply add the Subsurface Scattering node group:

1. Add an **Add Shader** node (press *Shift + A* and navigate to **Shader | Add Shader**) and paste it between the **Mix Shader** node and the **Material Output** node. Switch the connection from the first socket to the second socket (this is actually not required in this case because the shaders are added anyway).

2. Connect the output of the SSS_group node to the first socket of the **Add Shader** node as shown in the following screenshot:

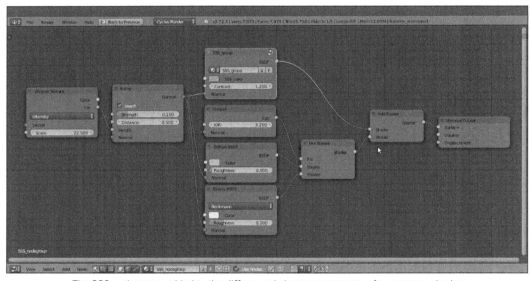

The SSS node group added to the diffuse and glossy components of an average shader

How it works...

The key of this material is obviously the **Light Path** node, with its several kinds of output. In this case, we are interested in two of them:

- The **Ray Length** and **Is Camera Ray** output of the **Light Path** node are added together. **Ray Length** defines the thickness of the mesh, and it's also clamped by the first **Multiply** node and the **Power** node. The **Is Camera Ray** output gets Cycles to render only those surface points that are directly hit by light rays emerging from the Camera. When added to each other, the two types of output produce a stencil effect, gray-scale values distributed according to the thickness of the mesh.

- Next, the **Backfacing** output of the **Geometry** node is added to take into consideration the color of the back mesh faces. All of this is multiplied by the second **Power** node for the **Contrast** value and further clamped by the **ColorRamp** node.

- At this point, the result is mixed with the **Subsurface Scattering_color** output by the **Overlay** node, and finally connected to the **Color** input socket of the **Translucent BSDF** shader, resulting in the semi-transparent-looking shader of the first image at the beginning of this recipe.

8

Creating Organic Materials

In this chapter, we will cover the following topics:

- ▶ Creating an organic-looking shader with procedurals
- ▶ Creating a wasp-like chitin material with procedural textures
- ▶ Creating a beetle-like chitin material with procedural textures
- ▶ Creating tree shaders – the bark
- ▶ Creating tree shaders – the leaves
- ▶ Creating a layered human skin material in Cycles
- ▶ Creating fur and hair
- ▶ Creating a gray alien skin with procedurals

Introduction

Following on from the natural materials we have seen in *Chapter 3, Creating Natural Materials in Cycles,* and in *Chapter 5, Creating Complex Natural Materials in Cycles*, it's now time to take a look at organic shaders.

Once again, while building the materials, we tried to use only the Cycles procedural textures. In several cases, this hasn't been the case by the way: on one side, because it hasn't been possible, and on the other side, because image maps usually work better than procedurals.

In any case, procedurals have often been added to the shader to refine the details or to add a natural-looking randomness to a pattern that repeats too much.

Creating an organic-looking shader with procedurals

In this recipe, we will create a sort of organic, disgusting-looking material, as shown in the following screenshot:

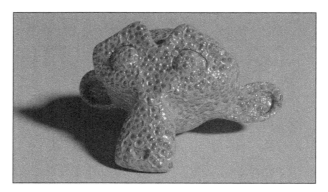

The disgusting organic material as it appears in the final rendering

Getting ready

Start Blender and open the 99310S_08_start.blend file, where there is an already set scene with an unwrapped **Suzanne** primitive object leaning on a Plane, an Emitter mesh-light, and a Camera.

Go to the **Render** window, and in the **Sampling** subpanel, change **Pattern** from **Sobol** to **Correlated Multi-Jitter**.

How to do it...

Let's go straight to the material creation by using the following steps:

1. Click on the **New** button in the **Node Editor** window toolbar or in the **Material** window under the main **Properties** panel and rename the new material Organic.

2. In the **Material** window, switch the **Diffuse BSDF** shader with a **Mix Shader** node, and label it as Mix Shader2. In the first **Shader** input socket, select a **Mix Shader** node and label it as Mix Shader1, and in the second one, select an **Add Shader** node.

3. Go to the **Mix Shader1** node, and in the first **Shader** input socket, load a **Diffuse BSDF** node, and in the second one, load a **Glossy BSDF** node. Change the **Glossy BSDF** shader node's **Distribution** to **Ashikhmin-Shirley**, and set the **Roughness** value to 0.100.

4. Add a **Subsurface Scattering** node (press *Shift + A* and navigate to **Shader |
    Subsurface Scattering**). Set the **Falloff** value to **Gaussian**, the **Scale** value to 0.060,
    and the **Radius** values to 4.000, 2.000, and 1.000 (top to bottom).

5. Connect the **Mix Shader1** output to the first **Shader** input socket of the **Add Shader**
    node, and the output of the **Subsurface Scattering** node to the second **Shader** input
    socket of the **Add Shader** node.

6. Add a **Layer Weight** node (press *Shift + A* and navigate to **Input | Layer Weight**) and
    connect its **Facing** output to the **Fac** input socket of the **Mix Shader2** node. Set the
    Blend value to 0.100.

7. Add a **Fresnel** node (press *Shift + A* and navigate to **Input | Fresnel**) and connect its
    output to the **Fac** input socket of the **Mix Shader1** node. Set the **IOR** value to 5.950
    as shown in the following screenshot:

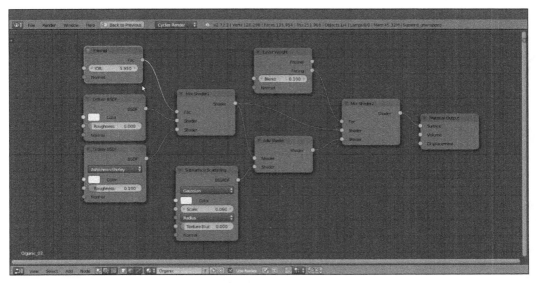

The basic shader nodes

8. Add a **Texture Coordinate** node (press *Shift + A* and navigate to **Input | Texture
    Coordinate**), a **Mapping** node (press *Shift + A* and navigate to **Vector | Mapping**),
    and a **Voronoi Texture** node (press *Shift + A* and navigate to **Texture | Voronoi
    Texture**). Connect the **Object** output of the **Texture Coordinate** node to the **Vector**
    input socket of the **Mapping** node, and the output of this to the **Vector** input of the
    Voronoi Texture node. Set the **Scale** value of the **Mapping** node to 1.500 for the
    three axes.

9. Add three **ColorRamp** nodes (press *Shift + A* and navigate to **Converter |
    ColorRamp**) and label them as ColorRamp1, ColorRamp2, and ColorRamp3.
    Connect the **Color** output of the **Voronoi Texture** node to the **Fac** input sockets of
    the three **ColorRamp** nodes.

10. In the **ColorRamp1** node, set **Interpolation** to **B-Spline**, the black color stop to the `0.400` position, and the white color stop to the `0.700` position. In the **ColorRamp2** node, set **Interpolation** to **B-Spline** as well. Leave the black color stop at the `0.000` position, and move the white color stop to the `0.300` position. In the **ColorRamp3** node, set **Interpolation** to **Cardinal**, leave the black color stop at the `0.000` position, and move the white color stop to the `0.805` position.

11. Add a **MixRGB** node (press *Shift + A* and navigate to **Color | MixRGB**), set **Blend Type** to **Add** and the **Fac** value to `1.000`, and then connect the **Color** output of the **ColorRamp1** node to the **Color1** input socket, and the **Color** output of the **ColorRamp2** node to the **Color2** input socket.

12. Press *Shift + D* to duplicate the **Add** node and change **Blend Type** of the duplicate to **Multiply**. Connect the output of the **Add** node to the **Color1** input socket, and the **Color** output of the **ColorRamp3** node to the **Color2** input socket.

13. Add a **Bump** node (press *Shift + A* and navigate to **Vector | Bump**) and connect the output of the **Multiply** node to the **Height** input socket of the **Bump** node. Connect the **Normal** output of this to the **Normal** input sockets of the **Diffuse BSDF**, **Glossy BSDF**, and **Subsurface Scattering** nodes. Enable the **Invert** option on the **Bump** node, as shown in the following screenshot:

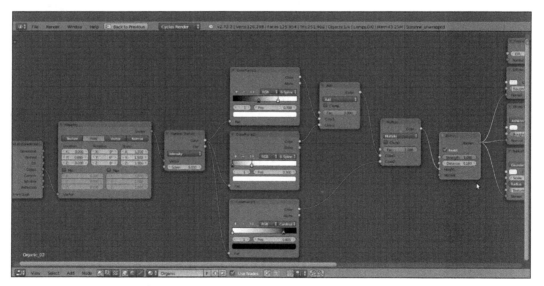

The Bump node

14. Now, box-select (press the *B* key) the **Texture Coordinate** node and the **Mapping** nodes, and move them to the left to make room for new nodes.

15. Add a **MixRGB** node (press *Shift + A* and navigate to **Color | MixRGB**) and label it as `Vector_deform`. Paste it between the **Mapping** and **Voronoi Texture** nodes.

16. Add a **Noise Texture** node (press *Shift + A* and navigate to **Texture | Noise Texture**), connect to its **Vector** input socket the **Mapping** node output, and set the **Scale** value to 7.200. Connect the **Noise Texture** node's **Color** output to the **Color2** input socket of the **Vector_deform** node. Set the **Fac** value of the **Vector_deform** node to 0.080, as shown in the following screenshot:

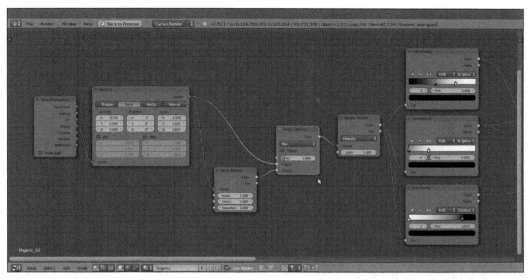

Deforming the mapping coordinates of the bump textures through a procedural noise

17. Add an **RGB** node (press *Shift + A* and navigate to **Input | RGB**) and a new **MixRGB** node (press *Shift + A* and navigate to **Color | MixRGB**). Label the **MixRGB** node

18. as Color_Diffuse.

19. Press *Shift + D* to duplicate the **Color_Diffuse** node and label the duplicate as Color_Glossy.

20. Connect the **Color_Diffuse** node's output to the **Color** input socket of the **Diffuse BSDF** shader node, and the **Color_Glossy** node's output to the **Color** input socket of the **Glossy BSDF** shader node.

21. Connect the output of the **RGB** node to the **Color1** input sockets of both the **Color_Diffuse** and **Color_Glossy** nodes. Connect the **RGB** node also to the **Color** input socket of the **Subsurface Scattering** node.

22. Press *Shift + D* to duplicate the **Color_Diffuse** node, set **Blend Type** of the duplicate to **Multiply**, and label it as Multiply_Diffuse; then, paste it between the **Color_Diffuse** and **Diffuse BSDF shader** nodes.

23. Connect the **Color** output of the **ColorRamp2** node to the **Color2** input socket of the **Multiply_Diffuse** node. Set the **Fac** value of this to 0.770.

24. Go to the **Color_Diffuse** node and set the **Fac** value to `0.830`, and change the **Color2** value of **R** to `0.315`, **G** to `0.500`, and **B** to `0.130`.

25. Go to the **Color_Glossy** node and set the **Fac** value to `0.770`, and change the **Color2** values of **R** to `0.860`, **G** to `0.611`, and **B** to `0.203`.

26. Go to the **RGB** node and set the **Color** values for **R** to `0.900`, **G** to `0.123`, and **B** to `0.395`, as shown in the following screenshot:

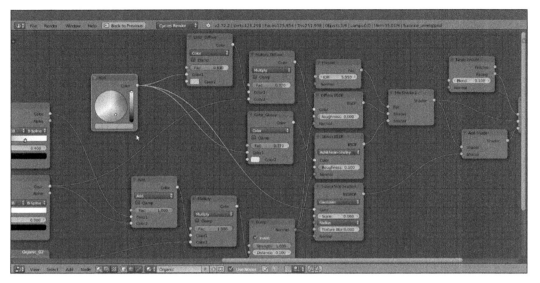

Adding the color nodes

27. Save the file as `99310S_organic.blend`.

How it works...

▶ From step 1 to 7, we built a shader that is very similar to the shaders that we have already seen for `SSS_materials`.

▶ From step 8 to 13, we built the bump pattern by using a single **Voronoi Texture** node tuned through three **ColorRamp** nodes with different settings.

▶ From step 14 to 16, we added, through the very low value of a **MixRGB** node, the values of a **Noise Texture** node to the vector of the **Voronoi Texture** node to obtain a less regular pattern.

▶ From step 17 to 25, we built the color pattern by establishing a base color by the **RGB** node and introducing a variation through the **MixRGB** nodes connected to the **Color** input sockets of the shader components. Note that the base pink color set in the **RGB** node goes straight to the SSS node. The **MixRGB** varied greenish color is multiplied by one of the bump outputs and then goes to the diffuse component of the shader, while the varied yellowish color is for the glossy component instead.

Creating a wasp-like chitin material with procedural textures

In this recipe, we will create a material similar to chitin (the characteristic substance of the exoskeletons of insects) colored with a yellow and black pattern like a wasp, as shown in the following screenshot:

The insect wasp-like material as it appears in the final rendering

Getting ready

Start Blender and open the `9931OS_08_start.blend` file, where there is an already set scene with an unwrapped **Suzanne** primitive object leaning on a Plane, an Emitter mesh-light, and a Camera.

Go to the **World** window and enable the **Ambient Occlusion** item with the **Factor** value `0.10`.

How to do it...

Let's start immediately with the material creation using the following steps:

1. Click on the **New** button in the **Node Editor** window toolbar or in the **Material** window under the main **Properties** panel to the right, and rename the new material `chitin_wasp`.

2. Now, in the **Material** window, switch the **Diffuse BSDF** shader with a **Mix Shader** node, and label it as `Mix Shader2`. In the first **Shader** slot, select a new **Mix Shader** node. In the second one, select a **Glossy BSDF** shader node. Label the new **Mix Shader** node as `Mix Shader1`, and the **Glossy BSDF** node as `Glossy BSDF_2`.

3. Go to the **Mix Shader1** node, and in the first **Shader** slot, select a **Diffuse BSDF** shader, and in the second one, select a new **Glossy BSDF** shader node. Label the latter as `Glossy BSDF_1`, and set its **Roughness** value to `0.100` and **Distribution** to **Beckmann**, and change the **Color** value for **R** to `0.039`, **G** to `0.138`, and **B** to `0.046`.

4. Set the **Glossy BSDF_2** node's **Roughness** value to `0.040` and **Distribution** to **Beckmann**, and change its **Color** values for **R** to `0.500`, **G** to `0.440`, and **B** to `0.086`. Set the **Fac** value of the **Mix Shader2** node to `0.025`.

5. Add a **Layer Weight** node (press *Shift + A* and navigate to **Input | Layer Weight**) and connect its **Facing** output to the **Fac** input socket of the **Mix Shader1** node. Leave the **Blend** value as `0.500`, as shown in the following screenshot:

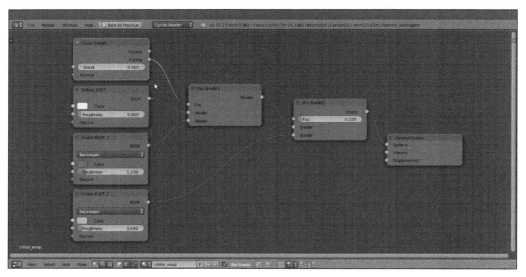

The nodes for the base shader

6. Add a **Texture Coordinate** node (press *Shift + A* and navigate to **Input | Texture Coordinate**) and a **Mapping** node (press *Shift + A* and navigate to **Vector | Mapping**). Connect the **UV** output of the **Texture Coordinate** node to the **Vector** input of the **Mapping** node. Label the latter as `Mapping1`.

7. Add a **Voronoi Texture** node (press *Shift + A* and navigate to **Texture | Voronoi Texture**) and a **Noise Texture** node (press *Shift + A* and navigate to **Texture | Noise Texture**). Connect the **Mapping1** node's **Vector** output to their **Vector** input sockets. Set the **Scale** values of both the texture nodes to `300.000` and then label the **Noise Texture** node as `Noise Texture1`.

8. Add a **Bump** node (press *Shift + A* and navigate to **Vector | Bump**) and connect the **Color** output of the **Voronoi Texture** node to the **Height** input socket of the **Bump** node. Connect the **Normal** output of this node to the **Normal** input sockets of the **Diffuse BSDF** node and both **Glossy BSDF** shader nodes. Set the **Bump** node's **Strength** value to `0.500`.

9. Add a **ColorRamp** node (press *Shift + A* and navigate to **Converter | ColorRamp**), label it as `ColorRamp1`, and paste it between the **Voronoi Texture** node and the **Bump** node. Set **Interpolation** to **Ease** and move the white color stop to the 0.059 position.

10. Add a **Math** node (press *Shift + A* and navigate to **Converter | Math**), set **Operation** to **Multiply**, and connect the **Fac** output of the **Noise Texture1** node to the first **Value** input socket of the **Math** node. Set the second **Value** to 0.100 and connect the **Value** output to the **Displacement** input socket of the **Material Output** node, as shown in the following screenshot:

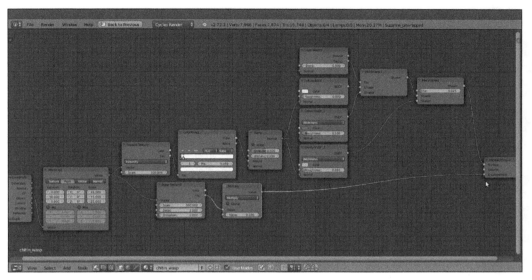

Textures connected either as per the shader bump and the total bump to the Displacement input socket of the Material Output node

11. Add a new **Mapping** node (press *Shift + A* and navigate to **Vector | Mapping**), label it as `Mapping2`, and connect the **UV** output of the **Texture Coordinate** node to its **Vector** input socket. Set the **Rotation** value for **Y** to 90° and the **Rotation** value of **Z** to 45°. Set the **Scale** value for all three axes to 5.000.

12. Add a **Noise Texture** node (press *Shift + A* and navigate to **Texture | Noise Texture**) and a **ColorRamp** node (press *Shift + A* and navigate to **Converter | ColorRamp**). Label them as `Noise Texture2` and `ColorRamp2`.

13. Connect the output of the **Mapping2** node to the **Vector** input socket of the **Noise Texture2** node, and the **Fac** output of this node to the **Fac** input socket of **ColorRamp2**. Connect the output of this node to the **Color** input socket of the **Diffuse BSDF** shader node.

14. Go to the **Noise Texture2** node and set the **Scale** and **Distortion** values to 2.000. Go to the **ColorRamp2** node and set **Interpolation** to **Constant**, select the white color stop, and change the **Color** values for **R** to 1.000, **G** to 0.429, and **B** to 0.000.

15. Click on the **+** icon button to add new color stops until you have eight color stops almost evenly spaced along the slider (that is: color stop **0** at the 0.000 position, **1** at the 0.125 position, **2** at the 0.250 position, then 0.357, 0.491, 0.626, 0.745, and 0.886).

16. Select the last color stop, put the mouse pointer on the color slider, and press *Ctrl + C* to copy the yellow color; then, select the color stops numbered **1**, **3**, and **5**, and paste the color (press *Ctrl + V*) so as to have a slider subdivided in eight parts, four black and four yellow, as shown in the following screenshot:

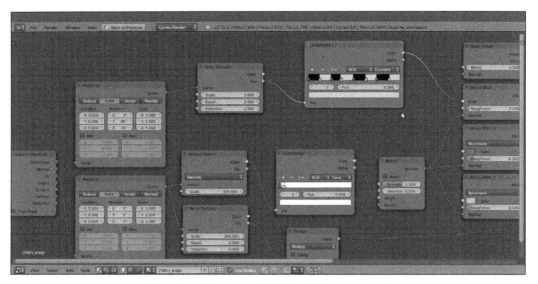

The color pattern connected to the diffuse component

How it works...

▶ From step 1 to 5, we built the basic shader using two **Glossy BSDF** shaders with different colors to mimic a color shifting in the specularity areas.

▶ From step 6 to 10, we built the chitin bump, assigning the pores to the per-shader bump but a general noise pattern to the displacement output (which, in this case, still works as a simple bump).

▶ From step 11 to 16, we built a simple and random wasp-colored pattern; obviously, this can be changed and modified as you prefer, and actually should also be used on a more appropriate model; in this case, it would be better to make use of a painted color texture map to build a more appropriate and symmetrical color pattern.

Creating a beetle-like chitin material with procedural textures

In this recipe, we will create a material similar to iridescent chitin (found in some kinds of beetles), as shown in the following screenshot:

The beetle chitin-like material as it appears in the final rendering

Getting ready

Start Blender and open the `9931OS_08_start.blend` file, where there is an already set scene with an unwrapped **Suzanne** primitive object leaning on a Plane, an Emitter mesh-light, and a Camera.

Go to the **World** window and enable the **Ambient Occlusion** option with the **Factor** value as `0.10`.

How to do it...

Let's start immediately with the material creation using the following steps:

1. Click on the **New** button in the **Node Editor** window's toolbar or in the **Material** window under the main **Properties** panel to the right, and rename the new material as `chitin_beetle`.

2. Now, in the **Material** window, switch the **Diffuse BSDF** shader with a **Mix Shader** node and label it as `Mix Shader2`. In the first **Shader** slot, select a new **Mix Shader** node; in the second **Mix Shader** node, select a **Glossy BSDF** shader node. Label the new **Mix Shader** node as `Mix Shader1`, and the **Glossy BSDF** one as `Glossy BSDF_2`.

3. Go to the **Mix Shader1** node, and in the first **Shader** slot, select a **Diffuse BSDF** shader, and in the second one, select a new **Glossy BSDF** shader node; label this node as `Glossy BSDF_1` and set its **Roughness** value to `0.200` and **Distribution** to **Beckmann**, and change the **Color** values for **R** to `1.000`, **G** to `0.000`, and **B** to `0.562`.

4. Set the **Glossy BSDF_2** node's **Roughness** value to `0.100` and **Distribution** to **Beckmann**, and change its **Color** values for **R** to `0.800`, **G** to `0.574`, and **B** to `0.233`.

5. Add a **Layer Weight** node (press *Shift + A* and navigate to **Input | Layer Weight**), label it as `Layer Weight1`, and connect its **Facing** output to the **Fac** input socket of the **Mix Shader2** node. Leave the **Blend** value at `0.500`.

6. Add a second **Layer Weight** node (press *Shift + A* and navigate to **Input | Layer Weight**), label it as `Layer Weight2`, and connect its **Facing** output to the **Fac** input socket of the **Mix Shader1** node. Leave the **Blend** value at `0.800`, as shown in the following screenshot:

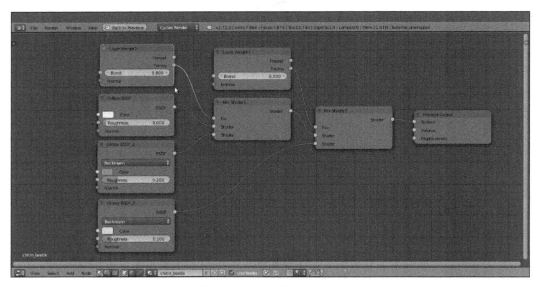

The shader part of the material

7. Add a **Texture Coordinate** node (press *Shift + A* and navigate to **Input | Texture Coordinate**) and a **Mapping** node (press *Shift + A* and navigate to **Vector | Mapping**). Connect the **UV** output of the **Texture Coordinate** node to the **Vector** input of the **Mapping** node.

8. Add a **Voronoi Texture** node (press *Shift + A* and navigate to **Texture | Voronoi Texture**) and a **Noise Texture** node (press *Shift + A* and navigate to **Texture | Noise Texture**); connect the **Mapping** output to their **Vector** input sockets. Set the **Scale** values of both the texture nodes to `300.000`.

9. Add a **Bump** node (press *Shift + A* and navigate to **Vector | Bump**) and connect the **Color** output of the **Voronoi Texture** node to the **Height** input socket of the **Bump** node; connect the **Normal** output of this node to the **Normal** input sockets of **Diffuse BSDF** and of both the **Glossy BSDF** shader nodes. Set the **Bump** node's **Strength** value to 0.500.

10. Add a **ColorRamp** node (press *Shift + A* and navigate to **Converter | ColorRamp**) and paste it between the **Voronoi Texture** node and the **Bump** node. Set **Interpolation** to **Ease** and move the white color stop to the 0.059 position.

11. Add a **Math** node (press *Shift + A* and navigate to **Converter | Math**), set **Operation** to **Multiply**, and label it as Multiply1; connect the **Fac** output of the **Noise Texture** node to the first **Value** input socket of the **Math** node. Set the second **Value** to 0.075 and connect the **Value** output to the **Displacement** input socket of the **Material Output** node, as shown in the following screenshot:

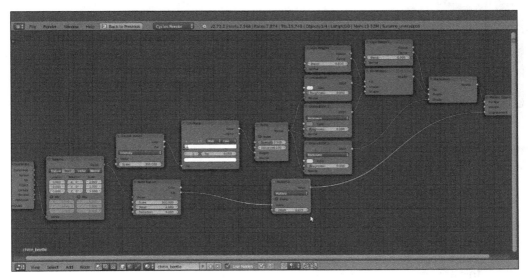

The bump is both "per shader" and as "total" bump (as in the previous wasp material recipe)

12. Add a new **Layer Weight** node (press *Shift + A* and navigate to **Input | Layer Weight**), two **Math** nodes (press *Shift + A* and navigate to **Converter | Math**), and a **Hue Saturation Value** node (press *Shift + A* and navigate to **Color | Hue/Saturation**); label the new **Layer Weight** node as Layer Weight3.

13. Connect the **Facing** output of the **Layer Weight3** node to the first **Value** input socket of one of the **Math** nodes; set its **Operation** to **Multiply** and the second **Value** to 0.700, and label it as Multiply2.

14. Connect the **Multiply2** node's output to the first **Value** input socket of the second **Math** node, and the output of this node to the **Hue** input socket of the **Hue Saturation Value** node; connect the output of this node to the **Color** input socket of the **Diffuse BSDF** shader node.

15. Change the **Hue Saturation Value** node's **Color** values for **R** to `0.103`, **G** to `0.500`, and **B** to `0.229`, and just for this example, leave the other values as they are, as shown in the following screenshot:

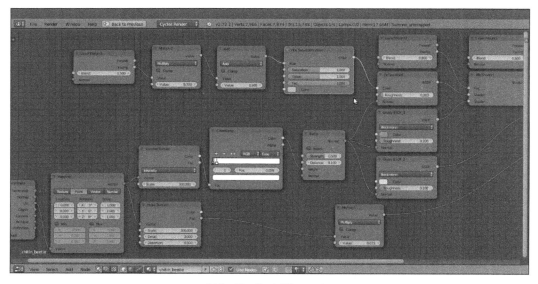

Adding the final diffuse color

How it works...

▸ The introductory steps of this shader work almost the same as for the `chitin_wasp` material, that is, the basic shader from step 1 to 6 and the chitin bump from step 7 to 11.

▸ From step 12 to 15, we build the color component coming from the **Hue Saturation Value** node, and thanks to the combination of the **Layer Weight3** and **Math** nodes, this appears mainly in the mesh faces perpendicular to the point of view, sliding in the other spectrum colors on the facing-away mesh sides, basically behaving as a sort of Fresnel effect. The addition of the **Hue Saturation Value** node allows for further color tweaking.

Creating tree shaders – the bark

There are several different ways to make trees in a 3D package: starting from the simpler low-poly objects, such as the billboards used in video games (simple planes mapped with tree images on a transparent background), to middle complex objects where a trunk mesh is attached to a foliage mass made of little alpha textured planes, each one representing a leaf or even a twig, to more complex and heavy meshes, where every little branch and leaf is actually modeled.

In case you need them, you can find several free tree models in the Blender format and also their billboard versions at `http://yorik.uncreated.net/greenhouse.html`.

For this two-part tree shader recipe, we will instead use a model coming from the many environment assets of the CG short *Big Buck Bunny*, the second open movie produced by the Blender Foundation. All the movie assets are free to be downloaded, distributed, and reused even for commercial projects because the short is licensed under the Creative Commons Attribution 3.0 license (refer to its official website at `http://creativecommons.org/licenses/by/3.0/`).

The general shape of the tree and the leaves is pretty toyish. This is because they are elements that have been drawn to match the toon style of the furry characters, but it's actually perfectly suited for our demonstration purposes. The final rendered tree from *Big Buck Bunny* is shown in the following screenshot for your reference:

The final rendered tree from *Big Buck Bunny*

The tree model is composed of several parts: on the first layer, there are the **tree_trunk**, the **tree_branch**, and the **tree_branches** meshes, and on the second layer are the leaves, made by a single leaf object dupliverted on the tiny faces of the **leaves_dupli** object. (That is, the **leaf_tobeswitched** object is parented to the **leaves_dupli** object, and then, in the **Object** window and under the **Duplication** subpanel, the **Faces** duplication method has been selected, the **Scale** item checked, and the **Inherit Scale** value set to `1110.000`. This way, the **leaf_tobeswitched** object is instanced on the **leaves_dupli** object's many faces according to their location, rotation, and scale.)

On the 11th layer, there are three leaf objects with three different levels of detail: a simple flat Plane, a subdivided and curved Plane, and a modeled leaf. Their presence is only to supply the low, middle, and high resolution mesh data. By selecting the **leaf_tobeswitched** object and by going to the **Object data** window, it is possible to switch between the **leaf_generic_low**, **leaf_generic_mid**, and **leaf_generic_hi** foliage levels of detail.

In the first part of this two-part recipe, we will create the material for the bark, as shown in the following screenshot:

The bark material

Getting ready

Start Blender and open the `99310S_08_tree_start.blend` file. For this recipe, deactivate the second layer, and in **Outliner**, select the **tree_trunk** object.

How to do it...

Let's start by creating the bark material using the following steps:

1. Click on the **New** button in the **Node Editor** window toolbar or in the **Material** window, and rename the material as `bark`.

2. Still in the **Material** window, switch the **Diffuse BSDF** shader with a **Mix Shader** node, and label it as `Mix Shader_bark1`. In the first **Shader** slot, select a **Diffuse BSDF** shader node, and in the second one, select a **Glossy BSDF** shader node; then, label them as `Diffuse_bark1` and `Glossy_bark1`. Set the **Glossy_bark** distribution to **Beckmann**, the **Roughness** value to `0.800`, and the **Mix Shader_bark1** node's **Fac** value to `0.200`.

3. Add a **Texture Coordinate** node (press *Shift + A* and navigate to **Input | Texture Coordinate**), a **Mapping** node (press *Shift + A* and navigate to **Vector | Mapping**), and an **Image Texture** node (press *Shift + A* and navigate to **Texture | Image Texture**); label the last two as `Mapping1` and `Bark_color1`.

4. Connect the **UV** output of the **Texture Coordinate** node to the **Vector** input socket of the **Mapping1** node, and the output of this node to the **Vector** input socket of the **Bark_color1** node. Connect the **Color** output of the **Bark_color1** node to the **Color** input sockets of both the **Diffuse_bark1** and **Glossy_bark1** shader nodes.

5. Click on the **Open** button of the **Bark_color1** node, browse to the `textures` folder, and load the `bark_color_tile.png` image.

6. Press *Shift + D* to duplicate the **Bark_color1** node, label it as `Bark_normal1`, and connect the **Mapping1** node output to its **Vector** input socket. Make the image datablock single-user by clicking on **2**, which appears on the right side of the image name. Click on the **Open Image** button (the one with the folder icon), browse again to the `textures` folder, and load the `bark_norm_tile.png` image. Set **Color Space** to **Non-Color Data**.

7. Add a **Normal Map** node (press *Shift + A* and navigate to **Vector | Normal Map**), label it as `Normal Map1`, and connect the **Color** output of the **Bark_normal1** node to the **Color** input socket of the **Normal Map1** node, and then set the **Strength** value to `2.000`. Click on the **UV Map for tangent space maps** button upwards of the **Strength** one and select **UVMap** (the trunk mesh has two different sets of UV coordinates, which we'll see later).

8. Connect the **Normal** output of the **Normal Map1** node to the **Normal** input sockets of both the **Diffuse_bark1** and the **Glossy_bark1 shader** nodes, as shown in the following screenshot:

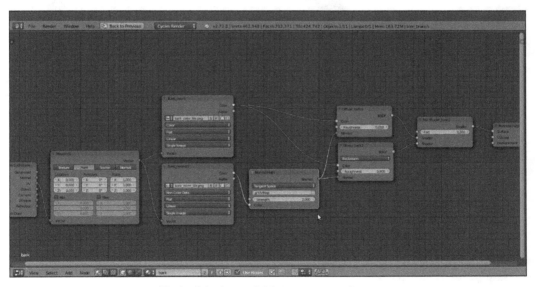

The basic bark material that uses a normal map

9. Now, box-select (press the *B* key and then draw a rectangle) all the nodes except for the **Texture Coordinate** and **Material Output** nodes and press *Shift + D* duplicate them. Move them down and change their labels by substituting the 1 suffix with 2. Connect the **UV** output of the **Texture Coordinate** node to the **Vector** input socket of the duplicated **Mapping2** node, and set the **Scale** of this node to `0.350` for all three axes.

10. Add a **Mix Shader** node (press *Shift + A* and navigate to **Shader | Mix Shader**), label it as `Mix Shader_bark3`, and paste it right before the **Material Output** node. Connect the output of the **Mix Shader_bark2** node to the second **Shader** input socket of the **Mix Shader_bark3** node.

11. Add a **Noise Texture** node (press *Shift + A* and navigate to **Texture | Noise Texture**), connect the **UV** output of the **Texture Coordinate** node to the **Vector** input socket of the **Noise Texture** node, and connect the **Fac** output of this node to the **Fac** input socket of the **Mix Shader_bark3** node.

12. Set the **Noise Texture** node's **Scale** value to `15.000`, as shown in the following screenshot:

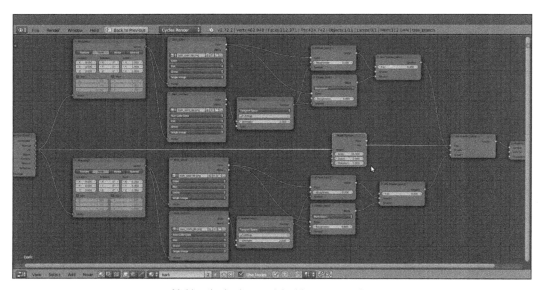

Making the bark material a bit more complex

13. Now, press *Shift* and select the **tree_branch** and **tree_branches** meshes, and as the last one, reselect the **tree_trunk** mesh to make it the active object; then, press *Ctrl + L*. In the **Make Links** pop-up menu, select the **Materials** item to assign the bark material to the other two meshes.

How it works...

▸ For this material, we built a simple shader using two tileable image maps, a color one for the Diffuse and the Glossy components, and a normal map for the bump.

▸ Then, we duplicated everything and mixed the second material copy with different scale values to the first one by the factor of a Noise procedural texture, to add variety to the bark pattern and to avoid that unpleasant repeating effect that often shows up with tileable image textures.

There's more...

At this point, if you look carefully at the **Rendered** view of the tree trunk, you'll see that sadly, there are ugly seams where the trunk's main body joins the big low branches as shown in the following screenshot:

The visible seams at the branches joining

This is due to the fact that the unwrap of the mesh has separated the branches' UV islands from the main trunk ones. Although the effect can be barely visible, let's say that you absolutely want to avoid this; that's why we are now going to see a solution for the problem, by using a second set of UV coordinates and a Vertex Color layer.

This is what we are going to do:

1. Select the **trunk** mesh and go into the **Vertex Paint** mode; the mesh turns totally white, because that is the color assigned to the vertexes by default. Start to paint with pure black on the vertexes located at the joining of the low branches with the trunk, achieving this result:

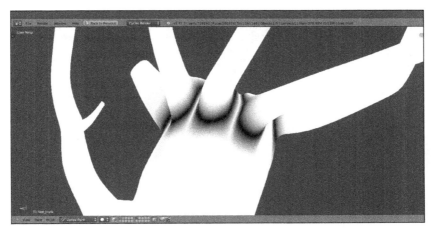

The trunk model seen in the Vertex Paint mode

2. As you can see, the joining vertices edge loops are black but are smoothly blending into the white of the default mesh vertex color. This will be used as a stencil map to blend two different instances of the same bark material mapped on different UV coordinates. Go to the **Object data** window and rename the **Vertex Color** layer as `Join_branches`.

3. Switch to **Edit Mode** and select all the faces including the necessary vertices' edge loops; in the **Object data** window, under the **UV Maps** subpanel, click on the **+** icon (add **UV Map**) and rename the new UV coordinates layer as `UVMap2`. Place the mouse cursor on the 3D viewport, press **U**, and select **Unwrap** in the **UV Mapping** pop-up menu, as shown in the following screenshot:

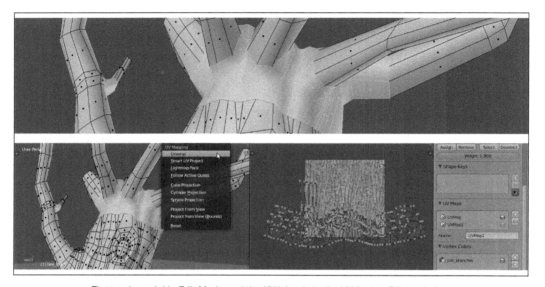

The trunk model in Edit Mode and the UV islands in the UV/Image Editor window

4. Go out of **Edit Mode**. Click on the user number to the right of the material data block in the **Node Editor** window toolbar and rename the new material as `bark_seamless`.

Now, by looking at the following screenshot, it is clear what we have to do:

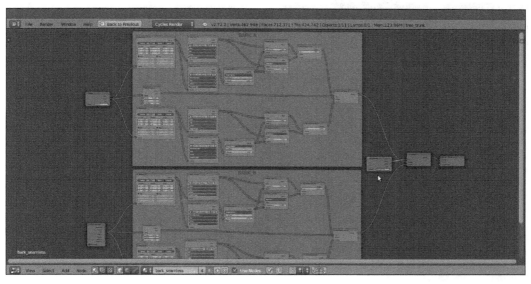

Two identical bark materials mapped on different UV layers and mixed on the ground of the Vertex Paint output

5. Make a duplicate of the bark material and blend the two shaders (inside the **BARK_A** and **BARK_B** frames respectively) using a **Mix Shader** node, modulated by the **Join_branches** vertex color stencil. Use an **Attribute** node both for the **Vertex Color** layer output and to set the **UVMap2** coordinates layer for the copy of the bark material. Now, the output looks similar to what is shown in the following screenshot:

The final result: no more seams

As you can see in the preceding screenshot, there are no more visible seams; the two differently UV mapped materials smoothly blend together.

Creating tree shaders – the leaves

In this second tree recipe, we will create the leaves shaders, as shown in the following screenshot:

The leaves as they appear in the final rendering

Getting ready

Carrying on with the blend file of the previous recipe, now, activate (hold *Shift* while clicking) the 2nd and the 11th scene layers, and in **Outliner**, select the **leaf_generic_mid** object.

How to do it...

Let's proceed with the creation of the leaves shaders:

1. Click on the **New** button in the **Node Editor** window toolbar or in the **Material** window, and rename the material as `leaf_alpha`.

2. In the **Material** window, switch the **Diffuse BSDF** shader with a **Mix Shader** node and label it as **Mix Shader Cutout**; in the first **Shader** slot, select a **Transparent BSDF** shader node, and in the second one, select a new **Mix Shader** node, which will be labeled as **Mix Shader Add Translucency**.

3. Add an **Image Texture** node (press *Shift + A* and navigate to **Texture | Image Texture**), label it as `MASK`, and connect its **Alpha** output to the **Fac** input socket of the **Mix Shader Cutout** node.

4. Click on the **Open** button of the **MASK** node, browse to the `textures` folder, and load the `leaf_generic_mask.png` image (which actually is a simple black leaf silhouette with a transparent alpha channel). Set **Color Space** to **Non-Color Data**.

5. Add a **Diffuse BSDF** node (press *Shift + A* and navigate to **Shader | Diffuse BSDF**), a **Glossy BSDF** node (press *Shift + A* and navigate to **Shader | Glossy BSDF**), and a **Translucent BSDF** node (press *Shift + A* and navigate to **Shader | Translucent BSDF**).

6. Add two new **Mix Shader** nodes (press *Shift + A* and navigate to **Shader | Mix Shader**), and label them as `Mix Shader1` and `Mix Shader2`.

7. Connect the output of the **Diffuse BSDF** shader to the first **Shader** input socket of the **Mix Shader1** node, and the output of the **Glossy BSDF** shader to the second **Shader** input socket. Set the **Glossy BSDF** node's **Distribution** to **Beckmann**, and change the **Color** values for **R** to `0.794`, **G** to `0.800`, and **B** to `0.413`, and the **Roughness** value to `0.500`.

8. Connect the output of the **Mix Shader1** node to the first **Shader** input socket of the **Mix Shader2** node, and the output of the **Translucent** node to the second one; connect the output of the **Mix Shader2** node to the second **Shader** input socket of the **Mix Shader Add Translucency** node.

9. Connect the output of the **Diffuse BSDF** shader node to the first **Shader** input socket of the **Mix Shader Add Translucency** node. Set its **Fac** value to `0.300` (this value establishes the amount of translucency in the shader).

10. Add an **Image Texture** node (press *Shift + A* and navigate to **Texture | Image Texture**), label it as `TRANSLUCENCY`, and connect its **Color** output to the **Fac** input socket of the **Mix Shader2** node. Click on the **Open** button, browse to the usual `textures` folder, and load the `leaf_generic_trans.png` image. Set **Color Space** to **Non-Color Data**.

11. Add a **Fresnel** node (press *Shift + A* and navigate to **Input | Fresnel**), connect it to the **Fac** input socket of the **Mix Shader1** node, and set **IOR** to `1.500`.

12. Add an **Image Texture** node (press *Shift + A* and navigate to **Texture | Image Texture**), label it as `COLOR`, and connect its **Color** output to the **Color** input socket of the **Diffuse BSDF** shader node and to the **Color** input socket of the **Translucent BSDF** node. Click on the **Open** button, browse to the `textures` folder, and load the `leaf_generic_col.png` image.

13. Add a **Hue Saturation Value** node (press *Shift + A* and navigate to **Color | Hue/Saturation**) and paste it between the **COLOR** image texture node and the **Translucent BSDF** shader node. Set the **Hue** value to `0.350` and **Value** to `2.000`.

14. Add a last **Image Texture** node (press *Shift + A* and navigate to **Texture | Image Texture**) and label it as `BUMP`; add a **Bump** node (press *Shift + A* and navigate to **Vector | Bump**) and connect the **BUMP** image node's **Color** output to the **Height** input socket of the **Bump** node, and the **Normal** output socket of this node to the **Normal** input sockets of the **Diffuse BSDF**, **Glossy BSDF**, and **Translucent BSDF** shader nodes.

15. Click on the **Open** button, browse to the `textures` folder, and load the `leaf_generic_bump.png` image. Set **Color Space** to **Non-Color Data** and the **Bump** node's **Strength** value to `0.200`, as shown in the following screenshot:

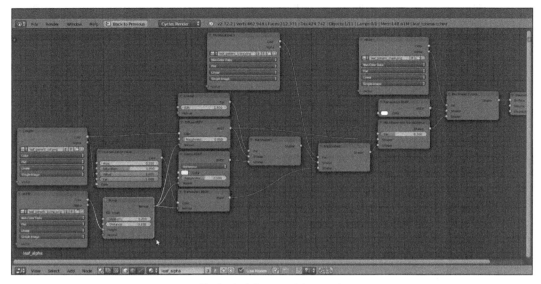

The leaf_alpha material network

How it works...

▸ From step 1 to 11, we built the basic shader of the leaf, using an image that has alpha channel data to cut out the leaf shape on the Plane and a gray-scale image to drive the translucency effect.

▸ From step 12 to 15, we added the color of the leaf, using it also with a hue and intensity variation for the translucency color, and then we added the bump.

There's more...

Now, assign the same material to both the `leaf_generic_low` and `leaf_generic_hi` meshes on the 11th layer.

The modeled leaf mesh doesn't need the alpha channel, so select the **leaf_generic_hi** object, and in the toolbar of the **Node Editor** window, click on **user data number** to make it **single-user**. Rename the new material as `leaf` and delete the **MASK** and **Transparent BSDF** nodes, and then press *Alt + D* to remove the **Mix Shader Cutout** node from the link and delete it as well.

Remember that the examples in the preceding and following images are made with very stylized models that come from the *Big Buck Bunny* short movie; real objects have more subtle details and more random repeating patterns, but in this case, this just depends on the image textures you are going to use for your material.

Such a shader is of good use not only for leaves, but also for other kinds of plants; in many cases, it's enough to give variations to the color.

Creating a layered human skin material in Cycles

In this recipe, we will create a layered skin material by using the open-content character Sintel.

Sintel is the main character of the third open movie of the same name produced by the Blender Foundation; the Sintel character and all the other movie assets are licensed under the Creative Commons Attribution 3.0 license (`http://creativecommons.org/licenses/by/3.0/`). The following screenshot is of Sintel's face:

Sintel's face in the final rendering

Getting ready

Start Blender and open the `9931OS_08_skin_start.blend` file, where there is an already set scene with the Sintel character standing on a Plane, a Sun lamp, and a Camera.

Except for Sintel's body skin, all the other mesh objects have either gesso-like materials or eyes already assigned.

How to do it...

Let's start with the layered skin shader creation:

1. Be sure to have the **Sintel** object selected, and then click on the **New** button in the **Node Editor** window toolbar or in the **Material** window under the main **Properties** panel and rename the material as `skin_layered`.

2. In the **Material** window, switch the **Diffuse BSDF** shader with a **Mix Shader** node; go to the **Active Node** panel to the right of the **Node Editor** window (if not present, put the mouse in the **Node Editor** window and press *N* to make it appear), and in the **Label** slot, rename the **Mix Shader** as `Mix Shader1`.

3. In the first **Shader** slot of this new **Mix Shader1** node, select a **Diffuse BSDF** shader node, and in the second one, select an **Add Shader** node; label this node as `Add SPEC`.

4. Add two **Glossy BSDF** shader nodes (press *Shift + A* and navigate to **Shader | Glossy BSDF**) and label them as `Glossy BSDF_1` and `Glossy BSDF_2`. Set their **Distribution** to **Ashikhmin-Shirley**, and then connect their output to the first and second **Shader** input sockets of the **Add SPEC** node respectively.

5. Add a **Fresnel** node (press *Shift + A* and navigate to **Input | Fresnel**) and connect it to the **Fac** input socket of the **Mix Shader1** node. Set **IOR** to `1.450`.

6. Press *Shift + D* to duplicate the **Mix Shader1** node, label the duplicate as **Mix Shader2**, and paste it between the **Mix Shader1** and the **Material Output** nodes.

7. Press *Shift + D* to duplicate the **Add SPEC** node, label the duplicate as `Add SSS`, and connect its output to the first **Shader** input socket of the **Mix Shader2** node, so that the connection that comes from the **Mix Shader1** node automatically switches to the second **Shader** input socket. Connect the output of the **Mix Shader1** node also to the second **Shader** input socket of the **Add SSS** node.

8. Add a **Subsurface Scattering** node (press *Shift + A* and navigate to **Shader | Subsurface Scattering**) and connect its output to the first **Shader** input socket of the **Add SSS** node. Set **Falloff** to **Gaussian**; **Scale** to `0.050`; **Radius** to `4.000`, `2.000`, and `1.000`; and the **Texture Blur** value to `0.100`, as shown in the following screenshot:

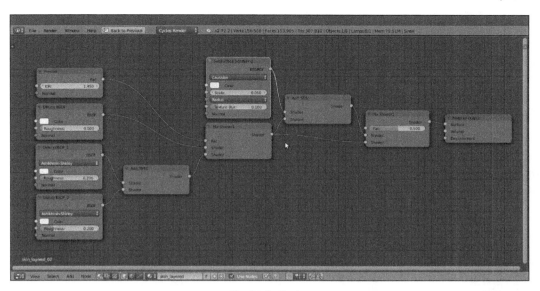

The basic shader

9. Add an **Image Texture** node (press *Shift + A* and navigate to **Texture | Image Texture**) and label it as EPIDERMIS; connect its **Color** output to the **Color** input sockets of the **Diffuse BSDF** and **Subsurface Scattering** nodes and the two **Glossy BSDF** nodes.

10. Click on the **Open** button of the **EPIDERMIS** image texture node, browse to the textures folder, and load the sintel_skin_diff.png image.

11. Add two **ColorRamp** nodes (press *Shift + A* and navigate to **Converter | ColorRamp**) and label them as ColorRamp_Spec1 and ColorRamp_Spec2. Connect the **Color** output of the **EPIDERMIS** node also to the **Fac** input socket of both the **ColorRamp** nodes.

12. Connect the **Color** output of the **ColorRamp_spec1** node to the **Roughness** input socket of the **Glossy BSDF_1** shader node; set **Interpolation** to **Ease**, and move the black color stop to the 0.550 position and the white color stop to the 0.000 position.

13. Connect the **Color** output of the **ColorRamp_spec2** node to the **Roughness** input socket of the **Glossy BSDF_2** shader node; set **Interpolation** to **B-Spline**, and move the white color stop to the `0.100` position and the white color stop to the `0.000` position, as shown in the following screenshot:

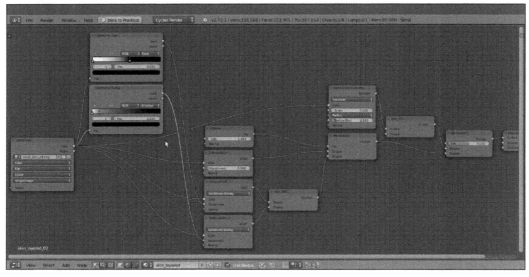

Sintel's color map is directly connected to the shader nodes but is modulated through ColorRamp nodes for the roughness of the glossy nodes

14. Add a **Hue Saturation Value** node (press *Shift + A* and navigate to **Color | Hue/Saturation**), label it as `Hue Saturation Value DERMIS`, and paste it between the **EPIDERMIS** and **Subsurface Scattering** nodes. Set the **Hue** value to `0.470`, the **Saturation** value to `1.500`, and **Value** to `1.200`.

15. Add a new **Image Texture** node (press *Shift + A* and navigate to **Texture | Image Texture**) and a **Bump** node (press *Shift + A* and navigate to **Vector | Bump**); label this **Image Texture** node as `BUMP`, and connect its **Color** output to the **Height** input socket of the **Bump** node, and the **Normal** output of this node to the **Normal** input sockets of the **Diffuse BSDF** node, of the two **Glossy BSDF** nodes, and of the **Subsurface Scattering** nodes.

16. Click on the **Open** button of the **BUMP** image texture node, browse to the `textures` folder, and load the `sintel_skin_bmp.png` image. Set **Color Space** to **Non-Color Data** and the **Bump** node's **Strength** value to `0.100`, as shown in the following screenshot:

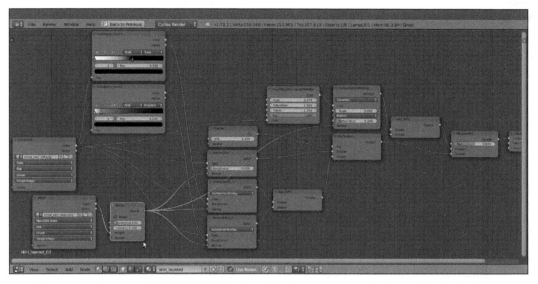

The same color map modified for the SSS node and the bump map connected as per the shader bump

How it works...

In this recipe, we used a layered approach to build the human skin shader, but what does layered mean exactly?

It means that the shader tries to simulate the behavior of real human skin in the most effective possible way. I'm referring to the fact that the human skin is composed of several different overlapping and semi-transparent layers that reflect and absorb light rays in various ways, giving the reddish coloration to certain areas due to the famous subsurface scattering effect.

Now, a perfect reproduction of the real human skin model is not necessary; usually, it's enough to use different image maps for the key components of the shader, each one added on top of the other: the base color, the dermis blood layer, the specularity map, and the bump map.

In our case, we had at our disposal only two image maps, the `sintel_skin_diff.png` color one and the `sintel_skin_bmp.png` gray-scale map, which we used straight for the bump; we could have obtained the missing maps with the aid of an image editor (such as, for example, GIMP), but for the sake of this exercise, to obtain the required missing images, we used the nodes: so, starting from the **EPIDERMIS** layer, that is the color map, we obtained via the **Hue Saturation Value DERMIS** node the blood-vessel layer that lies beneath the epidermis, as shown in the following screenshot:

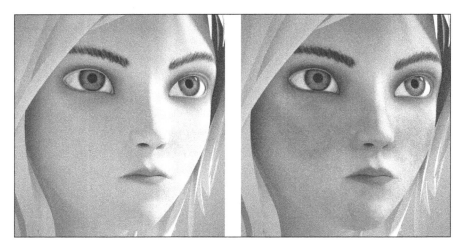

The normal color map and the blood-vessel version rendered separately

By the use of the two **ColorRamp** nodes and the two gray-scale versions for the specularity component, one sharp specularity map and a softer one are shown in the following screenshot:

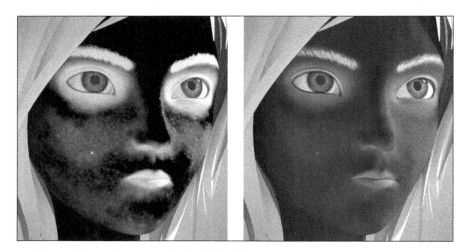

The two different glossy maps obtained from the same color map and rendered separately

Then, the `sintel_skin_bmp.png` map has been connected to the **Bump** node for the per-shader bump effect.

Note that because we used the color map to obtain all the others, certain areas of the images are wrong; for example, the eyebrows, shown in pure white on the specularity maps, should have been removed. In any case, this doesn't show that much on the final render, and the result is more than acceptable.

Creating fur and hair

Fur, in the world of computer graphics, is considered among the most difficult things to recreate, both because it's generally quite expensive from a memory management point of view (a single character can easily have millions of hair strands) and also because it can be quite a task to make a believable shader that can work under different light conditions.

Blender is not new to fur creation; the exact goal of the open movie *Big Buck Bunny* was to add tools for fur creation to the Blender Internal rendering engine, and it did it through a new type of primitive, strands, which have to be enabled in the **Particle** panel (the **Strand render** item); strands are very instanced on the particle system, but they can be edited, combed, and tweaked in several ways to obtain the best possible result.

Almost the same concept applies for the Cycles rendering engine; there's no need to enable the **Strand render** item anymore, because strands are rendered automatically by Cycles when the **Hair** item is selected as **Particle Type**.

In fact, once the **Hair** item's **Particle Type** has been selected, you will find two more subpanels at the bottom of the **Particle** window: **Cycles Hair Rendering** and **Cycles Hair Settings**. Here is a screenshot of the teddy bear Suzanne in the **Rendered** view:

The Rendered teddy bear Suzanne

Getting ready

Start Blender and open the 9931OS_08_hair_start.blend file; in the scene, there is a Suzanne primitive (**Suzanne_teddybear**) with a **Hair** particle system already named **teddybear** and set (go to see it in the **Particle** window) to resemble the fur of a cuddly toy.

The **Suzanne_teddybear** mesh is already unwrapped and has a **Vertex Group** named **density**, used in the **Particle** window (the **Vertex Groups** subpanel) to establish the **Density** distribution of the fur on the mesh (in short, to avoid fur on the eyes, the nose, and inside the mouth) as shown in the following screenshot:

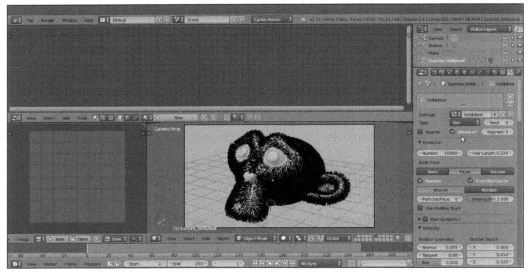

A screenshot of the particle system as it appears in the Solid viewport shading mode and the settings to the left

How to do it...

We are going to add three different materials to the **Suzanne_teddybear** object: **base_stuff**, which is the basic material for the raw mesh, an eyes material, and the **teddybear** material for the fur, using the following steps:

1. Select the **Suzanne** mesh and click on the **New** button in the **Node Editor** window toolbar or in the **Material** window to the right; rename the material as base_stuff.

2. Press *Tab* to go into **Edit Mode** and select the eyes vertices (put the mouse pointer over the interested part and press the *L* key to select all the linked vertices); click on the little **+** icon to the right of the **Material** window (add a new material slot) and add a new material. Click on the **New** button and rename the new material eyes, and then click on the **Assign** button. Press *Tab* to go out of **Edit Mode**.

3. Click again on the little **+** icon to the right of the **Material** window (add a new material slot) to add a third material (not to be assigned to any vertex or face; in fact, we are out of **Edit Mode**); click on the **New** button and rename the new material as `teddybear`.

4. Go to the **Particle** window at the top of the **Render** subpanel, and click on the **Material Slot** button (Material slot used to render particles), where at the moment, **Default Material** is selected instead of the `teddybear` material.

5. Go to the **Cycles Hair Rendering** subpanel to be sure that the **Primitive** item is set to **Curve Segments**, and set **Shape** to **Thick**; then, go to **Cycles Hair Settings** to be sure that the **Shape** value is `-0.50`, the **Root** value is `1.00`, the **Tip** value is `0.05`, the **Scaling** value is `0.01`, and the **Close Tip** item is checked.

6. Now, in the **Material** window, select the **base_stuff** material; in the **Node Editor** window, add a **Texture Coordinate** node (press *Shift + A* and navigate to **Input | Texture Coordinate**), a **Mapping** node (press *Shift + A* and navigate to **Vector | Mapping**), an **Image Texture** node (press *Shift + A* and navigate to **Texture | Image Texture**), a **Glossy BSDF** node, and a **Mix Shader** node (press *Shift + A* and navigate to **Shader | Texture Coordinate**; repeat similar steps to add other nodes).

7. Connect the **UV** output of the **Texture Coordinate** node to the **Vector** input socket of the **Mapping** node, and the output of this node to the **Vector** input socket of the **Image Texture** node. Paste the **Mix Shader** between the **Diffuse BSDF** and the **Material Output** nodes and connect the output of the **Glossy BSDF** shader to the second **Shader** input socket of the **Mix Shader** node.

8. Connect the **Color** output of the **Image Texture** node to the **Color** input socket of the **Diffuse BSDF** shader node and of the **Glossy BSDF** shader node; click on the **Open** button and browse to the `textures` folder to load the `teddybear.png` image (a simple color map painted directly in Blender). Set **Distribution** of the **Glossy BSDF** node to **Ashikhmin-Shirley**, the **Roughness** value to `0.300`, and the **Mix Shader** node's **Fac** value to `0.400`.

9. Back in the **Material** window, select the **eyes** material and switch the **Diffuse BSDF** shader with a **Mix Shader** node; in the first **Shader** slot, select a **Diffuse BSDF** shader, and in the second one, select a **Glossy BSDF** shader node.

10. Set the **Mix Shader** node's **Fac** value to `0.200`; change the **Diffuse BSDF** node's **Color** values for **R** to `0.010`, **G** to `0.003`, and **B** to `0.001`; and change the **Glossy BSDF** node's **Roughness** value to `0.100`.

In the following screenshot, the **teddybear** particle system has been hidden by disabling the viewport's visibility in the **Object modifiers** window:

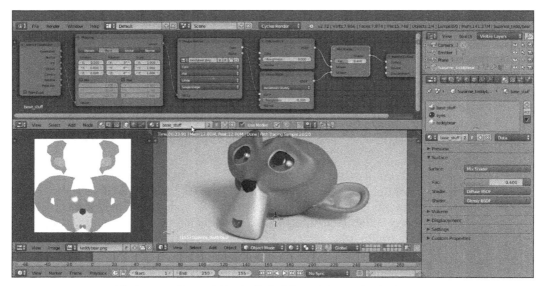

The base_stuff material in the Node Editor window and in the Preview

11. In the **Material** window, select the **teddybear** material and switch the **Diffuse BSDF** node with a **Mix Shader** node, and label it as `Mix Shader1`; in the first **Shader** slot, select another **Mix Shader** node, and in the second one, select a **Transparent BSDF** node.

12. Label the second **Mix Shader** node as `Mix Shader2`; then, in the first **Shader** slot, select a **Diffuse BSDF** shader node, and in the second one, select a **Glossy BSDF** shader node. Set the **Glossy BSDF** node's **Distribution** to **Ashikhmin-Shirley**, and its **Roughness** to `0.200`.

13. Add a **Fresnel** node (press *Shift + A* and navigate to **Input | Fresnel**) and connect it to the **Fac** input socket of the **Mix Shader2** node; set **IOR** to `1.580`. Add a **Hair Info** node (press *Shift + A* and navigate to **Input | Hair Info**), and connect the **Intercept** output to the **Fac** input socket of the **Mix Shader1** node.

14. Add an **Image Texture** node (press *Shift + A* and navigate to **Texture | Image Texture**), and connect its **Color** output to the **Color** input socket of the **Diffuse BSDF** node; click on the little arrows to the left of the **Open** button to select the already loaded `teddybear.png` image map.

15. Add a **MixRGB** node (press *Shift + A* and navigate to **Color | MixRGB**), set **Blend Type** to **Add** and the **Fac** value to `1.000`, and paste it between the **Image Texture** node and the **Diffuse shader** node. Set the **Color2** values for **R** to `0.277`, **G** to `0.179`, and **B** to `0.084` and then connect its output also to the **Color** input socket of the **Glossy BSDF** shader node.

16. Optionally, add a **Texture Coordinate** node (press *Shift + A* and navigate to **Input | Texture Coordinate**) and a **Mapping** node (press *Shift + A* and navigate to **Vector | Mapping**), and connect the **UV** output of the **Texture Coordinate** node to the **Vector** input socket of the **Mapping** node and the output of the latter to the **Vector** input socket of the **Image Texture** node, as shown in the following screenshot:

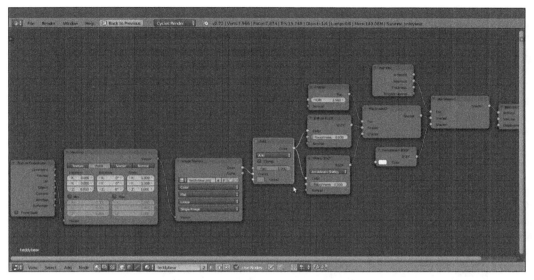

The teddy bear material network; note the transparency driven by the Intercept output of the Hair Info node

How it works...

From step 1 to 3, we prepared the three materials to be used; we went into **Edit Mode** to assign the second material, **eyes**, to the eyes vertices of the mesh, and then we went back in **Object Mode** to add a third material that doesn't need to be assigned to any face of the mesh because they are only to be used for hair rendering.

In steps 4 and 5, we made sure that the right particle system settings for the material are to be rendered as fur.

From step 6 to 8, we built the base_stuff material, a simple basic shader made by the Diffuse and Glossy components mixed by the **Mix Shader** node and colored by the UV mapped teddybear image texture; note that the texture we used in this first material is also used to give the right color to the hair; it is useful to have it also on the underlying mesh, to cover any hole or missing part in the particle system.

In steps 9 and 10, we built the eyes shader, which is again a very basic material made of the dark Diffuse color and the light gray Glossy components simply mixed by the **Mix Shader** node.

From step 11 to 16, we built the shader to be used by the particle system for the fur, mixing the already used `teddybear.png` image map, mapped on the UV coordinates, with a **MixRGB** node brownish color outputted to the usual **Diffuse/Glossy** basic shader; note that the **Diffuse/Glossy** shader is then mixed with the **Transparent BSDF** shader by the **Intercept** value of the **Hair Info** node along the length of each hair strand.

There's more...

The `teddybear.png` image texture has been used both in the `base_stuff` and in the **teddybear** materials; this is often not necessary, because in Blender, the particle system hairs get the textures from the surface they are emitted from, so it would have been enough to use the `base_stuff` material also for the fur (by selecting it in the **Material Slot** under the **Render** subpanel in the **Particle** window, because we had more than one material on the **Suzanne** mesh); we had to make a new and different material because we wanted to add a **MixRGB** brownish color to the UV-mapped image and we had to make the shader fade and become transparent towards the strands' tips.

Note that in the **Hair Info** node, there is also the Boolean **Is Strand** output that, similar to the outputs of the **Light Path** node (**Is Camera Ray**, **Is Shadow Ray**, and so on) can be used alternatively to the **Material** button in the **Particle** window to assign a material value of **0** to the emitter mesh and a material value of 1 to the fur strands (`9931OS_08_hair_isstrand.blend`) as shown in the following screenshot:

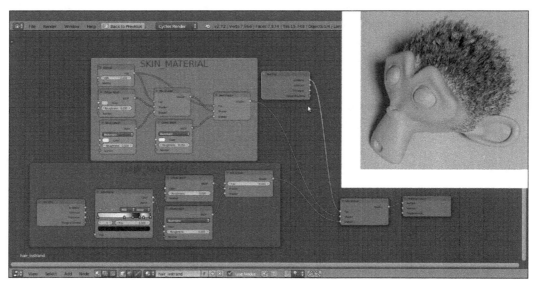

The set up for the hair_isstrand material and the rendered result

This also means that obviously we can also use different image textures to obtain fur materials different from the material of the particle emitter: for example, in the following screenshot, the `tiger.png` image texture has been used only for the fur, whereas the `base_stuff` material still uses the `teddybear.png` texture (and, honestly, this is blatantly visible... better to use the same image both for fur and emitter):

The rendered Suzanne_tiger object

The **Suzanne_tiger** object also has two different particle systems to create the fur, **tigerfur_long** and **tigerfur_short**, and three **Vertex Groups** to modulate the fur appearance, **density_long**, **density_short**, and **length**.

To take a look at the **Suzanne_tiger** object, open the `9931OS_08_tiger.blend` file.

See also

- http://wiki.blender.org/index.php/Doc:2.6/Manual/Render/Cycles/Hair_Rendering
- http://wiki.blender.org/index.php/Doc:2.6/Manual/Render/Cycles/Nodes/More
- http://blenderdiplom.com/en/tutorials/all-tutorials/536-tutorial-fur-with-cycles-and-particle-hair.html
- http://cgcookie.com/blender/2014/04/24/using-cycles-hair-bsdf-node/

Creating a gray alien skin material with procedurals

In this recipe, we will create a gray alien-like skin shader as shown in the following screenshot, using Cycles procedural textures:

The alien Suzanne as it appears in the final rendering

Getting ready

Start Blender and open the `99310S_08_alienskin_start.blend` file, where there is an already set scene with an unwrapped **Suzanne** primitive object.

The **Suzanne_unwrapped_alien** mesh has been modified by a shape key, to morph its monkey features into the head of a gray alien–like creature; in fact, in the **Object data** window, under the **Shape Keys** subpanel, there are the alien shape keys, with **Value** of `1.000`; sliding the slider towards `0.000` gradually restores the original Suzanne shape.

The **Suzanne** mesh also has a **Vertex Colors** layer named **Col** and is obtained by the **Dirty Vertex Colors** tool.

On the second layer, there are two Planes tracked (by a Damped Track constraint, in the **Object Constraints** window) to the Camera to stay perpendicular to its point of view; the **star_backdrop** object is used to create a simple star backdrop for our alien Suzanne, and the **star_backdrop.001** object is used simply to create something to be reflected by the alien-like Suzanne's eyes.

Press *Shift + F1* (or go through the **File | Append** main menu) to append the **SSS_group** node from the `99310S_07_SSS_ngroup.blend` file.

How to do it...

Let's start by first setting the background image material using the following steps:

1. Select the **star_backdrop** Plane and click on the **New** button in the **Node Editor** window toolbar or in the **Material** window. Rename the material `star_backdrop`, and in the **Material** window, switch the **Diffuse BSDF** shader with an **Emission** shader. Set the **Strength** to `0.500`.

2. Add an **Image Texture** node (press *Shift + A* and navigate to **Texture | Image Texture**) and connect the **Color** output to the **Color** input socket of the **Emission** node. Click on the **Open** button and browse to the `textures` folder and load the `centre-of-milky-way_tile_low.png` image.

3. Add an **RGB Curves** node (press *Shift + A* and navigate to **Color | RGB Curves**) and paste it between the **Image Texture** and **Emission** nodes. Click on the **curve** window to add a control point and set these coordinates: **X** to `0.36667` and **Y** to `0.12778`. Click again to add a second control point and set these coordinates: **X** to `0.65556` and **Y** to `0.81111`.

4. Add a **Mix Shader** node (press *Shift + A* and navigate to **Shader | Mix Shader**) and paste it between the **Emission** and **Material Output** nodes; switch the connection that comes from the **Emission** node to the second **Shader** input socket of the **Mix Shader** node; leave the first **Shader** input socket empty.

5. Add a **Light Path** node (press *Shift + A* and navigate to **Input | Light Path**) and connect the **Is Camera Ray** output to the **Fac** input socket of the **Mix Shader** node.

6. Go to **Outliner** and select the **star_backdrop.001** object; click on the double arrows icon to the left side of the data block name (*Browse Material to be linked*) in the **Node Editor** toolbar, and select the `star_backdrop` material; click on the **2** icon button to make it single-user.

7. In the new **star_backdrop.001** material, select the **Mix Shader** node and press *Ctrl + X* to delete it and keep the connection; then, also delete the **Light Path** node.

8. Go to the **Object data** window, and in the **Ray Visibility** subpanel, uncheck all the items except for the **Glossy** one.

   Now, let's get started with the creation of the alien skin shader (also with a different material for the eyes).

9. Select the **Suzanne_unwrapped_alien** object; click on the **New** button in the **Node Editor** window toolbar or in the **Material** window, and rename the material `alienskin`.

10. Go into **Edit Mode**, select the eyes vertices, and click on the **+** icon on the right of the **Material** window to add a second material. Click on the **New** button and rename the material as `alieneyes`; then, click on the **Assign** button to assign it to the selected vertices. Go out of **Edit Mode**.

11. Switch the **Diffuse BSDF** shader with a **Mix Shader** node; in the first **Shader** slot, select a **Diffuse BSDF** shader, and in the second one, select a **Glossy BSDF** shader. Set the **Mix Shader** node's **Fac** value to `0.600` and the **Diffuse BSDF** node's **Color** values for **R** to `0.010`, **G** to `0.006`, and **B** o `0.010`; set the **Glossy BSDF** node's **Distribution** to **Beckmann**, change the **Color** values for **R** to `0.345`, **G** to `0.731`, and **B** to `0.800`, and change the **Roughness** value to `0.100`.

12. Select the **alienskin** material, and in the **Material** window, switch the **Diffuse BSDF** shader with an **Add Shader** node (label it as `Add Shader1`); in the first **Shader** slot, select a **Mix Shader** node, and in the second one, load the appended **SSS_group** node. In this node, set the **Contrast** value to `3.000` and change the **Color** values for **R** to `0.834`, **G** to `0.263`, and **B** to `0.223`.

13. Go to the **Mix Shader** node, and in the first **Shader** slot, select a **Diffuse BSDF** node, and in the second one, select a new **Add Shader** node (label it as `Add Shader2`). Set the **Diffuse BSDF** node's **Roughness** value to `0.800`.

14. In both the **Shader** slots of the **Add Shader2** node, select a **Glossy BSDF** shader node; label the first one as **Glossy BSDF 1** and the second as **Glossy BSDF 2**; set **Distribution** of both to **Beckmann**, and then set the **Roughness** value of the first one to `0.600` and that of the second one to `0.300`.

15. Add a **Fresnel** node (press *Shift + A* and navigate to **Input | Fresnel**) and connect its output to the **Fac** input socket of the **Mix Shader** node. Set the **IOR** value to `1.300`, as shown in the following screenshot:

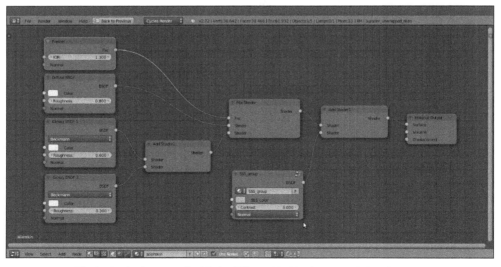

The basic shader network with the SSS provided by the appended node group

Now that we have set the basic shader for the alien skin, let's set an important component of the material, that is, the bump, by following these steps:

16. Add a **Texture Coordinate** node (press *Shift + A* and navigate to **Input | Texture Coordinate**) and two **Mapping** nodes (press *Shift + A* and navigate to **Vector | Mapping**); connect the **UV** output of the **Texture Coordinate** node to the **Vector** input socket of both the **Mapping** nodes, labeled as Mapping1 and Mapping2 respectively.

17. Set the **Rotation** value of **Y** of the **Mapping1** node to 60°; set the **Rotation** value of **Y** of the **Mapping2** node to 20°.

18. Add two **Voronoi Texture** nodes (press *Shift + A* and navigate to **Texture | Voronoi Texture**) and label them as Voronoi Texture1 and Voronoi Texture2. Connect the **Mapping1** node output to both their **Vector** input sockets. Set the **Scale** value of the **Voronoi Texture1** to 100.000 and the **Scale** value of the **Voronoi Texture2** to 20.000.

19. Add two **Wave Texture** nodes (press *Shift + A* and navigate to **Texture | Wave Texture**) and label them as Wave Texture1 and Wave Texture2. Connect the **Mapping1** node output to the **Vector** input socket of the **Wave Texture1** node. Set the texture **Scale** value to 20.000, **Distortion** to 10.000, **Detail** to 16.000, and **Detail Scale** to 0.300.

20. Connect the **Mapping2** node output to the **Wave Texture2** node's **Vector** input socket, and set all the texture values exactly as in the previously described one.

21. Add a **Noise Texture** node (press *Shift + A* and navigate to **Texture | Noise Texture**) and label it as Noise Texture1. Connect the **Mapping2** node output to its **Vector** input socket, and set the texture **Scale** value to 120.000 and the **Detail** value to 7.000.

22. Add a **ColorRamp** node (press *Shift + A* and navigate to **Converter | ColorRamp**), label it as ColorRamp1, and connect the **Voronoi Texture1** node's **Color** output to its **Fac** input socket. Set **Interpolation** to **Ease** and move the white color stop to the 0.126 position.

23. Add a **Math** node (press *Shift + A* and navigate to **Converter | Math**), change **Operation** to **Multiply**, and label it as Multiply1. Connect the **Color** output of the **ColorRamp1** node to the first **Value** input socket of the **Multiply1** node, and set the second **Value** to 0.050.

24. Add a **MixRGB** node (press *Shift + A* and navigate to **Color | MixRGB**) and connect the **Color** output of the **Voronoi Texture2** node to the **Color1** input socket, and the **Color** output of the **Wave Texture1** node to the **Color2** input socket. Set **Blend Type** to **Difference** and the **Fac** value to 1.000, and then label it as Difference1.

25. Add a second **MixRGB** node (press *Shift + A* and navigate to **Color | MixRGB**) and connect the **Color** output of the **Voronoi Texture2** node to the **Color1** input socket, and the **Color** output of the **Wave Texture2** node to the **Color2** input socket. Again, set the **Blend Type** to **Difference** and the **Fac** value to 1.000 and label it as Difference2.

26. Add two **ColorRamp** nodes (press *Shift + A* and navigate to **Converter | ColorRamp**), and label them as `ColorRamp2` and `ColorRamp3`; connect the **Difference1** node output to the **Fac** input socket of the **ColorRamp2** node, and the output of the **Difference2** node to the **Fac** input socket of the **ColorRamp3** node.

27. Set **Interpolation** to **B-Spline** for both of them, and for both of them, move the white color stop to the `0.255` position.

28. Add a **MixRGB** node (press *Shift + A* and navigate to **Color | MixRGB**) and connect the **Color** output of the **ColorRamp2** node to the **Color1** input socket and the **Color** output of the **ColorRamp3** node to the **Color2** input socket. Set the **Blend Type** to **Multiply** and the **Fac** value to `1.000`. Label it as `Multiply2`.

29. Press *Shift + D* to duplicate the **Multiply1** node and label the duplicate as `Multiply3`. Connect the output of the **Multiply2** node to the first **Value** input socket of the **Multiply3** node. Set the second **Value** to `0.050`.

30. Press *Shift + D* to duplicate the **Multiply3** node and label the duplicate as `Multiply4`. Connect the **Color** output of the **Noise Texture** node to the first **Value** input socket of the **Multiply4** node, and set the second **Value** to `0.175`.

31. Add a **Math** node (press *Shift + A* and navigate to **Converter | Math**) and label it as `Add1`. Connect the output of the **Multiply1** node to the first **Value** input socket and the output of the **Multiply3** node to the second **Value** input socket.

32. Press *Shift + D* to duplicate the **Add1** node and label the duplicate as `Add2`; connect the output of the **Add1** node to the first **Value** input socket and the output of the **Multiply4** node to the second **Value** input socket.

33. Add a **Bump** node (press *Shift + A* and navigate to **Vector | Bump**) and connect the output of the **Add2** node to the **Height** input socket of the **Bump** node; set its **Strength** value to `4.000` and connect its **Normal** output to the **Normal** input sockets of the **Diffuse BSDF** node, of the two **Glossy BSDF** nodes, and of the **SSS_group** node, as shown in the following screenshot:

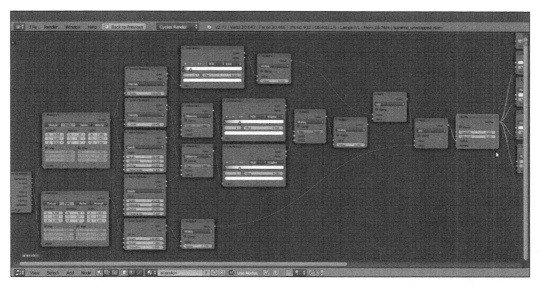

The apparently complex bump network to be connected as per the shader bump

We are done with the bump part, so now, let's set the color pattern using the following steps:

34. Add a **ColorRamp** node (press *Shift + A* and navigate to **Converter | ColorRamp**), label it as `ColorRamp4`, and connect the **Color** output of the **Multiply2** node to its **Fac** input socket. Set **Interpolation** to **Ease** and move the black color stop to the `0.495` position, and the white color stop to the `0.000` position.

35. Add a **MixRGB** node (press *Shift + A* and navigate to **Color | MixRGB**), set the **Blend Type** to **Add**, and label it as `Add3`. Connect the **Color** output of the **ColorRamp4** node to the **Fac** input socket and set the **Color2** values for **R** to `0.553`, **G** to `0.599`, and **B** to `0.473`.

36. Add a **Noise Texture** node (press *Shift + A* and navigate to **Texture | Noise Texture**) and label it as `Noise Texture2`. Connect the **Mapping1** node output to its **Vector** input socket and set the texture's **Scale** value to `60.000` and the **Detail** value to `7.000`.

37. Add a **ColorRamp** node (press *Shift + A* and navigate to **Converter | ColorRamp**), label it as `ColorRamp5`, and connect the **Noise Texture2** color output to its **Fac** input socket. Set **Interpolation** to **B-Spline** and move the black color stop to the `0.486` position and the white color stop to the `0.771` position.

38. Press *Shift + D* to duplicate the **Add3** node, label the duplicate as `Add4`, and connect the **Color** output of the **ColorRamp5** node to its **Fac** input socket; connect the output of the **Add3** node to the **Color1** input socket and set the **Color2** values for **R** to `0.235`, **G** to `0.198`, and **B** to `0.132`.

39. Press *Shift + D* to duplicate the **Add4** node, label the duplicate as `Overlay`, and change **Blend Type** to **Overlay** as well. Set the **Fac** value to `1.000` and connect the output of the **Add4** node to the **Color1** input socket.

40. Add an **Attribute** node (press *Shift + A* and navigate to **Input | Attribute**) and connect its **Color** output to the **Color2** input socket of the **Overlay** node; in the **Name** field, write `Col` (the **Vertex Colors** layer).

41. Connect the output of the **Overlay** node to the **Color** input socket of the **Diffuse BSDF** shader node.

42. To make them more easily readable, frame the three groups of nodes, **SHADER**, **BUMP**, and **COLOR**, as shown in the following screenshot:

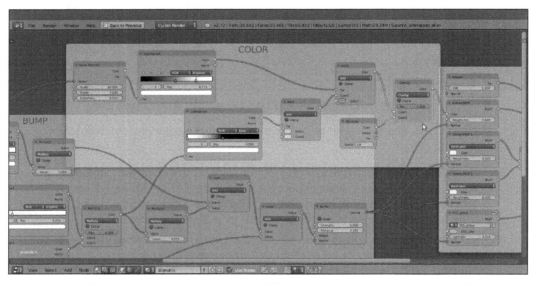

The simpler color pattern to be connected only to the Diffuse shader node and the nodes grouped by frames

43. Save the file as `9931OS_08_alienskin_final.blend`.

How it works...

▶ From step 1 to 8, we built a simple and quick shader for the starry background and for the Plane in front of the **Suzanne_unwrapped_alien** mesh to be reflected in the eyes; note that the background Plane material works as a shadeless material. To see how to set a bright but not emitting light background, that is, a shader that behaves as the shadeless material you have in the Blender Internal engine, go to *Chapter 9, Special Materials*.

▶ From step 9 to 15, we built the basic shader for the alien Suzanne's skin; the diffuse component is mixed and modulated by the **Fresnel** output, with a specular component made by two summed **Glossy BSDF** nodes with different roughness values, so as to have a crisper specular effect on a more diffuse one, and with the additional help of the **SSS_group** node to simulate a reddish *Subsurface Scattering* effect.

▶ From step 16 to 33, we built the quite complex bump pattern for the skin by mixing the outputs of three different types of procedural textures with the help of both the **Math** and **MixRGB** nodes, and the variations provided by the **ColorRamp** nodes.

▶ Finally, from step 34 to 41, a simple grayish color pattern is modulated through the **Dirty Vertex Colors** layer data that comes from the mesh and that uses the first part of the bump pattern to add variation.

9

Special Materials

In this chapter, we will cover the following recipes:

- ► Using Cycles volume materials
- ► Creating a cloud volumetric material
- ► Creating a "fire and smoke" shader
- ► Creating a shadeless material in Cycles
- ► Creating a fake immersion effect material
- ► Creating a fake volume light material

Introduction

In this final chapter, we are going to see some special materials, that is, materials that can be used for special effects or for situations where very realistic results are not required, for example, creation of volumetric effects (fire, smoke, mist, volumetric light, and so on) and special materials to obtain peculiar results (shadeless images, alpha backgrounds, and so on).

Using Cycles volume materials

In all the recipes we have seen so far, Cycles used the **Surface** input socket and (very rarely) the **Displacement** input socket for the bump effects of the **Material Output** node to make the renderings. Assigning colors or textures to the surface of an object clearly means that interaction between a ray of light and an object happens only at the surface level of the object, and until this surface doesn't show what should be inside, that's OK. The surface attribute is enough for a realistic rendering.

Things get more complex when there is a need to show what's inside an object, for example, water inside a glass container, smoke and clouds in a thick atmosphere, and so on.

Usually, these are effects that require the use of the volume attribute more than the surface attribute to be effectively rendered.

So, in the first recipes of this chapter, we are going to see the use of the **Volume** input socket of the **Material Output** node. Rather than covering a specific material, this recipe is more of a "tour" to show the possibilities related to the **Volume** shader assigned to a mesh object. Have a look at the following screenshot:

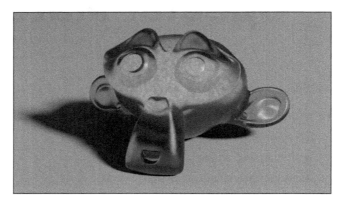

A glass Suzanne containing some kind of liquid

Getting ready

Start Blender and open the 99310S_09_start.blend file, with the usual Suzanne object leaning on a Plane, a mesh-light Emitter, and the Camera.

1. Go to the **Render** window, and under the **Sampling** subpanel, set **Samples** for **Preview** to 50 and for **Render** to 100. Switch **Pattern** from **Sobol** to **Correlated Multy-Jitter**.

2. Still in the **Render** window, go to the **Volume Sampling** subpanel, and under the **Heterogeneous** item, set the **Step Size** value to 0.25. The default value is 0.10. Increasing this will make the rendering of volumes less accurate but faster, and lowering it will result in the opposite.

How to do it...

First, let's see the Volume applied to our usual Suzanne mesh primitive by performing the following steps:

1. Move the mouse to the **Camera** view and press *Shift + Z* to switch the **Viewport Shading** mode to **Rendered**.

2. Make sure that you have the **Suzanne_unwrapped** object selected, and click on the **New** button in the **Node Editor** toolbar, or in the **Material** window under the main **Properties** panel.

3. In the **Node Editor** window, press *Ctrl* and click and drag a line onto the link connecting the **Diffuse BSDF** shader to the **Material Output** node to cut it away. Because nothing is connected to the **Material Output** node sockets, in the **Camera** view, the **Suzanne** object turns pitch black as shown in the following screenshot:

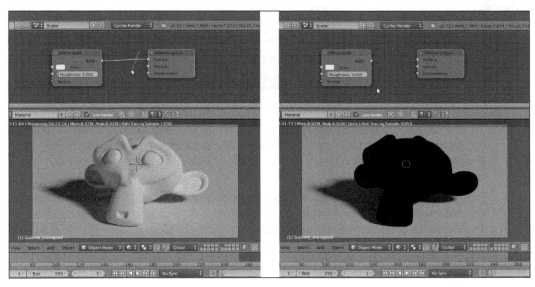

The Diffuse shader connected and disconnected from the Material Output node

4. Select and delete the **Diffuse BSDF** shader node. Still in the **Node Editor** window, add a **Volume Scatter** node (press *Shift + A* and navigate to **Shader | Volume Scatter**) and connect its output to the **Volume** input socket of the **Material Output** node.

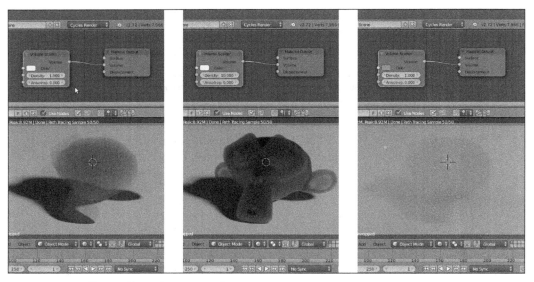

Different effects of the Volume Scatter node obtained by changing density and color

5. Try to increase the **Density** value to `10.000`, either in the node interface in the **Node Editor** window, or in the slot under the **Volume** subpanel in the main **Properties** panel. Suzanne's volume looks more solid, as shown in the middle of the preceding screenshot.

6. Change the **Density** value back to the default `1.000` and change the **Color** values of the **Volume Scatter** node for **R** to `1.000`, **G** to `0.000`, and **B** to `0.000` (a red color). The **Suzanne** object now appears as complementary colored smoke (on the right side of the preceding screenshot) because light is scattered (note that the shadow on the Plane gets the same color).

7. Add a **Glass BSDF** shader (press *Shift + A* and navigate to **Shader | Glass BSDF**) and connect its output to the **Surface** input socket of the **Material Output** node. Set the **IOR** value to `1.440` and the **Roughness** value to `0.100`.

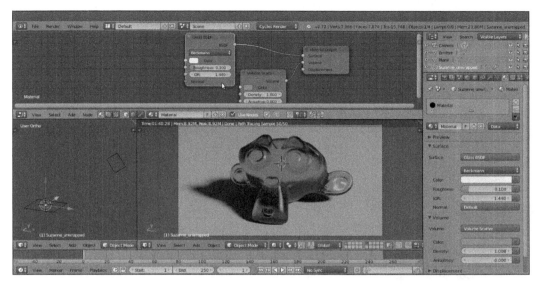

Adding a glassy envelope to the bluish, scattered glassy volume

8. Now you have to temporarily remove the connection of the **Glass BSDF** shader node to the **Surface** input socket of the **Material Output** node, take back the **RGB** value and set it to `0.800` for the **Color** of the **Volume Scatter** node.

9. Add a **Texture Coordinate** node (press *Shift + A* and navigate to **Input | Texture Coordinate**), a **Voronoi Texture** node (press *Shift + A* and navigate to **Texture | Voronoi Texture**), and a **Math** node (press *Shift + A* and navigate to **Converter | Math**).

10. Connect the **Object** output of the **Texture Coordinate** node to the **Vector** input socket of the **Voronoi Texture** node, and the **Fac** output of this node to the first **Value** input socket of the **Math** node. Set the second **Value** to `10.000`, set **Operation** to **Multiply**, and connect its output to the **Density** input socket of the **Volume Scatter** node as shown in the following screenshot:

The Density value of the Volume Scatter node driven by a Voronoi texture output

11. Add a **ColorRamp** node (press *Shift + A* and go to | **Converter** | **ColorRamp**) and paste it between the **Voronoi Texture** and the **Math** nodes. Move the black color stop to position `0.195` and the white color stop to position `0.100` as shown in the following screenshot:

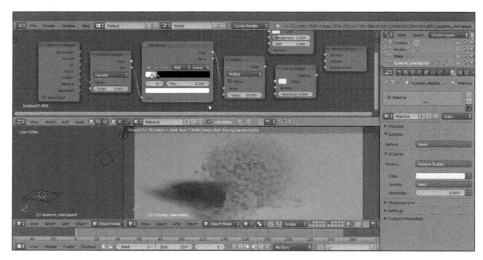

Enhancing the contrast of the texture output

12. Set the **Voronoi Texture** node's **Scale** value to 11.500, and reconnect the **Glass BSDF** shader node output to the **Surface** input socket of the **Material Output** node. Change the **Color** values of the **Volume Scatter** node for **R** to 1.000, **G** to 0.000, and **B** to 0.000 as shown in the following screenshot:

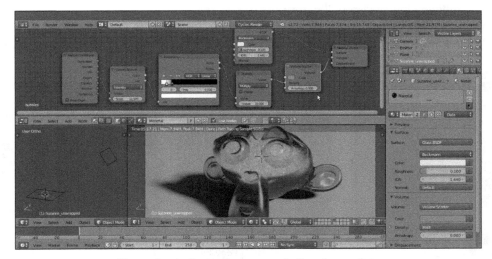

The previously cloudy volume covered with a glass surface

13. Rename the material as Bubbles and save the file by naming it 99310S_09_volume.blend. Have a look at the following screenshot:

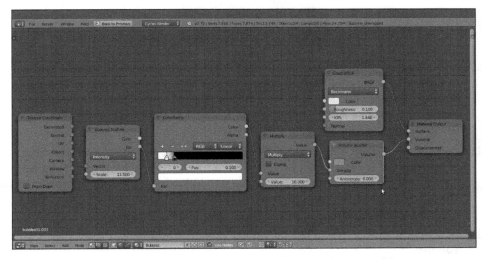

The overall network for the combined surface and volume material

So, for the previous material named Bubbles, we used the **Volume Scatter** node. What about the **Volume Absorption** node?

14. In the **Node Editor** toolbar, enable *fake user* for the Bubbles material, and click on the **X** icon button to delink the datablock. Then click on the **New** button.

15. Delete the **Diffuse BSDF** shader node and add a **Volume Absorption** node (press *Shift + A* and navigate to **Shader | Volume Absorption**). Then connect it to the **Volume** input socket of the **Material Output** node.

16. To make a comparison with the **Volume Scatter** node, raise the **Density** value of the **Volume Absorption** node to 10.000 and set the **Color** values for **R** to 1.000, **G** to 0.000, and **B** to 0.000. Have a look at the following screenshot:

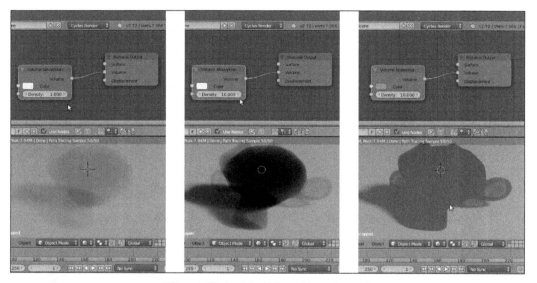

Different effects of the Volume Absorption node

17. Add a **Texture Coordinate** node (press *Shift + A* and navigate to **Input | Texture Coordinate**), a **Voronoi Texture** node (press *Shift + A* and navigate to **Texture | Voronoi Texture**), two **Math** nodes (press *Shift + A* and navigate to **Converter | Math**), and a **Glass BSDF** shader (press *Shift + A* and navigate to **Shader | Glass BSDF**).

18. Connect the **Object** output of the **Texture Coordinate** node to the **Vector** input socket of the **Voronoi Texture** node, and the **Fac** output of this node to the first **Value** input socket of the first **Math** node. Set the second **Value** to 0.100, set **Operation** to **Less Than**, and connect its output to the first **Value** input socket of the second **Math** node. Set the second **Value** to 12.800 and the **Operation** to **Multiply**.

19. Connect the output of this **Multiply-Math** node to the **Density** input socket of the **Volume Absorption** node, and rename the material as algae. Here is a screenshot for your reference:

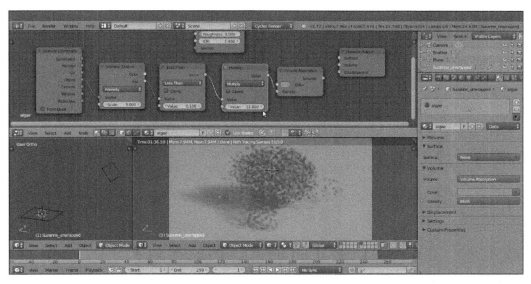

The density of the Volume Absorption node driven by the Voronoi Texture output

20. Set the **Scale** value of the **Voronoi Texture** node to 3.500, change the **Color** of the **Volume Absorption** node for **R** 0.045, **G** 0.800, and **B** 0.113, and connect the output of the **Glass BSDF** shader node to the **Surface** input socket of the **Material Output** node. Set the **IOR** value to 1.440 and the **Roughness** value to 0.100 as shown in the following screenshot:

Different colors and a glass cover for the absorption volumetric material

21. In the **Node Editor** toolbar, enable *fake user* for the `algae` material, and then click on the **2** icon (**Display number of users for this data**) to create a duplicate of the material, named `algae.001`.

22. Rename the material as `emitting_volume` and substitute the **Volume Absorption** node with an **Emission** node (press *Shift + A* and go to | **Shader** | **Emission**). Connect the output of the **Multiply-Math** node to the **Color** input socket, and set the **Strength** value to `0.050`.

23. Disable the visibility of the sixth scene layer to hide the **Emitter** mesh-light, and go to the **Render** window. In the **Light Paths** subpanel, enable both the **Reflective Caustics** and **Refractive Caustics** items. Here is a screenshot for your reference:

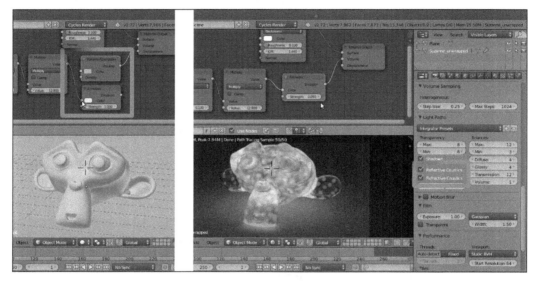

Substituting the Volume Absorption node with an Emission node as the volume material

24. Enable *fake user* for the `emitting_volume` material and save the file.

How it works...

In this tour recipe, we saw the three shaders used for the volumetric attribute of a material in Cycles, that is, the **Volume Scatter**, **Volume Absorption**, and **Emission** shaders (we have already seen the **Emission** shader the previous chapters, and it is commonly used in Lamps and mesh-lights).

The **Volume Scatter** and **Absorption** shaders do exactly what their names say, as we saw in the examples. If we give them a color other than black, gray, or white, the **Volume Scatter** shader returns a complementary hue, while the **Volume Absorption** shader returns the same hue we set up.

About the **Density** value, remember that the higher the value, the more particles inside the volume. This allows for simulation of very light and rarefied vapors or very dense clouds of smoke, where the material looks almost solid.

There's more...

A Volume can be associated not only with objects but also with the World. This allows for several effects, for example, mist, or the famous God's rays. They are obtained by simply scattering light in the air of a Spot lamp.

The setup is really simple and intuitive: a **Volume Scatter** node connected to the **Volume** input socket of the **World Output** node. Have a look at the following screenshot:

The cone of a Spot lamp visible through the ambient volume material

The **Density** value of the **Volume Scatter** node in this case is set very low (0.010) to allow the light of the Spot lamp to shine through.

Open the 9931OS_09_volume_ambient.blend file to have a look.

See also

► http://wiki.blender.org/index.php/Doc:2.6/Manual/Render/Cycles/ Materials/Volume

Creating a cloud volumetric material

The natural consequence of a volumetric material is (quite obviously) clouds.

A simple way to create clouds in Cycles is by modeling the desired shape and then assigning an appropriate volumetric material. In the following screenshot, you can see this method applied to the usual Suzanne mesh:

The volumetric Suzanne cloud as it appears in the final rendering

Getting ready

Start Blender and open the `99310S_09_cloud_start.blend` file, where there is the **Suzanne_cloud** object with two **Emitter** mesh-lights and a bright **World** set with a **Sky Texture**.

1. Go to the **Object modifiers** window and raise the **Subdivisions** level of the **Subdivision Surface** modifier from 2 to 3 for both **Preview** and **Render**.

2. Assign a new **Subdivision Surface** modifier. Set the **Subdivisions** level to 2.

3. Assign a **Displace** modifier. Click on the **Show texture in texture tab** button to the right of the **New** button to switch to the **Texture** window.

4. Click on the **New** button under the **Displace** item, then click on the **Type** slot to switch from **Image or Movie** to **Clouds**. Set the **Size** to 0.35 and the **Depth** to 3.

5. Go back to the **Object modifiers** window and click on the **Vertex Group** slot to select the **rest** item. Then set the **Strength** value to 0.400.

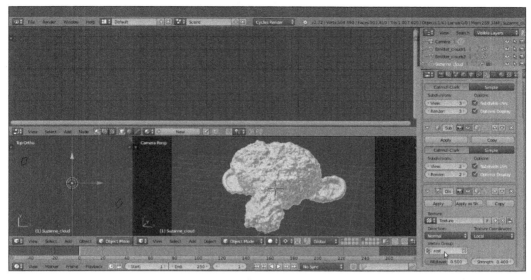

The displaced Suzanne cloud seen in the Solid Viewport Shading mode and the assigned modifiers in the main properties panel to the right

How to do it...

After creating the cloud shape, let's make a start on the material:

1. Ensure that the **Suzanne_cloud** object is still selected, and click on the **New** button in the **Node Editor** toolbar or in the **Material** window under the main **Properties** panel.

2. In the **Node Editor** window, select and delete the **Diffuse BSDF** shader node.

3. Add a **Volume Scatter** node (press *Shift + A* and navigate to **Shader | Volume Scatter**), a **Volume Absorption** node (press *Shift + A* and navigate to **Shader | Volume Absorption**), and an **Add Shader** node (press *Shift + A* and navigate to **Shader | Add Shader**).

4. Connect the output of the **Volume Absorption** node to the first **Shader** input socket of the **Add Shader** node, and the **Volume Scatter** output to the second **Shader** input socket. Connect the output of the **Add Shader** node to the **Volume** input socket of the **Material Output** node.

5. Add a **Mix Shader** node (press *Shift + A* and navigate to **Shader | Mix Shader**) and paste it between the **Add Shader** node and the **Material Output** node. Connect the output of the **Volume Scatter** node to the second **Shader** input socket of the **Mix Shader** node. Set the **Fac** value to 0.700.

6. Add a **Value** node (press *Shift + A* and navigate to **Input | Value**) and an **RGB** node (press *Shift + A* and navigate to **Input | RGB**). Connect the **Value** output to both the **Density** input sockets of the **Volume Absorption** and **Volume Scatter** nodes. Set the input value to 5.000.

7. Connect the output of the **RGB** node to the **Color** input sockets of the **Volume Absorption** and **Volume Scatter** nodes. Set the color values for **R** to 0.890, **G** to 0.866, and **B** to 0.832.

8. Under the **Material** windows, go to the **Settings** subpanel and enable the **Homogeneous** item.

9. Go to the **Scene** window, and under the **Color Management** subpanel, enable the **Use Curves** item. Then click on the curves window to create a new control point. Set its coordinates as **X** to 0.67206 and **Y** to 0.88125. Click again to create a new control point, and set the coordinates as **X** to 0.31579 and **Y** to 0.46875. Have a look at the following screenshot:

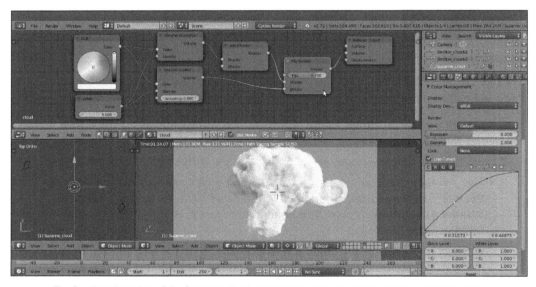

The Rendered preview of the Suzanne cloud and the material network in the Node Editor window

How it works...

Most of the effect of this material is because of the **Displace** modifier deforming the Suzanne mesh in order to resemble the shape of a Suzanne cloud. The material itself is simply a combination of the **Volume Scatter** and the **Volume Absorption** shader, first added by the **Add Shader** node and then with a **Mix Shader** node to further control the mixing of the scattering in the whole shader.

The **Vertex Group, rest**, selected in the **Displace** modifier slot is simply a group with lower weight going towards the ears, because they are quite thin, and the displacement we're using can easily cause bad mesh intersections.

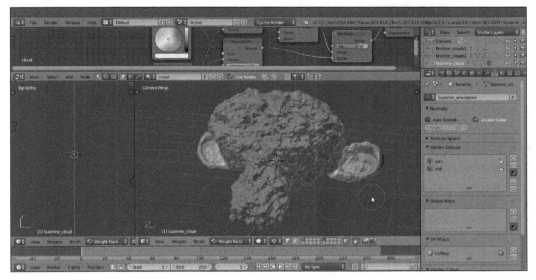

The Rest Vertex Group visible in the Weight Paint mode

In the last step, we enabled curves for the Color Management to obtain a brighter and more contrasted rendering of the cloud against the sky.

Creating a fire and smoke shader

In this recipe, we are going to see one of the most exciting effects we can obtain in Cycles—a fire and smoke simulation effect:

The fire and smoke shader as it appears in the final rendering when assigned to the Suzanne mesh

Getting ready

Start Blender and open the 9931OS_09_fire_smoke_start.blend file, where there is the **Suzanne_unwrapped** object leaning on a Plane and surrounded by five small Cubes, a Spot lamp, the Camera, and a medium-intensity World with a **Sky Texture**.

1. Go to the **Render** window, and under the **Sampling** subpanel, set the **Preview** samples to 50 and the **Render** samples to 100. Then go to the **Dimensions** subpanel and set the **End Frame** to 80. Under the **Light Paths** subpanel, enable the **Reflective** and **Refractive Caustics** items.

How to do it...

Let's start by creating the smoke simulation by a shortcut:

1. Select the **Suzanne_unwrapped** object, click on the **Object** item in the 3D viewport toolbar to go to **Quick effects**, and select the **Quick Smoke** item. Alternatively, press the spacebar, and in the search window, start typing Quick. Then select the **Quick Smoke** item from the menu as shown in the following screenshot:

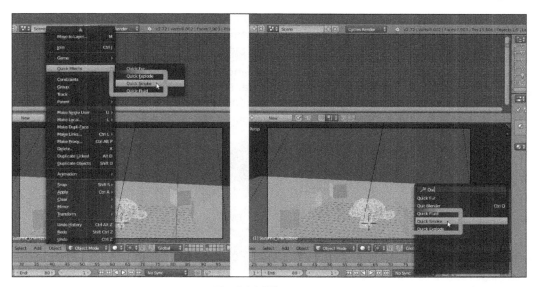

The Quick Effects menu

2. A **Smoke Domain** (the selected wire box around the **Suzanne** object) with a prepared
    fire/smoke material (`Smoke Domain Material`) is automatically set up on the
    selected object, and when you press the **Play** button in the **Player Control** on the
    Timeline toolbar, the smoke simulation starts. Have a look at the following screenshot:

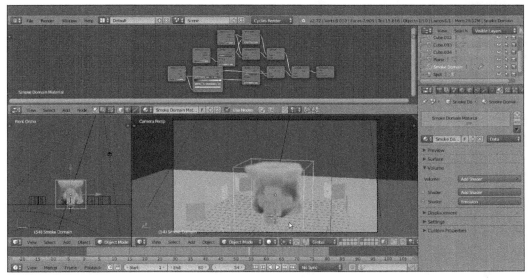

The smoke simulation: in the upper Node Editor window, the material being automatically created by the
Quick Effects tool

3. Go back to frame **1** and scale the **Smoke Domain** to a larger size on the global *z* axis such that its top goes out of the Camera frame boundary. Scale it by 3.000 (press *S*, enter digit 3.000, then press *Enter*). Then move it 5 units upwards.

4. Go to the **Physics** window, and under the **Smoke** subpanel, set the **Divisions** value to 64. Then go to the **Smoke Flames** subpanel and set the **Speed** value to 2.00000, **Smoke** to 0.50000, and **Vorticity** to 1.00000. Restart the **Play** button to recalculate the cache. Have a look at the following screenshot:

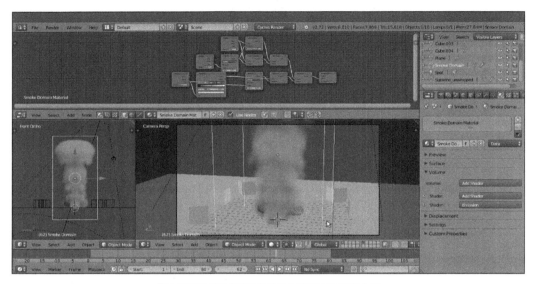

The smoke simulation inside a bigger domain box

5. As all the 80 frames have been cached, go to the **Physics** window, and under the **Smoke Cache** subpanel, click on the Current Cache to Bake button.

6. Enable the **Smoke Adaptive Domain** and the **Smoke High Resolution** subpanels. Leave the default settings as they are.

7. With the mouse arrow in the **Camera** view, press *Shift + Z* to switch to the **Rendered** viewport shading mode. Have a look at the following screenshot:

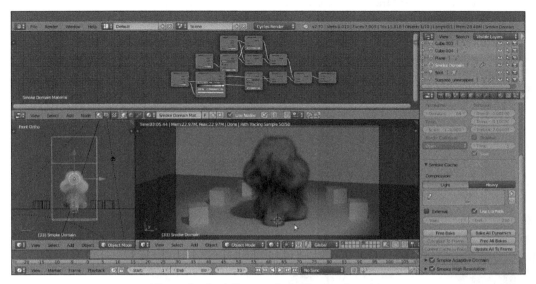

The smoke simulation seen in the Rendered preview

In the **Rendered** preview (be careful that the smoke is not supported by GPU yet), we can see the dark grey smoke, but what about the fire?

8. In the **Physics** window, under the **Smoke Cache** subpanel, click on the **Free All Bakes** button.

9. Go to the **Outliner** to select the **Suzanne _unwrapped** item. Then go to the **Physics** window again. Under the **Smoke** subpanel, click on the **Flow Type** slot and switch from **Smoke** to **Fire + Smoke**. Then click on the **Smoke Color** slot and change the color values for **R** to 0.700, **G** to 0.317, and **B** to 0.335. Have a look at the following screenshot:

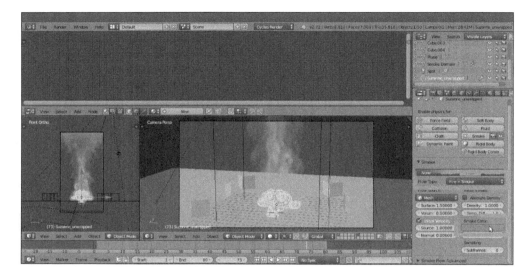

10. Reselect the **Smoke Domain** object and click on the **Play** button to cache the smoke simulation again, this time with reddish smoke and also the fire. Then click on the **Current Cache to Bake** button again.

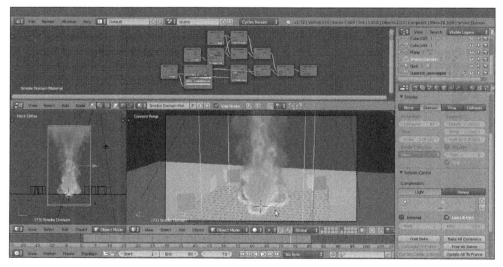

The new smoke (and fire) simulation

But this is a Cookbook about materials, so let's put aside the smoke simulation settings and concentrate on the material. To better understand how this works, let's delete the ready-made material and create a new material from scratch.

11. In the **Node Editor** toolbar, press *Shift* and click on the **X** button to unlink the Smoke Domain Material. Set the users to zero.

    Now, setting the **Camera** view shading mode to **Rendered** shows only the Smoke Domain box as a solid object because no material is assigned to the simulation.

12. Click on the **New** button in the **Node Editor** window toolbar. Delete the **Diffuse BSDF** shader node and add a **Volume Scatter** node (press *Shift + A* and navigate to **Shader | Volume Scatter**). Connect it to the **Volume** input socket of the **Material Output** node.

13. Add an **Attribute** node (press *Shift + A* and navigate to **Input | Attribute**) and connect its **Fac** output to the **Density** input socket of the **Volume Scatter** node. In the **Name** field of the **Attribute** node, write density.

14. Add a **Math** node (*Shift + A* | **Converter** | **Math**), set the **Operation** to **Multiply**, and paste it between the **Attribute** and the **Volume Scatter** nodes. Set the second **Value** to 5.000.

Building the smoke density after deleting the default Quick Effects material

15. Press *Shift + D* to duplicate the **Attribute** node, connect the duplicated node's output to the **Color** input socket of the **Volume Scatter** node. In the **Name** field, write `color`.

The smoke color

As you can see in the rendered preview, the smoke gets a bluish coloration, with the complementary color (orange) getting scattered.

1. Add a **Volume Absorption** node (*Shift + A* | **Shader** | **Volume Absorption**) and an **Add Shader** node (*Shift + A* | **Shader** | **Add Shader**). Paste the **Add Shader** node between the **Volume Scatter** and the **Material Output** nodes. Then connect the **Volume Absorption** output to the second **Shader** input socket of the **Add Shader** node.

2. Connect the **Color** output of the **Color-Attribute** node to the **Color** input socket of the **Volume Absorption** node, and the output of the **Multiply** node to the **Density** input socket of the **Volume Absorption** node as shown in the following screenshot:

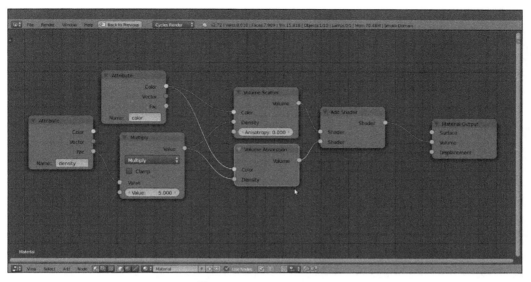

The complete smoke network

3. Parent all of these nodes, except the **Material Output** node, to a **Frame**. Label it as SMOKE.

4. Duplicate or add a new **Attribute** node, and in the **Name** field, write **flame**. Add an **Emission** shader (press *Shift + A* and navigate to **Shader | Emission**) and connect the **Fac** output to both the **Strength** and the **Color** input sockets of the **Emission** shader node.

5. Add a **ColorRamp** (*Shift + A* | **Converter** | **ColorRamp**) and paste it between the **Attribute** output and the **Color** input socket of the **Emission** node. Set the black color stop values for **R** to 1.000, **G** to 0.000, and **B** to 0.010. Then set the white color stop values for **R** to 1.000, **G** to 0.724, and **B** to 0.224. Add a new color stop and move it to the 0.290 position. Set the color values for **R** to 1.000, **G** to 0.280, and **B** to 0.000.

6. Add a **Math** node and paste it between the **Attribute** output and the **Strength** input socket of the **Emission** node. Set the **Operation** to **Multiply** and the second **Value** to 5.000.

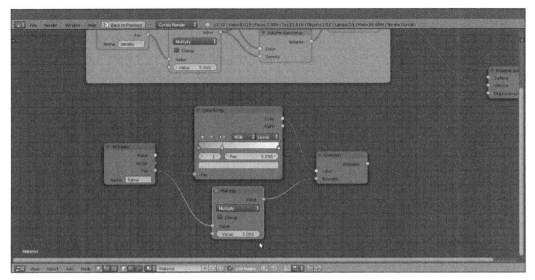

Starting to build the fire shader

7. Parent these four nodes to a new **Frame** labeled as FLAME.

8. Add an **Add Shader** node (press *Shift + A* and navigate to **Shader | Add Shader**) and paste it between the output of the **Add Shader** inside the **SMOKE** frame and the **Material Output**. Connect the output of the **Emission** shader inside the **FLAME** frame to the second **Shader** input socket of the last **Add Shader** node.

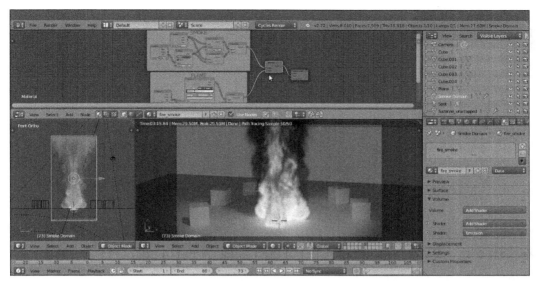

Smoke and fire shaders added

9. Rename the material as `fire_smoke` and save the file as `99310S_09_fire_smoke_final.blend`.

How it works...

Considering that we basically used the default settings for the fire and smoke simulation, the result was pretty good. To find out more about the different settings and types of smoke, take a look at the links provided in the *See also* section of this chapter.

We used the Quick Effects menu to let Blender automatically set up the smoke simulation for us. The steps usually involved are as follows:

▶ For the simulation domain, set an object that defines the bounds of the simulation volume. In our case, it was the **Smoke Domain** box in the wireframe viewport shading mode. It could be scaled, moved, or rotated if necessary.

▶ For the flow, set an object that determines where the smoke will be produced from, that is, the **Suzanne_unwrapped** object.

▶ Assign a material to the smoke. In our case, it was the automatically created `Smoke Domain Material`, which we then remade as the `fire_smoke` material.

▶ Bake the simulation by computing the cache for the required frames and then clicking on the **Current Cache to Bake** button.

▶ Save the blend file.

The `fire_smoke` material we set in the **Node Editor** is made exactly as shown in the previous volume recipes of this chapter. It consists of all the three shader nodes that can be used for a Volume: the **Volume Scatter**, the **Volume Absorption** and the **Emission** shaders, driven by the **flame**, **density** and **color** attributes we wrote in the **Name** field of the **Attribute** nodes and coming from the smoke simulation.

See also

- ▸ http://wiki.blender.org/index.php/Doc:2.6/Manual/Physics/Smoke
- ▸ https://cgcookie.com/blender/lessons/02-cycles-fire-and-smoke/
- ▸ http://www.blendernation.com/2014/04/14/rendering-smoke-and-fire-in-cycles/

Creating a shadeless material in Cycles

In this recipe, we will create a shadeless material, which is a material that behaves as self-illuminated but does not actually emit any light on the nearby objects.

In the following screenshot, we can see the difference between a Plane with a shadeless material and a Plane with an emitting material:

A shadeless Plane and an emitting Plane in comparison

At the top, the cloudy sky image is perfectly self-illuminated and visible, but it's neither affecting the Spheres or the Suzannes nor the floor Plane (nevertheless slightly visible because of a low intensity World).

This is the reason a shadeless material is perfect for backdrop elements mapped on Planes (or more often on unwrapped half-spheres called domes) to simulate skies, clouds, and even distant trees. It can also simulate forests and mountains in the background of a scene.

In Blender Internal, obtaining a shadeless material is very simple. Enabling the appropriate item in the material panel is enough. In Cycles, there are two methods to obtain this effect: one based on the material and the other based on the **Ray Visibility** subpanel in the **Object** window, under the main **Properties** panel.

Getting ready

Start Blender and open the `99310S_09_start.blend` file. Then follow these steps:

1. Go to the **Render** window, and under the **Sampling** subpanel, set the **Samples** to `50` for **Preview** and `100` for **Render**.

2. Set the **Camera** view to the **Rendered** shading mode by pressing *Shift + Z* with the mouse arrow in the viewport.

3. Go to the **World** window and set the **Background** strength to `0.200`.

4. Go to **Outliner** and select the **Emitter** object. In the **Node Editor** window, set the **Strength** of the **Emission** shader node to `0.100`.

5. Select the **Plane** object, and in the **Material** window under the main **Properties** panel to the right, replace the **Diffuse BSDF** shader with a **Glossy BSDF** shader node. Switch the **Distribution** of this node from **GGX** to **Beckmann** and set the **Roughness** value to `0.200`.

6. Select the **Suzanne_unwrapped** object and click on the **New** button in the **Node Editor** window toolbar, or in the **Material** window under the main **Properties** panel to the right.

7. With the mouse arrow in the bottom-left corner of the 3D window, press the *7* key in the numeric keypad to switch to the **Top Ortho** view. Press *Shift + D* to duplicate the Suzanne mesh, and move it to the left of the scene. Rotate it to accommodate it close to the original mesh. Click on the **2** button to the side of the **Material** datablock in the **Node Editor** window toolbar to make it single-user.

8. In the **Material** window, switch the **Diffuse BSDF** node with a **Mix Shader** node. In the first **Shader** slot, select a **Diffuse BSDF** node, and in the second **Shader** slot, select a **Glossy BSDF** shader node. Set the **Glossy** distribution to **Beckmann**, the **Roughness** value to `0.100`, and the **Fac** value of the **Mix Shader** node to `0.900`. Rename the material as `mirror`.

9. Press *Shift + D* to duplicate the `mirror` Suzanne mesh, and move it to the right of the scene, close to the original mesh.

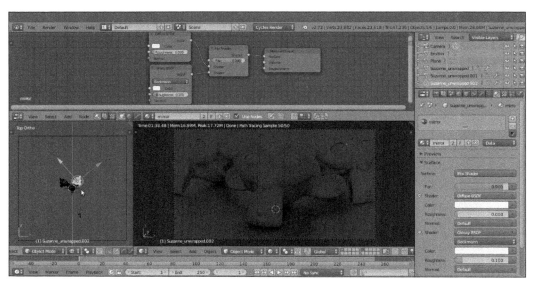

The three Suzannes on the floor Plane in the dark

How to do it...

Let's start with the first method, based on the material:

1. Select the original **Suzanne_unwrapped** mesh, which is in the middle, and click on the **New** button in the **Node Editor** window toolbar. In the **Material** window, switch the **Diffuse BSDF** shader with an **Emission** shader. Add an **Image Texture** node (press *Shift + A* and navigate to **Texture | Image Texture**) and connect its **Color** output to the **Color** input socket of the **Emission** node.

2. In the **Rendered Camera** view, the original Suzanne mesh is emitting pink light on the scene. Pink is the default color that Blender uses to tell us that we haven't loaded an image texture yet.

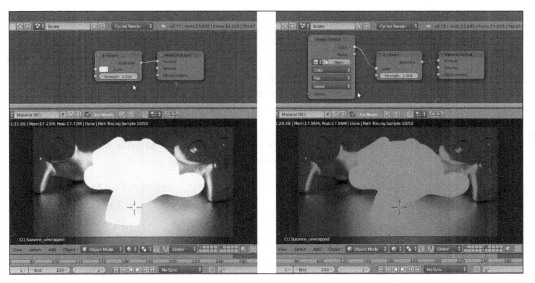

Suzanne emitting light and the texture being missing

3. Click on the **Open** button of the **Image Texture** node, browse to the `textures` folder, and load the `teddybear.png` image (which was used in *Chapter 8, Creating Organic Materials*).

Suzanne with the UV-mapped texture

4. In the **Node Editor** window, add a **Mix Shader** node (press *Shift + A* and navigate to **Shader | Mix Shader**) and paste it between the **Emission** node and the **Material Output** node.

5. Add a **Light Path** node (press *Shift + A* and navigate to **Input | Light Path**) and connect its **Is Camera Ray** output to the **Fac** input socket of the **Mix Shader** node. The Suzanne mesh turns totally black (no material) but still lights the scene based on the teddybear.png image's values.

6. Switch the connection of the **Emission** node from the first **Shader** input socket of the **Mix Shader** node to the second **Shader** input socket.

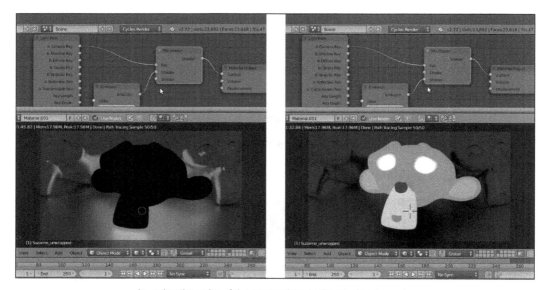

Inverting the order of the connections in the Mix Shader node

At this point, the shadeless Suzanne is still affecting the surrounding objects. It's reflected as a black object by the floor and by the mirror Suzannes. In fact, the output of the first empty input socket of the **Mix Shader** node is a black color because there is no material at all.

To prevent the shadeless Suzanne from getting reflected, follow these steps:

1. Add a **Transparent** shader node (press *Shift + A* and navigate to **Shader | Transparent BSDF**) and connect it to the first **Shader** input socket of the **Mix Shader** node.

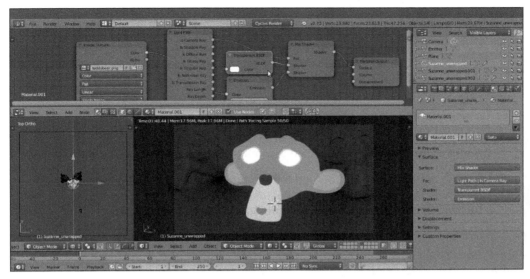

The totally shadeless Suzanne

2. Rename the material as shadeless and save the file as 9931OS_09_shadeless. blend.

How it works...

Thanks to the **Is Camera Ray** output of the **Light Path** node, all the light rays from the Camera that directly hit the Suzanne mesh are rendered with the **Emission** material brightness (because this material has a value equal to 1, which is due to its connection to the second **Shader** socket of the **Mix Shader** node). For the other kind of rays (reflected, transmitted, and so on, first socket = 0 value) there is no emitting material coming from the Suzanne mesh. Actually, there is initially no material at all, and this gives a black, reflected Suzanne. Following this, to avoid the black reflections, a **Transparent BSDF** shader has been connected to the first socket of the **Mix Shader** node.

There's more...

The second method to obtain a shadeless object is as follows:

1. Starting from the preceding file, select the **Suzanne** mesh, and in the toolbar of the **Node Editor** window, click on the **F** button on the right side of the material name data block to assign a *fake user* (this is to keep the material saved in the blend file even if not assigned to anything). Then click on the **X** icon (to unlink the datablock).

2. Now click on the **New** button to create a new material. In the **Material** window under the **Properties** panel, switch the **Diffuse BSDF** with an **Emission** shader node.

3. In the **Node Editor** window, add an **Image Texture** node (press *Shift + A* and navigate to **Texture | Image Texture**) and connect its **Color** output to the **Color** input socket of the **Emission** shader.

4. Click on the **Open** button on the **Image Texture** node to load the `teddybear.png` image texture.

   At this point, we are at the same stage as step 2 of the first method. We have created a light emission material based on the image texture mapped on the Suzanne mesh.

5. Now go to the **Object** window under the main **Properties** panel to the right of the screen. In the **Ray Visibility** subpanel (usually the last at the bottom) uncheck the **Diffuse**, **Glossy**, **Transmission**, **Volume Scatter** and **Shadow** items.

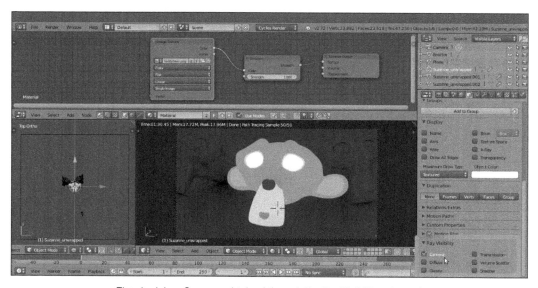

The shadeless Suzanne obtained through the Ray Visibility subpanel

So basically, only the **Camera** item is active now. Simple, quick, and effective!

Creating a fake immersion effect material

In this recipe, we will create a material to give the effect of an object immersed in a substance becoming more and more opaque as the depth increases, for example, murky water.

The murky water effect as it appears in the final rendering

Getting ready

Start Blender and open the `9931OS_09_start.blend` file. Then follow these steps:

1. Go to the **World** window and click on the little dotted square on the right side of the color slot. From the menu, select **Sky Texture**. Then set the **Strength** value to `0.500`.

2. Select the Plane, rename it as **water**, and move the **Location** value of **Z** to `1.17000`. Then press *Shift + D* to duplicate it, rename it as `bed`, and move the **Location** value of **Z** to `-2.00000`.

How to do it...

Let's go ahead and create the different materials:

1. Go to the **Material** window and select the **Suzanne_unwrapped** mesh. In the **Node Editor** window toolbar, click on the **New** button, and rename the material as (simply) `Suzanne`. In the **Material** window under the main **Properties** panel, switch the **Diffuse BSDF** shader with a **Mix Shader** node. In the first **Shader** slot, select a **Diffuse BSDF** shader node, and in the second **Shader** slot, select a **Glossy BSDF** shader node.

2. Set the **Glossy** distribution to **Beckmann** and the **Roughness** value to `0.100`. Then set the **Fac** value of the **Mix Shader** node to `0.600`.

3. Select the **bed** Plane and click on the **New button** in the **Node Editor** window toolbar. Rename the material as bed.

4. In the **Material** window, switch the **Diffuse BSDF** shader with an **Emission** shader node. Set the **Color** values for **R** to 0.800, **G** to 0.659, and **B** to 0.264. Then set the **Strength** value to 0.100.

5. Select the **water** Plane and click on the **New** button in the **Node Editor** window toolbar. Rename the material as water.

6. In the **Material** window, switch the **Diffuse BSDF** shader with a **Mix Shader** node. In the first **Shader** slot, select a **Glass BSDF** shader node, and in the second **Shader** slot, select a **Transparent BSDF** node.

7. Set the **Glass BSDF** node's **Roughness** value to 0.600 and the **IOR** to value 1.333. Then set the **Color** values for **R** to 0.185, **G** to 0.611, and **B** to 0.800.

8. Add a **Light Path** node (press *Shift + A* and navigate to **Input | Light Path**) and a **ColorRamp** node (press *Shift + A* and navigate to **Converter | ColorRamp**). Connect the **Ray Length** output to the **Fac** input socket of the **ColorRamp** and invert the position of the black-and-white color stops (that is, move the black color stop to the extreme right and the white color stop to the extreme left of the slider).

9. Connect the **ColorRamp** output to the **Fac** input socket of the **Mix Shader** node.

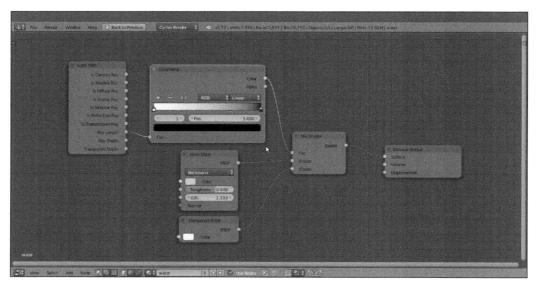

The murky water material network

How it works...

The effect happening on the `water` material is due to the **Ray Length** output, which returns the length of the light rays passing through an object, thus giving the thickness of that object. In our case, the distance from the water mesh surface to the far distance (from the Camera point of view, because the light rays originate from the Camera).

The gradient of the **ColorRamp** is mapped on the length of this **Ray Length** output (also clamped and inverted by the same **ColorRamp** node), connected to the **Fac** input socket of the **Mix Shader** node in order to work as a stencil map to smoothly blend the amount of the **Glass** shader with the amount of the **Transparent BSDF** shader node.

Thus, the transition from the **Transparent** shader to the **Glass** shader returns the impression of a volume of water becoming murkier as the distance of the object from the surface increases.

Creating a fake volume light material

In this recipe, we will create a material to fake the typical effect of a cone of light visible when passing through the dust suspended in the air, or falling from the sky on a cloudy day (the so-called God's rays) different from the real volumetric effect described in the *There's more* section of the *Using Cycles volume materials* recipe. This is a fake—just a mesh and not a real light to be used for the scene. Therefore, a matching Lamp must be set for the real lighting, as shown in the already made blend file.

The fake volume cone of light as it appears in the final rendering

Getting ready

Start Blender and open the 9931OS_09_volumelight_start.blend file, where there is a scene set with a ground Plane, a Cube, the volumetric cone mesh (**volume_light**), a spot mesh object (**spot_mesh**), and an effective Spot lamp parented to the **volume_light**. The Spot lamp cone follows the shape of the **volume_light**, and its purpose is to light the Cube leaning on the ground Plane.

The volume light objects also have a brief animation of 98 frames. To see it, move the Time Cursor inside the **Timeline** window; to point the cone of light to the Cube, go to frame **81**.

How to do it...

Let's go ahead with creating the light cone material:

1. Select the **volume_light** object and click on the **New** button in the **Node Editor** window toolbar, or in the **Material** window under the main **Properties** panel to the right. Rename the material as volume_light.

2. In the **Material** window, switch the **Diffuse BSDF** shader node with a **Mix Shader** node. Label it as Mix Shader1.

3. In the first **Shader** slot of the **Mix Shader1** node, select a new **Mix Shader** node. Label it as **Mix Shader2**. In the second **Shader** slot, select a **Transparent BSDF** shader node.

4. Go to the **Mix Shader2** node, and in the first **Shader** slot, select a **Mix Shader** node again (**Mix Shader3**). Connect the output of the **Transparent BSDF** node to the second **Shader** slot of the **Mix Shader2** node.

5. Go to the **Mix Shader3** node, and in the first **Shader** slot, select one more **Mix Shader** node (label it Mix Shader4). Connect the output of the **Transparent BSDF** node to the second **Shader** slot.

6. Go to the **Mix Shader4** node, and in the first **Shader** slot, select one **Emission** node. Connect the output of the **Transparent BSDF** node to the second **Shader** slot of the **Mix Shader4** node.

7. Set the color values of the **Emission** node for **R** to 0.769, **G** to 0.800, and **B** to 0.592. Then set the **Fac** value of **Mix Shader4** to 0.800.

8. Add a **Layer Weight** node (press *Shift + A* and navigate to **Input | Layer Weight**) and connect its **Facing** output to the **Fac** input socket of the **Mix Shader3** node. Set the **Blend** value to 0.900.

9. Add a **ColorRamp** node (press *Shift + A* and navigate to **Converter | ColorRamp**) and connect its color output to the **Fac** input socket of the **Mix Shader2** node. Set the **Interpolation** to **B-Spline** and move the black color stop to position 0. Then move the white color stop to the extreme left.

10. Add a **Value** node (press *Shift + A* and navigate to **Input | Value**), label it as `Intensity`, and connect it to the **Fac** input socket of the **Mix Shader1** node. Set the value to `0.400`.

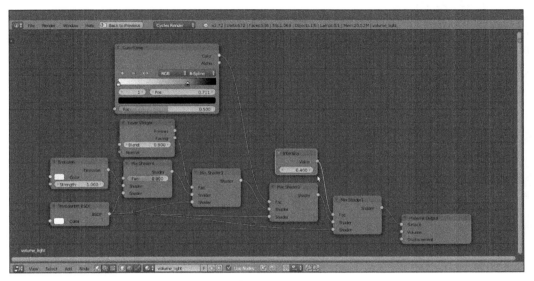

The entire material network

11. Save the file as `99310S_09_volumelight_final.blend`.

How it works...

The effect of light blending with the night is obtained by the various factors of blending of the **Mix Shader** nodes that cause the mixing of the **Emission** shader with the **Transparent** shader. The purpose of connecting the **Value** node to the **Fac** input of the **Mix Shader1** node is to establish the intensity of the fake volumetric light. A value of `1.000` turns it off completely (be careful not to go beyond `1.000`, otherwise the cone mesh will show up as a dark silhouette). On the contrary, values towards `0.000` (or even negative values) make it appear more and more intense.

Be careful with this simulation because being a mesh emitting light, it can produce strange and unrealistic effects if not carefully planned. Suppose you go to frame **62** and start the rendering. Then you will see that the volumetric cone mesh is intersecting the Cube even in those areas where a real light would create shadows.

See also

Since Cycles has been added to Blender, many artists have posted screenshots and tests for almost every possible kind of material. Especially on the Blender Artists forum, you will find a plethora of data and will discover different (and often better) ways to create the same materials that you have seen in this Cookbook.

Now it's up to you to create new, amazing materials and renderings that no one can avoid staring at. Blend on!

Index

Thank you for buying
Blender Cycles: Materials and Textures Cookbook
Third Edition

About Packt Publishing

Packt, pronounced 'packed', published its first book, *Mastering phpMyAdmin for Effective MySQL Management*, in April 2004, and subsequently continued to specialize in publishing highly focused books on specific technologies and solutions.

Our books and publications share the experiences of your fellow IT professionals in adapting and customizing today's systems, applications, and frameworks. Our solution-based books give you the knowledge and power to customize the software and technologies you're using to get the job done. Packt books are more specific and less general than the IT books you have seen in the past. Our unique business model allows us to bring you more focused information, giving you more of what you need to know, and less of what you don't.

Packt is a modern yet unique publishing company that focuses on producing quality, cutting-edge books for communities of developers, administrators, and newbies alike. For more information, please visit our website at www.packtpub.com.

About Packt Open Source

In 2010, Packt launched two new brands, Packt Open Source and Packt Enterprise, in order to continue its focus on specialization. This book is part of the Packt open source brand, home to books published on software built around open source licenses, and offering information to anybody from advanced developers to budding web designers. The Open Source brand also runs Packt's open source Royalty Scheme, by which Packt gives a royalty to each open source project about whose software a book is sold.

Writing for Packt

We welcome all inquiries from people who are interested in authoring. Book proposals should be sent to author@packtpub.com. If your book idea is still at an early stage and you would like to discuss it first before writing a formal book proposal, then please contact us; one of our commissioning editors will get in touch with you.

We're not just looking for published authors; if you have strong technical skills but no writing experience, our experienced editors can help you develop a writing career, or simply get some additional reward for your expertise.

Blender 3D Basics Beginner's Guide

Second Edition

ISBN: 978-1-78398-490-9   Paperback: 526 pages

A quick and easy-to-use guide to create 3D modeling and animation using Blender 2.7

1. Explore Blender's unique user interface and unlock Blender's powerful suite of modeling and animation tools.

2. Learn how to use Blender, and also the principles that make animation, lighting, and camera work come alive.

3. Start with the basics and build your skills through a coordinated series of projects to create a complex world.

Blender Compositing and Post Processing

ISBN: 978-1-78216-112-7   Paperback: 114 pages

Learn the techniques required to create believable and stunning visuals with Blender Compositor

1. Explore Blender compositor to create spectacular visuals.

2. Make the most out of Blender's node-based compositing architecture.

3. Step-by-step guide full of practical examples.

Please check **www.PacktPub.com** for information on our titles

Blender Cycles: Lighting and Rendering Cookbook

ISBN: 978-1-78216-460-9   Paperback: 274 pages

Over 50 recipes to help you master the Lighting and Rendering model using the Blender Cycles engine

1. Get acquainted with the lighting and rendering concepts of the Blender Cycles engine.

2. Learn the concepts behind nodes shader system and get the best out of Cycles in any situation.

3. Packed with illustrations and a lot of tips and tricks to make your scenes come to life.

Three.js Essentials

ISBN: 978-1-78398-086-4   Paperback: 198 pages

Create and animate beautiful 3D graphics with this fast-paced tutorial

1. Acquire thorough knowledge of the essential features of Three.js, explained using comprehensive examples.

2. Animate HTML5 elements directly from Three.js using the CSS3 3D renderer.

3. Visualize information such as sound and open data in beautiful 3D.

Please check **www.PacktPub.com** for information on our titles